Attention and Avoidance

Heinz Walter Krohne (Editor)

Attention and Avoidance

Strategies in Coping with Aversiveness

Hogrefe & Huber Publishers
Seattle · Toronto · Göttingen · Bern

EDITOR
Heinz W. KROHNE
Psychologisches Institut
Abteilung Persönlichkeitspsychologie
Johannes Gutenberg-Universität
Saarstraße 21/Staudinger Weg 9
D-6500 Mainz 1, Germany

Library of Congress Cataloging-in-Publication Data
is available via the Library of Congress Marc Database under the
LC Catalog Card Number 92-074344

Canadian Cataloguing in Publication Data
Main entry under title:
Attention and avoidance
ISBN 0-88937-108-3
1. Stress (Psychology). I. Krohne, Heinz W.
BF575.S75A88 1992 155.9'042 C92-095237-2

ISBN 0-88937-108-3
Hogrefe & Huber Publishers, Seattle · Toronto · Göttingen · Bern

ISBN 3-8017-0664-8
Hogrefe Göttingen · Bern · Toronto · Seattle

USA: P.O. Box 2487, Kirkland, WA 98083-2487, Phone (206) 820-1500, Fax (206) 823-8324
CANADA: 12 Bruce Park Avenue, Toronto, Ontario M4P 2S3, Phone (416) 482-6339
SWITZERLAND: Länggass-Strasse 76, CH-3000 Bern 9, Phone (031) 242533,
Fax (031) 243380
GERMANY: Robert-Bosch-Breite 25, D-3400 Göttingen, Phone (0551) 49609-0,
Fax (0551) 49609-88

Printed and bound by Dieterichsche Universitätsbuchdruckerei W. Fr. Kaestner GmbH & Co. KG,
D-3400 Göttingen-Rosdorf.
Printed in Germany on acid-free paper.

Contents

Contributors

HASIDA BEN-ZUR, Ray D. Wolfe Centre for Study of Psychological Stress, University of Haifa, Mount Carmel, Haifa, Israel.

THOMAS D. BORKOVEC, Department of Psychology, The Pennsylvania State University, University Park, PA, USA.

SHLOMO BREZNITZ, Ray D. Wolfe Centre for Study of Psychological Stress, University of Haifa, Mount Carmel, Haifa, Israel.

CHARLES S. CARVER, Department of Psychology, University of Miami, Coral Gables, FL, USA.

R. LORRAINE COLLINS, Research Institute on Alcoholism, Buffalo, NY, USA.

CHRISTOPHER COMBS, Department of Psychology, Temple University, Philadelphia, PA, USA.

DIETER FERRING, Fachbereich I - Psychologie, Universität Trier, Trier, Germany.

SIGRUN-HEIDE FILIPP, Fachbereich I - Psychologie, Universität Trier, Trier, Germany.

RUTH HASHMONAY, Ray D. Wolfe Centre for Study of Psychological Stress, University of Haifa, Mount Carmel, Haifa, Israel.

MICHAEL HOCK, Psychologisches Institut, Abteilung Persönlichkeitspsychologie, Johannes Gutenberg-Universität, Mainz, Germany.

VOLKER HODAPP, Institut für Physiologische Psychologie, Heinrich-Heine-Universität, Düsseldorf, Germany.

THOMAS KLAUER, Fachbereich I - Psychologie, Universität Trier, Trier, Germany.

PETER P. KLEEMANN, Klinik für Anästhesiologie, Johannes Gutenberg-Universität, Mainz, Germany.

JOACHIM F. KNOLL, Institut für Physiologische Psychologie, Heinrich-Heine-Universität, Düsseldorf, Germany.

CARL-WALTER KOHLMANN, Psychologisches Institut, Abteilung Persönlichkeitspsychologie, Johannes Gutenberg-Universität, Mainz, Germany.

HEINZ WALTER KROHNE, Psychologisches Institut, Abteilung Persönlichkeitspsychologie, Johannes Gutenberg-Universität, Mainz, Germany.

LINDA KRUUS, Department of Psychology, Temple University, Philadelphia, PA, USA.

ELAINE A. LEVENTHAL, Department of Medicine, Robert Wood Johnson School of Medicine, Rutgers University, New Brunswick, NJ, USA.

HOWARD LEVENTHAL, Institute for Health, Health Care Policy, and Aging Research/Department of Psychology, Rutgers University, New Brunswick, NJ, USA.

JAMES D. LYONFIELDS, Department of Psychology, The Pennsylvania State University, University Park, PA, USA.

ANDREW MATHEWS, MRC Applied Psychology Unit, Cambridge, England, UK.

SUZANNE M. MILLER, Department of Psychology, Temple University, Philadelphia, PA, USA.

MICHAEL F. SCHEIER, Department of Psychology, Carnegie Mellon University, Pittsburgh, PA, USA.

KERSTIN SLANGEN, Psychologisches Institut, Abteilung Persönlichkeitspsychologie, Johannes Gutenberg-Universität, Mainz, Germany.

JERRY SULS, Department of Psychology, University of Iowa, Iowa City, IA, USA.

GERDI WEIDNER, Department of Psychology, State University of New York at Stony Brook, NY, USA.

Preface

Research on stress and coping has established two concepts central to an understanding of the *cognitive* response to an aversive situation: *attention* and *avoidance*. This volume is designed to develop a framework which demonstrates how concepts and empirical data concerning these two central coping strategies fit together with the current research on stress and coping. A central purpose of this book is to elaborate a more integrated approach in the study of vigilant and avoidant coping. Special attention has been given to the following topics:

1. theoretical approaches to vigilance and avoidance;
2. research and measurement strategies;
3. the role of attentional processes in the self-regulation of behavior;
4. uncertainty and emotional arousal as determinants of vigilance and avoidance;
5. flexibility and individual consistency in coping;
6. gender, age, and coping; and
7. vigilant/avoidant coping and health status.

I believe the reader will agree that these objectives have been achieved, although one will never be totally satisfied in such a complex field.

This book brings together authors distinguished by their substantial theoretical contributions and empirical investigations in the areas mentioned. Early versions of most of the chapters were presented and discussed at an invitational conference held in Mainz, Germany, September 12 - 15, 1990. Three contributions (Leventhal, Suls, & Leventhal; Filipp, Klauer, & Ferring; Carver & Scheier) could not be presented at the conference. However, the authors have graciously submitted their papers for inclusion in this volume.

This volume is directed at students (especially graduate students), researchers, and professionals in the fields of clinical psychology, health psychology, behavioral medicine, psychophysiology, personality, social psychology, and education.

Several individuals, groups, and organizations have helped to make this book possible. First of all, I would like to thank the distinguished contributors. I am also grateful to the Volkswagen-Stiftung (Volkswagen Foundation) and the Johannes Gutenberg-Universität Mainz for supporting the conference on which this volume is based. Furthermore, I am endebted to those graduate students from my university including Boris Egloff, Silke Richter, Pamela A. Tabbert, and Anja Tausch, who have provided substantial help in editing the final manuscript. Last, but not least, the support from the staff of my department has been greatly appreciated.

Heinz Walter Krohne

Johannes Gutenberg-Universität
Mainz,
November 1991

PART I.

INTRODUCTION

Chapter 1

Attention and Avoidance. Two Central Strategies in Coping with Aversiveness

Heinz Walter Krohne

Overview

Current studies on stress and coping, particularly within the scope of *health research*, have established two concepts central to an understanding of the cognitive response to an aversive situation: *attention*, i.e., being oriented toward the threat-related aspects of a situation, and (cognitive) *avoidance*, that is turning attention away from threatening cues (cf. Janis, 1983; Krohne, 1978; Krohne & Rogner, 1982; Roth & Cohen, 1986; Singer, 1990; Suls & Fletcher, 1985). Formulations corresponding to these concepts are, among others, "Sensitization/Repression" (Byrne, 1964), "Monitoring/Blunting" (Miller, 1980, 1987), "Attention/Rejection" (Mullen & Suls, 1982), and "Vigilance/Cognitive Avoidance" (Krohne, 1986, 1989).

Without going into detail, research on these two concepts can be characterized by three trends:

A first research trend follows the tradition of the repression-sensitization construct as elaborated by Byrne (1964; cf. Bell & Byrne, 1978). Recent efforts in this field focus on a *methodological* improvement of this approach. Byrne's strongly criticized unidimensional-bipolar conception (for an overview cf. Chabot, 1973; Krohne & Rogner, 1985) has been extended to a multivariable assessment of coping dispositions (cf. Asendorpf & Scherer, 1983; Krohne & Rogner, 1985; Weinberger, Schwartz, & Davidson, 1979). In comparison with this, *theoretical* considerations concerning the concepts repression (or cognitive avoidance, respectively) and sensitization (or vigilance) become less important. If they are advanced, they then reflect an adherence to certain neo-psychoanalytical propositions, such as those formulated by Anna Freud (1946). (See, for example, Haan, 1977; Horowitz, 1988; or Vaillant, 1977.)

A second trend is represented by a multitude of empirical studies linked to theoretical models only loosely and, at best, post hoc. This trend includes, on the one hand, the numerous studies with coping inventories constructed without any stronger theoretical foundation, and, on the other hand, studies which deal with specific topics such as "illness and denial".

The third trend in attention and avoidance research is manifested by some promising theoretical approaches (e.g., information processing models, systems theories) which were, however, developed in relative isolation from one another. These circumstances have so far blocked the elaboration of a more comprehensive theory about (in particular cognitive) coping strategies, a fact which has in turn had negative consequences for the development of theory-based applied approaches (e.g., in the field of coping, illness, and health).

Efforts to create a more comprehensive theoretical integration of these diverse approaches are therefore necessary. The following formulations appear to be particularly appropriate in contributing to such an integration:

1. The information processing model of anxiety formulated by Mathews, MacLeod, and colleagues (e.g., Eysenck, MacLeod, & Mathews, 1987; MacLeod & Mathews, 1988; Williams, Watts, MacLeod, & Mathews, 1988).

2. Conceptions about the relationship between the processes of "worrying" and imagery and the maintenance of anxiety, as they have been presented by Borkovec (1985; cf. Borkovec & Hu, 1990; Borkovec & Inz, 1990).

3. Miller's "Monitoring-Blunting" approach (1980, 1987, 1990).

4. The model of "coping modes" (Krohne, 1986, 1989; cf. Krohne, Hock, & Kohlmann, 1991).

5. Research on the perception of emotions and symptoms conducted by Pennebaker (1982) and Leventhal (cf. Baumann & Leventhal, 1985; Leventhal, 1987).

6. Systems-theoretical approaches to behavior regulation, as proposed in regard to the processing of aversive information among others by Carver and Scheier (1981, 1986, 1990) and Leventhal (1970, 1984; cf. Leventhal & Nerenz, 1983).

Researchers who have substantially advanced the elaboration of these approaches will present their work in this volume. In addition, contributions will be presented which examine specific aspects of these approaches. These studies determine and perhaps specify the scope of central assumptions of several models. They also illustrate the methodological approaches of different research groups. They include studies about:

a) coping dispositions, direction of attention, and anxiety states conducted by Hock;

b) the relationship between denial of failure-related information and the Type-A Behavior Pattern investigated by Breznitz, Ben-Zur, and co-workers; and

c) the importance of coping dispositions for the perception of internal somatic processes as outlined both by Hodapp, Knoll, and co-workers and by Kohlmann.

Besides the presentation and discussion of theoretical fundamentals and empirical findings about the coping strategies "vigilance" and "avoidance", a further objective of this volume is to determine the importance of these strategies in the origin, treatment, and prevention of disease. Three functional relationships are currently being discussed in the research literature and will be appropriately dealt with in this text (see also Friedman, 1990):

1. The influence of certain coping strategies on the *origin* as well as *manifestation* of disease (e.g., the role denial plays in the development of cancer or coronary heart disease).
2. The importance of certain strategies for *coping* with acute or chronic disease (e.g., after developing cancer or after surgical treatment).
3. Coping as a *mediator* between aversive events and stress reactions or health consequences, respectively (e.g., in the relationship between preoperative stress, coping, and intra- and postoperative adaptation).

Theoretical Approaches

Corresponding to this arrangement of the topics, the volume is divided into three main parts. In the part following this introduction (*Part II*), the central concepts of vigilance and cognitive avoidance as well as certain theoretical approaches which have been developed in this context will be presented. In the chapters by Krohne and by Miller, Combs, and Kruus, the central concepts in the description of cognitive reactions to aversive events (vigilance or monitoring, respectively, and cognitive avoidance or blunting) are outlined in more detail.

In Krohne's contribution the attempt is made to venture beyond a mere description so as to establish a theoretical foundation (the model of "coping modes"). Habitual preferences for vigilance and cognitive avoidance are explained by the constructs *intolerance of uncertainty* and *intolerance of emotional arousal*. Individuals high in intolerance of uncertainty should tend to employ vigilant coping, while intolerance of emotional arousal is supposedly associated with cognitive avoidant strategies. Since the model postulates a detached functioning of the dimensions intolerance of uncertainty (vigilant coping) and intolerance of emotional arousal (cognitive avoidant coping), specific configurations of intolerances (or dispositional preferences for coping strategies, respectively) can be considered. In comparison with the traditional unidimensional personality construct repression-sensitization, this two-dimensional conceptualization has the advantage that one can distinguish between those people who employ an increased amount of vigilance *and* cognitive avoidance in stressful situations (i.e., who are highly intolerant of both uncertainty and emotional arousal) and those who do not tend toward these basic forms of coping (i.e., who are tolerant of uncertainty and emotional arousal).

The contribution by Miller and co-workers explores the motivations and consequences of adopting a *monitoring* (vigilant) versus *blunting* (avoidant) style of coping, particularly in the face of *medically-related stressors*. Three possible mechanisms for monitoring are considered by the authors: (1) executing controlling actions; (2) modulating negative affect; and

(3) reducing uncertainty. It is proposed that monitors remain vigilant to threat, despite its arousing consequences, partly to access competent others and partly to reduce uncertainty. Sustained arousal may stem from the way in which information is processed, since it entails cognitive rehearsal of threatening cues along with increased attention to the individual's own negative affective state. In addition, it is postulated that vigilance often activates unsuccessful attempts to avoid, which may interfere with full emotional processing of the stressor.

Leventhal, Suls, and Leventhal (Chapter 4) propose that research on coping strategies such as vigilance or cognitive avoidance requires a theoretical framework that allows one to treat coping responses as having *multiple functions*. These functions vary with the type of problem and the specific point in the course of a problem episode. The authors propose a hierarchical model of coping in which the different levels are related to one another *functionally*. The uppermost level consists of generalized coping intentions. An intermediate level contains overlearned coping strategies (i.e., learned sequences for controlling problems and regulating the problem-solving system), while a lower level is defined by specific coping responses. It is argued that these levels differ qualitatively, i.e., they involve different memory codes and modes of information processing. Leventhal et al. substantiate their model by presenting data relevant to differences in coping in cohorts sampled from different areas of the life-span.

The subsequent chapter by Borkovec and Lyonfields examines the relationships between *worry cognitions* and cognitive avoidant processes in anxiety maintenance. The authors suggest that worry is a conceptual avoidance response which is reinforced by the reduction of somatic anxiety activation and thereby contributory to the maintenance of anxious meanings. Although worriers will claim that their worry functions to avoid future catastrophe, evidence presented by Borkovec and Lyonfields indicates that worrisome conceptual activity prior to the presentation of aversive material eliminates cardiovascular response to that material. The authors assume that worry may suppress efferent command and therefore emotional processing via its avoidance of aversive imagery. They present a theoretical model of anxiety emphasizing the role of *behavioral inhibition, physiological inhibition*, and *excessive conceptual avoidance* in an effort to integrate recent research in evaluative conditioning, unconditioned stimulus revaluation, and imagery-anxiety interactions. Using this model, it may be possible to integrate research on cognitive forms of coping and on cognitive anxiety reactions which, up to now, has largely been conducted concurrently.

A remarkably similar orientation underlies Mathews' information processing model (Chapter 5). In this model, operating at a microanalytic level, vigilance and cognitive avoidance are related to the study of cognitive processes that are characteristic of *highly anxious subjects*. It is argued that, because threatening events must first attract attentional resources, be interpreted for personal meaning, and then sometimes further elaborated, there are several points at which *individual differences* may emerge. Evidence is summarized to show that highly anxious subjects selectively attend to threat cues and tend to interpret ambiguous events as more threatening than do less anxious individuals. However, other evidence is presented which suggests that anxiety can also be associated with cognitive avoidance at a subsequent stage of processing, so that despite selective encoding of the threatening meaning of events, further elaboration may be inhibited. Mathews therefore concludes that vigilance at one processing stage is not incompatible with avoidance at another. Obviously, the deployment of cognitive resources (vigilance or avoidance) is a function of the interaction between the different stages in the information processing continuum, the degree of trait anxiety, and the level of the emotional state. Mathews presents experimental information-processing designs which allow for a more fine-grained and objective analysis of cognitive coping than is available from self-report alone. Such methods provide a useful way of testing hypotheses about the nature and consequences of cognitive coping that could not otherwise be addressed.

The Processing of External and Internal Information

In *Part III*, the focus is on empirical findings about the role of vigilant and avoidant coping in the processing of aversive (external and internal) information. In the first contribution, Hock bases his work on the model of coping modes presented in Chapter 2 (Krohne). This model differentiates between four dispositionally determined configurations of the response to threatening stimuli: sensitization, repression, high trait anxiety, and nondefensiveness. Hock applies this conception to the simultaneous analysis of state anxiety and attentional reactions. His central goal is to determine *intraindividual dependencies* between both of these reaction forms and to relate them to the coping modes mentioned. To deal with this task, methods have to be established which allow for a continuous assessment of emotional and attentional changes within a person. Regarding attention, Hock proposes the *looking behavior* of individuals, directed toward or away from a source of threatening information, as a promising starting point for such an analysis. Looking behavior has a two-fold function: as a part of a person's *warning system* and as an *arousal regulation device*. Hock presents two studies which analyze dispositional coping determinants of looking at or away from a source of (social) threat. In an elaborate conceptual and methodological analysis, he finally addresses the topic of *inter*individual differences in the *sequential relationships* between attentional orientation and somatic arousal during the anticipation of a potentially aversive event.

In the contribution by Ben-Zur, Breznitz, and Hashmonay, an attempt is made to associate processes of cognitive avoidance to the *Type-A Behavior Pattern*. The Type-A person is characterized by the following pattern of coping reactions: the ability to focus attention on task information while ignoring aversive bodily cues (such as fatigue or pain) and the ability to allocate attention to the important task or environmental aspect while ignoring peripheral information (such as failure feedback). The authors conclude that for

Type-A persons the denial (cognitive avoidance) of failure functions to maintain efforts and persistance while struggling for success and achievement. It seems to be very promising to apply this reaction pattern to both the previously mentioned model of the coping dimensions "vigilance" and "cognitive avoidance" and to the description of worry processes as a special form of avoidance, i.e., as a suppression of emotional information.

Hock addresses an almost "classic" question in this field: the influence of interindividual differences on the processing of *external* aversive information. In dealing with this question, he proposes innovative experimental and statistical methods of analysis. Ben-Zur et al. expand on this general approach by considering the contribution of individual differences to the processing of both external (failure feedback) and *internal* (e.g., pain, fatique) aversive stimulation. The analysis of the relationship between coping variables and the processing of internal (somatic) information has largely been neglected up to now. However, as is obvious in the application of this relationship to the Type-A Behavior Pattern (cf. Ben-Zur et al.), processing of internal stimuli has become an important applied topic, especially in health research. The way individuals identify somatic states and the role personality variables play in this process have increasingly become central topics in health psychology (cf. Barr, Pennebaker, & Watson, 1988; Baumann & Leventhal, 1985; Leventhal, 1987; Pennebaker, 1982). Consequently, the final two chapters of Part III (Hodapp & Knoll; Kohlmann) deal with the relationships between dispositional coping variables and the perception of somatic reactions (or states, respectively).

Using heartbeat perception as an example, Hodapp and Knoll begin their chapter with a critical discussion of questions and methods in *interoception* research. They continue with the presentation of a study which investigates the influence of heartbeat perception ability and coping dispositions (vigilance and cognitive avoidance) on emotional reactions during the presentation of neutral and aversive information. Of special interest is the way avoidance and vigilance are related to the ability to perceive internal processes. While some authors assume that highly vigilant persons perceive somatic processes more sensitively and avoidant subjects less sensitively (cf. chapter by Miller et al.), Hodapp and Knoll report a positive relationship between cognitive avoidance and heartbeat perception ability and a negative one between vigilance and this ability. This finding is in accordance with the assumption proposed in the model of coping modes (cf. Krohne, Chapter 2) that avoiders should exhibit a heightened sensitivity for arousal-related information. Since Hodapp and Knoll's findings refer, however, to a specific aspect of the perception of somatic processes (heartbeat), further investigations are needed in order to generalize the results to other areas of interoception.

Kohlmann relates coping variables to accuracy in blood pressure estimation. By distinguishing two types of accuracy (*level accuracy*, i.e., the overall discrepancy between average estimated blood pressure and mean actual blood pressure, and *covariation accuracy*, i.e., the degree to which fluctuations of estimated blood pressure covary with actual blood pressure fluctuations), Kohlmann achieves a differentiated pattern of results. While coping strategies are unrelated to level accuracy, cognitive avoidance proves to be a relevant variable for covariation accuracy. The percentage of variance in estimated blood pressure accounted for by *external situational cues* (e.g., performing a physical exercise task) is significantly higher for avoiders than for nonavoiders. Kohlmann sees this result as support for the hypothesis that cognitive avoidant behavior is motivated by "intolerance of emotional arousal" (cf. Krohne, Chapter 2). As a consequence of this intolerance, avoiders withdraw attention from internal bodily cues and exclude somatic-affective information from further processing (see also Borkovec & Lyonfields, Chapter 5).

Besides investigating coping variables, Kohlmann also relates the processing of internal information to *gender differences*. While no gender differences can be observed when the *direct perception* of somatic states is tested, some support is found for the hypothesis that women rely more markedly than men on external cues when estimating blood pressure. Further interesting gender differences emerge when level accuracy is assessed for different situational contexts (e.g., cognitive tasks, physical exercise, rest periods). Kohlmann's results point to the important role gender differences and situational contexts play in addition to coping variables when investigating the processing of somatic information.

Coping and Health

The chapters in *Part IV* deal with the relationship between cognitive coping reactions and health status. They thereby build a bridge between basic coping research and applied approaches. The first chapter in this section (Weidner & Collins) follows Kohlmann's contribution in so far as it also deals with a topic long neglected by researchers, the significance of gender differences in coping. Consequently, Weidner and Collins' analysis of the association between coping factors and health-related variables also takes into account differences manifested by men and women in certain coping reactions. The authors are particularly interested in determining whether the different prevalence rates for major health variables (e.g., depression, heart disease, alcohol consumption) among men and women are somehow related to gender differences in coping styles (e.g., anger expression, avoidance). While the analysis in terms of vigilance and cognitive avoidance has proven successful for coronary-prone individuals (see also chapter by Ben-Zur et al.), this has not been the case with depression. The hypothesis assuming relationships between vigilance, avoidance, and depression definitely has a speculative value but, at the moment, little empirical support.

Weidner and Collins follow a *prevention-oriented* perspective when dealing with the relationship between coping and health. In particular, they aim at establishing a causal chain, beginning with (social-psychologically determined) gender differences in the types of stressors a person encounters, followed by the gender-specific employment of certain coping strategies, and closing with different prevalence rates of certain illnesses in men and women. The contribution by Filipp, Klauer, and Ferring, on the other hand, is concerned with the influence certain coping reactions have on the *progression* of an illness. They address the question of how self-focused attention (or self-consciousness) interferes with the coping process in patients suffering from a malignant disease.

The authors report results from a large study with cancer patients which suggest (1) that private self-consciousness mediates the activation of coping efforts and (2) that relationships between certain indicators of medical stress (e.g., multimorbidity) and measures of psychosocial adjustment are dependent on interindividual differences in self-consciousness. Whether self-focused attention functions as a risk factor concerning adaptation (as one might expect) or as a protective factor depends on a number of specific circumstances discussed in their chapter.

A topic, which has become an almost "classical" area in research examining the influences of coping variables on health status, is the way in which patients cope with *surgical stress*. The final two chapters of this volume address this topic. Although vigilance and avoidance have been frequently studied in this area, there has been little detailed theoretical work done to determine when these coping strategies lead to the most favorable adaptational outcomes, i.e., under which conditions and in which phase of the surgical situation. Equally inconsistent are the results reported in the literature, although cognitive avoidance is generally viewed, at least in the pre-operative phase, as a relatively adaptive coping strategy. Additional problems arise, however, when one attempts to pinpoint factors which indicate the quality of adaptation to the surgical situation.

Carver and Scheier present a view of vigilant and avoidant coping which is derived from their model of behavioral self-regulation (Carver & Scheier, 1981). In this model effort gives way to disengagement as expectancy of success declines. From this viewpoint the authors conducted several studies of coping, two of which were relevant to discussions of vigilance and avoidance. Subjects in these studies were men undergoing nonemergency coronary artery bypass and women undergoing surgery for breast cancer. Before surgery and about one week later, the patients reported what they had been thinking about and what they had tried not to think about. These reports were then related to measures of distress and a range of other variables surrounding the surgery and recovery period.

Among the complex pattern of results, three findings seem to be especially worth mentioning: (1) Manifestations of vigilance were related to high levels of distress, both before and after surgery. In particular, the tendency to focus on emotional reactions and physical symptoms seems to have adverse effects. (2) Avoidant tactics were also associated with distress but to a lower degree than vigilance was. (3) The effects of vigilance and avoidance on distress can both be distinguished from the effect of *disengagement*, which is a central mechanism in Carver and Scheier's model of self-regulation.

In the final chapter Slangen, Kleemann, and Krohne outline three studies on surgery which have two major goals: (1) an analysis of the relationship between coping variables and the patient's adaptational status, which is based on a theory of vigilance and cognitive avoidance presented in the model of coping modes (cf. Krohne, Chapter 2), and (2) the determination of indicators for the adaptational status at different levels (self-report, physiological parameters, medical data) and at different time points in the surgical process (pre-, intra-, postoperative).

In all three studies the pattern of relationship was complex and not very consistent. For example, while the first two studies established the expected stress-reducing effect of cognitive avoidance, the third study could not confirm it. Obviously, hypotheses concerning effects of avoidant or vigilant coping on the adaptational status of surgical patients need further scrutiny. In particular, the following topics have to be addressed: (1) the limiting conditions of an established relationship (such limiting conditions could be, for example, the specific structure or the temporal extension of a stress event); (2) the context in which coping takes place, e.g., the amount of social support available to the patient; and (3) different aspects of vigilance and cognitive avoidance and their specific functional relationships with different stress indicators.

Future Directions

The approaches presented in this volume often coincide but there are also some discrepancies. Obviously, the contributors share the opinion that vigilance (i.e., the orientation towards threat-relevant aspects of a situation) and cognitive avoidance (i.e., turning attention away from threatening cues) are two central (albeit not the only) mechanisms for regulating stress. Most authors also emphasize that the prime goal of cognitive avoidance is to regulate emotional arousal, while vigilance aims at reducing the state of uncertainty. (Of course, these are not the only goals of coping. Other general objectives are, e.g., to keep or to regain decisional control in aversive situations or to maintain positive self-esteem.)

It remains to be clarified whether these two behavioral classes should be related to stable (i.e., dispositional) interindividual differences. But even those authors who are critical of a personality-based view of coping occasionally employ dispositionally oriented instruments to assess coping (cf. contribution by Filipp et al.). Critics of a dispositional (or "trait") approach argue that persons can react vigilantly *as well as* avoidantly, albeit at different stages of a stressful encounter (cf. Mathews). Approaches which regard vigilance and cognitive avoidance not as poles of a unidimensional continuum but as two separate personality dimensions (cf. Krohne) might help to settle this matter.

Models which suggest that individuals can *habitually* tend towards vigilance as well as cognitive avoidance (Krohne, Miller et al.) have so far provided only a meager answer to one important question: Can characteristic sequences of vigilance and cognitive avoidance during a stressful encounter be empirically related to personality dispositions and can these relationships be theoretically substantiated? In my judgment, Mathews' approach seems to be suitable for clarifying this issue: individuals high in trait anxiety react vigilantly in an early stage of a threatening encounter and avoidantly in a later one. They are assumed to be subject to an "automatic vigilant bias", i.e., ambiguous events are interpreted (in a more or less *automatic* way) as threatening in an early stage of processing. At a subsequent stage, however, anxious persons (voluntarily or *strategically*) avoid the elaboration of the meaning of such stimuli. Suitable for such a sequential view is also Borkovec and Lyonfield's idea that worry functions to avoid aversive imagery in order to regulate somatic activation (see also contribution by Hock).

Marked inconsistencies among the single contributions become obvious if one considers the hypothesized and empirically observed relationships between vigilance/cognitive avoidance and behavioral consequences (e.g., level of distress after surgery, health status, performance level, degree of emotional arousal). To name only a few examples, some studies report favorable effects of cognitive avoidance on level of distress in surgical patients (Slangen et al., Studies 1 and 2), others yield negative effects (Carver & Scheier), while still others observe no effects (Slangen et al., Study 3). Similarly inconsistent are the findings for vigilance (cf. Filipp et al., Miller et al.).

If one does not want to draw the conclusion that vigilance and cognitive avoidance are not actually meaningful constructs for coping research, the following stipulation has to be fulfilled in the future: hypotheses about the effects expected for vigilance and avoidance should only be formulated after that situation which supposedly initiates the *actualization* of these two coping dispositions has been carefully analyzed with respect to certain features. These features include:

1. The stage of an aversive episode the individual encounters. Investigations employing multiple points of measurement (Carver & Scheier; Hock; Slangen et al.; cf. also Mathews) demonstrate that the respective stage of an aversive encounter is decisive for the relationship expected between vigilance or cognitive avoidance and actual behavior.
2. The degree of controllability and predictability of a stressor which can, however, vary as the stress episode (e.g., a surgical treatment) progresses (see also Weidner & Collins).
3. If certain aspects of a task are used as performance criteria (e.g., amount of words recalled), a precise analysis of the *demands* of this task is necessary. For example, if differences in the automatic (early-stage) processing of information are of interest, the material to be processed has to first have a certain content (it has to contain *ambiguous* stimuli) and then specific recall tests suitable for assessing the *implicit memory* have to be applied. However, if differences in the voluntary or strategic (later-stage) processing of information are of prime interest, tests for the assessment of the *explicit memory* are necessary (cf. Mathews' chapter; see also Krohne et al., 1991).

Another reason for the somewhat inconsistent findings might be the fact that the *intentions* (or *goals*) underlying coping behavior have often been neglected.

These intentions define the range of intended and unintended effects, and, accordingly, govern the processing of feedback from these effects. The concepts "intention", "coping action", "effect", and "feedback" refer to a systems approach, i.e., a process-oriented view of coping. In their contribution, Leventhal et al. demonstrate how these different elements may be interconnected within a functional hierarchy. In my opinion, this is a very promising approach since it takes into account, on the one hand, very general personality dispositions (the intentions) and, on the other hand, rather specific feedback from coping reactions and emotional states. A very similar model has been put forward by Carver and Scheier.

The model of coping modes (Krohne) as well as the hierarchical conception proposed by Leventhal et al. point to the importance of *somatic information* in the coping process. This makes evident the significance of the fast developing field of interoception research (cf. Hodapp & Knoll, Kohlmann). If one argues that coping also refers to the control of emotional reactions, then it is obvious that this control depends on the perception, encoding, and processing of internal (somatic) stimuli (see also Borkovec & Lyonfields). Particularly important is of course the answer to the question of how individuals use *internal* and *external cues* in estimating their somatic state (Kohlmann) or in regulating their subsequent actions (Ben-Zur et al.). This opens a very promising avenue to an integration of personality psychology (or differential psychology), coping research, and health psychology. Examples of this kind of integration dealt with in this volume include the Type-A Behavior Pattern (Ben-Zur et al.) and gender differences (Kohlmann).

Gender is a variable which has been largely neglected in coping research. Its significance and possible relationships with coping-dependent characteristics (e.g., coronary heart disease, depression) have been elaborated by Weidner and Collins. Gender cannot be regarded however as an explicative personality construct. What is therefore needed is a general theory which is able to explain, for example, why men tend towards avoidance in certain situations while women react with vigilance.

Throughout this volume, much attention is devoted to methodological topics. Surprisingly, no one addressed the "laboratory vs. field research" controversy. It obviously remains undisputed that laboratory investigations are of utmost importance for testing central hypotheses. The same applies to field research, if we want to determine the value of certain statements acquired in the laboratory for explaining everyday behavior. However, we then have to determine which mechanisms can be transferred from the lab to field research.

Since coping occurs in a dynamic, continuously changing action field, there is a need for methods which allow for a continuous assessment of certain behavioral indicators (e.g., attentional changes, emotional states, cf. Hock's chapter). It is undisputed that the development of such process measures will have a great impact on future coping research. However, most statements on this topic remain on a programmatic level. At present, the process measurement which has been elaborated is confined to large-scale laboratory experiments (cf. contributions by Mathews; Hock; Hodapp & Knoll; Kohlmann). An economical employment for diagnostic purposes, e.g., to infer coping dispositions from certain processes, remains to be discovered. This has to be one major focus of future coping research.

References

Asendorpf, J. B., & Scherer, K. R. (1983). The discrepant repressor: Differentiation between low anxiety, high anxiety, and repression of anxiety by autonomic-facial-verbal patterns of behavior. *Journal of Personality and Social Psychology, 45*, 1334-1346.

Barr, M., Pennebaker, J. W., & Watson, D. (1988). Improving blood pressure estimation through internal and environmental feedback. *Psychosomatic Medicine, 50*, 37-45.

Baumann, L. J., & Leventhal, H. (1985). "I can tell when my blood pressure is up, can't I?". *Health Psychology, 4*, 203-218.

Bell, P. A., & Byrne, D. (1978). Repression-sensitization. In H. London & J. E. Exner (Eds.), *Dimensions of personality* (pp. 449-485). New York: Wiley.

Borkovec, T. D. (1985). The role of cognitive and somatic cues in anxiety and anxiety disorders: Worry and relaxation-induced anxiety. In A. H. Tuma & J. D. Maser (Eds.), *Anxiety and the anxiety disorders* (pp. 463-478). Hillsdale, NJ: Erlbaum.

Borkovec, T. D., & Hu, S. (1990). The effect of worry on cardiovascular response to phobic imagery. *Behaviour Research and Therapy, 28*, 69-73.

Borkovec, T. D., & Inz, J. (1990). The nature of worry in generalized anxiety disorder: A predominance of thought activity. *Behaviour Research and Therapy, 28*, 153-158.

Byrne, D. (1964). Repression-sensitization as a dimension of personality. In B. A. Maher (Ed.), *Progress in experimental personality research* (Vol. 1, pp. 169-220). New York: Academic Press.

Carver, C. S., & Scheier, M. F. (1981). *Attention and self-regulation: A control-theory approach to human behavior*. New York: Springer-Verlag.

Carver, C. S., & Scheier, M. F. (1986). Functional and dysfunctional responses to anxiety: The interaction between expectancies and self-focused attention. In R. Schwarzer (Ed.), *Self-related cognitions in anxiety and motivation* (pp. 111-141). Hillsdale, NJ: Erlbaum.

Carver, C. S., & Scheier, M. F. (1990). Origins and functions of positive and negative affect: A control-process view. *Psychological Review, 97*, 19-35.

Chabot, J. A. (1973). Repression-sensitization: A critique of some neglected variables in the literature. *Psychological Bulletin, 80*, 122-129.

Eysenck, M. W., MacLeod, C., & Mathews, A. (1987). Cognitive functioning and anxiety. *Psychological Research, 49*, 189 -195.

Freud, A. (1946). *The ego and the mechanisms of defense*. New York: International Universities Press.

Friedman, H. S. (Ed.). (1990). *Personality and disease*. New York: Wiley.

Haan, N. (1977). *Coping and defending. Processes of self-environment organization*. New York: Academic Press.

Horowitz, M. J. (1988). *Introduction to psychodynamics*. New York: Basic Books.

Janis, I. L. (1983). Stress inoculation in health care: Theory and research. In D. Meichenbaum & M. Jaremko (Eds.), *Stress reduction and prevention* (pp. 67-99). New York: Plenum.

Krohne, H. W. (1978). Individual differences in coping with stress and anxiety. In C. D. Spielberger & I. G. Sarason (Eds.), *Stress and anxiety* (Vol. 5, pp. 233-260). Washington, DC: Hemisphere.

Krohne, H. W. (1986). Coping with stress: Dispositions, strategies, and the problem of measurement. In M. H. Appley & R. Trumbull (Eds.), *Dynamics of stress. Physiological, psychological, and social perspectives* (pp. 209-234). New York: Plenum.

Krohne, H. W. (1989). The concept of coping modes: Relating cognitive person variables to actual coping behavior. *Advances in Behaviour Research and Therapy, 11*, 235-248.

Krohne, H. W., Hock, M., & Kohlmann, C.-W. (1991). *Coping dispositions, uncertainty, and emotional arousal*. Manuscript submitted for publication.

Krohne, H. W., & Rogner, J. (1982). Repression-sensitization as a central construct in coping research. In H. W. Krohne & L. Laux (Eds.), *Achievement, stress and anxiety* (pp. 167-193). New York: Mc Graw-Hill.

Krohne, H. W., & Rogner, J. (1985). Mehrvariablen-Diagnostik in der Bewältigungsforschung [Multivariate assessment in coping research]. In H. W. Krohne (Ed.), *Angstbewältigung in Leistungssituationen* (pp. 45-62). Weinheim: edition psychologie.

Leventhal, H. (1970). Findings and theory in the study of fear communications. In L. Berkowitz (Ed.), *Advances in experimental social psychology* (Vol. 5, pp. 119-186). New York: Academic Press.

Leventhal, H. (1984). A perceptual-motor theory of emotion. In L. Berkowitz (Ed.), *Advances in experimental social psychology* (Vol. 17, pp. 117-182). Orlando: Academic Press.

Leventhal, H. (1987). Symptom reporting: a focus on process. In S. McHugh & T. M. Vallis (Eds.), *Illness behavior. A multidisciplinary model* (pp. 219-237). New York: Plenum.

Leventhal, H., & Nerenz, D. (1983). A model for stress research with some implications for the control of stress disorders. In D. Meichenbaum & M. Jaremko (Eds.), *Stress reduction and prevention* (pp. 5-38). New York: Plenum.

MacLeod, C., & Mathews, A. (1988). Anxiety and the allocation of attention to threat. *Quarterly Journal of Experimental Psychology, 40*, 653-670.

Miller, S. M. (1980). When is a little information a dangerous thing? Coping with stressful life events by monitoring versus blunting. In S. Levine & H. Ursin (Eds.), *Health and coping* (pp. 145-169). New York: Plenum.

Miller, S. M. (1987). Monitoring and blunting: Validation of a questionnaire to assess styles of information seeking under threat. *Journal of Personality and Social Psychology, 52*, 345-353.

Miller, S. M. (1990). To see or not to see: Cognitive informational styles in the coping process. In M. Rosenbaum (Ed.), *Learned resourcefulness: On coping skills, self-regulation, and adaptive behavior* (pp. 95-126). New York: Springer.

Mullen, B., & Suls, J. (1982). The effectiveness of attention and rejection as coping styles: A meta-analysis of temporal differences. *Journal of Psychosomatic Research, 26*, 43-49.

Pennebaker, J. W. (1982). *The psychology of physical symptoms*. New York: Springer-Verlag.

Roth, S., & Cohen, L. J. (1986). Approach, avoidance, and coping with stress. *American Psychologist, 41*, 813-819.

Singer, J. L. (Ed.). (1990). *Repression and dissociation. Implications for personality theory, psychopathology, and health*. Chicago: University of Chicago Press.

Suls, J., & Fletcher, B. (1985). The relative efficacy of avoidant and non-avoidant coping strategies: A meta-analysis. *Health Psychology, 4*, 249-288.

Vaillant, G. E. (1977). *Adaptation to life*. Boston: Little, Brown.

Weinberger, D. A., Schwartz, G. E., & Davidson, R. J. (1979). Low-anxious, high-anxious, and repressive coping-styles: Psychometric patterns and behavioral and physiological responses to stress. *Journal of Abnormal Psychology, 88*, 369-380.

Williams, J. M. G., Watts, F. N., MacLeod, C., & Mathews, A. (1988). *Cognitive psychology and emotional disorders*. London: Wiley.

PART II.

GENERAL CONCEPTUAL ISSUES

Chapter 2

Vigilance and Cognitive Avoidance as Concepts in Coping Research

Heinz Walter Krohne

Coping Processes and Coping Dispositions

In this chapter, a personality-oriented model for analyzing coping will be presented. In recent years, coping approaches which focus on personality constructs have been subject to criticism. The main objection against personality-centered analyses, which has been put forward in particular by Lazarus and co-workers (cf. Folkman & Lazarus, 1985; Lazarus & Folkman, 1984a), points to the variability in behavior observed for the majority of individuals in stressful situations. Very few people universally employ the same coping strategies when confronted with different kinds of stressors.

Researchers such as Lazarus characterize this *intraindividual variability* in coping behavior, originating in situational demands, as a *process* (Folkman & Lazarus, 1985). They contrast this process with *structure*. Structure is supposed to refer to stable factors such as personality dispositions ("traits"). Since personality traits are assumed to be static, i.e., intraindividually invariable, it is argued that "structural approaches cannot reveal changes in stress-related phenomena ..." (Folkman & Lazarus, 1985, p. 151). Consequently, personality dispositions (or their empirical indicators, e.g., personality scales) are considered to be unsuitable for adequately explaining or predicting intraindividual variability in behavior (Lazarus & Folkman, 1984a). Lazarus, and others as well (cf. Filipp, Klauer, & Ferring, this volume), have therefore called for a shift away from personality dispositions as the focal point in the analyses of stress events. Instead, they demand that the emphasis should be placed on the contingencies of situational characteristics and specific behavior patterns, conceived of as processes (cf. Folkman, Lazarus, Dunkel-Schetter, DeLongis, & Gruen, 1986).

I have previously (Krohne, 1986, 1990c) attempted to demonstrate that an antagonism of *structure* (e.g., personality dispositions) to *process* (e.g., changes in coping behavior and emotional states during a stressful encounter) does not exist as it was described by Lazarus and co-workers. The most important arguments can be summarized as follows:

I would like to thank Michael Hock, Carl-Walter Kohlmann, and Lothar Laux for helpful comments on a draft of this chapter.

1. "Process" and "structure" are terms conceived to be on different conceptual levels. Process (at least as it is understood by Lazarus) refers to a stream of observed events, for example (a) the manifestation of an emotion of a certain intensity, (b) the execution of a coping act, (c) the subsequent decline in the intensity of this emotion, and (d) the emergence of another emotion. Structure refers to (a) the *regularity* which one might recognize in such a process and (b) the *constellation of inferred mechanisms* which effect this process. A prerequisite of structure and regularity is the term "system".

2. Change and stability do not exclude each other, since "stable" does not in any way mean only "static" (as Lazarus appears to have in mind). In connection with this, Herrmann (1973) introduced the concept of "stability of change". Accordingly there are stable and unstable changes. *Instability* refers to the inability to put a boundary on a system's states along the time course of some encounter (cf. Ashby, 1956). *Unstable changes* generally indicate the *breakdown* of a system. *Stability of change* implies that a *process is replicable.* However, this is only possible when the crucial effect mechanisms which this process is based on have been previously identified. With regard to the replicability of a process it should be pointed out that it is of course impossible for a person to be confronted with exactly the same situation more than once.

3. The crucial effect mechanisms are identified by using both induction and deduction. Using an exact, fine-grained analysis of a stream of events (e.g., emotions and coping behavior), it would be possible to obtain initial evidence for a cross-temporal or cross-situational consistency (i.e., stability) in this process (cf. Laux & Weber, 1987). In this manner, initial ideas about effect mechanisms could be *inductively* developed. However, regularity (stability) in the stream of behavior can only be detected by applying specific theoretical concepts to the behavioral analysis, i.e., by following *rules of deduction.* What appears to be irregular from a certain point of view can be described as an ordered (i.e., stable) sequence of events when a different theoretical construct is applied.

4. There is another reason why it is important to determine which effect mechanisms are crucial to a process (and thus to predict and replicate this process). The above-mentioned breakdown of a system is not the focus of research on stress, coping, and adaptation. Instead, such research deals with finding out how a system (a person) tries to regulate itself after a displacement, i.e., after the system is moved from one state (e.g., low anxiety) to another (e.g., high anxiety; see also Carver & Scheier, this volume). In order to intervene in this system (e.g., modify it), one cannot be satisfied with a mere description of the actual self-regulation. More importantly, it is necessary to identify the rules which the system follows in regulating itself. This is exactly the point where structure and process meet, i.e., (structural) personality research begins to focus on process.

In the next section, I will present a personality model which is based on two coping dimensions, i.e., structural aspects. However, the main theoretical assumptions relate to processes. It is thereby posited that changing factors may indicate personality characteristics if these changes yield *interindividual variability* and manifest a certain *stability*, i.e., can be replicated as a function of equivalent situational circumstances.

The Model of Coping Modes

The personality model of coping (Krohne, 1986, 1989) attempts to describe and explain person-specific differences in behavioral regulation under stressful conditions. The model concentrates on those processes of *attention orientation* which can be observed when an individual is confronted with threat cues. Based on fundamental conceptualizations in coping research (e.g., Byrne, 1964; Eriksen, 1966; Krohne, 1978; Miller, 1980; Roth & Cohen, 1986), the constructs "vigilance" and "cognitive avoidance" have been introduced to describe these processes. *Vigilance* refers to those strategies which are characterized by intensified intake and processing of threatening information. *Cognitive avoidance* is marked by a turning away from the threat-related cues. Subsequent to later developments in research on perceptual defense (cf. Erdelyi, 1974; Krohne, 1978), the allocation of attention in threatening situations is defined as a two-phase process; after a (perhaps only rudimentary) identification of threat-related cues, attention is turned toward or away from such stimuli.

In this model, coping is conceived as a *multi-level process* with feedback (cf. Figure 2.1). The intake and processing of threatening information is followed by the selection of strategies, the initiation of coping reactions or acts, as well as the registration of the (intended and unintended) effects of these reactions. The (partially preattentive, partially conscious) procedure by which information is processed and the strategic selection of coping reactions is dependent on specific goals (which will be presented later) and controlled by specific cognitive processes. The registered effects then act as feedback on both the subsequent process of coping and the experience of anxiety which is an emotion potentially concomitant with this process. (For a similar approach, also see the chapter by Mathews, this volume; cf. also the chapter by Borkovec and Lyonfields for a theoretical model of the worry process.)

The concepts central to the description of coping – *reaction*, *act*, and *strategy* – can be assigned to different levels (Krohne, 1989). For example, the *coping strategy* "distraction from threatening cues" can manifest itself in different *acts* (e.g., listening to music with closed eyes or participating in an animated discussion), which may not only be directed at different partial goals but can also be distinguished with regard to individual *reaction components* and their respective arrangement. Strategies, in turn, can also be categorized into behavioral classes of a higher order, so-called *superstrategies* (cf. Figure 2.4, p. 30, in the section on measurement of vigilance and cognitive avoidance). The model of coping modes is conceived of as a *partial-area theory*, i.e., it concentrates, as mentioned, on two specific higher-order classes: coping by

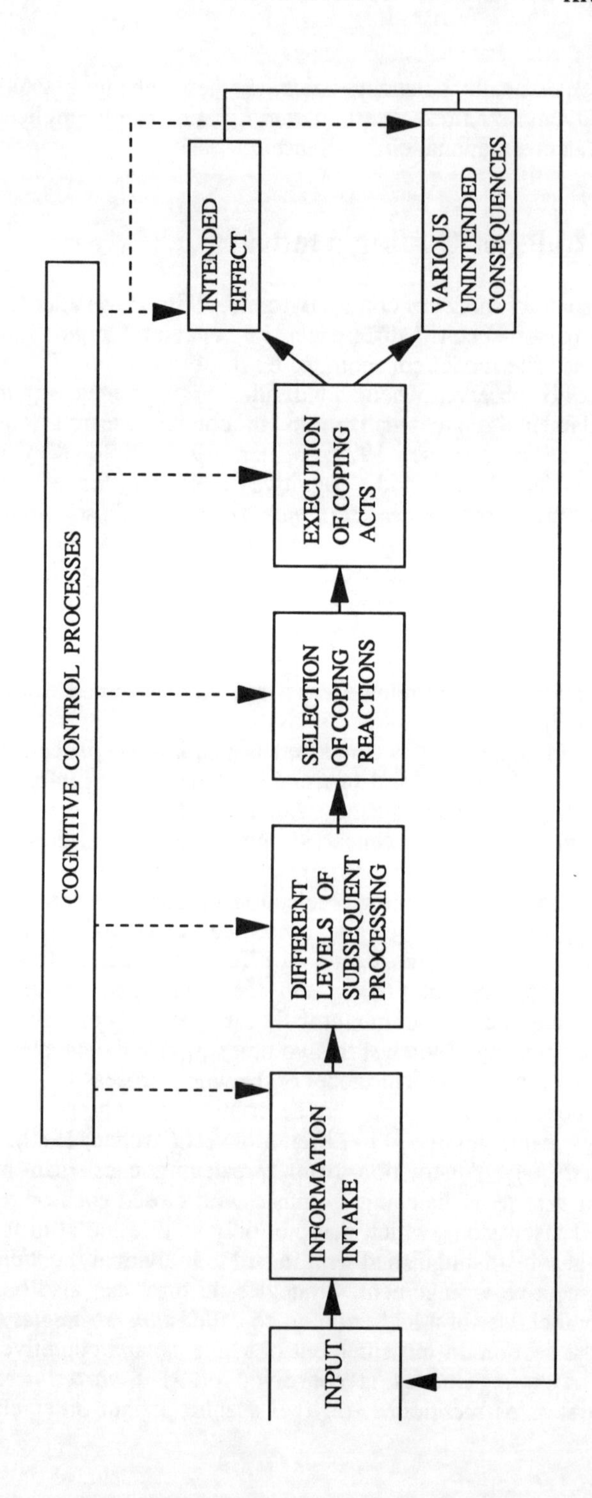

Figure 2.1. Conceptualization of the processing of aversive information and the execution of coping acts.

collecting and processing threatening information (vigilance) and by turning away from threat-related cues (cognitive avoidance).

It has to be emphasized that the hierarchy described (reaction, act, strategy, superstrategy, cf. Krohne, 1989; see also Figure 2.4, p. 30) is not meant to be a *functional model*, i.e., a model which conceptualizes *qualitatively different* processes and their functional relationships. (For a functional hierarchical model of coping, see Leventhal, Suls, and Leventhal, this volume.) Instead, as in a "philosophy of science" approach, it gives an idea how to organize (and differentiate) those concepts which must be taken into account when analyzing coping. It points out the necessity of distinguishing between *observable facts* (reactions and acts) and *theoretical concepts* (behavioral classes = strategies and superstrategies). It further stresses that observable facts do not integrate themselves (so to speak) into theoretical classes. Instead, this classification can either be achieved purely empirically (e.g., by factor analysis) or be based on theoretical considerations (with different theories leading to different classification systems).

The Dimensions Vigilance and Cognitive Avoidance

According to the central assumption of the model, individuals can be differentiated according to the way they *habitually* (dispositionally) react in threatening situations. They can react with either vigilant or cognitive avoidant strategies. Vigilance and cognitive avoidance are conceived conceptually and operationally as *separate personality dimensions*, i.e., on the habitual level, the employment of vigilant strategies and of avoidant ones do not preclude each other. The specific configuration of a person's standing on both personality dimensions (e.g., high vigilance and low cognitive avoidance) is called "*coping mode*".

The model extends beyond other similar approaches in coping research (e.g., the concept of "repression-sensitization", Byrne, 1964; or the "monitoring-blunting hypothesis", Miller, 1980, 1987; cf. Miller, Combs, & Kruus, this volume) in that it relates the *descriptive constructs* "vigilance" and "cognitive avoidance" to an *explicative basis*. According to a number of theoretical approaches and empirical studies (summarized in Epstein, 1972), most situations which evoke anxiety can be characterized by two general aspects: the *presence of aversive stimuli* (Epstein: "primary overstimulation") and a *high degree of ambiguity* ("cognitive incongruity"). Ambiguity in aversive situations is an important factor in triggering anxiety, because it counteracts the immediate employment of open reactions which are aimed at removing danger. Corresponding to these general aspects, it is postulated that two reactions will be triggered in persons confronted with an aversive situation (cf. Figure 2.2): the *experience of uncertainty* (as related to ambiguity) and the *perception of somatic arousal* (caused by the presence of aversive stimuli).

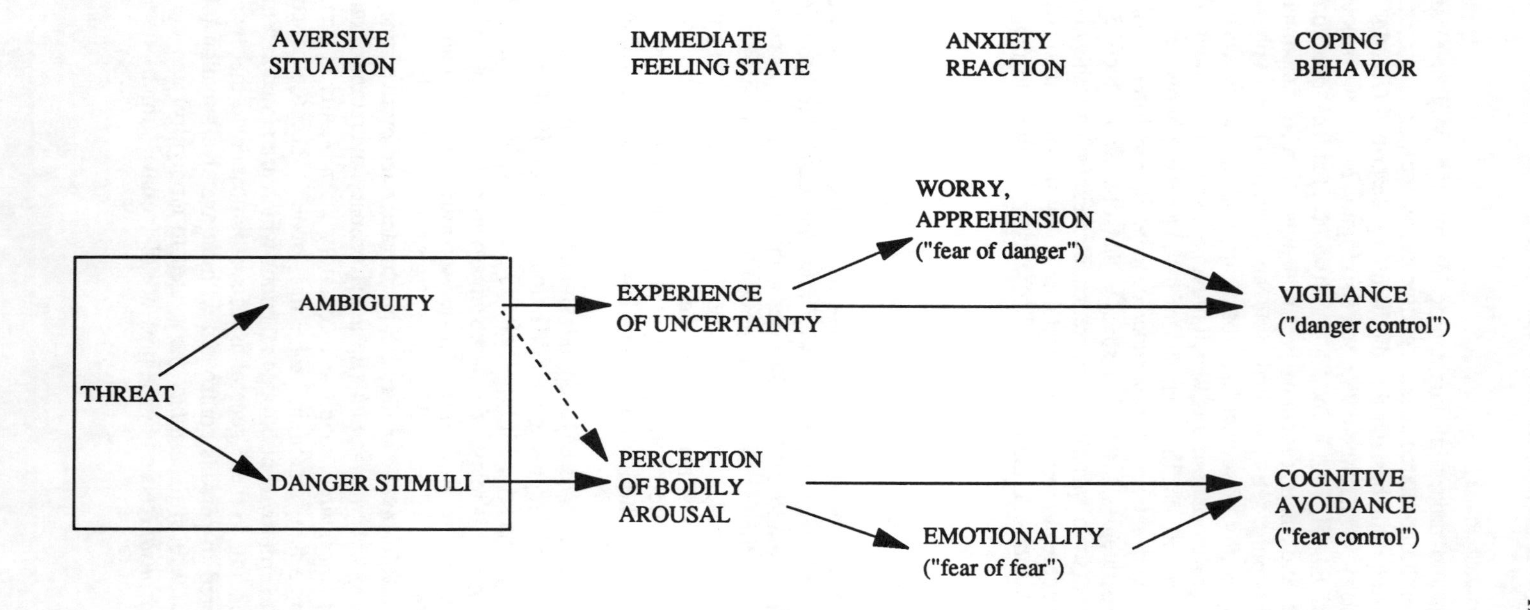

Figure 2.2. Hypothetical relationships between the components of an aversive situation, immediate experiences ("feeling states"), anxiety reactions, and coping.

For the present, these two reactions are viewed as very *elementary feeling states* which can, however, link with more complex anxiety reactions.[1] Thus, "elementary" uncertainty, which manifests itself in questions such as "What does that mean?", can lead to a more complex cognitive anxiety reaction as a result of "calculating" the relevant situational parameters, especially the imminence of a danger and the degree of predictability and controllability of the situation. This reaction can be described as, for example, apprehension about being surprised by negative developments in the situation (cf. Krohne, 1989). Other research groups (Breznitz, 1984) have designated this "fear of danger". The perception of somatic arousal when confronted with aversive stimuli, on the other hand, could lead to the expectation of a further increase in emotionality which might not be controllable as it arises. This type of expectation may also be called "fear of fear".

It is additionally postulated that the intensified experience of uncertainty (or "fear of danger") should release behavioral impulses characteristic of vigilance (or "danger control", Leventhal, 1970; Wilson, 1985). In contrast, the perception of intense somatic arousal, or at least the anticipation of the same ("fear of fear"), should initiate the tendency to avoid threat-related cues ("fear control"). In these cases, we are dealing with cognitive processes instead of open reactions like flight or attack, which are probably not possible because of situational ambiguity. It must, however, be pointed out that the processes depicted in Figure 2.2 are still purely speculative. In particular, the reciprocal influences of both processes, e.g., that of uncertainty on somatic arousal or arousal on apprehension, have been intentionally excluded from the flow chart.

At this point, vigilance can be more precisely defined as a class of coping strategies which are employed in order to reduce uncertainty or to prevent a further increase of the same. I call this *uncertainty-motivated* behavior. Thus, individuals strive to construct a schema of the aversive situation and its eventual course in order to prevent the possibility of being negatively surprised. Cognitive avoidance, in contrast, designates a class of coping strategies which are aimed at shielding the organism from stimuli which induce arousal (*arousal-motivated* behavior). An existing emotional state experienced as too intensive would thereby be reduced, or an impendent strong and possibly uncontrollable increase in arousal would be prevented.

When uncertainty and somatic arousal are high, we are dealing with two disturbances in system states which generally cannot be regulated at the same time. For example, the intensified preoccupation with information relevant to the encountered danger may succeed in reducing existing uncertainty. The price of this outcome, however, may be a simultaneous strong increase in arousal (cf. Krohne, 1989). Conversely, ignoring aversive stimuli could lower immediate arousal. However, since threatening situations are generally dynamic, the price of this desired state will be an increase in uncertainty shortly thereafter. In the

[1] It should be mentioned that there will be no discussion at this point about the differentiation between feelings and emotions, their respective definitions, and possibilities for classification (cf. also Mees, 1991; Ortony, Clore, & Collins, 1988).

next step in unfolding this model, vigilance and cognitive avoidance will be related to an explicative personality-oriented basis.

Intolerance of Uncertainty and Intolerance of Emotional Arousal

Habitual (dispositional) preferences for vigilance and cognitive avoidance are explained by the constructs *intolerance of uncertainty* and *intolerance of emotional arousal* (cf. Figure 2.3). Individuals are assumed to habitually vary in the extent to which they are able to tolerate uncertainty or emotional arousal (cf. also Rothbart & Mellinger, 1972). Individuals high in intolerance of uncertainty should tend to employ vigilant coping. On the other hand, intolerance of emotional arousal should be associated with cognitive avoidant strategies.

Individuals with the configuration "high intolerance of uncertainty, low intolerance of arousal" are especially affected by the ambiguity inherent in threatening situations. Their prime concern is to construct a cognitive schema of the impending danger and, hence, to avoid "negative surprise". Correspondingly, they manifest a comparatively consistent vigilant behavior and direct their attention continuously to the threat-relevant information (*consistent monitoring*, cf. Figure 2.3). Although emotional arousal is thereby unintentionally intensified, vigilant behavior can still stabilize, since persons of this mode are comparatively insensitive to such stress. Individuals with this configuration (cf. Figure 2.3) are called, following the traditional terminology in coping research, "sensitizers" (Krohne, 1986, 1989).

The emotional (somatic) arousal released by the perception of threat-related cues is the central problem for individuals with the configuration "high intolerance of arousal, low intolerance of uncertainty". They encounter this state by ignoring such cues (*consistent avoidance*) and endure the subsequent increase of uncertainty, because it is not particularly stressful for them. These individuals are called "repressers".

Those individuals who are highly intolerant of both arousal and uncertainty are able to withstand neither the uncertainty nor the emotional arousal induced by cues in aversive situations. When they try to reduce the uncertainty that they experience as stressful by increased preoccupation with the stressor, they simultaneously heighten their emotional arousal to a level exceeding that which they can tolerate. If they turn away from the stressor in order to reduce this unbearable state of arousal, then their uncertainty increases together with the stress resulting from it. Since the employment of vigilant as well as cognitive avoidant behavior means intolerable unintended consequences for individuals of this mode, they are faced with a conflict which should lead to coping actions of only short duration and, consequently, a *fluctuating* coping behavior. Individuals with such a fluctuating and therefore less efficient coping behavior could be designated as "high-anxious". As these individuals are preoccupied with both threats – being negatively surprised as well as being overwhelmed by strong emotions, they should be unable to wait and see if a strategy has been

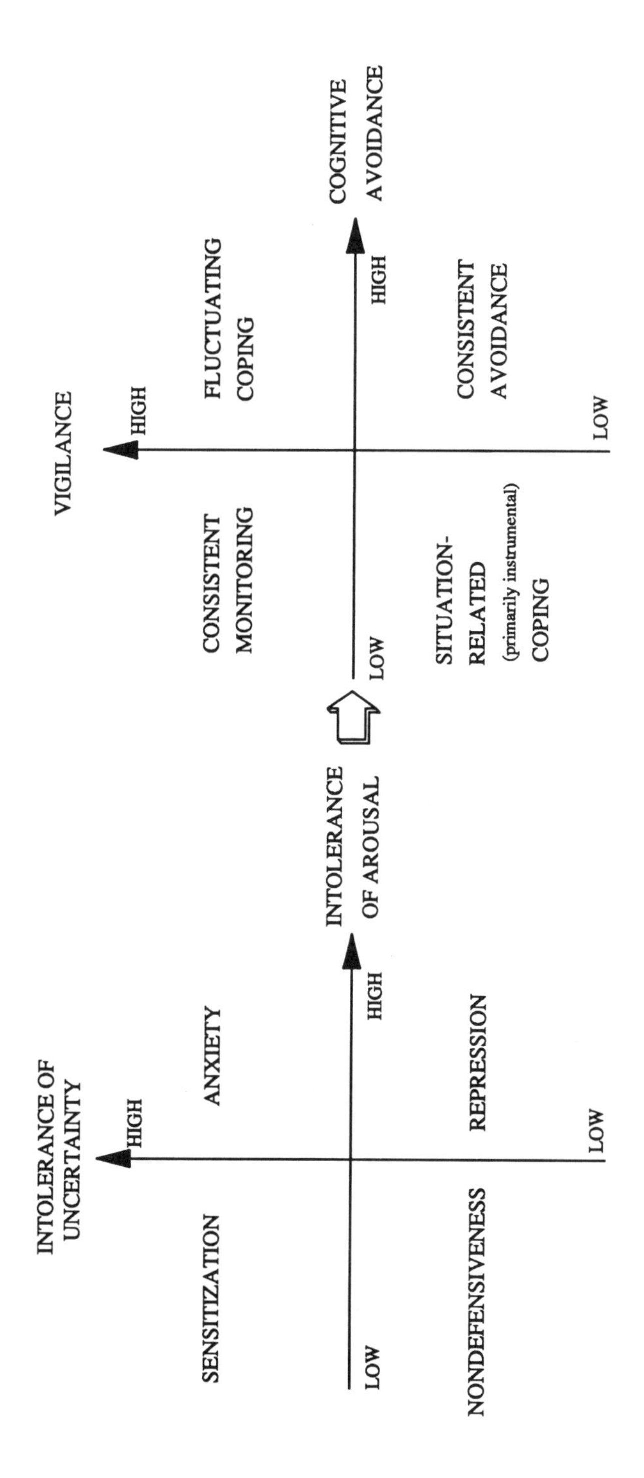

Figure 2.3. A two-dimensional model of coping.

effective. This should then hinder the employment of situation-related, particularly instrumental, coping behavior. This is assumed to be manifested in an *intensified tendency* to employ intrapsychic (vigilant *and* avoidant) coping. One should not, however, interpret Figure 2.3 as a one-to-one correspondence. Anxious individuals do tend toward the coping pattern "high vigilance and high avoidance", ***but not everyone with this pattern can be designated as "anxious"***.

Individuals, who are characterized by a low intolerance of both factors can withstand both uncertainty and arousal relatively well in aversive situations. Because of their relatively high tolerance for uncertainty and arousal, they can pursue a certain strategy long enough to determine if it is effective or not. Their orientation is not necessarily directed toward an analysis of all threat-relevant aspects of the situation or toward evasion of cues which induce arousal. Therefore, they are able to *flexibly* adapt their behavior to the important demands of each situation. For example, they intensify their search for information when this enables them to improve their control over the situation, they act instrumentally when this is the best way to bring about a desired effect, or they distract themselves from threat-related stimuli in an aversive situation whose eventual course is beyond their control. Such individuals are called "nondefensives". Regarding the relationship of this pattern to vigilance and cognitive avoidance, the same is true as for the anxious individuals. Nondefensives are characterized by a comparatively low employment of intrapsychic (vigilant or avoidant) coping strategies, but not all individuals with this coping pattern can be designated as "nondefensives". While the adaptiveness of coping behavior should generally increase with a simultaneous rise in the tolerance of uncertainty and emotional arousal, this relationship is presumably not linear. Extreme tolerance and thereby a low tendency to employ vigilant or avoidant coping behavior could also indicate a lack of sensitivity to uncertainty and emotional arousal and perhaps a general deficit in coping resources, as is the case for severely depressed individuals (cf. Seligman, 1975).

Concerning the configurations presented, it is necessary to point out the following:

1. The statements put forward are still of a largely hypothetical nature. This is true for the assumption about stable interindividual differences in the intolerance of uncertainty and arousal, the conception of the person-specific coping variables "vigilance" and "cognitive avoidance", and the proposed relationships between intolerance and coping dimensions.

2. The designations "sensitization", "repression", "high-anxiety", and "nondefensiveness" are merely tentative and have to be validated by experiments designed according to the formulated theory.

3. Besides the four configurations of habitual coping tendencies described, it would also be interesting to take into consideration those persons located in the middle of the distribution (i.e, with average scores on the variables "vigilance" and "cognitive avoidance"). It is possible that these individuals are also nondefensives.

The Measurement of Vigilance and Cognitive Avoidance

Problems and Approaches in Coping Measurement

As already described (cf. p. 21), it is posited that the circumstances which must be taken into account when measuring coping should be conceptualized in terms of a hierarchical organization (cf. Figure 2.4). The base is defined by actual coping behavior ("behavioral level"). This can be further differentiated into two sublevels. On a more microscopic level, narrowly defined coping reactions are investigated. Typical for this sublevel are experimental investigations which deal with the selection of coping reactions (e.g., listening to a music channel or monitoring a warning signal) when anticipating an imminent aversive event (cf. Averill, O'Brien, & DeWitt, 1977; Kohlmann, 1990; Krohne & Fuchs, 1991). However, the microanalytic approach is not confined only to laboratory studies. Some real-life investigations may also be termed microanalytic, for example those conducted by Lazarus and co-workers aimed at registering "associations between fluctuating factors across a multitude of time points for one person" (DeLongis, Folkman, & Lazarus, 1988; Folkman et al., 1986; Lazarus, 1990).

A macroscopic analysis, in contrast, operates on a higher level of aggregation. While in the laboratory situation one generally deals with single, narrowly circumscribed, and temporally brief coping reactions (e.g., monitoring a warning tone which proceeds an electric shock), the behavior patterns observed in real-life situations are more complex and extend over longer periods of time (e.g., informing oneself in detail about the diet necessary when suffering from a certain illness; see also Filipp et al., this volume, on coping with cancer). In contrast to the microscopic coping reactions, I designate these more macroscopic units as "coping acts". Coping acts generally represent organized sequences of coping reactions (see Figure 2.4).

As previously mentioned, the registration of reactions and acts operates on the *behavioral level* of analysis. As we now advance within our hierarchy to the coping strategies and superstrategies, we enter the *conceptual level*. Based on theoretical considerations, coping reactions and acts are assigned to behavioral classes. We call these classes "coping strategies". As indicated in Figure 2.4 by the dashed lines, different theoretical approaches can lead to differing classifications.

Nevertheless, it should be emphasized that integrating coping reactions into strategies on the basis of theoretical deductions is a route depicted comparatively seldom. The more frequent procedure lies in grouping the individual coping strategies on the basis of statistical (generally factor-analytical) classifications into superordinate units (see, e.g., Endler & Parker, 1990; Janke, Erdmann, & Kallus, 1985; McCrae, 1984). However, such classifications are not only relatively arbitrary (and hence can, in general, be replicated only seldom) but also frequently have little connection to the

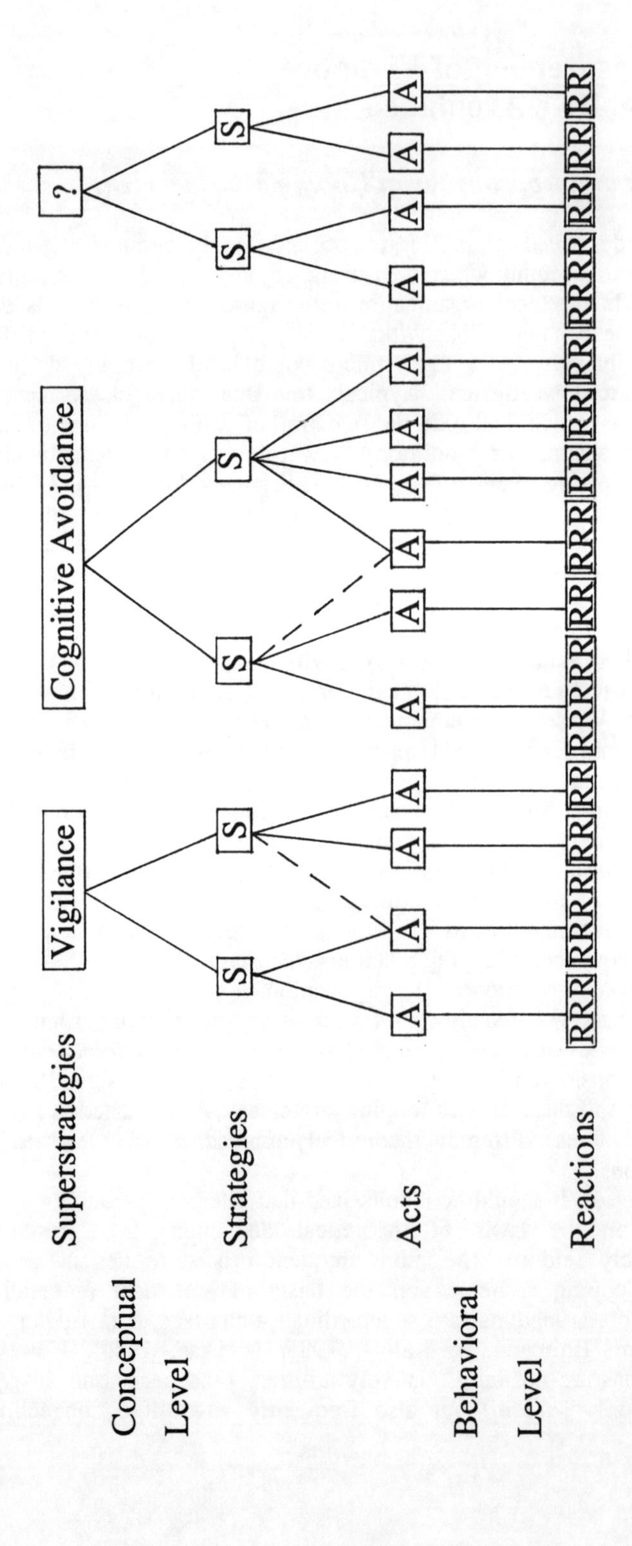

Figure 2.4. Hierarchical organization of different concepts employed in the analysis of coping. (Question mark indicates that other models may specify further superstrategies.)

theoretical model the author has advanced for his empirical work. A typical example of this is Lazarus' approach: On the theoretical level, Lazarus and Launier (1978) proposed a classification of coping processes which could not be confirmed empirically (i.e., by factor analysis, cf. Folkman & Lazarus, 1985; for more details see Laux & Weber, 1990). Furthermore, Lazarus has postulated a complex (reciprocal) relationship between different elements ("the stress process is a relationship constantly changing as a result of a continual interplay between the person and the environment", Lazarus, 1990, p. 4). In contrast to this, he has developed instruments for operationalizing these constructs (e.g., the "Ways of Coping Checklist", Folkman & Lazarus, 1985), whose internal structure was determined factor-analytically (i.e., according to a linear-additive model) and whose content has only a tenuous relationship to the theoretical basis. (For an approach which is similarly problematic, cf. McCrae, 1984; McCrae & Costa, 1986). I am not arguing against factor analysis as an instrument for determining the different components of a specific psychological phenomenon, such as coping. I am only trying to point out that (a) factor analysis must be carried out on the basis of theoretical assumptions and that (b) the results of such a classification must be again related to those same theoretical assumptions (e.g., in order to modify or dismiss them).

As mentioned above, behavioral classes (or strategies) can be combined into strategies of a higher order (so-called *superstrategies*), depending on the goals of the research being conducted and the theoretical foundation of the particular study. In the literature on coping, different classes of such superstrategies have been described (Billings & Moos, 1981, 1984; Krohne, 1989; Krohne & Rogner, 1982; Lazarus & Folkman, 1984b; McCrae & Costa, 1986; Miller, 1980, 1987; Moos & Billings, 1982; Roth & Cohen, 1986), such as emotion-focused coping, instrumental coping, problem-solving, monitoring, and cognitive avoidance.

The level chosen when determining coping strategies has immediate consequences for specifying whether behavior is more consistent or more variable throughout situations. The narrower the investigated strategies (or their empirical indicators), the more unlikely it is that they (at least in real-life situations) will again appear in exactly this form (cf. Lazarus & Folkman, 1987). Correspondingly, the opposite relationship is valid for highly aggregated strategies. Hence, whether transsituational stability or variability is observed largely depends on the level of analysis selected (e.g., single, narrow reactions vs. the indicators of superstrategies).

One problem largely neglected in the assignment of individual coping reactions to strategies (and possibly superstrategies) is the *intention* the individuals have when they manifest certain reactions. As an example we can consider the "classical" experimental design advanced by Averill and co-workers (cf. Averill et al., 1977): Subjects, who anticipate a noxious event, can choose between listening to music on an acoustic channel (assumed to indicate "distraction" from the aversive situation) or gathering stressor-relevant information on a different channel (alleged "orientation" toward the stressor). Does selecting the "information channel" really represent a case of searching for information and thereby a manifestation of vigilant coping in every case? Perhaps, for some persons, the actual goal of orienting toward external information is to withdraw attention from internal somatic processes experienced as unpleasant or from distressing cognitions. The investigations conducted by Borkovec and co-workers (Heide & Borkovec, 1983, 1984; cf. Borkovec & Lyonfields, this volume) on relaxation-induced anxiety (primarily worry) suggest this possibility. People who are completely relaxed have little means of diverting their attention away from unpleasant internal states.

One and the same coping act can thus have very different intentions behind it (cf. Laux & Weber, 1987, 1990; Stone & Neale, 1984; see also chapters by Carver & Scheier, and by Leventhal et al., this volume). Actual coping behavior can therefore be split up into two components: act and intention. However, a specific dependency does exist between them: Only after a specific coping act has been registered can one also record the intentions behind it. (Of course, one can also proceed in reverse: ask which intentions a person has prior to a certain stress situation, e.g., before an exam, and then register how these intentions are transformed into coping behavior. In any case, act and intention are dependent on one another). As a result, the specific individual connection between act and intention must always be recorded on the level of actual behavior. Such connections represent the true basis for determining coping strategies. I do not currently know of an instrument able to record this specific connection in a manner which is *psychometrically acceptable*. Moreover, it appears to be questionable whether an unbiased assessment of intentions is even possible. At present, the call to record both coping act and intention is therefore only a program without a foundation in measurement methodology.

The "Mainz Coping Inventory"

I have already pointed out the possibility of determining coping dispositions by relying on specific coping processes. Yet in empirical investigations, this possibility refers more to the analysis of actual dependent variables. In this way, regularities could be discovered and related to theoretical concepts (e.g., dispositional high-anxiety; cf. chapters by Hock and by Mathews, this volume). However, when recording coping dispositions (e.g., on the dimensions vigilance and cognitive avoidance), it would be uneconomical to employ such a procedure. Instead, we should strive to construct a structurally oriented instrument which would however have to follow theoretical considerations about coping processes as closely as possible.

Taking the lead from stimulus-response inventories in anxiety research (cf. Endler, Hunt, & Rosenstein, 1962), our group constructed the "Mainz Coping Inventory" for the separate measurement of the dimensions "vigilance" and "cognitive avoidance" (MCI, Krohne, 1989; Krohne, Rösch, & Kürsten, 1989; Krohne, Wigand, & Kiehl, 1985; Schumacher, Krohne, & Kohlmann, 1989).

As a *first* step, descriptions of various situations potentially capable of eliciting anxiety were developed. On the one hand, these situations were

Table 2.1
Threat Situation and Coping Acts from the Mainz Coping Inventory

Imagine that you are riding in a car as a front-seat passenger next to an obviously inexperienced driver. Road conditions are poor due to snow and ice.

In this situation ...

1. I remember similar dangerous situations that I have experienced in the past . . . .
2. I tell myself: "Nothing terrible is going to happen." . . . .
3. I am glad that I don't lose my composure as easily as most others . . . .
4. I think: "I'm the one this always happen to." . . . .
5. I tell myself: "Thank goodness, he's not driving that fast." . . . .
6. I watch the driver carefully and try to tell in advance when he is going to make a mistake . . . .
7. I think that I don't cope with this kind of situation (for instance, by staying calm and relaxed) as well as most of my acquaintances . . . .
8. I just stop looking at the road and either think about something else, or look at the scenery . . . .
9. I stay completely calm . . . .
10. I tell myself: "In future, I'll only go on rides like this if I myself am the driver, never again as a passenger." . . . .
11. I'd very much like to say: "Stop, I want to get out." . . . .
12. I tell myself: "As a passenger, one often perceives the driver's way of driving as unsteady, whereas in fact, the driver isn't driving all that badly." . . . .
13. I tell myself: "I've been able to cope with situations that were far more trying than this one." . . . .
14. "I drive along with the driver", i.e., I act as if I myself were driving . . . .
15. I think about everything that could go wrong . . . .
16. I think: "Somehow this driver also has to have the opportunity to practice driving when road conditions are poor." . . . .
17. I tell myself: "When one has fastened one's seat belt and is moreover driving so slowly, not too much can go wrong." . . . .
18. I think about what I should do if the car should start to skid . . . .

supposed to represent the two large groups of threat described in the literature (see, e.g., Hodges, 1968) – *ego-threat* and *physical threat*. On the other hand, these situations had to contain varying degrees of controllability and predictability. In this manner, eight situations were collected, four of these representing ego-threat and four others physical threat. (For more details, see Krohne, 1989.)

Second, equally large repertoires of vigilant and cognitive avoidant coping strategies were assigned to every situational description. Examples of vigilant coping strategies are "anticipation of negative events", "information search", or "recalling negative events", while avoidant coping includes strategies such as "attentional diversion", "self-enhancement", or "denial" (cf. Krohne, 1989). The sequence of these 18 total coping strategies was always the same; only the concrete manner in which coping (e.g., denial) was expressed was matched with the description of the particular threat. A "true-false" scale served as the mode for responding to every strategy. (Table 2.1 lists one threat situation and the respective coping acts.)

Depending on the purpose of a study, only the parts "physical threat" or "ego-threat" are used. The answers that are summed up separately with regard to vigilance and cognitive avoidance items across the four situations of one part serve as scores of dispositional coping. Empirical investigations with this instrument, described in more detail elsewhere (Krohne, 1989; Krohne & Kürsten, 1989; Krohne et al., 1989; Schumacher et al., 1989), yielded the following results:

1. The four fictitious situations of each part met the criteria for variable predictability and controllability. The instrument contains situations that are described by our subjects as being both relatively predictable and controllable (e.g., driving with an inexperienced driver in ice and snow; cf. Table 2.1) as well as situations lacking predictability and controllability (e.g., a very rough flight, having the impression that "something is wrong"). Other configurations (e.g., high predictability and low controllability, for example, "in the dentist's waiting room") are also included in our instrument.

2. The reliabilities of the scores measuring dispositional coping proved to be satisfactory, with coefficients around .85 for internal consistency and around .65 for retest-reliability (with a time span of one week).

3. The results of principal component analyses, carried out to verify the dimensionality of the inventory, distinctly showed a two-factor solution for the physical-threat situations (cf. Krohne, 1989) and for women responding to the ego-threat part (cf. Schumacher et al., 1989). Based on this solution, a clear separation between vigilant and cognitive avoidant coping strategies could be achieved. These results support the assumption underlying the model of coping modes which postulates a detached functioning of the dispositional preferences for vigilant and avoidant coping. However, administering the ego-threat version to a male sample resulted in a three-factor solution (cf. Schumacher et al., 1989). While one factor, similar to the physical-threat part, only contained cognitive avoidant strategies, the vigilant responses were divided into two

dimensions. One contained strategies referring to a low self-efficacy expectancy when confronted with evaluative situations (e.g., recalling past failures or making negative comparisons with others). The other dimension was made up of strategies explicitly addressing an enhanced search for information. This last factor seems to correspond closely to the monitoring dimension described by Miller (1980, 1987; cf. Miller et al., this volume).

After having outlined central characteristics of the internal structure of our instrument for the assessment of cognitive coping strategies, the next part will refer to some studies centered around the concepts of vigilance and cognitive avoidance and conducted as a means of verifying hypotheses derived from the model of coping modes.

Empirical Findings

Our group has conducted laboratory studies as well as field research. In laboratory studies, the scope of the central assumptions of the model of coping modes is tested and the methodological approach of the research group is illustrated (cf. chapters by Hock and by Kohlmann). In field research, the following issues were analyzed:

Relationships between the two coping variables described and the degree of stress experienced prior to and following surgery were analyzed by Krohne (1990a) and Krohne, Kleemann, Hardt, and Theisen (1990). Since studies addressing this issue will be presented in detail in a separate chapter (Slangen, Kleemann, & Krohne, this volume), I will not deal with them any further at this point.

The effect of an athlete's coping behavior during critical situations occurring in the course of athletic competitions on the resulting athletic performance was investigated by Krohne and Hindel (1988, 1989, 1990). This real-life stress situation is of interest because, in contrast to many other situations, it contains a clear criterion for evaluating the efficiency of a coping strategy: the ensuing achievement. For example, we found that top table-tennis players who employed cognitive avoidant strategies to cope with critical situations occurring in the course of the match won more games in the especially critical tie-break situation than players who did not employ such strategies (Krohne & Hindel, 1988).

An as yet unpublished investigation analyzed the relationship between coping modes and academic achievement. 105 boys and girls from four classes in grade 8 took a classroom test in German (orthography and grammar). This test was announced ten days prior to administration and was identical for each class. Two classes were assigned to a "structured preparation" condition (n = 49), i.e., they received a specially developed booklet containing those rules to be tested in the exam. The remaining two classes (n = 56) were assigned to the "unstructured preparation" condition. They were informed that the test would cover topics taught during the past weeks. No special material was handed out to them. Among other variables, we measured appraised importance of the exam, expected success (self-efficacy), and rated difficulty of the test immediately prior to and after the exam. As a measure of performance, the number of mistakes were recorded.

Just a few results will be mentioned at this point. Sensitizers (i.e., high vigilance, low avoidance) appraised the exam as being more important and difficult than repressers (low vigilance, high avoidance). Moreover, an interesting treatment by coping interaction on appraised importance emerged. While repressers react consistently across conditions, sensitizers respond to differences in the degree of structure the preparation had. They assess the test with the well-structured preparation as being more important than the other exam situation. One may suppose that sensitizers consider a test which the teacher rigorously prepares for to be a very important one.

Concerning self-efficacy, repressers score significantly higher than sensitizers. This self-appraisal seems to be well-founded, as repressers performed significantly better on the test than sensitizers. This finding again demonstrates the higher efficiency of avoidant strategies in achievement situations (cf. Krohne & Hindel, 1988). However, an interesting treatment by coping interaction emerged (cf. Figure 2.5). While both groups performed equally well in the structured condition, sensitizers significantly decreased and repressers significantly increased in their performance in the unstructured preparation condition.

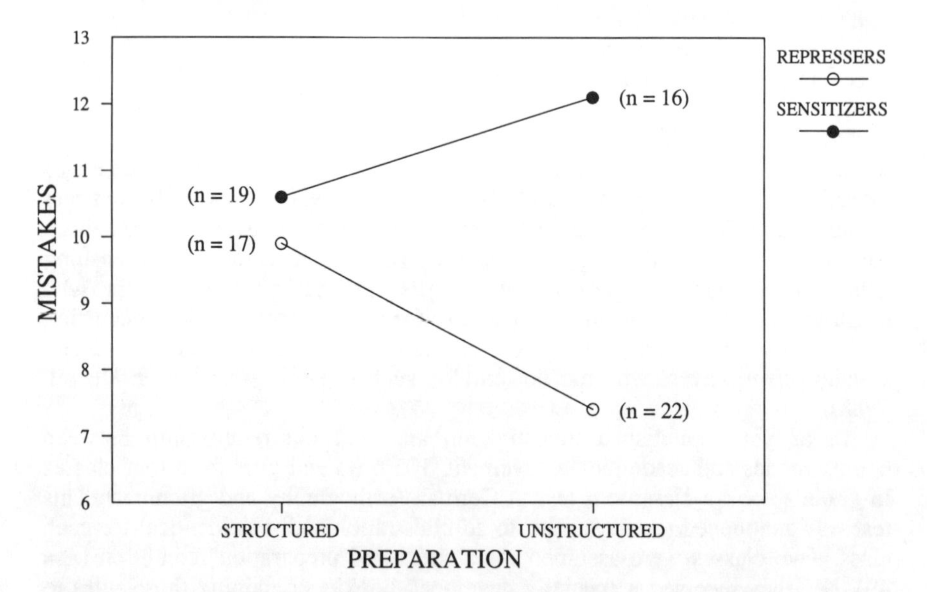

Figure 2.5. Relationship between coping modes (repression, sensitization), type of preparation for a classroom test, and achievement on this test (number of mistakes).

This result is in accordance with assumptions from the model of coping modes presented above. A situation of high ambiguity (= unstructured preparation) is especially problematic for sensitizers. It stimulates strong behavioral impulses to employ vigilance, which in turn leads to an intake of too much, especially irrelevant, information. This should then be associated with a decline in the efficiency of their problem-solving behavior. On the other hand, this preparation condition contains relatively few danger cues and thus stimulates few impulses to employ cognitive avoidance. Correspondingly, repressers, who experience little stress, should function well in such a situation. Repressers, on the other hand, should experience the structured condition as more stressful (because of the clear danger cues in the preparation) while sensitizers find it comparatively relieving (because of the amount of relevant information and the resulting low ambiguity). The performance of the first group should therefore decline while that of the second group improves.

Two further investigations (Kohlmann & Krohne, 1991; Krohne & Kohlmann, 1991) on the relationship between coping dispositions and the reporting of symptoms and emotions represent a transition between field research and controlled experiment.

Kohlmann and Krohne (1991) report four studies which relate vigilance and cognitive avoidance to several measures of symptom reporting (cf. Pennebaker, 1982). In the first study, 107 subjects completed a symptom-emotion checklist five times per day for seven consecutive days. The symptom-emotion checklist consisted of ten symptoms and eight emotions, each of which was to be rated on a 7-point unipolar scale. Because subjects were required to complete the questionnaire five times per day, the self-reports reflect the subjects' condition in a wide array of settings over time. Data were aggregated separately for each symptom and emotion during approximately 35 ratings. In addition to this state-based symptom measure, the subjects' general proclivity for reporting physical symptoms was assessed by the Pennebaker Inventory of Limbic Languidness (PILL, Pennebaker, 1982).

Interactions of vigilance and cognitive avoidance emerged for a subgroup of symptoms on the symptom-emotion checklist (i.e., headache, watering eyes, upset stomach, stomach-ache) and for the PILL. Subjects being characterized by the pattern "high vigilance and low cognitive avoidance" (i.e., sensitizers) exhibited the highest symptom scores.

The generalizability of these results was tested in three different replication studies. In the second study 42 students participated in eleven tasks (e.g., mental arithmetic, running in place, relaxation) in the laboratory. The tasks were varied along a number of dimensions in an attempt to manipulate physiological and mood state. Following each task, blood pressure readings were taken while subjects estimated their systolic blood pressure and rated the intensity of several symptoms on a symptom-emotion checklist. The third study was similar to the previous laboratory study; 64 students additionally responded to the PILL. The reporting of symptoms in the context of social situations was examined in the fourth study (59 students). Verbal scripts for two episodes were applied (cf. Laux & Weber, 1991), one to elicit anger (i.e., the subject is unfairly compromised and betrayed by a fellow student in the presence of others) and one to elicit anxiety (i.e., the subject is attending a party when he or she is suddenly confronted with the task of acting out some scene to entertain the party). The subjects were asked to vividly imagine themselves being the target person in the scripts. Applying item checklists, anxiety (e.g., insecurity, nervousness, worry), anger (e.g., anger, defiance, indignation), and bodily symptoms (e.g., palpitation, perspiration, changes in voice) were measured.

No further interactions between vigilance and cognitive avoidance on symptom reporting (trait, aggregated states, actual states in anger and anxiety eliciting situation) could be observed. However, some positive correlations between vigilance and symptom reporting in the anger and anxiety situations emerged.

Since previous research has demonstrated that an avoidant mode of coping is associated with a discrepancy between subjective and physiological responses to stress (i.e., avoiders report low levels of anxiety compared to their physiological arousal, cf. Weinberger, Schwartz, & Davidson, 1979; for an overview, see Kohlmann, 1990), anxiety, anger, and symptoms (each of which was measured in the anxiety and anger situations) were *z*-transformed. The differences between these scores (i.e., anxiety - symptoms, anger - symptoms) were subjected to a 2×2 ANOVA (vigilance × cognitive avoidance) with the within-subject factors situation (elicitation of anxiety or anger) and emotion (anxiety, anger). For vigilance, no effects on the discrepancy scores emerged. High avoiders, however, exhibited a significant discrepancy between anxiety and symptoms in that they showed only low levels of anxiety relative to the amount of symptoms reported. For the anger emotion, however, no such discrepancy emerged.

Krohne and Kohlmann (1991) investigated associations between vigilance and cognitive avoidance and the reporting of positive and negative affects as assessed by a German adaptation of the "Positive and Negative Affect Schedule" (PANAS; Watson, Clark, & Tellegen, 1988). The subjects were asked to indicate on a 5-point scale ranging from "not at all" to "very much" the extent to which they had experienced each of 20 affective states during a given time frame. Six different temporal instructions were used: "at the moment", "today", "during the past days", "during the past weeks", "during the last year", and "in general". 137 subjects (60 male, 77 female) responded individually first to the PANAS and then to the MCI.

In the male sample, a significant vigilance by avoidance by quality of affect interaction emerged. While *S*s high in vigilance and low in cognitive avoidance (sensitizers) reported an about equal amount of positive and negative affects, the remaining three coping modes scored significantly higher for positive than for negative affects. Additionally, *S*s low in vigilance and in cognitive avoidance (nondefensives) were significantly lower than sensitizers for negative affects. In the same sample, another significant interaction emerged between vigilance and time frame. Differences between *S*s high and low in vigilance increased (with vigilant *S*s reporting more intense affects) as the time frame lengthened. For the shorter time frames ("moment", "today"), no differences between vigilant and nonvigilant persons were observed. In the female sample, the interaction between cognitive avoidance, quality of affect, and time frame yielded a significant effect. While *S*s high and low in cognitive avoidance were not different in the reporting of positive affects, a significant time by avoidance interaction emerged for negative affects. Only in the case of the longer time frames (past days, weeks, year) did avoiders report a lower amount of negative affects than nonavoiders. This finding is analogous to the one reported for the variable "vigilance" in the male sample.

The results of this investigation permit several (tentative) conclusions. First, as the relationships between coping dispositions and the *actual experience* of affects are not very marked (highest coefficient: vigilance / positive affect in the male sample, $r = -.30$, $p < .05$), a simple interpretation of vigilance and cognitive avoidance in terms of the constructs "negative affectivity" or "positive affectivity" (cf. Tellegen, 1985) does not seem to be meaningful. As an alternative, a model of the representation of emotional information (situations and affective states) in memory (encompassing the processes of encoding, storage, and recollection) should be considered (see also chapters by Leventhal et al., and by Mathews, this volume). Second, negative affects may be more representative of mood states for highly vigilant persons than they are for individuals low in vigilance. Persons high in vigilance could therefore overestimate the occurrence of these states. Third, it may, however, also be possible that the self-assessment of affective states is only based on certain salient and infrequent emotional experiences. The longer the time frame, the more likely it is that persons are confronted with these experiences. Additionally, one might assume that individuals with specific coping dispositions (e.g., high avoidance) experience certain affect-related situations less often than persons with other coping modes do.

The results of both investigations suggest the following additional assumptions which should be tested in future research. Persons differing in coping dispositions probably process internal bodily information in different ways. In two recent studies it could be demonstrated that avoiders, to a much smaller degree than non-avoiders, base their estimation of physiological arousal (cf. Kohlmann, this volume) as well as their experience of anxiety (cf. Krohne, Hock, & Kohlmann, 1991) on internal bodily cues. Results indicate that coping dispositions may be relevant person variables in a cognitive-perceptual model of health (cf. Cioffi, 1991). For example, subjects high versus low in cognitive avoidance do not seem to differ in their *ability* to perceive bodily symptoms but in the way they *further process* this information.

A laboratory experiment on the dimensions vigilance and cognitive avoidance was conducted by Krohne and Fuchs (1991; for further experiments cf. Kohlmann, 1990; Krohne et al., 1991; see also chapters by Hock, and by Kohlmann, this volume).

The authors investigated the interaction between dispositional coping modes and types of pre-impact information on emotional, cognitive, and instrumental reactions of subjects awaiting an aversive event. As regards the information, two forms were realized: "valid" information which improved cognitive control over the impending stressor, and "redundant" information which did not increase potential control over the stressor. 40 subjects (university students) who were randomly assigned to the two information conditions had the option of either listening to information about the impending aversive stimulus or of choosing distraction by listening to music while anticipating an aversive event (an unpleasant, loud noise).

As expected, persons high in vigilance and low in cognitive avoidance (sensitizers) exhibited the highest degree of instrumental as well as cognitive orientation towards the aversive event. With subjects low in vigilance and high in avoidance (repressers), however, expectations were only confirmed for the cognitive, not for the instrumental coping reactions. Instead, repressers showed a comparatively high amount of orientation toward information related to the aversive event. In their case, however, it is possible that they tuned to the available information mainly to bridge the unpleasant waiting period. This has to be tested in future experiments by systematically assessing the *intentions* underlying the selection of specific options. Despite their low level of cognitive orientation toward the threat, repressers exhibited a high degree of emotional arousal, thus confirming the above-mentioned discrepancy hypothesis for repressers (cf. Kohlmann, 1990). For sensitizers, however, instrumental, cognitive, and autonomic reactions were in accordance with each other.

Conclusions and Questions for Future Research

Vigilance and cognitive avoidance are relevant personality dimensions for describing the intake of aversive information as well as processes which determine the short-term and long-term effects of this information (cf. Krohne et al., 1991). This is true for both the processing of *external* threat-related cues (cf. Kohlmann, 1990; Krohne & Fuchs, 1991; see also chapters by Hock, and by Slangen et al., this volume) and for experiencing *symptoms* and *emotions* (cf. Kohlmann & Krohne, 1991; Krohne & Kohlmann, 1991; see also chapters by Hodapp & Knoll, and by Kohlmann, this volume). The constructs *intolerance of uncertainty* and *intolerance of emotional arousal* appear to be relevant for explaining disposition-related differences within these areas.

In comparison with the traditional one-dimensional construct repression-sensitization (Byrne, 1964), the two-dimensional conceptualization presented in this chapter has the advantage that one can distinguish between those people who employ an increased amount of vigilance *and* cognitive avoidance in aversive situations and those who infrequently rely on any of these basic coping forms. Both of these groups become especially interesting when one refers to the patterns of intolerances postulated for them: high intolerance of uncertainty *and* emotional arousal in the first group and the reverse for the second.

In connection with the concept of variable tolerances for uncertainty and emotional arousal and the coping dimensions vigilance and cognitive avoidance related to them, the following questions, among others, should be dealt with in future research:

1. How are both intolerance dimensions *associated* with both coping variables, and how are these four same characteristics related to behavioral adaptivity in aversive situations?
2. How can the dimensions intolerance of uncertainty and intolerance of emotional arousal, which have been only very globally addressed, be more precisely *defined*?
3. What ideas exist with regard to the *changeability* of the personality dispositions (or "traits") mentioned as the consequence of feedback received during specific coping acts?
4. How can this model be used for *applied* questions?

Associations. The relationships between both intolerance dimensions and both coping dispositions have, up to now, been assumed to be monotone: As intolerance of uncertainty increases, more behavioral impulses to employ vigilance should be released, and, similarly, as intolerance of emotional arousal rises, the number of behavioral impulses to employ cognitive avoidance should also increase. The relationships between both of the intolerance dimensions (as well as both coping variables) and behavioral adaptability have been only loosely defined: High levels on both dimensions should be less adaptive, low levels more adaptive.

The precise analysis of the relationships between dispositional intolerances and the *dispositional* coping characteristics is actually not of central importance. Instead, the model requires that first both intolerance dimensions (conceived as personality variables) have to be more precisely defined conceptually. If, in this manner, two intolerance dimensions can actually be established and reliably defined operationally, then it would be of only secondary importance to deal further with the *personality* dimensions vigilance and cognitive avoidance. Instead of that, one could investigate the *actual* coping behavior more precisely and (taking the specific, situational characterisitics into account) relate it to both intolerance dimensions.

With regard to the relationship between the personality dimensions and behavioral adaptivity, the concept of linear associations is certainly too simple. The frequent use of vigilant (and also cognitive avoidant) coping strategies as well as their seldom use (or very high or low tolerances of uncertainty and emotional arousal) are apparently not adaptive. For example, people who are high in tolerance of uncertainty *and* of emotional arousal will fail to timely identify relevant threat-related cues and act in accordance with them. On the other hand, persons who are high on both dimensions may, as described above, also fail to act adaptively in aversive situations, albeit for different reasons. Moreover, one should consider not only linear and nonlinear but also interactive models of the influence of intolerance dimensions on behavior. If one wants to make theoretical predictions in this respect, it is necessary however to define both intolerance dimensions more exactly.

Definition. The concept of variable tolerance suggests the idea of different sensitivities (thresholds) for the ambiguity as well as danger inherent in an aversive situation. Intolerance of emotional arousal would then mean that such persons are especially susceptible to danger stimuli in an aversive situation while individuals with high intolerance of uncertainty are especially sensitive to the ambiguity inherent in that situation. One could also imagine that the variable thresholds do not relate to the sensitivity to specific aspects of the aversive situation but to the perception of immediate feeling states triggered by it. High intolerance would then mean a low threshold for the perception of emotional arousal or ambiguity, respectively.

Moreover, it is also possible that there are not really any differences in the thresholds but that persons with high intolerance react with the corresponding components of the elementary feeling state in a particularly strong way. High intolerance of emotional arousal would then mean that such persons in aversive situations react particularly by manifesting arousal and the consequent anxiety component, emotionality, whereas persons with intolerance of ambiguity would react by experiencing strong uncertainty and the consequent cognitive anxiety reactions, worry and rumination.

A combination of both ideas could also be possible. Particularly low thresholds for the perception of ambiguity and danger could trigger respectively strong reactions in the feeling states mentioned.

A third possibility is that individuals are not different with respect to threshold or the strength of their (elementary) reaction but in their *interpretation* of the feeling states and their subsequent *anticipations*. For example, for the same feeling states, the possibility of becoming even more strongly aroused could be unpleasant for one person whereas the possibility of being "negatively surprised", i.e., not knowing how an aversive situation will develop, could be extremely threatening for another.

The different interpretations (or expectations) which are connected to the states of emotional arousal and uncertainty could have been developed as a consequence of a person's past social learning experiences. For example, it is imaginable that certain parents continually point out to their children how important it is to carefully monitor aversive situations and to predict their further development ("You have to watch out!" - "You should have known that!" - "Be more careful!"). In addition, their child-rearing style (for example, higher aversiveness with simultaneously high ambiguity, i.e., little predictability) could cause the child to especially fear being negatively surprised. In contrast, other parents may emphasize the negative aspects of high emotionality ("You shouldn't get so upset!" - "Don't always get so nervous!" - "Don't be a scaredy-cat!"). In this way, the child learns to fear states of high emotional arousal and to consequently pay more attention to the appropriate cues.

These alternatives for defining intolerance do not exclude each other. It is possible that the thresholds (as well as the strength of the emotional reactivity) change as a consequence of a certain experience. Of course, it is also possible that there is a biological (hereditary) foundation for thresholds and reactivity. I, however, favor the assumption that the different interpretations and anticipations in aversive situations are obtained by social learning (cf. Krohne, 1990b).

Changeability. How do concrete experiences with actual (e.g., cognitive avoidant) coping affect the coping disposition? Certain forms of coping (e.g., consistent cognitive avoidance or fluctuating coping) could have disadvantages for the individual. How do individuals deal with encountering such disadvantages? Do they change their preference for specific coping strategies, i.e., do they change dispositionally? One could, on the other hand, also imagine that certain dispositions (e.g., the tendency to monitor consistently) become increasingly consolidated in the course of coping experiences. Do such people eventually manifest pathological behavior? Perhaps these questions can be answered if one considers how persons with different coping modes function in aversive situations.

The way people function in aversive situations can be described by drawing on action-theory models (cf. Kaminski, 1981). Central concepts in such models are "goal", "means", and "intended and unintended effects" (cf. Figure 2.1).

If one summarizes the previous descriptions, the sensitizers' (high vigilance, low avoidance) action plan in an aversive situation would appear as follows: The *goal* of their actions can be stated as "Nothing aversive may occur which I am not prepared for." The *motive* for formulating such a goal could be based on the expectation that the appearance of unanticipated events means a *loss of control over the situation.* This anticipated loss of control causes *actual fear* ("fear of danger"), which vigilant behavior is directed against.

As a *means* of preventing the appearance of unexpected aversive events and the loss of control connected with them, sensitizers attempt to construct an *internal model* of the entire course of the aversive event. In order to do this, they collect as much information related to the aversive event as possible; in particular, they monitor signals which reliably indicate the events about to occur.

The *intended* effect of this behavior is to always be able to predict an immediately impendent aversive event. Thus, the fear of losing control over the situation should decrease. The *unintended* effects are that sensitizers neglect the neutral (and probably also the positive) aspects of the situation and instead emphasize the threatening elements. This preoccupation with aversive information results in an intensified assessment of the danger as well as an increase in the excitability in such situations. This excitability appears immediately after the vigilant strategy is employed and cannot be reduced if the sensitizers' plan is to be carried out. Therefore, one could assume that sensitizers gradually adapt to the unintended effect of high excitability, i.e., acquire a higher tolerance of arousal.

The repressers' (high cognitive avoidance, low vigilance) action could be founded on the following *goal*: "I mustn't become strongly aroused". The *motive* behind formulating this goal is the expected loss of control over emotional reactions when arousal is high. This anticipated loss of control causes actual fear ("fear of fear"), which cognitive avoidance is directed against.

As a *means* of preventing the appearance of more intense emotional arousal, repressers employ mechanisms which cause threat-related information to be "faded out" during information gathering, i.e., they stop dealing with the aversive aspects of the situation.

By employing this behavior, the individual wants to prevent a confrontation with signals that indicate impending arousal. The fear of losing control over emotional reactions is thereby reduced. The *unintended* effects are that repressers neglect the threatening aspects of the situation and emphasize the neutral (and probably also the positive) elements of the situation instead. The consequence is that they are readier to approach the anticipated event both spatially and temporally. At the same time, repressers experience in general less stress while approaching such events. However, it is also possible that, while they are approaching an event, strong signals and even unconditioned pain-fear-stimuli appear and release fear. However, this effect is - in contrast to the unintended effect in the case of vigilance - not yet present and, furthermore, one that has only a certain probability. It is therefore not actually represented cognitively ("repressed"). Consequently, adaptation to this effect, in contrast to the vigilants' reaction to emotional arousal, is difficult to achieve.

This effect could also be responsible for the finding reported by some authors that repressers in threatening situations manifest low scores on the self-report level but relatively high scores on indicators of autonomous arousal (for a critical overview of data cf. Kohlmann, 1990). Since repressers do not pay attention to cues at the beginning of a potentially aversive episode and therefore expect that the situation is not dangerous, they are occasionally "overpowered" by massive danger cues. Because of their general tendency to ignore weak threat cues, they only construct an inadequate repertoire for coping with stronger stimulation which they cannot block out. Correspondingly, repressers should experience more helplessness when facing clear threats. In addition to the strong expectation that situations are harmless, repressers would formulate a second weaker expectation (cf. Krohne, 1978): "There are some threatening events which occur suddenly and which I'm not really capable of dealing with". The combination of the constant attempt to avoid threat-related information and the activation of this second anxiety-inducing hypothesis could be the reason for the mentioned discrepancy between the indicators of subjective and autonomous arousal.

While sensitive coping is directed by hypotheses which are confirmed both by positive and negative outcomes of an aversive encounter and thereby stabilize the system (in the case of harmless outcomes, this can be related to vigilant endeavours to prepare, in the case of dangerous outcomes to the general expectation of numerous dangers), repression is a comparatively *vulnerable system* of coping.

The sensitive coping mode should therefore represent a comparatively stable system in dealing with stressors. In principle this should also be true for the repressive system when one considers that (1) the cognitive "fading out" of danger cues does in general represent an adaptive mechanism (one should recall the advantage in performance situations reported for avoiders, cf. p. 36, see also Krohne & Hindel, 1988) and (2) individuals do not only encounter confrontations passively; they also attempt to actively organize their environment so that they can function as optimally as possible. For repressers this would mean that they seek out situations in which the chance of encountering a confrontation is very low.

Application. We do not expect that persons who manifest repressive or sensitive coping can change their disposition significantly or manifest pathological behavior. Long-term negative consequences are however possible on the level of health status (cf. Weidner & Collins, this volume). In conclusion, analyses of associations which could perhaps exist in this area should illustrate ways to apply the model of coping modes. I will first address the consequences that the greater vulnerability assumed for repressive coping could have on health status in particular.

Recently a so-called Type-C pattern has been described as a biobehavioral risk factor in cancer development (cf., among others, Greer & Watson, 1985; Temoshok, 1987, 1990). The most marked characteristic of this pattern is the suppression of negative feelings or the inability to express emotions, particularly anger. Other characteristics include the avoidance of conflicts, a harmonizing and conformable behavior as well as a marked tendency to react in a socially desirable way. That this disposition, also called the "antiemotional" personality, is equivalent to the coping mode repression is obvious. It is now posited, although still very speculatively, that this coping behavior is, on the one hand, appropriate for maintaining a behavioral and psychological homeostasis (e.g., a positive self-image) but that, on the other hand, it is followed by more severe disturbances (resulting mainly from the chronic suppression of emotions) in the neuroendocrine and immune systems. Since the immune system plays an important role in cancer development, it is hypothesized that avoidant coping (Type C) thereby raises an individual's vulnerability to carcinogenic influences. These assumptions are however, as already mentioned, still very speculative. In addition, the corresponding empirical investigations have significant methodological deficits (cf. Temoshok, 1990).

Expectations about the associations with health status can be formulated not only for repressers but also for sensitizers. For example, Kneier and Temoshok (1984) have speculatively conceived the Type-A behavior pattern, a risk factor for cardiovascular disease, as a coping style which is the converse of that displayed by Type-C individuals. The word "converse" is used here to express that the Type-A pattern, just as for Type C, is a less adaptive form of coping with stress but that the mechanisms which are used to cope (open expression of hostility, competitiveness, setting high standards of performance and constant attention to the time factor while working) operate in the opposite way as those of the Type C. (The adaptive form would be the Type-B pattern, falling in between the other two on a continuum; cf. Bonanno & Singer, 1990; Contrada, Leventhal, & O'Leary, 1990.)

Moving from the behavioral level to a closer description of the underlying psychological processes, we would expect certain characteristics which should correspond to those manifested by sensitizers. These expectations are supported by studies conducted by Glass (1977) and Matthews (1982). Glass pointed out that Type-A persons always strive to control the stress-relevant aspects of their environment. Matthews especially emphasized that the Type A's characteristic behavioral manifestations are mainly directed at removing unclear information when evaluating one's own behavior. Matthews and Brunson (1979) could also show that Type-A persons direct their attention particularly to external performance cues and simultaneously neglect bodily signals (e.g., fatigue, intensified autonomous arousal). This corresponds to the pattern of sensitive coping presented (intolerance regarding situational uncertainty while, at the same time, higher tolerance of negative bodily signals).

It is however still unclear whether Type-A persons can tolerate negative bodily signals relatively well or whether they actively deny them, i.e., employ cognitive avoidant strategies when facing such signals. Furthermore, it still remains to be investigated whether the clarification of information with respect to the Type A's performance is achieved by orienting attention very specifically, namely with an intensified sensitivity for positive cues and a simultaneously reduced receptivity for negative feedback. This is suggested by data reported by Ben-Zur, Breznitz, and Hashmonay (this volume).

Although many questions with regard to the use of the coping model in the two fields presented – research on the "antiemotional personality" and the "Type-A behavior pattern" – remain unanswered, it still appears to be of interest to include coping dispositions as relevant variables in a cognitive-perceptual-behavioral model of health. Approaches using such a model have recently been presented by, among others, Cioffi (1991; cf. Leventhal et al., this volume).

References

Ashby, W. R. (1956). *An introduction to cybernetics*. London: Chapman & Hall.

Averill, J. R., O'Brien, L., & DeWitt, G. W. (1977). The influence of response effectiveness on the preference for warning and on psychophysiological stress reactions. *Journal of Personality, 45*, 395-418.

Billings, A. G., & Moos, R. H. (1981). The role of coping responses and social resources in attenuating the impact of stressful life events. *Journal of Behavioral Medicine, 4*, 139-157.

Billings, A. G., & Moos, R. H. (1984). Coping, stress, and social resources among adults with unipolar depression. *Journal of Personality and Social Psychology, 46*, 877-891.

Bonanno, G. A., & Singer, J. L. (1990). Repressive personality style: Theoretical and methodological implications for health and pathology. In J. L. Singer (Ed.), *Repression and dissociation. Implications for personality theory, psychopathology, and health* (pp. 435-470). Chicago: University of Chicago Press.

Breznitz, S. (1984). *Cry wolf: The psychology of false alarms.* Hillsdale,NJ: Erlbaum.
Byrne, D. (1964). Repression-sensitization as a dimension of personality. In B. A. Maher (Ed.), *Progress in experimental personality research* (Vol. 1, pp. 169-220). New York: Academic Press.
Cioffi, D. (1991). Beyond attentional strategies: A cognitive-perceptual model of somatic interpretation. *Psychological Bulletin, 109,* 25-41.
Contrada, R. J., Leventhal, H., & O'Leary, A. (1990). Personality and health. In L. A. Pervin (Ed.), *Handbook of personality. Theory and research* (pp. 638-669). New York:Guilford.
DeLongis, A., Folkman, S., & Lazarus, R. S. (1988). The impact of daily stress on health and mood: Psychological and social resources as mediators. *Journal of Personality and Social Psychology, 54,* 486-495.
Endler, N. S., Hunt, J. M., & Rosenstein, A. J. (1962). An S-R inventory of anxiousness. *Psychological Monographs, 76*(17, Whole No. 536).
Endler, N. S., & Parker, J. D. (1990). Multidimensional assessment of coping: A critical evaluation. *Journal of Personality and Social Psychology, 58,* 844-854.
Epstein, S. (1972). The nature of anxiety with emphasis upon its relationship to expectancy. In C. D. Spielberger (Ed.), *Anxiety: Current trends in theory and research* (Vol. 2, pp. 291-337). New York: Academic Press.
Erdelyi, M. H. (1974). A new look at the New Look: Perceptual defense and vigilance. *Psychological Review, 81,* 1-25.
Eriksen, C. W. (1966). Cognitive responses to internally cued anxiety. In C. D. Spielberger (Ed.), *Anxiety and behavior* (pp. 327-360). New York: Academic Press.
Folkman, S., & Lazarus, R. S. (1985). If it changes it must be a process: Study of emotion and coping during three stages of a college examination. *Journal of Personality and Social Psychology, 48,* 150-170.
Folkman, S., Lazarus, R. S., Dunkel-Schetter, C., DeLongis, A., & Gruen, R. J. (1986). The dynamics of a stressful encounter: Cognitive appraisal, coping, and encounter outcomes. *Journal of Personality and Social Psychology, 50,* 992-1003.
Glass, D. C. (1977). *Behavior patterns, stress, and coronary disease.* Hillsdale, NJ: Erlbaum.
Greer, S., & Watson, M. (1985). Towards a psychobiological model of cancer: Psychological considerations. *Social Science and Medicine, 20,* 773-777.
Heide, F. J., & Borkovec, T. D. (1983). Relaxation-induced anxiety: Paradoxical anxiety enhancement due to relaxation training. Journal of *Consulting and Clinical Psychology, 51,* 171-182.
Heide, F. J., & Borkovec, T. D. (1984). Relaxation-induced anxiety: Mechanisms and theoretical implications. *Behaviour Research and Therapy, 22,* 1-12.
Herrmann, T. (1973). *Persönlichkeitsmerkmale: Bestimmung und Verwendung in der psychologischen Wissenschaft* [Personality concepts: Definition and use in psychology]. Stuttgart: Kohlhammer.
Hodges, W. F. (1968). Effects of ego threat and threat of pain on state anxiety. *Journal of Personality and Social Psychology, 8,* 364-372.
Janke, W., Erdmann, G., & Kallus, W. (1985). *Streßverarbeitungsfragebogen (SVF). Handanweisung* [Coping Questionnaire (SVF). Manual]. Göttingen: Hogrefe.
Kaminski, G. (1981). Überlegungen zur Funktion von Handlungstheorien in der Psychologie [Reflections on the function of action theories in psychology]. In H. Lenk (Ed.), *Handlungstheorien - interdisziplinär: Vol. 3. Verhaltenswissenschaftliche und psychologische Handlungstheorien. Erster Halbband* (pp. 93-121). München: Fink.
Kneier, A. W., & Temoshok, L. (1984). Repressive coping reactions in patients with malignant melanoma as compared to cardiovascular disease patients. *Journal of Psychosomatic Research, 28,* 145-155.

Kohlmann, C.-W. (1990). *Streßbewältigung und Persönlichkeit. Flexibles versus rigides Copingverhalten und seine Auswirkungen auf Angsterleben und physiologische Belastungsreaktionen* [Coping and personality. Flexible versus rigid coping behavior and its effects on anxiety and physiological stress reactions]. Bern: Huber.

Kohlmann, C.-W., & Krohne, H. W. (1991, July). *The coping dispositions vigilance and cognitive avoidance: Associations with symptom reporting*. Paper presented at the 6th annual meeting of the International Society for Research on Emotions, Saarbrücken, Germany.

Krohne, H. W. (1978). Individual differences in coping with stress and anxiety. In C. D. Spielberger & I. G. Sarason (Eds.), *Stress and anxiety* (Vol. 5, pp. 233-260). Washington, DC: Hemisphere.

Krohne, H. W. (1986). Coping with stress: Dispositions, strategies, and the problem of measurement. In M. H. Appley & R. Trumbull (Eds.), *Dynamics of stress. Physiological, psychological, and social perspectives* (pp. 209-234). New York: Plenum.

Krohne, H. W. (1989). The concept of coping modes: Relating cognitive person variables to actual coping behavior. *Advances in Behaviour Research and Therapy, 11*, 235-248.

Krohne, H. W. (1990a, July). *Coping dispositions and stress reactions before and after surgery*. Paper presented at the 5th annual meeting of the International Society for Research on Emotions, New Brunswick, NJ.

Krohne, H. W. (1990b). Parental child-rearing and anxiety development. In K. Hurrelmann & F. Lösel (Eds.), *Health hazards in adolescence* (pp. 115-130). Berlin, New York: Walter de Gruyter.

Krohne, H. W. (1990c). Personality as a mediator between objective events and their subjective representation. *Psychological Inquiry, 1*, 26-29.

Krohne, H. W., & Fuchs, J. (1991). Influence of coping dispositions and danger-related information on emotional and coping reactions of individuals anticipating an aversive event. In C. D. Spielberger, I. G. Sarason, J. Strelau, & J. M. T. Brebner (Eds.), *Stress and anxiety* (Vol. 13, pp. 131-155). Washington, DC: Hemisphere.

Krohne, H. W., & Hindel, C. (1988). Trait anxiety, state anxiety, and coping behavior as predictors of athletic performance. *Anxiety Research, 1*, 225-234.

Krohne, H. W., & Hindel, C. (1989). *Streßbewältigung und sportlicher Erfolg* [Coping and athletic success] (Final Report to the Bundesinstitut für Sportwissenschaft). Mainz: Johannes Gutenberg-Universität, Psychologisches Institut.

Krohne, H. W., & Hindel, C. (1990). *Effizienz situationsspezifischen Bewältigungsverhaltens* [Efficiency of situation-specific coping behavior] (Final Report to the Bundesinstitut für Sportwissenschaft). Mainz: Johannes Gutenberg-Universität, Psychologisches Institut.

Krohne, H. W., Hock, M., & Kohlmann, C.-W. (1991). *Coping dispositions, uncertainty, and emotional arousal*. Manuscript submitted for publication.

Krohne, H. W., Kleemann, P. P., Hardt, J., & Theisen, A. (1990). Relations between coping strategies and presurgical stress reactions. In L. R. Schmidt, P. Schwenkmezger, J. Weinman, & S. Maes (Eds.), *Theoretical and applied aspects of health psychology* (pp. 423-429). London: Harwood.

Krohne, H. W., & Kohlmann, C.-W. (1991, July). *Vigilance, cognitive avoidance, and the reporting of positive and negative affects*. Paper presented at the 6th annual meeting of the International Society for Research on Emotions, Saarbrücken, Germany.

Krohne, H. W., & Kürsten, F. (1989). *Die Messung von Angstbewältigungsdispositionen: III. Die Erfassung erlebter Kontrollierbarkeit und Vorhersagbarkeit von Belastungssituationen* [The assessment of coping dispositions: III. Measurement of perceived controllability and predictability of stress situations] (Mainzer Berichte zur Persönlichkeitsforschung No. 24). Mainz: Johannes Gutenberg-Universität, Psychologisches Institut.

Krohne, H. W., Rösch, W., & Kürsten, F. (1989). Die Erfassung von Angstbewältigung in physisch bedrohlichen Situationen [The assessment of coping in physical-threat situations]. *Zeitschrift für Klinische Psychologie, 18*, 230-242.

Krohne, H. W., & Rogner, J. (1982). Repression-sensitization as a central construct in coping research. In H. W. Krohne & L. Laux (Eds.), *Achievement, stress and anxiety* (pp. 167-193). New York: Mc Graw-Hill.

Krohne, H. W., Wigand, A., & Kiehl, G. E. (1985). Konstruktion eines multidimensionalen Instruments zur Erfassung von Angstbewältigungstendenzen [Construction of a multidimensional instrument for the assessment of coping tendencies]. In H. W. Krohne (Ed.), *Angstbewältigung in Leistungssituationen* (pp. 63-77). Weinheim: edition psychologie.

Laux, L., & Weber, H. (1987). Person-centred coping research. *European Journal of Personality, 1*, 193-214.

Laux, L., & Weber, H. (1990). Bewältigung von Emotionen [Coping with emotions]. In K. R. Scherer (Ed.), *Enzyklopädie der Psychologie: Serie Motivation und Emotion: Band 3. Psychologie der Emotion* (pp. 560-629). Göttingen: Hogrefe.

Laux, L., & Weber, H. (1991). Presentation of self in coping with anger and anxiety: An intentional approach. *Anxiety Research, 3*, 233-255.

Lazarus, R. S. (1990). Theory-based stress measurement. *Psychological Inquiry, 1*, 3-13.

Lazarus, R. S., & Folkman, S. (1984a). Coping and adaptation. In W. D. Gentry (Ed.), *The handbook of behavioral medicine* (pp. 282-325). New York: Guilford.

Lazarus, R. S., & Folkman, S. (1984b). *Stress, appraisal, and coping*. New York: Springer.

Lazarus, R. S., & Folkman, S. (1987). Transactional theory and research on emotions and coping. *European Journal of Personality, 1*, 141-169.

Lazarus, R. S., & Launier, R. (1978). Stress-related transactions between person and environment. In L. A. Pervin & M. Lewis (Eds.), *Perspectives in interactional psychology* (pp. 287-327). New York: Plenum.

Leventhal, H. (1970). Findings and theory in the study of fear communications. In L. Berkowitz (Ed.), *Advances in experimental social psychology* (Vol. 5, pp. 119-186). New York: Academic Press.

Matthews, K. A. (1982). Psychological perspectives on the Type A behavior pattern. *Psychological Bulletin, 91*, 293-323.

Matthews, K. A., & Brunson, B. I. (1979). Allocation of attention and the Type A coronary-prone behavior pattern. *Journal of Personality and Social Psychology, 37*, 2081-2090.

McCrae, R. R. (1984). Situational determinants of coping responses: Loss, threat, and challenge. *Journal of Personality and Social Psychology, 46*, 919-928.

McCrae, R. R., & Costa, P. T. (1986). Personality, coping, and coping effectiveness in an adult sample. *Journal of Personality, 54*, 385-405.

Mees, U. (1991). *Die Struktur der Emotionen* [The structure of emotions]. Göttingen: Hogrefe.

Miller, S. M. (1980). When is a little information a dangerous thing? Coping with stressful life events by monitoring versus blunting. In S. Levine & H. Ursin (Eds.), *Health and coping* (pp. 145-169). New York: Plenum.

Miller, S. M. (1987). Monitoring and blunting: Validation of a questionnaire to assess styles of information seeking under threat. *Journal of Personality and Social Psychology, 52*, 345-353.

Moos, R. H., & Billings, A. (1982). Conceptualizing and measuring coping resources and processes. In L. Goldberger & S. Breznitz (Eds.), *Handbook of stress: Theoretical and clinical aspects* (pp. 212-230). New York: The Free Press.

Ortony, A., Clore, G. L., & Collins, A. (1988). *The cognitive structure of emotions*. New York: Cambridge University Press.

Pennebaker, J. W. (1982). *The psychology of physical symptoms*. New York: Springer-Verlag.

Roth, S., & Cohen, L. J. (1986). Approach, avoidance, and coping with stress. *American Psychologist, 41*, 813-819.

Rothbart, M., & Mellinger, M. (1972). Attention and responsivity to remote dangers: A laboratory simulation for assessing reactions to threatening events. *Journal of Personality and Social Psychology, 24*, 132-142.

Schumacher, A., Kohlmann, C.-W., & Krohne, H. W. (1989). *Die Messung von Angstbewältigungsdispositionen: IV. Angstbewältigung in selbstwertbedrohlichen Situationen* [The assessment of coping dispositions: IV. Coping in ego-threat situations] (Mainzer Berichte zur Persönlichkeitsforschung No. 25). Mainz: Johannes Gutenberg-Universität, Psychologisches Institut.

Seligman, M. E. P. (1975). *Helplessness. On depression, development, and death.* San Francisco, CA: Freeman.

Stone, A. A., & Neale, J. M. (1984). New measure of daily coping: Development and preliminary results. *Journal of Personality and Social Psychology, 46*, 892-906.

Tellegen, A. (1985). Structures of mood and personality and their relevance to assessing anxiety, with an emphasis on self-report. In A. H. Tuma & J. D. Maser (Eds.), *Anxiety and the anxiety disorders* (pp. 681-706). Hillsdale, NJ: Erlbaum.

Temoshok, L. (1987). Personality, coping style, emotion and cancer: Towards an integrative model. *Cancer Surveys, 6*, 545-567.

Temoshok, L. (1990). On attempting to articulate the biopsychosocial model: psychological-psychophysiological homeostasis. In H. S. Friedman (Ed.), *Personality and disease* (pp. 203-225). New York: Wiley.

Watson, D., Clark, L. A., & Tellegen, A. (1988). Development and validation of brief measures of positive and negative affect: The PANAS scales. *Journal of Personality and Social Psychology, 54*, 1063-1070.

Weinberger, D. A., Schwartz, G. E., & Davidson, R. J. (1979). Low-anxious, high-anxious, and repressive coping-styles: Psychometric patterns and behavioral and physiological responses to stress. *Journal of Abnormal Psychology, 88*, 369-380.

Wilson, J. F. (1985). Stress, coping styles, and physiological arousal. In S. R. Burchfield (Ed.), *Stress. Psychological and physiological interactions* (pp. 263-281). Washington, DC: Hemisphere.

Chapter 3

Tuning In and Tuning Out: Confronting the Effects of Confrontation

Suzanne M. Miller, Christopher Combs,
and Linda Kruus

Introduction

The twin concepts of attention and avoidance have been one of the cornerstones of the intersecting fields of clinical, personality, and health psychology. At the same time, however, there is probably no other area that has engendered as much - or as sharp - debate. While Freud tended to focus on the negative consequences of avoidant-like processes, such as repression, a good deal of research points to the adaptive value of selective inattention (Krohne, 1986; Miller, 1990; Suls & Fletcher, 1985; see also Filipp, Klauer, & Ferring, this volume; Slangen, Kleeman, & Krohne, this volume; Weidner & Collins, this volume). The challenge currently is to not only identify, but also to predict, when and for whom avoidance may be associated with healthy outcomes, as well as to determine when the opposite might be true.

In our own research, we have been interested in understanding the nature and development of self-regulation in the face of a variety of perceived or actual medical and nonmedical life events. In particular, we have tried to elucidate the impact of divergent attentional styles (vigilance vs. avoidance) when dealing with complex emotions in the face of potential loss of life and health (Miller, 1989, 1990, in press-a, in press-b). Consider the following example:

Imagine that you have just recently learned that you have an abnormal Pap smear or that you have tested positive for the HIV (AIDS) virus. Do you tune into the threat, show up for regular screening visits, scan your body for symptoms, and generally explore what you can do to protect yourself? That is, do you adopt a "monitoring" or vigilant mode of coping?

Alternatively, do you tune out from threat, avoid or delay screening check-ups, ignore bodily symptoms, and suppress thoughts about your predicament or its consequences? That is, do you adopt a "blunting" or avoidant mode of coping? How do these attentional processes impact on how you use information to problem-solve, rearrange your life, and take account of future consequences?

This research was supported in part by grant CA46591 from the National Cancer Institute to the first author. Its contents are solely the responsibility of the authors and do not necessarily represent the official views of the National Cancer Institute. We thank Gregg Hurst, Anand Athavale, and Richard Sommers for their assistance.

Perhaps most critically, when would each strategy best help you to reduce stress while at the same time enabling you to adhere effectively to screening, treatment, and preventive regimens?

The history of research in this area has generated a broad range of sometimes conflicting findings that have proven difficult to tie together (Auerbach, 1989; Suls & Fletcher, 1985). We have been pursuing a program of research that has attempted to provide a coherent framework for understanding these issues, by adopting a person by situation approach to the study of coping (Mischel, 1979). Rather than proceeding on the assumption that one mode of approach is necessarily "good" and the other "bad", this work has been concerned with delineating when and under what circumstances monitoring and blunting modes have adaptive consequences for the individual and when they do not.

In this chapter, we concentrate on elaborating the motivations for - and consequences of - the monitoring end of the coping spectrum. We propose three main possible mechanisms that may underlie and motivate this type of coping, that are not mutually exclusive, and consider evidence for and against each of these alternatives. These include: (1) monitoring in order to execute controlling actions; (2) monitoring to modulate negative affect; and (3) monitoring to reduce uncertainty. We then go on to consider circumstances under which monitoring may become inappropriately excessive and maladaptive. In particular, we evaluate the role of both intrusive ideation and of avoidant ideation in sustaining uncontrolled vigilance for threat.

Monitoring to Exercise Control

Direct Exercise of Control

In aversive situations, individuals are naturally motivated to minimize the maximum danger to themselves. That is, they are concerned with making the "best of a bad situation." Hence, they often prefer and feel better when the threat is controllable. This is because they are generally ensured of a lower maximum danger when control responses are personally available to them than when they are unavailable. According to the *Minimax Hypothesis*, in situations where individuals have control over an aversive event, they are able to attribute the cause of relief to an internal source they consider predictable: i.e., their own response. This means that, in the future, they have a reliable predictor that danger will be minimized to the fullest extent possible. In contrast, if the attribution of relief is to some external, potentially unpredictable or unstable factor, then there is no guarantee that future danger will be restricted to any minimum level (Miller, 1979, 1980).

Monitors may be tuned into threatening cues in order to be in an optimal position to execute controlling actions. That is, information seeking may be undertaken in order to efficiently identify and perform instrumental actions that will, in some way, directly decrease the aversiveness of the stressor for them. This possibility does not appear to have much support, however. Monitors have been found to scan for informational cues in the face of threatening events, even when they know that there are no potential responses available for avoiding, escaping, or otherwise mitigating the stressor (Kohlmann, 1989; Miller, 1987; Slangen et al., this volume).

Problem-Solving Efforts

Another, related possibility is that monitors remain vigilant in order to attempt to consider and formulate plans at a more cognitive level and make decisions that will improve their situation. However, the available data also go against this view. In a study of patients attending a primary care facility for acute medical problems (e.g., flues, headaches, etc.), monitors were found to desire more information, reassurance, and support than blunters did. Despite this, monitors actually desired to play a less active role in the care of their medical problem, preferring instead to allow the physician to make most of the decisions for them (Miller, Brody, & Summerton, 1988).

This - more passive - orientation has been replicated in a study of gynecologic patients undergoing aversive diagnostic evaluation for abnormal Pap smears (Miller, Rodoletz, & Stoddard, 1990). Moreover, preliminary findings suggest that monitors not only prefer to rely on the physician, but actually claim to have played a less active role in their health-care. In addition, monitors believe that they have less control over the course of their medical condition than blunters do.

Hence, monitors appear to be more dependent and compliant in the face of short-term medical threats than blunters are. This seems to represent a more generalized problem-focused stance. Problem-focused strategies represent attempts to deal directly with the stressful problem itself (Carver, Scheier, & Weintraub, 1989). For example, in addition to planning, the individual may take active steps to change the problem, suppress ongoing competing activities, and remain behaviorally engaged in resolving the situation.

A study with undergraduates showed that while monitors were more likely to remain behaviorally engaged when they were under a lot of stress (that is, they kept trying to reach their goals), they did not actually engage in more active coping or planning. Instead, they sought out someone else who could give them advice or do something concrete about the problem on their behalf (Carver et al., 1989). That is, they engaged in social support seeking for instrumental reasons (in order to modify the situation), rather than for simply emotional (in order to obtain sympathy and understanding, to discuss one's feelings, etc.) reasons.

More recent work has explored the relation between monitoring and the use of problem-focused coping when dealing with chronic and potentially lethal health-care threats. For example, among HIV-positive gay men, preliminary findings suggest that monitors and blunters differ in the strategies they use in their everyday lives to cope with their health status. As a whole, the HIV-positive patients do not differ significantly from population norms. When we look at the coping process in a more fine-grained manner, exploring the distinctive profiles of monitors and blunters, a more discriminating pattern emerges (Miller, Robinson, & Combs, 1991).

Initial results show that monitors are more likely to adopt a rather ineffective problem-solving stance, compared with blunters. They are more likely to suppress competing activities, but they are less likely to try to cope actively with their problem. That is, they stop doing other things, but they do not necessarily turn their attention toward a creative solution to the problems engendered by their HIV-status. This is consistent with data on chronic worrying. While worriers tend to elaborate numerous potential problem scenarios, they are actually poorer at decision-making and problem-solving (Borkovec, 1985; Borkovec & Lyonfields, this volume). Interestingly, recent findings suggest that monitors are more likely to engage in worrying than blunters are (Davey, Hampton, Farrell, & Davidson, in press).

Indirect Exercise of Control

Perhaps monitors inappropriately evaluate their strategies as being more efficacious than they really are, and it is this that sustains information seeking. However, some data argue against this possibility (Miller et al., 1990). Alternatively, the Minimax Hypothesis may offer some clues to the behavior of monitors (Miller, 1979, 1980). This view predicts that individuals should only opt for control when they believe that their own responses can put an upper limit on how bad the situation can become. They should choose to yield control when they believe that some other, external factor can more reliably limit the danger for them.

Monitors may have come to believe that other people can more effectively resolve their problems than they themselves can. This may be particularly evident in cases where there are identified experts, as in the health-care setting. Remaining alert to threat may be part of the price for obtaining relevant information about when, with whom, and how to make contact. Indeed, as more information is accumulated, monitors may become more painfully aware of the limits of personal control in some settings (Miller et al., 1988). This should prompt them to transfer control to a more competent other and to experience a sense of relief when they do.

In ongoing work, it will be important to determine when attempts to exert secondary control (i.e., putting oneself in the hands of someone more competent) are, in fact, most closely linked with a vigilant style. Toward this end, it is critical to investigate in depth the nature and meaning of various behaviors that may appear to tap assertiveness or the lack of it. Repetitive question-asking, for example, may be viewed as a form of assertiveness in the health-care setting. However, it may instead reflect attempts to select and remain connected with a competent health-care provider and not be indicative of an active (controlling) orientation to threat.

An especially challenging and difficult situation for monitors may arise when no identified expert or competent other is available to help shoulder the burden of managing the crisis at hand. Under these conditions, monitors may be prone to perpetual information seeking in an attempt to locate such an individual. They may also attempt to consider and reach decisions about the various options by themselves. However, this may simply render them mentally and behaviorally stuck, given their low sense of self-efficacy in this domain and their lack of available skills (Bandura, 1985; Miller, in press-a, in press-b).

Monitoring to Modulate Negative Affect

Arousal Regulation

One of the prime concerns for individuals confronted with a range of stressful situations is to reduce indices of arousal and anxiety and to smooth the process of adjustment, especially in response to events that are largely uncontrollable. One possibility is that monitors initiate information seeking attempts, at least in part, in an effort to somehow make themselves feel more psychologically at ease in the situation. On the other hand, a case can be made that attending to threat-relevant information should increase, rather than decrease, negative affective state (Krohne, Chapter 2 in this volume).

According to the Monitoring and Blunting Hypothesis, information with little or no instrumental value should be arousing, since it forces the individual to remain in the psychological presence of a danger he or she cannot avoid (Miller, 1990). Engaging in a variety of cognitive avoidance techniques, such as distraction, can help individuals to selectively process aversive events in a less negative way. This, in turn, can be arousal-reducing (Miller, Combs, & Stoddard, 1989).

A number of studies have shown that monitors and blunters manifest equivalent levels of arousal in response to baseline or non-threat conditions (Miller, 1987; Phipps & Zinn, 1986; Sparks & Spirek, 1988). In contrast, the groups frequently differ in response to environmental challenges, but the monitors appear to be a more at-risk population in these circumstances than the blunters are.

First, in a number of health-care contexts, the coping style groups differ in how distressed they become in response to necessary diagnostic and treatment protocols. In one set of studies, we have been investigating in detail the affective reactions of women who have been referred for follow-up evaluation because of an abnormal Pap smear (Miller et al., 1990). These patients typically must undergo diagnostic screening at regular intervals to test for cancerous and precancerous forms of cervical cell abnormality. Treatment interventions are also sometimes required.

Overall, our preliminary results show that patients referred for ongoing diagnostic evaluation because of an abnormal Pap smear show elevations in anxiety, depression, anger, fatigue, and confusion, and reductions in vigor, compared with a healthy gynecologic sample undergoing a routine examination. Strikingly, these elevations are consistent with - and in the case of anxiety, anger, and confusion even greater than - those shown by gynecologic cancer patients during routine diagnostic testing prior to surgery (Andersen, Anderson, & deProsse, 1989).

In addition, within our sample, monitors show consistently greater self-reported elevations in depression, anger, and anxiety - both before and after the procedure - than blunters do. Similar findings have been obtained with a variety of medical populations. Monitors with at-risk pregnancies show greater increases in negative affect in response to genetic screening and amniocentesis than at-risk blunters and than monitors who are not at risk (Phipps & Zinn, 1986); monitors who are being treated for various cancers report greater distress and experience more severe side-effects of chemotherapy than blunters who are equally ill, despite the fact that they use greater amounts of medication designed to prevent the emergence of these effects (Gard, Edwards, Harris, & McCormack, 1988; Lerman et al., 1990); and monitors undergoing aversive diagnostic examinations manifest more behavioral indications of distress during the procedure (e.g., more overt signs of muscular tension), as well greater reports of pain, more use of analgesics, and slower recovery after the procedure (Miller & Mangan, 1983; Miller et al., 1991).

Monitors not only appear to be more affected by medical and nonmedical threats, they also appear to be more concerned about their own internal bodily cues. One study looked at patients attending a primary care setting, for new or changing physical symptoms (Miller et al., 1988). Monitors were far more likely to visit the doctor for medically trivial problems than blunters were. Despite the fact that their symptoms were less serious, according to the physician, monitors expressed equal concerns about their nature and meaning as blunters did (see also Miller et al., 1989; see also Leventhal, Suls, & Leventhal, this volume).

In addition to differential arousal and concerns in response to short-term threats, procedures, and treatments, monitors in at-risk groups show some signs of more long-term dysfunction than blunters do. For example, among women at risk for cervical cancer, monitors express greater loneliness and less optimism than their blunting counterparts. They do not differ in measures of trait anxiety or depression (Miller et al., 1990). Among HIV-positive patients who are asymptomatic, monitors experience greater depression and greater loneliness than blunters do. They also spend more days in bed because of not feeling well, although they are at the same level of disease progression (Miller et al., 1991).

Studies conducted in laboratory settings confirm these results. For example, in one study, subjects watched a frightening film for the first time. Monitors showed a significantly greater increase from baseline in skin conductance, reflecting greater physiological arousal in response to the film than blunters did (Sparks & Spirek, 1988). This effect was most pronounced during high stress segments of the film. In addition to displaying greater physiological and subjective arousal to threatening films (Sparks, 1989; Sparks & Spirek, 1988), Monitors also show greater distress under the threat of electric shock (Miller, 1987) and less tolerance for the cold pressor task (Efran, Chorney, Ascher, & Lukens, 1989).

Taken together, monitoring appears to increase, rather than decrease, negative affect and accompanying arousal. This result is most evident during the anticipatory and recovery phases of a stressful encounter, particularly in the short-term. These findings suggest that, in some instances, information seeking is undertaken despite - not because of - its arousal consequences (Krohne, Chapter 2 in this volume). On the other hand, monitors may, at times, have an advantage. Under some circumstances, monitoring appears to help offset arousal during the actual impact of a stressful event (e.g., Miller & Mangan, 1983; Steketee, Bransfield, Miller, & Foa 1989; Weisenberg & Caspi, 1989; see also Carver & Scheier, this volume). However, the boundaries of this effect are not well-understood.

Self-Efficacy

It is possible that monitors have somehow formed the erroneous belief that a focus on threat will enable them to effectively contain negative emotion, even though their strategy is often more arousal-inducing or arousal-sustaining than that of blunters. Some evidence argues against this possibility. Preliminary results confirm that monitors tend to use strategies of a more information-oriented nature when dealing with an unpleasant medical diagnostic procedure. They are more likely to focus on their bodily sensations, to talk to the staff about their physical feelings, to think about what the doctor is doing, and to think about how necessary the procedure is. They are less likely to use strategies of a more avoidant nature, such as relaxing themselves by taking deep breaths or thinking about things unrelated to the procedure or their gynecologic condition.

In comparison with blunters, however, they indicate that their strategies are not as helpful in making themselves feel better during the procedure (Miller et al., 1990). In addition, in response to a laboratory pain stimulus (the cold pressor task), monitors do not benefit as much from an information-oriented strategy (attending to the sensations in their hands) as blunters do from an avoidance-oriented strategy (turning attention away from pain-related sensations) (Efran et al., 1989). While both monitors and blunters report that they used the suggested techniques, monitors say that they had less confidence in the effectiveness of their strategy.

Other work has shown that blunters undergoing an aversive medical treatment (cancer chemotherapy) appear to benefit more from stress management interventions that emphasize relaxation (Lerman et al., 1990; see also Avants, Margolin, & Salovey, 1991). Overall, monitors appear to both experience heightened anxiety and to evaluate their strategies as being less useful to them in the modulation of that anxiety. Indeed, their lack of self-efficacy surrounding their own coping repertoire may be one of the factors that sustains anxiety (Bandura, 1985).

Monitoring to Reduce Uncertainty

Information Seeking

As outlined above, individuals generally prefer to distract themselves and engage in other cognitive avoidance activities in the face of an uncontrollable threat, in an effort to lower subsequent anxiety and arousal. However, some individuals typically find it too difficult or undesirable to distract themselves. According to the Monitoring and Blunting Hypothesis, these people should prefer and benefit from threat-relevant information. Information at least provides them accurate expectations about the severity, probability, nature, course and duration of the aversive event (Miller et al., 1988). This reduces uncertainty, identifies potential safety signals, and thereby helps to offset accompanying anxiety and arousal among monitoring individuals (Berlyne, 1960; Weiss, 1970).

There is a good deal of evidence to suggest that monitors are more inclined toward uncertainty reduction than blunters are. For example, prior to an aversive diagnostic procedure to determine the presence and severity of abnormal cervical tissue, initial results indicate that monitors are more likely than blunters to request higher levels of both sensory and procedural information (Miller et al., 1990).

Miller et al. (1988) studied patients visiting a primary care setting for acute medical problems. On arrival at the physician's office, patients were asked what information they considered is essential to obtain during the visit, given that the doctor had only a limited amount of time to spend with them. Results showed that all patients wanted to know their current diagnosis. In addition, monitors desired more detailed information about the cause of their medical problem, how healthy they were in general, what they could do to prevent future medical problems, and possible medication side-effects.

Information seeking preferences have also been studied in laboratory research. For example, when threatened with a low probability (unavoidable) electric shock to the finger, monitors prefer to listen for a warning signal that predicts the onset of shock, rather than to distract themselves with music. Blunters show the opposite preference (Miller, 1987). Similar results emerge with the use of more high probability aversive events (Kohlmann, 1989). Further, monitors are more likely to scan for information about their ongoing performance when undertaking a threatening cognitive task (Miller, 1987). Hence, they show greater preferences for information in response to both physically and psychologically aversive events.

Satisfaction with Information

Monitors not only desire more voluminous information than their blunting counterparts, they also often seem to demonstrate superior knowledge about upcoming threats. Steptoe and O'Sullivan (1986) studied women about to undergo gynecologic surgery. They found that monitors both claimed to have more factual knowledge and actually had more knowledge about the procedure than blunters did. Despite the fact that monitors know more, however, they are nonetheless less satisfied with their level of information. For example, the monitoring surgery patients in the Steptoe and O'Sullivan study were more likely to say that they would have preferred to have greater amounts of information.

Among patients with metastatic cancer, monitors were more likely than blunters to express dissatisfaction about the information that had been communicated to them about their symptoms, tests, and treatment (Steptoe, Sutcliffe, Allens, & Coombes, 1991). Similarly, two studies found that monitors undergoing an aversive diagnostic test for cervical cancer wanted more sensory and procedural information than had been provided to them (Miller & Mangan, 1983; Miller et al., 1990). The preliminary results of a follow-up study revealed that monitors and blunters were equally satisfied with the strictly medical, technical aspects of their care. However, monitors were more dissatisfied with the nonmedical aspects of their care (Miller et al., 1991).

With cardiac catheterization patients, blunters were far more likely than monitors to feel satisfied with the adequacy of the information provided, even those receiving minimal procedural information. Further, while monitors desired to receive information about all the potential risks associated with the procedure, only a minority of blunters wanted this information. Blunters (but not monitors) also indicated that hearing information about possible complications made them feel considerably more anxious about undergoing the catheterization (Watkins, Weaver, & Odegaard, 1986).

Dissatisfaction among monitors may be due, in part, to the fact that reasonable levels of information are not always readily available within the medical context. When monitors are provided with maximal procedural and sensory information, they are more likely to rate the information as being adequate (Watkins et al., 1986). Sensory information focuses on the sensations to be experienced, while procedural information focuses on the specific procedures to be followed. The combination enables the patient to accurately encode incoming sensations and experiences and to match them with expected occurrences, thereby reducing uncertainty and accompanying arousal (Leventhal, 1989; Suls & Wan, 1989; see also Leventhal et al., this volume).

In primary care doctor-patient interactions, monitors are more likely to request a health-care provider who treats them with kindness and respect and who attends to their concerns about their medical problem (Miller et al., 1988). Clearly, patients may believe that such a provider will take their case more seriously and give them the best possible medical attention. Monitoring patients may also feel that a doctor who manifests these traits will be more attentive to the nontechnical aspects of the health-care interaction. In addition to providing emotional support, such a physician may be perceived to be more open to the patients' concerns and more willing to spend time outlining the diagnostic or treatment protocols to be followed, the rationale for the decisions that have been made, and their probable consequences.

Matching Informational Needs

There is evidence that when monitors are provided with voluminous amounts of preparatory information before an upcoming diagnostic procedure, they subsequently fare better than when only minimal information is provided. For example, monitors given detailed sensory and procedural information prior to an aversive diagnostic test for cervical cell abnormality subsequently showed lower physiological and subjective arousal during the procedure than monitoring patients receiving more minimal information (Miller & Mangan, 1983). Results consistent with this have been obtained with coronary patients undergoing cardiac catheterization (Watkins et al., 1986) and in laboratory studies (Sparks, 1989).

Monitors also appear to fare comparatively better than blunters in situations where the cues about threat are highly invasive and intrusive and/or where preparation is routine and emphasized as the norm. In the laboratory, monitors show less autonomic and subjective arousal than blunters under conditions where it seems most appropriate to monitor for cues about an impending stressor (Kohlmann, 1989). This is not an uncommon situation in the "real world." Women about to give birth, for example, are typically advised to be as aware of their situation as possible and are urged to attend classes that will prepare them fully for the experience. Not surprisingly, monitors rate the pain of labor and childbirth as less severe than blunters do (Weisenberg & Caspi, 1989; see also Steketee et al., 1989).

Monitors' drive toward uncertainty reduction appears to have another positive consequence. It encourages them to comply with health-care regimens that enable them to better clarify their medical status. For example, they are more likely to undergo regular Pap smears and breast self-exams and thereby determine whether they are at risk (Miller et al., 1990; Steptoe & O'Sullivan, 1986). Recent, preliminary data suggest that this may bear positively on the state of their health (Miller et al., 1991). On the other hand, they may be less likely to adhere to recommended preventive behaviors that entail the successful modulation of stress. For example, they have more trouble keeping their stress levels low, exercising regularly, eating a healthy diet, and getting sufficient sleep (Miller et al., 1990).

Hence, monitoring in the face of health threats may ultimately be somewhat of a double-edged sword. It appears to increase stress, particularly in the short-term, but it may simultaneously increase adherence to screening and treatment regimens. Whether this type of style is helpful or harmful to health may depend on the relative strength and persistence of stress versus adherence behaviors, the point in the disease process, and the value of available treatments and regimens (see also Filipp et al., this volume).

Monitoring Sustained by Intrusive Ideation

Rehearsal of Threat

As discussed above, one problem for monitors is that information may not always be presented in a sufficiently clear or structured fashion to enable the individual to interpret ongoing bodily sensations and medical protocols in an accurate and non-threatening manner. In addition, information may not always be provided in an ongoing and flexible enough form to adequately match patients' needs. As monitors progress through a threatening encounter, particularly of a medical nature, they may develop distinctive and changing informational agendas (Leventhal, 1989). Preparatory communications may often be too cursory and generalized to be of maximal use to such patients (Miller, in press-a; Miller et al., 1989).

However, monitors' inability to feel completely satisfied with information that is available to them also may be due to a variety of other factors. Even when situational limitations in the nature and manner of information delivery are ameliorated, monitors may still feel that they do not have sufficient awareness of the threats that befall them. This may be due, in part, to the way in which incoming information is encoded, processed, and remembered. Monitors may not only seek out greater amounts of information when encountering stressful situations than blunters do, they may also tend to ruminate over it more intently and replay it over and over again in their minds. This repetitive rehearsal of threatening cues may, to some extent, account for the increased arousal that monitors appear to suffer, especially under short-term stressors.

Initial data from a study of HIV-positive gay men show differences between the coping style groups in the extent to which they engage in intrusive ideation about their medical condition (Miller et al., 1991). In comparison with blunters, monitors are more prone to repetitively reexperience and relive their situation. That is, they are more likely to think about it when they don't mean to, to dream about it, to have trouble falling asleep because of it, to be reminded of it, and to have strong feelings about it. Indeed, over one-half of the monitors have symptoms in the clinical range, suggesting the presence of one of the cardinal symptoms of post-traumatic stress disorder, compared with only 22% of the blunters.

Another path toward exploring this is to compare the scores of monitors and blunters with population norms. Collapsing across the dimension of coping style, the HIV-positive patients in our sample show significantly greater intrusion scores than male medical students at a stressful period in their training (Horowitz, Wilner, & Alvarez, 1979). However, they show less severe intrusion than male patients at a stress clinic. The picture changes somewhat when the scores of monitors and blunters are reanalyzed separately. Monitors have scores that are as high as patients at a stress clinic. In contrast, blunters appear to fare better and score between the medical student sample and the stress clinic sample.

Attention to Negative Affective State

Monitors not only often engage in more intense and prolonged cognitive rehearsal of threat, but they also tend to focus more on their own negative affective state in response to aversive events. That is, in comparison with blunters, they are more likely to attend to whatever distress or upset they are experiencing and to ventilate those feelings. This effect has been observed in undergraduate populations (Carver et al., 1989) and in at-risk medical populations (Miller et al., 1991). While such an orientation can sometimes be adaptive, in this case it does not appear to facilitate adjustment. Monitors are less likely than blunters to fully accept and accommodate to what has happened (Miller et al., 1991). Hence, focusing on the distress may somehow exacerbate it and/or interfere with moving beyond it (Felton, Revenson, & Hinrichsen, 1984; Scheier & Carver, 1977).

Differences in attentional focus appear to be borne out even in response to threats that are not directly personal in nature. Following the explosion of the American space shuttle Challenger, monitors were significantly more likely to want to see videotaped replays of the astronauts' family members as they watched the launch sequence and to hear them talking about their own reactions to the incident (Sparks & Spirek, 1988).

It is possible that monitors are simply locked into a vicious cycle, in which they cannot escape from an orientation to threat. This may occur because of the salience of their negative state and/or because they lack effective skills for reliably removing themselves from the psychological presence of danger. Alternatively, they may somehow have come to believe that orienting to their feelings and reactions will eventually resolve the situation.

Yet, one of the potential negative consequences of a ruminative style may be the elaboration of new and changing aversive scenarios, such that the initiating situation is ultimately perceived to be worse than it really is. Further, it may make it difficult to decide when sufficient amounts of information have been obtained, thereby driving the search for more details about threat-relevant cues. Indeed, recent research shows that monitors are more likely to be chronic worriers than blunters are (Davey et al., in press). Worry has been found to perpetuate negative thoughts and to actually generate greater awareness of problems, while at the same time interfering with effective problem-solving and decision-making (Borkovec & Lyonfields, this volume).

Monitors have also been found to rate the severity and unpredictability of potentially aversive events as higher and somewhat more uncontrollable and imaginable (Van Zuuren & Wolfs, 1991). Similarly, when asked to evaluate the nature and probability of occurrence of various common but unpleasant experiences (e.g., losing one's wallet), monitors were more likely to overestimate the potential aversiveness and likelihood of such events (Baptista, Figueira, Lima, & Matos, 1990). It is possible that the process of monitoring itself may somehow sustain or drive these cognitions. Alternatively, these cognitive biases may render it more difficult for monitors to emotionally process the event and resign themselves to it (Foa & Kozak, 1986).

Consistent with the latter interpretation, individuals show a different pattern of accommodation to rationally-framed negative self-statements - which assert wishes and wants and acknowledge appropriate levels of regret - than they do to equally negative self-statements that are irrationally framed - which declare an absolute demand or dictate and involve catastrophizing (Ellis, 1977). Subjects show lower initial arousal and greater habituation over time to rational self-statements than they do to irrational self-statements (Master & Miller, in press). This suggests that individuals who tend spontaneously to evaluate stressful situations from a more irrational or exaggerated perspective may have more trouble successfully adapting to that event.

At this point, it is unclear exactly how the greater arousal manifested by monitors is influenced by such factors as a sustained focus on the stressor and/or one's own internal reaction to that stressor. In addition, in future studies, it will be important to explore at precisely what level or stage of information-processing monitors and blunters diverge (Mathews, this volume). A highly tentative conclusion that may be drawn from the available data is that the bias to attend to and elaborate threat may be activated at a fairly early phase of the stress encounter.

Monitoring Sustained by Avoidant Ideation

Suppression of Threat

As we have seen, monitoring strategies sometimes tend to increase arousal and impede habituation in the process of coping with threat. This may activate avoidance mechanisms in an attempt to short-circuit intrusive ideation, and thereby to moderate arousal and keep distress within tolerable limits. Indeed, a central feature of the worry process entails efforts to suppress or distract oneself from anxious thoughts (Borkovec & Lyonfields, this volume; Mathews, this volume).

However, engaging in repeated or prolonged avoidance efforts may actually work to keep threat alive (Wegner, Schneider, Carter, & White, 1987). Recent research has shown that individuals who become dysfunctional in the face of severe life threats - particularly of a highly catastrophic nature - tend to show a pattern that is simultaneously characterized by extreme vigilance for threat (re-experiencing the aversive event), along with extreme avoidance of threat (staying away from cues and reminders of it).

Patients confronting some kind of medical risk situation also appear to be characterized by such a pattern. For example, we have explored these symptoms in women who have some form of cervical cell abnormality and therefore are at risk for cervical cancer (Miller et al., 1990). Preliminary results suggest that in the days preceding an aversive diagnostic test, patients are more likely to engage in avoidant ideation, in comparison with population norms.

In addition, coping style interacts with, and determines the psychological impact of, cancer risk. As discussed above, we sometimes find that monitors are more disturbed by intrusive ideation than blunters are. In addition, and even more strikingly, monitors are more likely to engage in avoidance strategies in an attempt to curb their thoughts. For example, in the gynecologic situation, they are more likely to avoid thinking about their gynecologic health, to push thoughts of it out of their minds, to try to remove it from memory, to feel numb and as if it's not real, and to avoid reminders of it (Miller et al., 1990).

Indeed, 40% of the monitors score in the clinical range for avoidant ideation, compared with only 5% of the blunters. In comparison with population norms, the sample as a whole scores above female medical students but below female stress clinic patients (Horowitz et al., 1979). Considered separately, monitors actually show levels of avoidant ideation that are equivalent to those of the stress clinic patients (Miller et al., 1990). This pattern of results has been replicated with patients facing more lethal health threats, such as being positive for HIV (Miller et al., 1991).

Emotional Processing

Mathews (this volume) has speculated that the combination of early attention to threat combined with later avoidance of threat may be anxiety-sustaining or even enhancing. The early attentional bias builds in threat cues that serve as constant reminders of potential danger, while subsequent attempts to avoid such cues prevent full emotional processing (Foa & Kozak, 1986). At this point, it is unclear exactly where there may deficits in the attention-avoidance process for monitors compared with blunters.

It is possible that monitors engage in greater initial vigilance, which then prompts greater avoidance. Alternatively, blunters may initially attend to threat, but may do so in a manner that is less oriented toward the negative and hence less disturbing. A third possibility is that blunters have greater self-efficacy about their ability to distract themselves and so do not try as hard to suppress threat-relevant ideation (Miller, in press-b).

It is also important to remember that being diagnosed with cancer or the AIDS virus, from the patient's point of view, entails not a single global stressor but many discrete events. Individuals must somehow come to grips or deal with the diagnosis itself, their doctors' ability to control the disease via surveillance and treatment regimens, their own ability to control the disease via adherence to recommended protocols, their ability to control their own emotional response to the disease and its management, their ability to find meaning in their plight, to accomplish other life tasks, and so forth (cf. Filipp et al., this volume).

Some aspects of this experience may best be dealt with by a vigilant approach and some by a more avoidant approach, and this may change as the process of the disease unfolds. For example, the initial response to diagnosis may require efficient monitoring of the threat, as the individual makes important decisions about the appropriate medical expert to choose. After that, the individual may do better to leave the worrying to the expert and concentrate on lowering arousal and anxiety via a variety of emotion-focused techniques (see also Leventhal et al., this volume).

Similarly, at a more molecular level, the individual may need to switch in to the threat at regular intervals in order to schedule and attend necessary surveillance or treatment protocols. However, undergoing these protocols may be facilitated by a more avoidant strategy. The danger for monitors may be that they sometimes simultaneously engage in large amounts of attention and avoidance, in a cyclical fashion, irrespective of situational requirements. On the other hand, large amounts of attention can sometimes facilitate emotional-processing and reduce avoidance, particularly in the face of more catastrophic stressors (Solomon, Mikulincer, and Arad, 1991). Future research should help to pinpoint and untangle these effects (cf. Krohne, Chapter 2 in this volume).

Conclusions

In this chapter, we have explored the underlying mechanisms and motivations of adopting a monitoring style in the face of threat, with a view toward specifying when it has a positive impact on a variety of outcomes in response to health and nonhealth threats. Information seeking does not appear to be undertaken simply in the service of the direct execution of controlling responses. Indeed, the available data seem to indicate that monitors are more - not less - likely to relinquish control and to put themselves in the hands of a more competent other. Thus, monitors may be attentive to information as a means of exercising secondary control, by relying on identified experts.

There is also a considerable amount of evidence to suggest that monitors are motivated to seek information in order to reduce uncertainty. They scan for information even under uncontrollable stressors and manifest higher levels of threat-relevant knowledge than blunters do. They also tend to fare better with more voluminous detail about threat, whereas blunters fare better with more minimal details. On the other hand, monitors tend to be less satisfied with the level of available information than blunters are.

In part, this may be due to the fact that information is not always provided in a sensitive enough or ongoing fashion to match patients' needs. In addition, the way in which monitors attend to threat may leave them craving for a level of certainty and detail that is virtually impossible to obtain. Monitoring appears to entail a recurrent cognitive focus on the threat itself, as well as on the individual's feelings in the face of threat. This rehearsal of the internal and external aspects of threat - combined with a tendency to evaluate the stressor as more negative and uncertain than it actually is - may leave the individual more vulnerable to heightened and sustained arousal.

The fact that monitors appear to alternate intrusive thoughts about threat with attempts to avoid and suppress such thoughts may further put them at risk. While the thoughts continue to intrude on their consciousness, their avoidance efforts may preclude any effective emotional processing of threat. Hence, the individual is not able to fully adjust or accommodate to the experience, particularly in the face of more transient or common stressors.

An individual's motivation for monitoring - and its adaptiveness - may vary as a function of the particular aspect of the event that is being coped with. For example, monitoring the initial disease process may be done mainly to put oneself in the hands of identified experts. Later monitoring may be undertaken mainly in order to reduce the uncertainty associated with unpleasant tests and treatments.

At present, it is still unclear exactly which situations activate the negative arousal consequences of a monitoring style. Is it any medical or nonmedical stressor, those that require the most effortful adjustment because of their level of severity, those that require the most prolonged adaptation because of their chronicity, those where information is not readily available, those where expert sources appear remote or simply do not exist, those where the necessity to maintain a certain degree of vigilance (because of the need to adhere to screening or treatment protocols) drives accompanying avoidance initiatives, or some combination of the above? Ongoing research should help to pin down which of these possibilities is most influential.

In conclusion, we have focused on some fundamental issues in the study of the individual's attempt to adapt to threat that are of relevance to the processes involved in attention and avoidance. Whether or not particular attentional styles are associated with adaptive or maladaptive outcomes depends on a number of considerations. For example, moderators of this link include subject characteristics, developmental considerations, specific interactions between task requirements and subject characteristics, types of outcomes considered, etc. Thus the links between vigilance and avoidance as cognitive styles and health outcomes do not lend themselves to simplistic generalizations. Neither style is intrinsically good or bad, regardless of the individuals or contexts involved.

In our own work, we have explored when a vigilant mode of coping (monitoring) helps individuals in the process of adjustment and when it interferes with adjustment. Given the kinds of fine-grained interactions we have been able to delineate, we are excited about the potential implications of our work for research on "hot" cognition in the stress and health fields generally, and the kinds of patterns that emerge when individuals must somehow simultaneously accommodate to and manage emotionally hot potatoes.

References

Andersen, B. L., Anderson, B., & deProsse, C. (1989). Controlled prospective longitudinal study of women with cancer: II. Psychological outcomes. *Journal of Consulting and Clinical Psychology, 57*, 692-697.

Auerbach, S. M. (1989). Stress management and coping research in the health care setting: An overview and methodological commentary. *Journal of Consulting and Clinical Psychology, 57*, 388-395.

Avants, S. K., Margolin, A., & Salovey, P. (1991). Stress management techniques: Anxiety reduction, appeal, and individual differences. *Imagination, Cognition, and Personality, 10*, 3-23.

Bandura, A. (1985). *Social foundations of thought and action: A social cognitive theory.* Englewood Cliffs, NJ: Prentice-Hall.

Baptista, A., Figueira, M. L., Lima, M. L., & Matos F. (1990). Bias in judgement in panic disorder patients. *Acta Psiquiatrica Portuguesa, 36*, 25-35.

Berlyne, D. E. (1960). *Conflict, arousal, and curiosity.* New York: McGraw-Hill.

Borkovec, T. D. (1985). The role of cognitive and somatic cues in anxiety and anxiety disorders: Worry and relaxation induced anxiety. In A. H. Tuma & J. D. Maser (Eds.), *Anxiety and the anxiety disorders* (pp. 463-478). Hillsdale, NJ: Erlbaum.

Carver, L. S., Scheier, M. F., & Weintraub, J. K. (1989). Assessing coping strategies: A theoretically based approach. *Journal of Personality and Social Psychology, 56*, 267-283.

Davey, G. C. L., Hampton, J., Farrel, J., & Davidson, S. (in press). Some characteristics of worrying: Evidence for worrying and anxiety as separate constructs. *Personality and Individual Differences.*

Efran, J., Chorney, R. L., Ascher, L. M., & Lukens, M. D. (1989). Coping style, paradox, and the cold pressor task. *Journal of Behavioral Medicine, 12*, 91-103.

Ellis, A. (1977). Rational-emotive therapy: Research that supplants the clinical and personality hypothesis of RET and other modes of cognitive behavior therapy. *The Counseling Psychologist, 7*, 2-42.

Felton, B. J., Revenson, T. A., & Hinrichsen, G. A. (1984). Stress and coping in the explanation of psychological adjustment among chronically ill adults. *Social Science and Medicine, 18*, 889-898.

Foa, E. B., & Kozak, M. J. (1986). Emotional processing of fear: Exposure to corrective information. *Psychological Bulletin, 99*, 20-35.

Gard, D., Edwards, P. W., Harris, J., & McCormack, G. (1988). The sensitizing effects of pretreatment measures on cancer chemotherapy nausea and vomiting. *Journal of Consulting and Clinical Psychology, 56*, 80-84.

Horowitz, M., Wilner, N., & Alvarez, W. (1979). Impact of event scale: A measure of subjective stress. *Psychosomatic Medicine, 41*, 209-218.

Kohlmann, C.-W. (1989, July). *Rigid and flexible modes of coping and the goodness-of-fit hypothesis: The role of coping preferences.* Paper presented at the First European Congress of Psychology, Amsterdam, Netherlands.

Krohne, H. W. (1986). Coping with stress: Dispositions, strategies, and the problem of measurement. In M. H. Appley & R. Trumbull (Eds.), *Dynamics of stress: Physiological, psychological, and social perspectives* (pp.207-232). New York: Plenum.

Lerman, C., Rimer, B., Blumberg, B., Cristinzio, S., Engstrom, P. F., MacElwee, N., O'Conner, K., & Seay, J. (1990). Effects of coping style and relaxation on cancer chemotherapy side-effects and emotional responses. *Cancer Nursing, 13*, 308-315.

Leventhal, H. (1989). Emotional and behavioral processes in the study of stress during medical procedures. In M. Johnston & L. Wallace (Eds.), *Stress and medical procedures* (pp. 3-35). Oxford: Oxford University Press.

Master, S., & Miller, S. M. (in press). A test of RET theory using an RET theory based mood induction procedure: The rationality of thinking rationally. *Cognitive Therapy and Research.*

Miller, S. M. (1979). Controllability and human stress: Method, evidence, and theory. *Behaviour Research and Therapy, 17*, 287-304.

Miller, S. M. (1980). Why having control reduces stress: If I can stop the roller coaster, I don't want to get off. In J. Garber & M. Seligman (Eds.), *Human helplessness: Theory and applications* (pp.71-95). New York: Academic Press.

Miller, S. M. (1987). Monitoring and blunting: Validation of a questionnaire to assess styles of information seeking under threat. *Journal of Personality and Social Psychology, 52*, 345-353.

Miller, S. M. (1989). Cognitive informational styles in the process of coping with threat and frustration. *Advances in Behaviour Research and Therapy, 11*, 223-234.

Miller, S. M. (1990). To see or not to see: Cognitive informational styles in the coping process. In M. Rosenbaum (Ed.), *Learned resourcefulness: On coping skills, self-regulation, and adaptive behavior* (pp.95-126). New York: Springer.

Miller, S. M. (in press-a). Individual differences in the coping process: What to know and when to know it. In B. N. Carpenter (Ed.), *Personal coping: Theory, research and application.* New York: Praeger.

Miller, S. M. (in press-b). Monitoring and blunting in the face of threat: Implications for adaptation and health. In L. Montada, S.-H. Filipp, & M. J. Lerner (Eds.), *Life crises and experiences of loss in adulthood.* Hillsdale, NJ: Erlbaum.

Miller, S. M., Brody, D. S., & Summerton, J. (1988). Styles of coping with threat: Implications for health. *Journal of Personality and Social Psychology, 54*, 345-353.

Miller, S. M., Combs, C., & Stoddard, E. (1989). Information, coping and control in patients undergoing surgery and stressful, medical procedures. In A. Steptoe & A. Appels (Eds.), *Stress, personal control and health* (pp. 107-130). Chichester, England: Wiley.

Miller, S. M., & Mangan, C. E. (1983). The interacting effects of information and coping style in adapting to gynecologic stress: Should the doctor tell all? *Journal of Personality and Social Psychology, 45*, 223-236.

Miller, S. M., Robinson, R., & Combs, C. (1991). *Styles of coping with HIV-positive status.* Unpublished manuscript, Temple University, Philadelphia.

Miller, S. M., Rodoletz, M., & Stoddard, E. (1990). *Adjustment, coping and compliance in women at risk for cervical cancer.* Unpublished manuscript, Temple University, Philadelphia.

Mischel, W. (1979). On the interface of cognition and personality. *Psychological Review, 80*, 252-283.

Phipps, S., & Zinn, A. B. (1986). Psychological response to amniocentesis: II. Effects of coping style. *American Journal of Medical Genetics, 25*, 143-148.

Scheier, M. F., & Carver, C. S. (1977). Self-focused attention and the experience of emotion: Attraction, repulsion, elation, and depression. *Journal of Personality and Social Psychology, 35*, 625-636.

Solomon, Z., Mikulincer, M., & Arad, R. (1991). Monitoring and blunting: Implications for combat-related post-traumatic stress disorder. *Journal of Traumatic Stress, 4*, 209-221.

Sparks, G. G. (1989). Understanding emotional reactions to a suspenseful movie: The interaction between forewarning and preferred coping style. *Communications Monographs, 56*, 325-340.

Sparks, G. G., & Spirek, M. M. (1988). Individual differences in coping with stressful mass media: An activation-arousal view. *Human Communications Research, 15*, 191-216.

Steketee, G., Bransfield, S., Miller, S. M., & Foa, E. B. (1989). The effect of information and coping style on the reduction of phobic anxiety. *Journal of Anxiety Disorders, 3*, 69-85.

Steptoe, A., & O'Sullivan, J. (1986). Monitoring and blunting coping styles in women prior to surgery. *British Journal of Clinical Psychology, 25*, 143-144.

Steptoe, A., Sutcliffe, I., Allen, B., & Coombes, C. (1991). Satisfaction with communication, medical knowledge, and coping style in patients with metastatic cancer. *Social Science and Medicine, 32*, 627-632.

Suls, J., & Fletcher, B. (1985). The relative efficacy of avoidant and non-avoidant coping strategies: A meta-analysis. *Health Psychology, 4*, 249-288.

Suls, J., & Wan, C. K. (1989). The effects of sensory and procedural information on adaptation to stressful medical procedures and pain: A meta-analysis. *Journal of Consulting and Clinical Psychology, 57*, 372-379.

Van Zuuren, F. J., & Wolfs, H. M. (1991). Styles of information seeking under threat: Personal and situational aspects of monitoring and blunting. *Personality and Individual Differences, 12*, 141-149.

Watkins, L. O., Weaver, L., & Odegaard, V. (1986). Preparation for cardiac catheterization: Tailoring the content of instruction to coping style. *Heart and Lung, 15*, 382-389.

Wegner, D. M., Schneider, D. J., Carter III, S. R., & White, T. L. (1987). Paradoxical effects of thought suppression. *Journal of Personality and Social Psychology, 53*, 5-13.

Weisenberg, M., & Caspi, Z. (1989). Cultural and educational influences on pain of childbirth. *Journal of Pain and Symptom Management, 4*, 13-19.

Weiss, J. M. (1970). Somatic effects of predictable and unpredictable shock. *Psychosomatic Medicine, 32*, 397-409.

Chapter 4

Hierarchical Analysis of Coping: Evidence From Life-Span Studies

Elaine A. Leventhal, Jerry Suls,
and Howard Leventhal

Introduction

Our objective is to examine coping, i.e., how people act to solve problems, and to present some ideas that may help in the development of more comprehensive models of coping behavior. This will involve the following steps. First, we will discuss the definition of coping and review a number of early and more recent studies in the area. Second, we will examine the issues arising from the apparently weak relationship between measures of coping that are specific to particular situations and measures of individual differences in coping strategies or coping styles. Third, we will briefly examine Krohne's hierarchical model of coping which attempts to resolve some of the problems discussed under the second of our objectives. Following this, we present a revised, hierarchical model which may prove to be a more faithful representation of coping processes. Finally, we discuss some data relevant to differences in coping in cohorts drawn from different segments of the life-span. We will examine how people cope with health problems during the middle to later adult years. Although later life lacks the many rapid, cognitive and emotional changes that take place during infancy and childhood, studying this period from a life-span perspective provides a view of changes that take place from the time one's abilities are at a maximum, i.e., during early adulthood, through later years when some competencies are in gradual decline. But, while competency may be on a gentle downhill slope, individuals may learn how to enhance their coping skills to compensate for biological decline. Thus, an expanding range of life experience may enhance individual wisdom and thereby compensate, to varying degrees, for the biological declines in various competencies.

A key feature of coping is its situational specificity; coping is shaped by the situational demands. This suggests that the development of a comprehensive coping model may be a difficult task. A narrow escape from a threatened assault may elicit startle, an emotional response of fear, and help seeking, while a crisis at work, e.g., a patient suffering a coronary, may elicit systematic, task

---

Preparation of this manuscript was supported by a grant from the National Institute On Aging (AG 03501).

oriented responses in the very same person. In addition to situational specificity, the most likely and most available coping response at the early part of an unfolding episode or crisis may be quite different than the coping responses made during intermediate or later phases of the episode (Safer, Tharps, Jackson, & Leventhal, 1979; Stone & Neale, 1984). Thus, variations across situations and within situations over time will make it difficult indeed to identify the characteristic mode of coping for an individual or a life epoch, if indeed there is a characteristic mode.

A Model for Coping

The dictionary definition of coping, "To maintain a contest or combat usually on even terms or with success .... to deal with and attempt to overcome problems and difficulties..." (Webster, 1986), emphasizes vigorous and competitive action. But it is more than action, it is action in *problem or difficult* situations, and it is action that is *evaluated*, usually as successful or at least on "even terms". Thus, even the nontechnical definition of coping takes important steps toward defining a *model* of coping, suggesting that coping cannot be defined independent of a psychological theory. The dictionary and some theoreticians (Carver, Scheier, & Weintraub, 1989; Krohne, Chapter 2, in this volume; Lazarus & Folkman, 1984), also suggest it is important to distinguish between coping actions (covert and overt) and coping functions, that is, the goals these acts are intended to achieve and the problems they are intended to resolve. Failure to recognize and maintain the distinction between the actions and functions of coping has been a source of conceptual confusion and created problems in developing scales to assess coping (Endler & Parker, 1990; Lazarus & Folkman, 1984; Rohde, Lewinsohn, Tilson, & Seeley, 1990). We will give considerable attention to this problem in this chapter.

The model with which we are working is compatible with the elements of the dictionary definition. In this model, coping is defined as the *set of procedures*, overt and covert, that an individual uses for managing a problem situation (see Figure 4.1). An *outcome appraisal* following the planning and execution of these procedures can result in the reappraisal of the effectiveness of the procedure, leading to an increase or decrease in the likelihood of its use, a change in the *representation* of the problem, or a reappraisal of the adequacy of the individual's resources, both personal and social. Representations of problems are critical and their attributes shape coping. Thus, the indicators of the presence of a health threat (its *identity* or label and symptoms), the temporal expectations of its rate of development and decline (*time-lines*), and its perceived *consequences* and *causes* and expectations respecting its *controllability*, all define targets or goals for coping. These attributes also help to establish criteria for evaluating coping outcomes.

As the stressors we consider here are anticipated or current health crises that evolve over time, our model presumes that representations of events change and

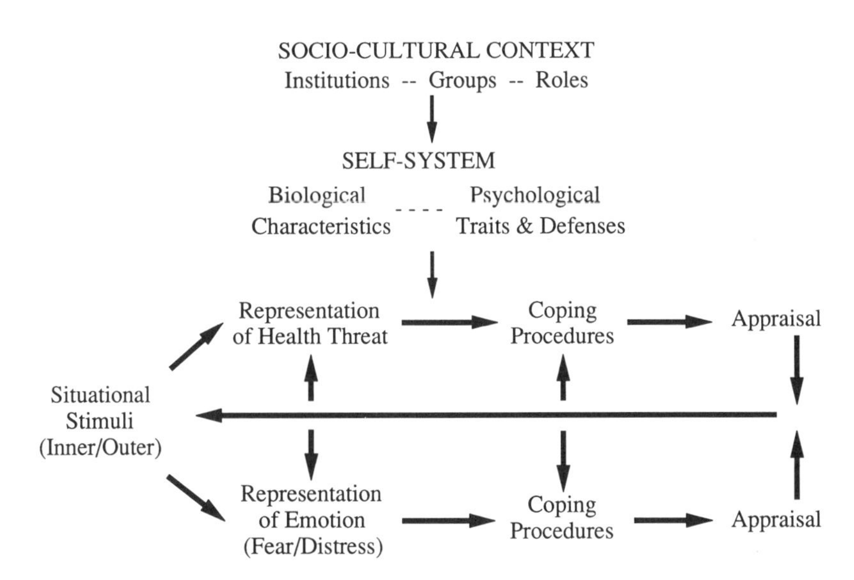

Figure 4.1. Systems model for analysis of adherence to health promotive and avoidance of health damaging behaviors. External and internal stimuli generate a multi-attribute representation (a subjective perception of a somatic problem) and an emotion, leading to coping procedures and appraisals of outcomes. Representations, e.g., targets for self-regulation, coping procedures, and appraisal rules are affected by self and social context.

are elaborated upon as a consequence of changes in the stressor (the underlying disease and its treatment). Thus, stressful events undergo an unfolding or elaboration which can be described in terms of stages (cf. Figure 4.2). The first stage that has been identified for many illness episodes is the *appraisal* stage, a period from just noticing a somatic change to deciding one is sick. The *illness* phase, or the period from deciding one is ill to the decision to seek professional care, is the second and it is followed by the *utilization* phase, or the period from appointment making to the time of medical contact. Medical contact initiates a *diagnostic and treatment* phase, the time from contact and beginning diagnostic procedures or treatment procedures till the end of contact, and a *rehabilitation* phase, or the time from the end of treatment to the return to everyday role activities (Alonzo, 1980; Cacioppo, Andersen, Turnquist, & Petty, 1986; Safer et al., 1979; Suchman, 1965).

The three stages, preparatory, impact or crisis, and post crisis or recovery phase, that have been described for stressors ranging from natural disasters to parachute jumping and exposure to electric shocks in laboratory settings (Epstein, 1973; Janis, 1958; Suls, 1982), overlap with, but are less detailed than, those elaborated for understanding the unfolding of health threats.

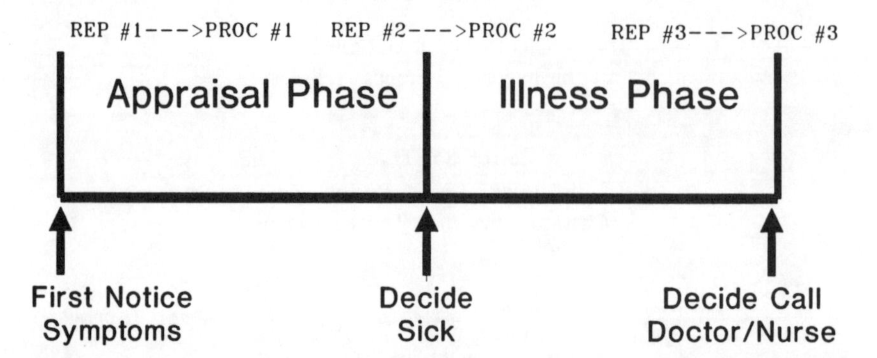

Figure 4.2. The first two phases of an illness episode. As illness episodes evolve over time, decision points appear which divide the episode into phases. Representations (REP) and coping procedures (PROC) change as the episode evolves, but the progression is not necessarily linear, i.e., representation attributes and procedures from earlier phases may appear at later ones.

The definitions of stages are clearly descriptive and subject to further differentiation and specification depending upon the particulars of the underlying disease and the organization and protocols of the health care system.

The model (Figure 4.1) also makes clear that all aspects of information processing, from the representation through procedures to outcome appraisals, take place within the context of the self and the social system. Thus, the individual's prior concrete experience and knowledge of illness and the social context shape every component of the processing system. Aspects of the social context, from the labels used to identify a disease to the institutional arrangements and exchanges of information occurring during the diagnosis and treatment of disease, shape every aspect of this self-regulative, information processing system. Hypertension provides an excellent example of the way labels affect the representation of a health threat; the term, hypertension, suggests symptoms (tension and anxiety), causes (stress), treatments (relaxation), and ways of appraising the value of treatments (feeling calm; Blumhagen, 1980; Meyer, Leventhal, & Gutmann, 1985), which may or may not have any bearing on the biological course of this disorder.

The model is similar to that proposed by Richard Lazarus, and both were developed over a similar time span and reflect the influence of a common zeitgeist (Lazarus, 1966; Lazarus & Folkman, 1984; Leventhal, 1970; Leventhal, Meyer, & Nerenz, 1980; Leventhal, Singer, & Jones, 1965).

The model we have described permits two quite different definitions for coping. First, it could refer to the performance of specific overt and covert actions (cognitive and emotional) involved in adapting to specific situations. Second, it could refer to the operation of the entire system during behavioral adaptation, i.e., to the content and organization of the representation, the selection and performance of coping procedures, and the criteria for the evaluation of response outcomes. When used in this latter sense, coping has an evaluative connotation, referring to the adaptive value or success of the coping performance. This latter meaning is salient in much every-day usage of the term as well as the dictionary definition, i.e., coping "..on even terms or with success..". In the present chapter, we will use the term coping in the first sense, that is as referring to overt and covert procedures for managing problems and feelings, and we will use the term adaptation to refer to the activity of the entire system. The distinction is important as the analysis of adaptation, i.e., of coping success and failure, requires attention to all components of the system. Thus, as our theory indicates, the representation of a problem or a threat establishes immediate, intermediate and remote goals which guide the selection of specific coping procedures, and these coping procedures cannot lead to successful adaptation unless the problem representation is valid. The representation also sets the framework for evaluating outcomes by setting targets for management (e.g., symptoms) and criteria and time frames for assessing change.

Emotion- and Problem-Based Functions of Coping

The concepts of emotion- and problem-based coping

There is more to system performance than the devising of procedures to manage a perceived problem. As the dictionary suggests, coping actions are designed to solve competitive and difficult problems, and these are problems which we would define as threatening or stress inducing. Because they are threatening, they stimulate a wide range of negative emotional reactions such as distress, fear, anger, disgust and depression. As these reactions can affect the overall performance of the system, they too can become targets for coping. Thus, an individual may engage in procedures to minimize or maximize one or another emotional response in the expectation that doing so will facilitate problem-solving, or he/she may act to minimize or amplify the emotion because its properties are experienced as unpleasant or pleasant. Because action can be directed toward the perceived problem or toward one's feelings, investigators have used terms such as danger control and fear control (Leventhal, 1970), or problem-based and emotion-focused coping (Folkman & Lazarus, 1980; Lazarus & Folkman, 1984; Lazarus & Launier, 1978). Although it is explicitly recognized that an individual may engage in both problem-focused and emotion-focused coping in the same situation (e.g., Folkman & Lazarus, 1980), the distinction clearly implies that different procedures are used to regulate problems and feelings. Hence, the bulk of published research on coping has focused on the identification and classification of coping behaviors as those used to deal with the perceived situation, i.e., the stressor (problem-based coping), and those designed to deal with the experienced, emotional reactions evoked by these stressors, such as avoidance coping, wishful thinking, and reinterpretation (Folkman & Lazarus, 1980, 1986).

We believe it logically impossible and empirically self-defeating to continue to tag procedures as consistently problem-focused or emotion-focused because virtually any action can serve multiple functions. For example, an individual may close his eyes to reduce the emotional distress provoked while watching a surgical operation, an emotion-focused function, and he may also close his eyes to avoid distractions and concentrate on touch while attempting to listen to heart sounds, a problem-focused function. Sometimes the same attention-regulating response can have affective or problem-based functions in the same situation. For example, seeking social support is often considered as an emotion-focused strategy, but simultaneously may be an attempt to obtain information to solve the problem. A stimulant such as amphetamine can be used as a mood enhancer to overcome depressed feelings and to control emotion, or the drug can be used to enhance problem-based performance by increasing mental activation when over-tired. Although the latter example pertains to a problem internal to the physical organism, they are no less problem-based than procedures to acquire information or social support. Moreover, both information seeking and social support can be emotion-focused (Carver et al., 1989; Pearlin, 1985): A person can enhance his mood by searching for humorous information and by calling on an especially good-humored friend. Thus, while an ontology of coping functions seems a realistic possibility, the versatility and multiple functions of specific behaviors create difficulties for the development of a taxonomy of coping procedures. Indeed, we think this difficulty is reflected in the empirical literature, and we concur that ".... many of the items used in previous coping inventories were ambiguous, at least in terms of the coping concepts .. explored. How an item was viewed (by respondents) was based not only on its objective content, but on how the person imagined using it." (Stone, Helder, & Schneider, 1988). We will have more to say about this issue later.

Recent studies of emotion- and problem-based coping

We believe that our pessimism regarding the construction of coping inventories to assess problem- and emotion-based coping is confirmed by the data. Early efforts to investigate coping made use of various coping checklists such as that for measuring "Ways of Coping" (WOC; Folkman & Lazarus, 1980). Responses to the 168 items WOC inventory were obtained in adult (Folkman & Lazarus, 1980) and college age populations (Folkman & Lazarus, 1985) and factor analyzed using principle component analysis (Aldwin, Folkman, Schaefer, Coyne, & Lazarus, 1980; Folkman & Lazarus, 1985; Folkman, Lazarus, Dunkel-Schetter, DeLongis, & Gruen, 1986; Vitaliano, Russo, Carr, Maiuro, & Becker, 1985). These analyses agree in four areas. First, each generated five (Vitaliano et al., 1985) to eight factors (Folkman & Lazarus, 1985). Second, each yielded a greater number of factors focused on the regulation of emotion, e.g., four (Vitaliano et al., 1985) to six (Folkman & Lazarus, 1985), and a smaller number (one or two) focusing upon the regulation or solution of problems (Folkman & Lazarus, 1985; Vitaliano et al., 1985). Third, each accounted for a relatively limited amount of variance (less than 30%) in the response space. Fourth, and last, somewhat different factors emerged in different analyses, e.g., a self-control factor was found in a study of community residents coping with a variety of major and minor stressors (Folkman, Lazarus, Gruen, & DeLongis, 1986) but not found among students coping with an examination (Folkman & Lazarus, 1985). In addition, some items loaded on different factors from one sample to the next. Thus, although the studies on the Ways of Coping checklist suggested that there may be some stability in the structure of coping, the overall picture did not suggest a high level of consistency across time and/or population.

In our judgment, recent efforts by three different groups of investigators made only minor improvements upon the empirical picture described above. All three began by using items taken from the Ways of Coping checklist and similar scales (Billings & Moos, 1981). One group, Endler and Parker (1990), conducted two principal component analyses, the first using 70 items, the second 44 of the 70, and found three factors, Task, Emotion, and Avoidance Coping, which accounted for 27.8% and 35.8% of the variance respectively in the two item sets. Using two additional samples of undergraduates, they found associations between their three factors and similarly labelled factors among the eight reported by Folkman and Lazarus (1985). They also found associations between the three factors and measures of depression and anxiety; the Task factor was weakly, but negatively associated with measures of emotional distress, especially among women undergraduates, and the Emotion factor was positively associated with measures of emotional distress for both genders (correlations mainly in the middle .30, with some correlations reaching .50 and above).

The second group, Rohde et al. (1990), also investigated the relationship of coping to depression. They administered and factor analyzed the responses of 742 community dwelling adults to 65 coping items. They found three factors which accounted for 25.3% of the item variance and labeled them: Cognitive Self-Control, Ineffective Escapism, and Solace Seeking. Although these factors appear similar to those found by Endler and Parker, e.g., Task Coping with Cognitive Self-Control, Emotion Coping with Ineffective Escapism, and Avoidant Coping with Solace Seeking, it is truly close only for the second pair, i.e., Emotion Coping and Ineffective Escapism. The modest correspondence between the two results is likely due to use of different items, as Rohde et al. used only six items from Folkman and Lazarus' (1980) Ways of Coping questionnaire whereas Endler and Parker made use of the entire set. Rohde et al. (1990) also found a significant association between concurrent depression and Ineffective Escapism, confirming Endler and Parker's (1990) results and supporting the correspondence between Ineffective Escapism and Emotion Coping. More important, Rohde et al. (1990) found that Ineffective Escapism and the combination (interaction) of life-stress and Ineffective Escapism predicted future depression.

The results reported by these two sets of investigators are similar in three important ways. First, the factors account for under 30% of the total item variance before the elimination of items which do not show expected loadings on a single factor (cf. Rohde et al., 1990); this occurs even though the scales have satisfactory internal consistency (*alphas* in excess of .70) and good test retest reliability (*r*'s near .60). Second, while criteria used for factor extraction produced a smaller number of factors in each study (three) than found by Lazarus's research group, an examination of the item content shows that most of the items with high loadings focused on the management of emotional states rather than the management of situational and/or life problems. Indeed, Endler and Parker (1990) eliminated three items from their task-focused coping factor ("try to calm myself down"; "think about ways to avoid the problem"; "pray for help") as the items clearly lacked face validity as measures of task-based coping. As this is the one factor that most clearly assesses problem-based coping, it suggests that procedures that appear to assess emotion coping, may have important functions in problem-solving, supporting our hypothesis that it may prove difficult if not impossible to identify coping procedures with only a single function.

The third similarity between the two studies is the reported association between what the authors call "maladaptive coping", i.e., Emotion Coping and Ineffective Escapism, with concurrent measures of depression, and the relationship of Ineffective Escapism to future depression (Rohde et al., 1990); depression as measured by the CES-D (Radloff, 1977) and diagnosed by interview. The concurrent and prospective relationship between coping and depression has two related implications, the first that individual differences in coping procedures may be related to individual differences in personality, and second that individual differences in coping procedures may be consistent over time.

Direct evidence of stability in individual differences in coping should be problematic if, as we have asserted, coping processes are situationally specific and variable. Different stressors should require different kinds of responses. Lazarus reported relatively low test-retest reliabilities with the highest being in the forties (Folkman, Lazarus, Gruen, & DeLongis, 1986). However, as noted above, both Endler and Parker as well as Rohde et al. found moderate test-retest reliabilities in the .60's and .70's, over two months or two years, respectively. Hence, recent studies provide evidence of consistency over time.

Additional evidence bearing on the structure and stability of coping comes from the studies by a third group of investigators (Carver et al., 1989), who found modest (r = .20 to .39), but statistically significant associations between coping scales and personality factors such as optimism, control, self-esteem, hardiness and anxiety (cf. Carver & Scheier, this volume). Their data also suggest some consistency in coping as they found adequate test-retest reliabilities for their coping scales (.42 to .89) and moderate associations (mainly .20 and .30) between assessments of "usual" coping behavior and reports of situationally specific coping behavior taken three weeks later. Their results differ from those of the Endler and Lewinsohn group, however, as Carver et al. (1989) report eleven interpretable factors with eigenvalues greater than one and, as before, seven can be interpreted as functional for coping with emotion and fewer, only three, can be interpreted as functional for problem-based coping. The eleventh factor involved seeking social support for both instrumental and emotional reasons.

These recent studies open several issues worthy of discussion. An initial concern is why the groups of Lazarus and Carver found five to eleven interpretable factors while Endler and Parker and Rohde et al. found only three? Part of the explanation probably lies in the fact that Endler and Parker followed scree test criteria to determine the number of significant factors to retain (Cattell, 1966) while Lazarus and Carver did not. Cattell (1966) recommends scree testing as component analysis yields "hybrid" factors, particularly in the factors extracted later, because unique variance overlaps with common variance. Variance unique to each specific item creeps into all factors and the proportion in factors extracted later on can be so great as to swamp the variance common to the items on the factor. The scree test identifies the optimum number of factors which can be taken out before the intrusion of unique variance becomes serious. Prior to the scree testing, Endler and Parker found 19 factors with eigenvalues greater than 1.0. Rohde et al. (1990) did not mention using scree criteria, but state that a "number of factoring procedures" were used: "On the basis of principal-components factor analysis with varimax rotation ... three psychologically meaningful factors were extracted each of which accounted for at least 5% of the variance and contained a minimum of six items" (p. 503). In contrast, Lazarus's group appears not to have imposed a criterion for the number of items required to constitute a factor. During initial scale construction, Carver et al. used only four items for each hypothetically derived factor. In brief, then, differences in the factor analytic procedures probably account for the differences in the factor structures found by these research groups.

Another concern is whether the statistical correctness evident in the more recent studies may have lead to scales lacking construct and ecological validity. We make this statement on the basis of the following observations. First, there are some items that we view as curious. For example, two of Endler and Parker's items on their emotion-oriented factor are: "Blame myself for procrastinating" and "Preoccupied with aches and pains." An item on Rohde et al.'s Ineffective Escapism factor states "I often find it difficult to overcome my feelings of nervousness and tension without outside help." These items do not refer to behaviors employed to handle a problem; they are outcomes of stressor occurrence or signs of the failure of coping. Although such items do not constitute the majority of the items on their factors, one must consider, nonetheless, to what degree the reported association with depression reflects content overlap between the coping measure and the measure of depression (cf. Watson & Pennebaker, 1989). Second, a number of coping strategies are missing from the Endler and Rohde scales that would seem important on a conceptual basis. Carver et al. have a category of *restraint* coping (e.g., "I hold off doing anything about it until the situation permits") that is similar to Lazarus' self-controlling factor. Though Endler and Parker as well as Rohde et al. have a few items that are similar in meaning (e.g., "Take time off and get away from the situation", "When I feel I am too impulsive, I tell myself, 'Stop and think before you do anything' "), none of them conveys exactly the sense of restraint coping, and this concept failed to emerge as a factor. We suspect this is because Endler and Rohde's methods tend to exclude low frequency coping strategies. Frequency of use is, however, a problematic criterion for a coping taxonomy. Rarity does not necessarily constitute a lack of efficacy.

In summary, recent studies with more psychometric rigor find more stable and internally consistent factors, but some of the items in these newer scales may reflect the outcome of stress or poor coping attempts and not coping behaviors, and the variety of strategies may be underrepresented because they are infrequently used. And to an unknown degree, differences between the results also reflect differences in factorial methods. Finally, problem-based strategies are still greatly underrepresented.

A Re-Examination of Coping: Concept and Measurement

Although the newer studies offer minor improvements over prior factorial studies, (e.g., their factors are likely more reliable), they too fail to incorporate process notions into the empirical study of coping. This deficit has been present from the time of publication of earlier process notions (Janis, 1958; Lazarus, 1966; Leventhal, 1970), now well over 20 years, and persists despite the transactional emphasis of recent conceptualizations of coping (e.g., Carver & Scheier, 1981; Lazarus & Folkman, 1984; Lazarus & Launier, 1978; Leventhal et al., 1980; Leventhal & Nerenz, 1983; Stone & Neale, 1984; Suls & Fletcher, 1985). Virtually all theoretical discussions state or imply that coping involves a transaction between person and setting, that it is guided by the representation of the stress situation, and therefore is highly situationally specific. As many of these theoretical formulations view stressful episodes as dynamic and changing over time, they also predict variation in coping behaviors with changes in the episode and its representation (Alonzo, 1980; Cameron, Leventhal, Leventhal, & Schaefer, 1991; Safer et al., 1979; Stone et al., 1988; Suls & Fletcher, 1985). Indeed, Stone and his colleagues have now shown that responses to psychometric instruments may be made with reference to one or more stages of a stress episode and these differences may reflect individual differences, item differences, stressor differences, and interactions among these three factors. The consequence is that there remains considerable doubt as to the referent or meaning of item endorsements when respondents are asked to indicate which strategies were used to cope with a specific stress episode (Stone, Greenberg, Kennedy-Moore, & Newman, in press).

We believe that a more detailed model of the coping process and increased efforts to generate a closer match between process models and experimental design and measurement procedures can enhance the validity of our observations and improve our understanding of coping. Comparisons between the procedures for coping with health threats by older and younger cohorts, to be described later on, support our suggestions for the conceptualization and assessment of coping as well as providing data about the relationship of age to coping.

Coping in Situations versus Coping as a Trait

What are the implications of the situational specificity of coping for the assessment of individual differences in coping style and changes in coping over the life-span? The data discussed in the prior section show modest associations between reports of "usual" coping and reports of coping in specific situations, and similarly modest associations between coping reports and personality measures. The modest associations between reports of "usual" coping and reports of situational coping could be due to biases in the reports of usual coping. For example, the instructions to assess usual coping could elicit recall of stress episodes that are very remote in time but are highly memorable, perhaps because their outcomes were especially satisfying, or these instructions could elicit reports of coping procedures associated with outcomes that one usually hopes for, rather than procedures actually put into play in adapting to stressful settings. In any case, it is likely that the reports are biased toward reporting on the goals or functions of coping, rather than reporting actual coping behaviors (Stone et al., 1988; Williams, Suls, Alliger, Learner, & Wan, in press).

On the other hand, reports of coping in specific situations may also be subject to bias. An individual may engage vigorously in a number of coping responses that are clearly appropriate to and/or shaped by the demands of a situation, and best recall his or her "objectives" or evaluation of the outcome, rather than recall the details of his or her performance. Moreover, many coping reactions such as the responses used to check the meaning of somatic sensations, may be overlearned and automatic, and take place so rapidly and with so little premeditation and thought that they are not subject to monitoring and verbal report. The search for symptoms consistent with an underlying schema of an illness or an underlying schema of the body provide many examples; e.g., if my sore throat indicates a head cold, I would expect to have a stuffy nose, and to determine whether a lump is an abnormal growth and a sign of illness or a normal part of the physical self, I might search for a similar growth in a symmetrical region of the body. Self-diagnostic procedures such as these also may be more common during the early phase of an illness episode.

The combination of poor monitoring of automatic reactions and the high salience of more dramatic phases of illness episodes such as seeking care or diagnosis, suggest that retrospective reports of situationally specific coping will be biased toward reporting on crisis periods and under-reporting of the many active coping procedures in the early phases of the episode. These biases would be consistent with the hypothesis that actors focus on the external situation (Jones & Nisbett, 1971) and their report of behaviors is biased toward those actions that are consistent with their representation of the situation. It is clear that new techniques may be needed to sample coping during phases of episodes and that this must be done in different domains (see Stone et al., 1988).

One strategy may be to have subjects keep nightly diary recordings of naturally-occurring stressful events and what they did to handle them for extended periods, an approach used by Stone and Neale (1984). A related approach is to have subjects who are due to undergo a stressful experience, such as an important examination, keep diary records during anticipation, impact, and recovery. This has been done by Folkman and Lazarus (1985) and more recently by Bolger (1990). Even end-of-the-day records may be too distal from stressor occurrence, however. Suls and Rittenhouse (1990) have proposed using experience sampling methodology (ESM) whereby persons signaled by beepers or special watches on a random schedule several times a day make diary recordings about problems occurring within the last few minutes and how they handled them. This type of proximal measurement "in situ" has had some success in a recent study of the responses of working mothers to juggling tasks of career and family (Williams et al., in press).

The important point is the need for coping researchers to take heed from the lessons of the literature on person vs. situation influences on behavior (Epstein, 1980; Mischel, 1968). When behavior in one situation is correlated with behavior in another situation, the correlations are invariably low. This led Mischel to propose that there is little stability in personality. However, as Epstein (1980) pointed out, most single items of behavior have a high component of measurement error and a narrow range of generality. When measures of behavior are averaged over an increasing number of events, stability coefficients increase. Coping researchers rarely measure only a single occasion of behavior (i.e., coping), but the number of measures they typically take may still be too few to expect any appreciable consistency. This does not mean that high levels of consistency will emerge (for reasons we will explain below), only that the consistency of coping may not yet have received an optimal opportunity for assessment (Epstein & Meier, 1989).

A Hierarchy of Coping Procedures

Both our analysis and the data we have reviewed suggests that the problem of identifying situationally specific coping procedures and identifying individual differences in coping preferences will be most difficult for problem-based coping. We can expect problem-solving procedures to vary by domain and by the features of the problem and point in time toward solution. Thus, the specific actions taken to cope with interpersonal problems should differ from the actions taken to cope with work problems, financial problems, and so on (Pearlin & Schooler, 1978; Stone et al., 1988). And problem episodes within a domain, i.e., within the domain of illness, or work, or family (spousal vs. parent-child), will differ from one another.

The hierarchical model of coping proposed by Krohne (1989; and Chapter 2, this volume) presents a possible solution to obtaining a valid picture of both individual differences in coping strategies (a high level of conceptualization) and situationally specific coping actions (a low level of description). This approach may help to clarify the relationship between relatively stable personality traits and situationally specific actions. For example, assessments of the strategies of vigilance and cognitive avoidance should provide a valid view of individual differences, while specific reactions in a stressful situation, e.g., looking away from the site of an impending insertion of a needle during medical treatment or monitoring the movement of the needle and its sensory impact during insertion, are specific behavioral tactics reflecting these higher order strategies.

Krohne's model, which we have described only in part, clearly advances our view of the complexity of the coping process and the empirical studies by Krohne and his associates provide a valuable platform for further research. But we think a basic modification may be needed in the way the relationship between the levels of the hierarchical system is conceptualized. Specifically, Krohne's depiction and verbal description of the hierarchy (cf. Krohne, 1989, Figure 4.1) suggests that strategies are collections of lower level actions. His formulation is consistent with traditional descriptions of the link between traits and habits (see Eysenck, 1953) and consistent with the factorial descriptions of coping which he criticizes, i.e., styles are clusters of acts and acts are clusters of specific actions such as those enumerated by the Ways of Coping checklists. Hence, Krohne implicitly accepts two key points which he has criticized as errors in prior research: 1. The empiricist nature of factorial approaches to coping, which he argues are inadequate to describe process; and 2. the failure of prior studies to recognize that specific acts can reflect different intentions and have different functions. Krohne's retreat from his suggestion (see page 32, this volume) that we must assess intentions if we are to understand how situationally specific actions relate to higher order coping strategies, reflects his quite legitimate concern that it may be difficult and even impossible to assess intentions uninfluenced by conscious or unconscious bias.

Despite the conceptual limitation of the particular hierarchical schema that Krohne presents in this volume, he and his colleagues have generated much useful and interesting data on coping (cf. chapters by Hock, by Kohlmann, and by Slangen, Kleemann, & Krohne, this volume). They have postulated two dimensions underlying coping and articulated the different processes that underly each of the four cells formed by them. Indeed, their empirical successes may seem paradoxical in light of our criticisms. Thus, we must either explain how a flawed model can do well empirically, or reject our criticisms. Hopefully the following sections will do the former and provide another small step forward in the conceptualization of coping processes.

Hierarchies from a Control Systems Perspective

Systems approaches to self-regulation posit multiple levels of control processes (e.g., Carver & Scheier, 1981; Leventhal, 1984; Powers, 1973), but the hierarchies in these analyses differ in a critical way from that proposed by traditional factorial representations, as the processes at a higher level do not represent collections or aggregations of events or responses at a lower level; rather, the levels differ qualitatively (Figure 4.3). For example, our model of emotional processing suggests that higher level conceptual processes are semantic and propositional in nature and represent ways of talking and reasoning about events. The intermediate level, or schematic processing, represents conditioned, associative processes established by contiguity. This level forms memory structures of the perceptual features and responses that make up specific emotion episodes and it forms prototypes when episodes are repeated. The lowest level, or sensory motor processing, consists of innate motor reactions to sensory and perceptual patterns. These "unconditioned" reactions form a base for the acquisition of conditioned associations involved in schemata and can be represented in conceptual form as an individual learned about his or her emotional reactions to a variety of specific situations. Thus, the representations or memory structures at each level are different in kind (e.g., concepts and symbols, perceptual memories, and unconditioned reactions), function according to different rules, (e.g., flexible propositions, image-like associative processes, and relatively unchanging or pre-wired automatic

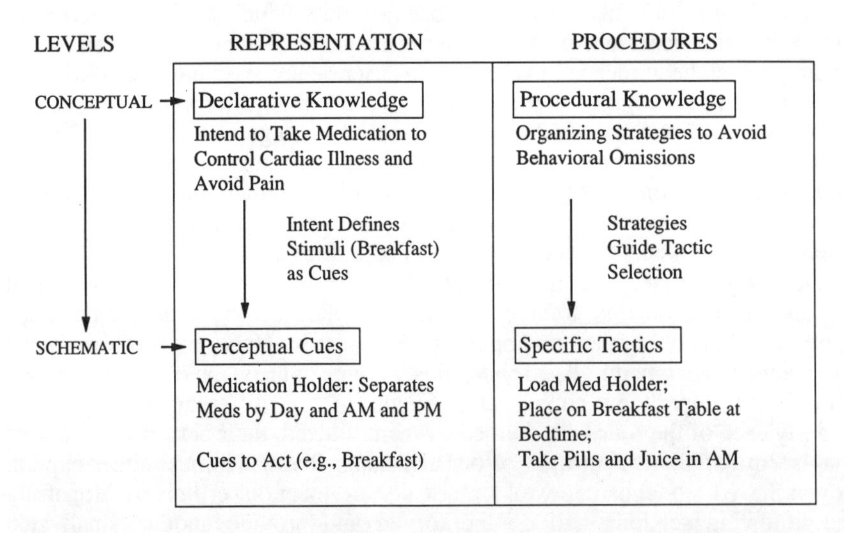

Figure 4.3. Representational and procedural knowledge at CONCEPTUAL and SCHEMATIC levels of processing. Conceptual representations, or intentions, direct attention and define stimuli to serve as cues for action. Procedural strategies define specific behavioral tactics. Although the figure emphasizes top-down processes, bottom-up processes occur simultaneously and are of equal importance for system maintenance. Top-down and bottom-up together form a coherent, homeostatic regulatory system.

reactions), and interact with one another in complex ways. The levels are more than a set of increasingly abstract clusters of reactions which subsume the groups below them.

Powers (1973) suggests that higher levels provide set points or targets for the activity of lower levels. For example, we can conceptualize the desire to complete this chapter as the highest, conceptual level of a multi-level behavioral program which establishes a set point for lower levels of regulation, these lower levels involving programs for getting up and dressing, walking to a car, driving to the office, and sitting down to the computer to proceed with writing. Each of the component acts is regulated by a sub-set of hierarchical programs, e.g., we drive on the right side of the road and look several hundred feet ahead of the vehicle to provide a stable target for steering, and these sub-programs are activated to satisfy a higher order *intention*. And the sub-systems controlling specific routines or actions, are highly flexible and able to serve many intentions.

Coping actions and the behavioral system as coping targets

If coping acts are situationally specific and have multiple functions and multiple intentions, how is it that investigators can assess individual differences in factors such as vigilance and avoidance, and relate these "trait-like" measures to coping reactions in specific situations? Do their operations predict outcomes without assessing process, or do they tap critical features of process? Can they tap process given the limitations in their current conceptual formulation and operational procedures? The answer, we suspect, is that they may succeed in predicting coping behavior and coping outcomes even though their conceptualizations are faulty, and their assessment procedures do not tap critical features of the coping process. An examination as to why this may be so is valuable as it will reveal added features of the coping process.

An important feature of coping is that it is performed in real time, and as stated earlier, it is shaped by the specific attributes of the situational representation. Thus, the procedures for coping with a health threat are guided by the *identity* of the threat, that is by the concrete perceptual cues that indicate the waxing and waning of the threat and by the meanings or labels placed on it. The presumed *cause*, expected *consequences*, perceived *time-line* (duration of onset and resolution), and the perceived *responsiveness of the threat to control* (see Bishop, 1987; Leventhal & Diefenbach, 1991) also guide coping. For example, the somatic cues of a headache will encourage self-treatment procedures such as taking Aspirin. These procedures will be adhered to as long as they result in reductions in sensory pain within an expected time period, and confirm the conceptual identity of the headache, i.e., as a cold or a stress headache and imply that the problem is controllable. Emotional reactions also may appear at different points during the episode. For example, the painful somatic sensations of a headache may elicit anger (Berkowitz, 1983), and the relief of the headache following specific procedures may elicit positive affect. Procedural failures may suggest alternative hypotheses respecting the identity and cause of the headache, e.g., that it might be a stroke due to over-exertion, and elicit fear and distress.

An important feature of this ongoing process is that both the representation of the situation and the affective reactions to it are *constructions of the individual* and are, therefore, amalgams of situational stimuli, i.e., what we presume is "out there", and the individual's behavioral operations. In short, the individual's earlier behaviors, e.g., his/her perceptions, interpretations and coping procedures, become part of the situational representation and are themselves targets for subsequent efforts at self-regulation. The same can be said of an individual's emotional reactions to a threat. Thus, anger, fear, disgust, and joy, are procedures for adapting to or coping with situations (Darwin, 1872; Scherer, 1984), and once elicited, emotions are part of the problem situation, that is they are both procedures for coping and targets for coping.

Because there are moderately stable individual differences in emotional responsivity, i.e., in both the type and intensity of affect manifested in a variety of settings (Kagan, Reznick, & Snidman, 1988; Larsen & Diener, 1987), an individual may experience similar coping problems over a fairly wide variety of situations, and therefore, adopt similar strategies for coping with these emotional reactions across several otherwise dissimilar situations. Moreover, our environments are relatively stable, both because the environment itself changes relatively slowly and because individuals create similar environments over time. Thus, both the problems we face and our emotional dispositions insure a modest degree of cross-situational stability in coping. It is possible, therefore, to assess emotional reactions and achieve a modest degree of predictions from that, however, understanding or describing the coping process. Moreover, as emotional reactions and several properties of emotional reactions, specifically their rapid, automatic occurrence in stressful settings and their frequent incongruity with socially appropriate norms, create conflict and the demand for control. Thus, the ability to regulate automatic, emotional reactions can become an important factor in adapting to stressful settings.

Finally, because emotions are interpersonal, knowledge of emotions and ways of managing emotions are shared knowledge and reflected in our language and discourse about stress and coping. Hence, individuals will be socialized to higher-order intentions and strategies for controlling emotional behaviors. These strategies will be reflected in individual differences in coping style and individuals can describe these strategies when responding to questions regarding their coping intentions (or functions) in general and in specific situations.

The above discussion may lead the alert reader to surmise that we are about to return to and accept the distinction between problem-based and emotional coping which we earlier criticized so forcefully; we will not. We have rejected the hypothesis that one can develop an orderly classification of coping responses as problem-based or emotion-based, and substituted the hypothesis that coping responses typically have multiple functions. Thus, from the perspective of coping as the adaptive activity of the organisms behavioral system, i.e., the management of the organism-environment fit, coping procedures will simultaneously satisfy at least two sets of goals: the management of the environment, as represented, and the management of the adaptive machinery. As we conceptualize the adaptive machinery as an information processing system, we will identify a variety of system management functions for coping procedures such as the following: 1. the control of information intake (e.g., attentional strategies of vigilance and avoidance); 2. the interpretation, elaboration and organization of stimuli into working representations of reality (interpreting stimuli as threatening or benign, identifying causal factors, creating simple or complex organizations, utilizing associative strategies and information prioritization to avoid information overload, etc.); 3. the identification of action possibilities depending upon the perceived controllability of the stressor and the controllability of the internal system; 4. setting outcome expectations for specific responses, the self and resources for social support; and 5. regulating emotional reactions.

Coping procedures, therefore, have dual objectives as they have functions in the problem space and in the information processing system, the latter set being broader but including the regulation of emotional states. Failure in the tasks of system management, i.e., failing to sustain attention to critical stressor cues or failure to sustain behavior or to store and properly mete out the resources needed for continued adaptation, can result in failure to adapt to the problem environment. Meta-analyses by Suls and colleagues (Suls & Fletcher, 1985; Suls & Wan, 1989) show that individuals will use different coping responses to achieve this adaptation at different points in the temporal unfolding of stressful episodes.

Situational elicitation of intentions and actions

The above analysis of the nature of intentions and their relation to actions lead to a number of hypotheses with regard to the use of specific coping procedures in stressful situations. First, we would suggest that individual differences in coping style should assess individual difference in conscious, preferred intentions, i.e., their preferred coping strategies rather than the strategies they typically employ. For example, we can conceptualize vigilance and avoidance as preferences to monitor or to avoid threatening stimuli (Krohne, Chapter 2, this volume, and Miller, Combs, & Kruus, this volume), stated tendencies to become fearful or angry as preferences to seek or not seek interpersonal assistance, a sense of control as a preference to actively manage the stressful settings (Rotter, 1954, 1966); hopefulness as a preference to expect positive outcomes (Scheier & Carver, 1987), and so forth. Individuals will differ in the degree to which they hold such intentions, and they will differ in the degree to which these intentions are manifest in the strategies and specific reactions they adopt in various domains and in specific situations within domains. And as Krohne (Chapter 2, this volume) suggests, dispositional preferences may be more or less rigid, i.e., applied more or less flexibly across situations and over time. The intentional level is the highest level of individual disposition in our revised hierarchical coping model (Figure 4.3).

Second, over a life-time, an individual will acquire response strategies that are closely connected to his or her intentional dispositions. Strategies, i.e., readinesses to enact overall sequences to satisfy specific intentions, will include combinations of attentional and interpretive orientations and readinesses to respond with specific sequences or alternations between problem and self-regulation. For example, an individual's typical action strategy may involve attempts to confront and control situational stressors as long as his/her emotional distress does not exceed a criterion or dose level; when distress exceeds that level, the action strategy may dictate that coping focus on system management to prevent system decompensation (Horowitz, 1976).

Third, intentions and strategies are instantiated in specific responses, and there will be considerable flexibility in response selection as a great variety of specific responses can satisfy both intentional and strategic demands. Various person by situation interactions provide cogent illustrations of this hypothesis. For example, an introverted person may disclose introversion by staying home and avoiding parties or may reveal it by going to public places to remain anonymous. Very different kinds of behaviors are enacted in the interest of the same higher-order construct. Indeed, though lower order behavioral programs will reflect both intentional and response strategies, they will be highly situationally specific and highly variable from setting to setting and over time in the same setting. Thus, the specific response selected for coping with a particular situation at a specific time reflects the individual's "assessment" (conscious or automatic) of the response that is compatible with his or her overall strategy and satisfies his or her operating intention. Most important, these assessments will be shaped by the representation of the situation, that is by the perceived attributes of the stressor and by the representation of the self (competencies and response availability) in that situation.

As we stated before, situational stressors can elicit emotional response strategies automatically and these strategies may or may not be congruent with higher-order intentions. When they are inconsistent with intentions, or with other acquired response strategies, the individual will act to make an adjustment to regulate the conflicting affect. This can involve any number of response adjustments such as those listed in the Ways of Coping checklist, including suppression of motor reactions, alterations in thought, and turning away. Because emotional coping procedures are partially innate, they will repeat in similar form across situations, and strategies acquired for emotional management also will generalize across settings.

It would be in error, however, to assume that emotions are always or even usually incompatible with intentions and response strategies elicited in a particular setting. An individual's initial automatic reaction of intense anger to a stressor such as an interpersonal assault may be compatible with his/her intentions (to injure or seek revenge on the attacker) and with other acquired response strategies. In this case, emotional expression and its accompanying instrumental actions form an active coping system. Emotions such as fear or disgust can also be highly adaptive even when they disrupt ongoing behavior, as the intentions and response strategies that are disrupted may no longer be appropriate to a changing situation. Indeed, emotions such as fear are typically brought into play by unexpected and threatening changes in situational appraisals, and their presence facilitates problem coping by disrupting ongoing behavior that is no longer appropriate for the changed situation (Leventhal & Scherer, 1987; Mandler, 1975; Scherer, 1984).

Monitoring as Emotion and Problem Coping

Because the present volume is focused on vigilance and avoidance, several prior studies from our laboratories provide an especially interesting view of the way in which a particular behavior, monitoring, can serve quite different functions. The data also illustrate the hierarchical nature of the adaptive system by showing that preferences to avoid can be over-ridden with experimental instructions, and when this happens, the strategies will affect lower level processes resulting in distress reduction even though monitoring was not the subject's preferred coping strategy.

In a series of laboratory (Johnson, 1973; Leventhal, Brown, Shacham, & Engquist, 1979) and field studies (Johnson & Leventhal, 1974; Leventhal, Leventhal, Shacham, & Easterling, 1989), it has been shown that providing subjects with information about the sensory features of an impending stressor, e.g., when your hand is in the ice-water, you will feel cold, pins and needles, and aching sensations, or instructing them to monitor and become familiar with the sensory features of the stressor, can lead to substantial reductions in stress responses during exposure to these noxious stimuli. These include laboratory stresses generated by ischemic pain (Johnson, 1973; Leventhal et al., 1979) and medical stressors such as gastroendoscopy (Johnson & Leventhal, 1974), cast removal (Johnson, Kirchhoff, & Endress, 1975) and childbirth (Leventhal et al., 1989). In all of these studies, monitoring led to distress reduction either by facilitating habituation of emotional reactions to the stressor or by facilitating other forms of active coping, e.g., swallowing the endoscopic tube (Johnson & Leventhal, 1974) and breathing and pushing in coordination with uterine contractions (Leventhal et al., 1989).

It would be incorrect, however, to describe monitoring as an information intake procedure that facilitates problem-based coping, as monitoring can have different effects depending upon what is monitored and how the monitored stimuli are *processed* or *interpreted*! (See also Miller et al., this volume.) Subjects instructed to monitor sensations who were told to expect pain, did not show reductions in distress (Leventhal et al, 1979), a finding also reported by Staub and Kellett (1972). When monitored sensations are interpreted as indicators of forthcoming pain, there is no habituation of emotional reactions (Leventhal et al., 1979). Monitoring is also ineffective in reducing distress if the subject monitors emotional reactions during exposure to cold pressor rather than monitoring the stressor induced sensations of coldness, pins and needles, etc. (Ahles, Blanchard, & Leventhal, 1983). Indeed, painful or catastrophic interpretations and monitoring emotion seem ideal conditions for sensitization or the intensification and prolongation of emotional reactions.

An unpublished dissertation by Linda Reinhardt (1979) provides a good illustration of the consequences of differential monitoring. In her first study, undergraduates were interviewed in detail about their thoughts and feelings following five minutes of exposure to cold-pressor. As expected, the majority of the subjects reported making active efforts to distract themselves from the noxious stimulus, but about 20% of the sample monitored rather than distracted. About half of the monitors said they attended to their emotional reactions and another half said they attended to their sensations. The subjects monitoring their emotional reactions reported high levels of distress throughout the five minute exposure while the latter group clearly adapted; their distress reports during exposure showed a precipitous decline about 2 minutes into the 5 minute trial. Post experimental interviews suggested that monitoring may be a learned reaction. Subjects who monitored their sensations said they did so because prior experience with pursuits such as ice fishing, had taught them that monitoring sensations would lead to reduced distress. On the other hand, those subjects monitoring their emotions said they did so because they couldn't help themselves; i.e., their emotional reactions were so salient that they could not be ignored.

While distraction appears to be quite automatic and unlearned, people can learn about it, i.e., they can observe their reactions and form the hypotheses that distraction will be effective for distress reduction. Thus, while avoident reactions may be automatic, intentions to avoid can be learned. Evidence for this can be seen in the study by Ahles et al. (1983). The authors gave the instructions for cold-pressor and its effects to a separate group of subjects and just before the trial was supposed to begin, asked these subjects to indicate how much distress they would experience if they monitored sensations and how much distress they would experience if they engaged in distraction (the experiment stopped after the ratings were made). The ratings showed nearly a 100 point difference with distraction (concentrate on positive imagery) rated an effective method of distress reduction (M = 40.7 on a scale where +100 means maximal effectiveness) and monitoring rated as ineffective (M = -56.4; -100 means least effective), and were inconsistent with the reports of distress obtained from subjects actually exposed to the stressor.

That distraction is widely believed to be effective for distress control was also seen in our study of monitoring and distraction during childbirth. Specifically, the expectant mothers were so reluctant to monitor their contractions that it took multiple revisions before the instructions were followed; the final form asked them to monitor the sensory properties of their contractions so they could tell the physician about them an hour later. And during the follow-up interviews, several mothers in the monitoring group expressed surprise that monitoring seemed to help. In short, distraction is generally the preferred (intentional) strategy, and monitoring is nonpreferred. Yet monitoring can be extremely helpful if conducted in an appropriate context, i.e., with benign interpretations of the somatic sensations monitored.

The data make clear, therefore, that the very same activity, i.e., monitoring, can serve different functions, affective observation versus stressor analysis, and have quite different outcomes for distress control and adjustment. Second, the data strongly support the hierarchical nature of coping, preferences for distraction (or monitoring) forming the "highest" conceptual level, actual monitoring an intermediate level of strategic performance, and the habituation processes associated with monitoring when expectations are benign, forming the lowest level at which habituation processes take place (Groves & Thompson, 1970). It also seems likely that intentions are complex; i.e., an intention to monitor is likely to include a variety of expectations respecting its function and outcome. Third, the data also show that while preferences usually direct strategies, i.e., people distract when they prefer to do so, *instructions can lead subjects to adopt nonpreferred strategies*, and when subjects adopt these strategies, they experience an unexpected alleviation of distress. Thus, the behavioral strategies bring the lowest level of habituation/coping effects into play even though the subject neither understands nor expects such outcomes. Finally, the results also suggest that preferences for specific coping responses such as distraction, are broadly shared if not culture-wide in their perceived utility. It is the most obvious aspect of coping, however, that is most readily shared; the more subtle and less observable consequences of monitoring will only be shared among people who have engaged in highly specialized activities.

Age-Related Changes at Different Levels of the Control System

Our comparisons of ways of coping with health problems over different age cohorts provides additional support for our hierarchical coping model. Age-related differences in both coping intentions (upper level of the hierarchical system) and specific coping reactions (lower levels of the system) can be observed when interviewing adults whose ages span the latter half of life. More important, perhaps, age appears to be related to the communication that takes place between levels.

Lower-level changes

The later years, post 65 and post 75, show substantial declines in a variety of organ systems reflecting reductions in ability to perform work. Thus, maximal achievable heart rate declines with age (Lakatta, 1987), pulmonary function declines with age (Kenney, 1989), and the elderly body is clearly less physically strong (Clarkson, Kroll, & Melchionda, 1981). These assessments of physiological function have their parallel in the levels of activity reported by older persons; they report engaging in less intense physical activity and having less endurance and strength. These age-related changes will impact on the individual's coping capacities as the older individual may lack the physical resources to use energy intrusion coping procedures given a smaller energy reserve. Reduced energy is likely responsible for age-related declines in the intensity of emotional reactions. Adults over 65 years of age report less intense positive, as well as less intense negative, emotional reactions (Larsen & Diener, 1987), report less fear and anxiety with regard to the possibility of contracting various illnesses (Leventhal & Prohaska, 1986), and show less anticipatory nausea, a conditioned aversive reaction partially based on fear and distress (Nerenz, Leventhal, Easterling, & Love, 1986). These changes observations are clearly consistent with the biological changes described above.

Upper-level, intentional, change

Finally, data suggest that many older adults, i.e., individuals 65 years of age or more, are aware of their declining energy level. Awareness of this change may be responsible for their endorsement of items suggesting their preference or intention to minimize emotional upset and emotional distress (Folkman, Lazarus, Pimley, & Novacek, 1987; Irion & Blanchard-Fields, 1987; McCrae, 1989; Prohaska, Keller, Leventhal, & Leventhal, 1987). The intention to conserve energy and to avoid taking unneeded risks with a more limited and fragile corpus seems to motivate a variety of specific coping strategies and tactics that can be described as risk aversion and conservation of resources. For example, persons over 65 appear to be swifter to use medical care and seem less likely to make use of distraction and avoidant strategies to reduce anxiety provoked by uncertainty regarding their physical conditions (Folkman et al., 1987; Leventhal, Leventhal, Schaefer, & Easterling, 1991). When uncertain and distressed, the elderly typically seek care as this "problem-based" coping response is an effective way of reducing both "objective" risk and the emotional distress associated with the knowledge of such risk. Avoidance and delay are more common in the middle-aged, and respondents in this cohort readily admit to delaying because of fears respecting the possible diagnosis and consequences of their medical conditions.

In summary, age-associated changes at the lower level, i.e., somatic strength and energy, affect coping procedures such as emotional displays to threat and emotion-related reactions to treatment. More importantly, however, older persons appear to be aware of these lower level changes and they adopt an intentional strategy of energy conservation and risk aversion consistent with their self-observations. Once adopted, risk averse or conserving intentions or outlooks set criteria for specific coping reactions resulting in marked changes in the perceived function or utility of these behaviors. Thus, approaching the medical care system, which is problem-solving and threat-inducing for the middle-aged individual, becomes problem-solving and threat-reducing when performed in the risk averse and conserving context of the older person. Our understanding of coping seems more complete when our models and data tap both intentions and functions as well as response strategies and specific coping actions.

Self-esteem/optimism and the selection of effective coping strategies
Our interpretation of the link between aging and conservation of energy and/or risk avoidance suggests that self-knowledge may be central to the wisdom of aging. This touches upon a broader set of issues, namely the division of the conceptual level of coping into a higher-order level of broadly based self-evaluations and self-reflective processes and a lower level of judgments of self-efficacy in specific domains. Thus, optimism (Scheier & Carver, 1985) and self-esteem (Rosenberg, 1965) may be interpreted as high-level self-appraisals based upon systematic self-reflection, and these processes may influence how an individual formulates domain-specific preferences and domain- and problem-specific coping strategies. For example, subjects high in self-esteem and high in optimism may prove more persistent and inventive in assessing their effectiveness in specific domains, and less likely to alter their generally positive outlook on themselves and the world because of failure to successfully cope with a particular problem in a specific domain. In one of our early studies, we found that using false feedback to bolster subjects' self-esteem enhanced their ability to manage smoking reductions after exposure to a threatening anti-smoking message (Rosen, Terry, & Leventhal, 1982). It had been shown that threat messages immobilized problem-based coping in low esteem subjects, even though these messages convinced them of their personal vulnerability to danger (Leventhal, 1970); negative emotions signal the low-esteem subject that he or she is unable to cope. Bolstering esteem appears to overcome this self-doubt and permit the individual to develop a self-appraisal and coping strategy effective for solving a particular problem (quitting smoking) in a particular domain (disease prevention and health enhancement).

Many attributional styles are likely conceptually similar and at a similar level of abstraction in relation to our concept of risk aversion, and these concepts are likely at the service of higher level of notions such as self-esteem and/or optimism. But as the aging data suggests, the direction of influence among these levels is not merely top-down, esteem to self-efficacy, it is also bottom-up, changes in biological competence to risk aversion. Much needs to be done to define and explore the relationships among these levels of cognitive process.

Conclusion

We began by proposing that research on coping requires a theoretical framework that allows us to treat coping responses or procedures as having multiple functions. The functions of specific procedures will vary with the type of problem and the specific point in the history of any single problem episode. Both prior and current approaches to coping fail to satisfy this demand as they adopt a highly empirical approach to coping assessment. This involves the factor analysis of elaborate coping response checklists in which coping responses are viewed as members of specific response classes that are labeled on the basis of their presumed functions. This approach conceives of coping procedures as falling into fixed function categories rather than viewing them as flexible options with changing and multiple functions varying with the ongoing transaction between individual and environment. The conceptual analyses of the methodology of coping research and data generated by Arthur Stone and his colleagues support the above arguments.

Following our critique, we attempted to build upon the theoretical ideas of Heinz Krohne by suggesting that the levels in a hierarchical model of coping should be different in kind, thus the uppermost levels will consist of the individual's generalized coping intentions, e.g., to reduce distress, to be vigilant to avoid risk, to solve problems at low cost and low effort, etc., and overarching notions such as self-esteem and optimism. Overlearned coping strategies, or learned sequences for controlling problems and regulating the problem-solving system, would be at a lower, intermediate, level while at a still lower level were specific coping responses would be at a still lower one. We argued that the levels involve different memory codes and different modes of information processing, and that they are related to one another functionally; upper levels are seen as setting targets or goals for lower levels of regulation, thus, levels do not relate to one another as increasingly abstract and inclusive ways of classifying behaviors. Data on changes in coping in the latter part of the life-span appear to be consistent with this hierarchical analysis. We also suggested that prior studies which did not use such a complex model achieved some degree of empirical success because emotional reactions, which are automatic coping procedures, are the initial reactions to many, if not most, stressful problems. Therefore, emotions become part of the problem for virtually all stressful situations, and assessments of coping have been informative and partially successful in making cross-situational and between-person predictions because emotional reactions are a common feature of most stress reactions and form a basis for the generalization of coping procedures.

Our analysis, if correct, suggests that studies which assess the frequency or intensity of performance [and there it is uncertain whether one or the other of these is assessed by current instruments (Stone et al., in press)] conceptualizing coping procedures as styles and traits, are conceptually limited and cannot give a true picture of the coping process. While we believe it essential to conceptualize coping as a multi-level process, we agree with Krohne that doing so complicates the assessment process (see Krohne, Chapter 2, this volume). Indeed, we wish to make clear that we view our suggestions as compatible with Krohne's theoretical approach. As Krohne (1990) points out, there are both stable and variable or situationally specific processes, the latter better predictors of action as they are variables in the current problem space. It is unclear, however, which of the higher-order dispositions are most stable or trait-like, i.e., the preferences or the coping strategies elicited by automatic emotional reactions.

The complication we have introduced suggests, therefore, that multivariate studies relying on self-reports of coping procedures in stress situations may have intrinsic limitations for testing specific hypotheses about the coping process whether the studies are cross-sectional or longitudinal. To achieve rigor and test hypotheses about coping in field studies, that predict the selection of coping reactions in longitudinal designs, one may have to focus on specific, well-understood stressor domains, as the subject's construction or representation of the stressor plays a key role in shaping the selection, performance, and evaluation of coping procedures. Thus, the functions or intent of a coping procedure are only visible in light of the representation of the problem it is intended to solve.

Our analysis also suggests that testing hypotheses about the causes and consequences of coping will proceed more effectively in well-controlled settings. Under these conditions we can examine interactions between independent variables such as coping intentions and coping strategies, etc., to the selection of specific coping acts and to the appearance of particular coping outcomes. We think it time, therefore, to re-examine some of our basic assumptions about coping behavior and to move forward with new, less psychometrically bounded, methodologies. Excellence in psychometrics has its place, particularly for the development of reliable and valid outcome measures for studies of parameters in large populations. Because scales are best designed to measure outcomes rather than ongoing process, psychometric rigor may prove to be a strait-jacket which can confine research and ignore the study of process. Given the attractiveness of scales and their ease of use, we are sure this constraint will be difficult to escape.

References

Ahles, T. A., Blanchard, E. B., & Leventhal, H. (1983). Cognitive control of pain: Attention to the sensory aspects of the cold pressor stimulus. *Cognitive Therapy and Research, 7*, 159-177.

Aldwin, C. M., Folkman, S., Schaefer, C., Coyne, J. C., & Lazarus, R. S. (1980, September). *Ways of Coping: A process measure*. Paper presented at the 88th annual convention of the American Psychological Association, Montreal, Canada.

Alonzo, A. A. (1980). Acute illness behavior: A conceptual exploration and specification. *Social Science and Medicine, 14*, 515-526.

Berkowitz, L. (1983). Aversively stimulated aggression: Some parallels and differences in research with animals and humans. *American Psychologist, 38*, 1135-1144.

Billings, A. G., & Moos, R. H. (1981). The role of coping responses and social resources in attenuating the stress of life events. *Journal of Behavioral Medicine, 4*, 139-157.

Bishop, G. D. (1987). Lay conceptions of physical symptoms. *Journal of Applied Social Psychology, 17*, 127-146.

Blumhagen, D. (1980). Hyper-tension: A folk illness with a medical name. *Culture, Medicine, and Psychiatry, 4*, 344-349.

Bolger, N. (1990). Coping as a personality process: A prospective study. *Journal of Personality and Social Psycholoyg, 59*, 525-537.

Cacioppo, J. T., Andersen, B. L., Turnquist, D. C., & Petty, R. E. (1986). Psychophysiological comparison processes: Interpreting cancer symptoms. In B. L. Andersen (Ed.), *Women with cancer* (pp. 141-171). New York: Springer-Verlag.

Cameron, L., Leventhal, E. A., Leventhal, H., & Schaefer, P. (1991). *Symptom representations and affect as determinants of care seeking*. Manuscript submitted for publication.

Carver, C. S., & Scheier, M. F. (1981). *Attention and self-regulation: A control-theory approach to human behavior*. New York: Springer-Verlag.

Carver, C. S., Scheier, M. F., & Weintraub, J. K. (1989). Assessing coping strategies: A theoretically based approach. *Journal of Personality and Social Psychology, 56*, 267-283.

Cattell, R. B. (1966). The scree test for the number of factors. *Multivariate Behavioral Research, 1*, 245-276.

Clarkson, P. M., Kroll, W., & Melchionda, A. M. (1981). Age, isometric strength, rate of tension development and fiber type composition. *Journal of Gerontology, 36*, 648-653.

Darwin, C. (1872). *The expression of emotion in man and animals*. London: Murray.

Endler, N. S., & Parker, J. D. A. (1990). Multidimensional assessment of coping: A critical evaluation. *Journal of Personality and Social Psychology, 58*, 844-854.

Epstein, S. (1973). Expectancy and magnitude of reaction to a noxious UCS. *Psychophysiology, 10*, 100-107.

Epstein, S. (1980). The stability of behavior. II. Implications for psychological research. *American Psychologist, 35*, 790-806.

Epstein, S., & Meier, P. (1989). Constructive thinking: A broad coping variable with specific components. *Journal of Personality and Social Psychology, 57*, 332-350.

Eysenck, H. J. (1953). *The structure of human personality*. London: Methuen.

Folkman, S., & Lazarus, R. S. (1980). An analysis of coping in a middle-aged community sample. *Journal of Health and Social Behavior, 21*, 219-239.

Folkman, S., & Lazarus, R. S. (1985). If it changes it must be a process: Study of emotion and coping during three stages of a college examination. *Journal of Personality and Social Psychology, 48*, 150-170.

Folkman, S., & Lazarus, R. S. (1986). Coping as a mediator of emotion. *Journal of Personality and Social Psychology, 54*, 466-475.

Folkman, S., Lazarus, R. S., Dunkel-Schetter, C., DeLongis, A., & Gruen, R. J. (1986). Dynamics of a stressful encounter: Cognitive appraisal, coping, and encounter outcomes. *Journal of Personality and Social Psychology, 50*, 992-1003.

Folkman, S., Lazarus, R. S., Gruen, R. J., & DeLongis, A. (1986). Appraisal, coping, health status, and psychological symptoms. *Journal of Personality and Social Psychology, 50*, 571-579.

Folkman, S., Lazarus, R. S., Pimley, S., & Novacek, J. (1987). Age differences in stress and coping processes. *Psychology and Aging, 2*, 171-184.

Groves, P. M., & Thompson, R. F. (1970). Habituation: A dual-process theory. *Psychological Review, 77*, 419-450.

Horowitz, M. (1976). *Stress response syndromes*. New York: Aronson.

Irion, J. C., & Blanchard-Fields, F. (1987). A cross-sectional comparison of adaptive coping in adulthood. *Journal of Gerontology, 42*, 502-504.

Janis, I. L. (1958). *Psychological stress*. New York: Wiley.

Johnson, J. E. (1973). Effects of accurate expectations about sensations on the sensory and distress components of pain. *Journal of Personality and Social Psychology, 27*, 261-275.

Johnson, J. E., Kirchhoff, K. T., & Endress, M. P. (1975). Altering children's distress behavior during orthopedic cast removal. *Nursing Research, 24*, 404-410.

Johnson, J. E., & Leventhal, H. (1974). Effects of accurate expectations and behavioral instructions on reactions during a noxious medical examination. *Journal of Personality and Social Psychology, 29*, 710-718.

Jones, E. E., & Nisbett, R. E. (1971). The actor and the observer: divergent perceptions of the causes of behavior. In E. E. Jones, D. E. Kanouse, H. H. Kelley, R. E. Nisbett, S. Valins, & B. Weiner (Eds.), *Attribution: Perceiving the causes of behavior* (pp. 79-94). Morristown, NJ: General Learning Press.

Kagan, J., Reznick, J. S., & Snidman, N. (1988). Biological bases of childhood shyness. *Science, 240*, 167-171.

Kenney, A. R. (1989). *Physiology of aging: a synopsis* (2nd ed.). Chicago: Year Book Medical Publishers.

Krohne, H. W. (1989). The concept of coping modes: relating cognitive person variables to actual coping behavior. *Advances in Behaviour Research and Therapy, 11*, 235-248.

Krohne, H. W. (1990). Personality as a mediator between objective events and their subjective representation. *Psychological Inquiry, 1*, 26-29.

Lakatta, E. G. (1987). Cardiovascular function and age. *Geriatrics, 42*, 84-94.

Larsen, R. J., & Diener, E. (1987). Affect intensity as an individual difference characteristic: A review. *Journal of Research in Personality, 21*, 1-39.

Lazarus, R. S. (1966). *Psychological stress and the coping process*. New York: McGraw-Hill.

Lazarus, R. S., & Folkman, S. (1984). *Stress, appraisal and coping*. New York: Springer.

Lazarus, R. S., & Launier, R. (1978). Stress-related transactions between person and environment. In L. A. Pervin & M. Lewis (Eds.), *Perspectives in interactional psychology* (pp. 287-327). New York: Plenum.

Leventhal, E. A., Leventhal, H., Schaefer, P., & Easterling, D. (1991). *Risk aversion: A possible explanation of age differences in delay in response to symptoms*. Manuscript submitted for publication.

Leventhal, E. A., Leventhal, H., Shacham, S., & Easterling, D. V. (1989). Active coping reduces reports of pain from childbirth. *Journal of Consulting and Clinical Psychology, 57*, 365-371.

Leventhal, E. A., & Prohaska, T. R. (1986). Age, symptom interpretation, and health behavior. *Journal of the American Geriatrics Society, 34*, 185-191.

Leventhal, H. (1970). Findings and theory in the study of fear communications. In L. Berkowitz (Ed.), *Advances in experimental social psychology* (Vol. 5, pp. 119-186). New York: Academic Press.

Leventhal, H. (1984). A perceptual motor theory of emotion. In K. R. Scherer & P. Ekman (Eds.), *Approaches to emotion* (pp. 271-291). Hillsdale, NJ: Erlbaum.

Leventhal, H., Brown, D., Shacham, S., & Engquist, G. (1979). Effects of preparatory information about sensations, threat of pain, and attention on cold pressor distress. *Journal of Personality and Social Psychology, 37*, 688-714.

Leventhal, H., & Diefenbach, M. (1991). The active side of illness cognition. In J. A. Skelton & R. T. Croyle (Eds.), *Mental representation in health and illness* (pp. 247-272). New York: Springer-Verlag.

Leventhal, H., Meyer, D., & Nerenz, D. R. (1980). The common-sense representation of illness danger. In S. Rachman (Ed.), *Contributions to medical psychology* (Vol. 2, pp. 7-30). Oxford: Pergamon.

Leventhal, H., & Nerenz, D. R. (1983). A model for stress research with some implications for the control of stress disorders. In D. Meichenbaum & M. Jaremko (Eds.), *Stress reduction and prevention* (pp. 5-38). New York: Plenum.

Leventhal, H., & Scherer, K. R. (1987). The relationship of emotion to cognition: A functional approach to a semantic controversy. *Cognition and Emotion, 1*, 3-28.

Leventhal, H., Singer, R., & Jones, S. (1965). Effects of fear and specificity of recommendation upon attitudes and behavior. *Journal of Personality and Social Psychology, 2*, 20-29.

Mandler, G. (1975). *Mind and emotion*. New York: Wiley.

McCrae, R. R. (1989). Age differences and changes in the use of coping mechanisms. *Journal of Gerontology, 44*, 161-169.

Meyer, D., Leventhal, H., & Gutmann, M. (1985). Common-sense models of illness: The example of hypertension. *Health Psychology, 4*, 115-135.

Mischel, W. (1968). *Personality and assessment*. New York: Wiley.

Nerenz, D. R., Leventhal, H., Easterling, D. V., & Love, R. R. (1986). Anxiety and drug taste as predictors of anticipatory nausea in cancer chemotherapy. *Journal of Clinical Oncology, 4*, 224-233.

Pearlin, L. I. (1985). Social structure and processes of social support. In S. Cohen & S. L. Syme (Eds.), *Social support and health* (pp. 43-60). Orlando, FL: Academic Press.

Pearlin, L. I., & Schooler, C. (1978). The structure of coping. *Journal of Health and Social Behavior, 19*, 2-21.

Powers, W. T. (1973). *Behavior: The control of perception*. Chicago: Aldine.

Prohaska, T. R., Keller, M. L., Leventhal, E. A., & Leventhal, H. (1987). Impact of symptoms and aging attribution on emotions and coping. *Health Psychology, 6*, 495-514.

Radloff, L. S. (1977). The CES-D Scale: A self-report depression scale for research in the general population. *Applied Psychological Measurement, 1*, 385-401.

Reinhardt, L. (1979). *Attention and interpretation in control of cold pressor pain distress*. Unpublished doctoral dissertation, University of Wisconsin, Madison.

Rohde, P., Lewinsohn, P. M., Tilson, M., & Seeley, J. R. (1990). Dimensionality of coping and its relation to depression. *Journal of Personality and Social Psychology, 58*, 499-511.

Rosen, T. J., Terry, N. S., & Leventhal, H. (1982). The role of esteem and coping in response to a threat communication. *Journal of Research in Personality, 16*, 90-107.

Rosenberg, M. (1965). *Society and the adolescent self-image*. Princeton, NJ: Princeton University Press.

Rotter, J. B. (1954). *Social learning and clinical psychology*. Englewood Cliffs, NJ: Prentice-Hall.

Rotter, J. B. (1966). Generalized expectancies for internal versus external control of reinforcement. *Psychological Monograph: General and Applied, 80* (1, Whole No. 609).

Safer, M. A., Tharps, Q. J., Jackson, T. C., & Leventhal, H. (1979). Determinants of three stages of delay in seeking care at a medical clinic. *Medical Care, 17*, 11-29.

Scheier, M. F., & Carver, C. S. (1985). Optimism, coping, and health: Assessment and implications of generalized outcome expectancies. *Health Psychology, 4*, 219-247.

Scheier, M. F., & Carver, C. S. (1987). Dispositional optimism and physical well-being: The influence of generalized outcome expectancies on health. *Journal of Personality, 55*, 169-210.

Scherer, K. R. (1984). On the nature and function of emotion: a component process approach. In K. R. Scherer & P. Ekman (Eds.), *Approaches to emotion* (pp. 293-318). Hillsdale, NJ: Erlbaum.

Staub, E., & Kellett, O. (1972). Increasing pain tolerance by information about aversive stimuli. *Journal of Personality and Social Psychology, 21*, 198-203.

Stone, A. A., Greenberg, M. M., Kennedy-Moore, E., & Newman, M. G. (in press). Self-report, situation-specific coping questions: What are they measuring? *Journal of Personality and Social Psychology*.

Stone, A. A., Helder, L., & Schneider, M. S., (1988). Coping with stressful life events. In L. H. Cohen (Ed.), *Research on stressful life events: Theoretical and methodological issues* (pp. 182-210). Beverly Hills, CA: Sage.

Stone, A. A., & Neale, J. M. (1984). New measure of daily coping: Development and preliminary results. *Journal of Personality and Social Psychology, 46*, 892-906.

Suchman, E. A. (1965). Social patterns of illness and medical care. *Journal of Health and Human Behavior, 6*, 2-16.

Suls, J. (1982). Social support, interpersonal relations, and health: Benefits and liabilities. In G. S. Sanders & J. Suls (Eds.), *Social psychology of health and illness* (pp. 255-277). Hillsdale NJ: Erlbaum.

Suls, J., & Fletcher, B. (1985). The relative efficacy of avoidant and nonavoidant coping strategies: A meta-analysis. *Health Psychology, 4*, 249-288.

Suls, J., & Rittenhouse, J. D. (1990). Models of linkages between personality and disease. In H. S. Friedman (Ed.), *Personality and disease* (pp. 38-64). New York: Wiley.

Suls, J., & Wan, C. K. (1989). Effects of sensory and procedural information on coping with stressful medical procedures and pain: A meta-analysis. *Journal of Consulting and Clinical Psychology, 57*, 372-379.

Vitaliano, P., Russo, J., Carr, J., Maiuro, R. D., & Becker, J. (1985). The Ways of Coping Checklist: Revision and psychometric properties. *Multivariate Behavioral Research, 20*, 3-26.

Watson, D., & Pennebaker, J. W. (1989). Health complaints, stress and distress: Exploring the central role of negative affectivity. *Psychological Review, 96*, 234-254.

Webster's new collegiate dictionary (9th ed.). (1986). Springfield, MA: Merriam-Webster.

Williams, K., Suls, J., Alliger, G., Learner, S., & Wan, C. K. (in press). Simultaneous role activity, mood disposition and daily mood states in working mothers: An experience sampling study. *Journal of Applied Psychology*.

Chapter 5

Worry: Thought Suppression of Emotional Processing

Thomas D. Borkovec and James D. Lyonfields

Introduction

Anxious individuals are highly vigilant, showing a pre-attentive bias toward threatening information and perceiving threat in many circumstances (see Mathews, this volume). How such biased, automatic processing of information develops is no doubt a function of a variety of genetic predispositions and environmental learning factors. However, few empirical results are available to offer convincing arguments for what these factors may be. It is possible, however, to investigate what it is that anxious people do in response to detected threat and how these strategic responses may contribute to the maintenance and/or strengthening of internal processes that underlie the experience of anxiety and maladaptive perceptions of threat. Our research program for the past several years has been devoted to attempting to understand certain types of strategic response to threat among both phobic subjects and generally anxious psychotherapy clients. It is our contention that the most important strategic responses that perpetuate vigilance to threat among anxious individuals are avoidant in nature and take place predominantly in their cognitive processes. Although behavioral avoidance has long been recognized as a maintainer of anxiety, cognitive avoidance is likely far more frequent across all anxiety disorders and is particularly salient in generalized anxiety disorder. Our view sees cognitive avoidance as no different in function and effect from behavioral avoidance. Both occur in response to detection of threat, both involve an appraisal of a lack of resources to adequately cope with the threat, and both function to remove the individual from the presence of threatening stimuli and the aversive emotional state elicited by those stimuli. More so than behavioral avoidance, however, cognitive avoidance is particularly associated with the detection of *internal* threat cues (thoughts, images, somatic reactions).

Our intention in this chapter is to review results that have to do with a certain type of strategic cognitive avoidance and to develop a theoretical model about this process in which to understand some of the maintaining factors responsible for the perseveration of severe anxiety disorders. That type of cognitive avoidance is referred to as worry.

Research reported in this chapter was supported in part by Grant MH-39172 to the first author from the National Institute of Mental Health.

Worry principally involves a stream of thoughts and images about possible future aversive events. The process is a commonly experienced psychological phenomenon in the general population. Indeed, it was one of only two indicators among several to show a worsening over a twenty-year longitudinal study of the mental health status of a large U.S. sample (Veroff, Douvan, & Kulka, 1981). Moreover, worry is pervasive throughout all of the anxiety disorders; 40-60% of clients with obsessive compulsive, simple phobia, agoraphobia, social phobia, and panic disorder report excessive worry about minor things (Barlow, 1988). And one additional DSM-III-R category, generalized anxiety disorder (GAD), is centrally defined by the chronic presence of worry about multiple life circumstances (American Psychiatric Association, 1987). Such ubiquity would suggest that, whatever is meant commonly or clinically by the construct of worry, experimental elucidation of its nature and functions would contribute considerably to our understanding of human behavior in general and of anxiety disorders in particular.

Despite its apparent pervasiveness, research on the construct has been minimal until recently. This may partly be due to the private nature of the phenomenon and the resulting difficulties in pursuing it experimentally. What research has been conducted, however, had led to some interesting possibilities about its nature and function. Our central thesis is that worry represents a strategic conceptual avoidance response which suppresses the processing of emotional information and thereby guarantees the maintenance of anxiety disorder.

The Nature of Worry

Worry is predominantly a conceptual, verbal-linguistic (as opposed to imaginal) process. We recently obtained data relevant to this conclusion from questionnaire results provided by 900 women, ranging in age from 18 to 45. The questionnaire included our Penn State Worry Questionnaire (Meyer, Miller, Metzger, & Borkovec, 1990) as well as the question, "When you do worry, does it involve mostly thoughts, mostly images, or both?" The predominance of thought or a mixture of thought and imagery over imagery alone was clear from their responses (51%, 46%, and 3%, respectively). A sample of 300 college students were asked the question in a different way: "When you worry, what percentage of the time are you *thinking* and what percentage of the time are you having *images*?" Again, clear dominance of thought was revealed: 70% vs 30%.

More convincingly, we now have data from a laboratory study which involved both dispositional group comparison and an experimental task manipulation with which to better document the predominance of thoughts in worry (Borkovec & Inz, 1990). GAD clients and nonanxious control subjects matched on gender, age, and education level underwent a 10-minute period of self-relaxation followed by a 10-minute period of worrying about a topic of current concern. During these periods, they were periodically contacted and asked to report whether their mental experience at the moment of contact was a thought, an image, both, or "unsure." The last category was rare, and the "both" category was evenly distributed over groups and periods. During relaxation, nonanxious subjects reported significantly more imagery than thought, whereas clients reported equivalent amounts of each. During worry, both groups displayed dominance of thought over imagery, with clients reporting the least amount of imagery. Ratings by the subjects of these mentation samples also showed significantly greater anxious valence during worry than during relaxation for the total group and among clients compared to nonanxious subjects during both relaxation and worry periods. The latter valence results replicated a study with chronic worriers (Pruzinsky & Borkovec, 1990): Thought samples of worriers obtained verbatim during a relaxation period were judged by objective raters to be significantly more negative and ambivalent in affective tone than those of nonworriers.

Thus, the inner life of clinical and nonclinical worriers is heavily loaded with negatively valenced, thought-predominating cognitive activity, even when relaxing. That inner life is modifiable, however: The GAD clients in the above study showed a dramatic normalization of thought/image frequencies and valence ratings during both relaxation and worry periods in a posttest re-assessment after twelve sessions of successful therapy intervention (Borkovec & Inz, 1990).

Establishing that worry is principally thought, as opposed to imagery, is of great importance, fundamental to an ultimate understanding of its function. As argued by Lang (1985) and Foa and Kozak (1986), imagery (especially imagery rich in response propositions) involves the accessing of memory structures that tie into affective/physiological response via efferent command. Thus, phobic exposures (*in vivo* or imaginal) that access much of the memory structure elicit strong autonomic response, yield habituation to repeated exposures, successfully predict therapeutic outcomes, and thus give evidence of more complete emotional processing than do exposures that fail to access the fear structure. Lang and his group have several demonstrations that verbal articulation of fear material produces little autonomic response, whereas imagination of the same material yields strong response (e.g., Vrana, Cuthbert, & Lang, 1986). Thus, the abstract conceptual system does not tie into the affective/physiological system as strongly as the imaginal system. There is good reason for this. Evolution has provided layers of information processing systems to facilitate the organism's adaptation to its environment; each layer provides increasing amounts of more finely discriminated information upon which to base responses. As one moves from simple, reflexive and conditioned stimulus-response connections to more richly developed emotional systems and to highly elaborated historical information stored in memory, there is an increased potential for delay in response to an immediate stimulus. The longer the delay, the more information can be retrieved, manipulated, and employed in the service of adaptive response selection. The abstract thought system, being a newcomer in evolutionary development, represents the system most remote from environmental demand. Indeed, a central function of the cortex is to inhibit action, thus providing for considerable delay between stimulus and response. Such inhibition allows for the varieties of higher cortical processes that give the human organism remarkable capabilities to experiment, create, and logically analyze. The products of these processes do not have to be immediately expressed behaviorally, until a chosen response is released. Thus, thought provides the potentiality of increased freedom from immediate external determinism. To do so, however, it cannot have strong and immediate connections to efferent command involved in the physiological, affective, and behavioral systems. If every thought was expressed, environmental consequences would quickly reduce the freedom of abstract conceptual processes and eliminate its adaptive advantages to experiment mentally without immediate external consequence.

While somewhat more isolated from the effects of environmental consequence, the conceptual activity of worry also appears to contain within its process mechanisms for its perseveration. Specifically, worry is self-perpetuating in the sense that certain durations of worrisome thinking result in a continuation of negative thought intrusions into subsequent periods. In one of our early studies (Borkovec, Robinson, Pruzinsky, & DePree, 1983), chronic worriers and nonworriers worried about a topic of current concern for 0, 15, or 30 minutes. On either side of this manipulation, subjects were instructed to spend 5 minutes focussing all of their attention only on their breathing. We chose this simple attentional task that requires little involvement of working memory in order to detect task-irrelevant thought intrusions under conditions where thought of any type was not required. Periodic contacts were made during these periods, and the subjects were asked to indicate whether at the moment of contact they were focussed on their breathing as instructed, or whether they were distracted by negative thought intrusion, positive thought intrusion, or some other distraction. While overall worriers reported significantly more negative thought intrusions than did nonworriers, the 15-minute worry period resulted for both worriers and nonworriers in an increase in number of negative intrusions during the posttest breathing-focus task, significantly greater than the decreases experienced by the other two conditions. Apparently, sufficiently long exposure to worry can result in some habituation, but brief worrying (characteristic of commonly experienced daily worry) can be self-perpetuating by as yet poorly understood mechanisms and disruptive of attention during subsequent tasks.

This self-perpetuation also appears to be predominantly due to the cognitive activity of worry rather than to the somatic accompaniments of anxious states (York, Borkovec, Vasey, & Stern, 1987). Three groups of subjects experienced 20 minutes of mood induction via Velten (1968) methods. One group was induced to experience worry, another to experience somatic anxiety, and a third to experience a neutral state. The worry condition resulted in significantly greater negative thought intrusions during the posttest breathing task than the neutral condition, whereas the somatic anxiety condition did not.

This perpetuation of negative thoughts due to worry has also been shown to influence information processing wherein working memory is involved. In their first of two experiments, Metzger, Miller, Cohen, Sofka, and Borkovec (1990) found that chronic worriers and nonworriers were not significantly different in reaction times to identifying clear examples of a target geometric shape or to clear nonexamples of the shape. As the ambiguity of the target shape increased, however, worriers took increasingly longer times to decide whether the stimulus was or was not a member of the target shape class, whereas nonworriers showed no change in decision times. In the second experiment, subjects spent 15 minutes either relaxing or worrying about a topic of current concern. Both nonworriers and worriers displayed increasing decision times to ambiguous target stimuli after worrying, whereas both groups showed consistently fast responding to all test stimuli if they had first been relaxed.

So, trait, as well as state, worry is associated with a predominance of thought activity that is negatively valenced in affective tone and that perpetuates itself into subsequent periods such that attentional and decision-making tasks are disrupted.

Functions of Worry

In a very general sense, worry seems to be a cognitive attempt to avoid future, negative outcomes. Clinical interviewing with worriers and GAD clients routinely reveals subject reports suggesting that this is the case, and further indicates that negative environmental as well as internal outcomes may be the targets of this avoidance. "As long as I expect the worst, I'll be prepared for the worst" is a common example. By adopting such a pessimistic approach, the individual is hoping to avoid untoward emotional and/or behavioral reactions to unwanted events. Equally common are reports that indicate that the worrying is an attempt to reduce the likelihood of possible negative external events. These come in three interesting and possibly interrelated forms. One is motivational, wherein worrying is used to activate adaptive but effortful behavior. This is commonly seen in achievement oriented workers and college students, who claim that worrying motivates them to work harder in order to obtain their goals. They fear that if they stop worrying, they will stop achieving. A second form is oriented toward problem solving. Worry is viewed as an attempt to anticipate the many negative outcomes that might happen regarding a particular area of concern, presumably so that solutions to each possibility might be found and thereby prevent those outcomes. In fact, the worry process appears to be mainly problem-generating with little actual engagement of effective problem solving or action decisions. The third form is superstitious in nature and is remarkedly commonly reported: "As long as I worry about it, it is less likely to happen." Functionally speaking, all of the above instances of avoidance through worry are indeed superstitiously strengthened quite often. Only rarely do the multiple "what-if" catastrophes or poor emotional coping commonly feared actually occur; thus, the anticipating worry is indeed frequently reinforced by the nonoccurrence of punishment and thus by the occurrence of relief (Denny, 1976).

So, at the molar level, worrying may be maintained by negative reinforcement. But it appears that worry is also an avoidance response at a more microscopic level and contains within itself, in any given episode, the dynamics for its own immediate reinforcement. The data reported above, wherein thought was found to increase and imagery to decrease as one moves from relaxed nonanxious subjects to worrying GAD clients (Borkovec & Inz, 1990), suggest that the function of excessive thought in worry is specifically to suppress the retrieval of further information, especially affective information, in the associative network related to the threat. Thus, worrisome thought is an avoidance of fearful imagery and the somatic anxiety consequential to the image's efferent commands.

Correlational support for this hypothesis was found in the questionnaire responses of the previously mentioned sample of 300 college students. In addition to indicating the percentage of thought and percentage of imagery when they worried, they were also shown a list of predominantly somatic symptoms from the DSM-III-R criteria for GAD and were to mark any of those which they often noticed when they felt anxious. The correlation between percentage of thoughts and number of symptoms was significant and negative. The more that worrying is composed of thinking, the fewer somatic symptoms are experienced when anxious. Shifting to thought suppresses imagery and somatic activation.

Experimental evidence for this function comes from a recent phobic imagery study (Borkovec & Hu, 1990). A group of speech phobic subjects were given preliminary training in imagining a fear-producing public speaking scene which included both stimulus and response propositions. They were then presented ten visualizations of this scene, each scene presented for ten seconds with 30 seconds between each scene. Three groups differed in what they were instructed to think about during the 30-seconds before each presentation: One group thought about relaxing words and situations, a second about neutral words and situations, and the third group about worrisome words and situations related to public speaking. The relaxation and neutral conditions showed cardiovascular reactions to the images similar to those found in prior phobic imagery research using deep muscular relaxation and neutral conditions (e.g., Borkovec & Sides, 1979): greater heart rate in response to the first scene presentation and signs of decline with repetition in the relaxed state. The worry condition displayed virtually no cardiovascular response at all throughout the ten scene presentations. These results occurred despite no differences among conditions at baseline or at samples obtained just before each image presentation. The effect may be due to the degree of discrepancy between imagery and its preceding thought periods. Gray's (1982) theory of anxiety suggests that the behavioral inhibition system is activated either when there is a mismatch between information expected and information received or when expected information is aversive. In worrisome states, less mismatch occurs and less information is processed. Such a mechanism may explain why worrisome thinking suppresses cardiovascular response to subsequently presented emotional material. From Lang's (1985) and Foa and Kozak's (1986) theoretical perspective, this outcome indicates that emotional processing of information is not taking place when a worrisome state is present, and thus change in the associated fear structure is precluded.

In a recently completed study, the relaxation and general worry conditions were repeated, while three additional conditions were employed. The latter groups involved an attempt to manipulate the predominance of type of experience during worry. All three groups were given pretraining, beginning with asking them to worry briefly and to notice the thoughts, images, and affect that occurred when they worried. One group (worry-thought) was then trained to worry by concentrating on generating only the thoughts of worry, one group (worry-image) on generating only the images involved in their worry, and the third group (worry-affect) on generating only the affective experience of worry. All five groups were then exposed to the ten phobic scene presentations while they engaged in their respective types of worrying or relaxation prior to each presentation. The relaxation condition again produced the greatest cardiovascular reaction to the first scene presentation and decline with repetition, whereas all worry groups showed suppression of heart rate response throughout the ten trials. The worry-thought subjects showed the greatest suppression and were significantly lower than the relaxation group on the first trial. The other three groups fell nonsignificantly between these two groups.

The untrained general worry condition, while resulting in little response to first scene presentation, was not significantly lower than the relaxation condition in heart rate response to the first scene, thus failing to replicate the original study. This appears to be partly due to the lower heart rate response of the second study's relaxation group relative to the first study (4.2 vs. 7.2 bpm). But it was also apparently due to a partial lack of effectiveness of the pretraining manipulation. As a manipulation check after each scene presentation, subjects reported the percentage of thought, image, and affect experiences noticed during the preceding period prior to the scene presentation. The worry-thought group reported significantly greater thought than the other four groups throughout the trials. The percentage of imagery reported, however, was equally high among both the worry-imagery and untrained general worry groups and significantly higher than the worry-thought and worry-affect groups. Thus, worrying without instruction or worrying with training in generating predominantly images did not differentially influence the amount of imagery experienced during worry. The greatest suppression of imagery occurred in the worry-thought condition, and only this condition suppressed heart rate response to phobic scene presentation relative to the relaxation condition.

Although not significantly different from either worry-thought or the other groups, the second unexpected outcome was the effectiveness of the worry-affect condition in suppressing emotional processing. This group alone reported a high percentage of affective experience during worry periods on the manipulation check, significantly higher than the other four conditions. Manipulation check also indicated that this condition led to a suppression of imagery during worry nearly as great as that occurring for the worry-thought group.

Thus, despite some ambiguities in the above results, the greatest suppression of emotional processing occurred among those subjects trained to emphasize thought during their worrying and among those groups wherein imagery during worry was most successfully reduced.The results from the worry-affect condition, however, raise an additional possibility, namely that under some circumstances attention to affect may also suppress emotional processing by the same or a different mechanism.

Physiological Activity in GAD

Our earlier studies (e.g., Borkovec, Robinson, Pruzinsky, & DePree, 1983) have failed to find any peripheral physiological differences between worriers and nonworriers or between resting and worry period conditions, unless imagery during worry is prompted (York et al., 1987). Such findings are in accord with the predominance of thought in worry and the partial independence of thought from peripheral efferent command. Yet EEG differences have been found which parallel the findings on conceptual versus imaginal activity in GAD-worry: Shift from rest to worry periods produces an increase in frontal beta activation for all subjects, and this frontal activation is particularly great in the left hemisphere of worriers compared to nonworriers (Carter, Johnson, & Borkovec, 1986). Analysis of heart and respiration rates of 13 (unmedicated) GAD clients and their matched nonanxious controls during a pre-therapy physiological session has revealed strikingly few differences between the two groups during our laboratory task periods (self-relaxation, worry, and three presentations of a phobic image) or at baselines before each task period (Elliott, 1990). In the meanwhile, Hoehn-Saric, McLeod, and Zimmerli (1988) have reported a remarkable finding: GAD clients do not generally show greater sympathetic activation overall or in response to stressors relative to nonanxious subjects. Rather, they show *inhibition* of some sympathetic systems, revealed in lower *variability* in heart rate and skin conductance, in response to stressors. This finding and their review of the few other autonomic studies of GAD led the authors to posit an autonomic rigidity hypothesis for this disorder wherein the habitual peripheral physiological response to environmental challenge involves reduced autonomic flexibility (Hoehn-Saric & McLeod, 1988). Such shut-down of peripheral activity fits nicely with our demonstrations that the worry of GAD clients involves predominance of thought and suppression of imagery and affective/physiological activity. Replication of the Carter et al. (1986) EEG results on a GAD sample would nicely complete the interesting, emerging picture that GAD-worry involves a mixture of inhibition and excitation of certain peripheral and cortical systems, reflective of their excessive dependence on *conceptual* defensive responses.

Very little EEG research has been conducted with GAD clients; extant studies implicate parietal and frontal functioning. We have been monitoring right and left frontal and parietal activity during baselines, self-relaxation, worry, and phobic imagery periods of our current lab session. Data from our first ten unmedicated, right-handed GAD clients has been recently contrasted with their matched nonanxious controls (Inz, 1990). Many significant results emerged; several correspond well with the Carter et al. (1986) findings, with our prior determination of thought predominance over imagery in GAD-worry, and with some hypotheses about cortical functioning, and are summarized below.

At rest, GADs show greater beta power in the left hemisphere (associated with verbal analytic processing), significantly greater than the controls' slightly greater power in the right hemisphere (associated with spatial, synthetic, and imaginal processing). Right parietal beta power (associated with attentional process) was lower in the GAD group than left parietal, relative to controls. And in a striking and important extension of Hoehn-Saric and McLeod's (1988) autonomic rigidity hypothesis, our clients showed few significant changes in EEG *variability* across our various tasks and baselines, whereas controls show significant shifts over virtually all tasks and recording sites. Thus, indeed, GAD clients display particular kinds of increased cortical (especially left hemisphere) activation in conjunction with peripheral shut-down, and they show an analogous inflexibility at the cortical level when faced with changing environmental demands.

A Theoretical Model of Worry Process

In a certain sense, anxiety begins with a perception of threat and continues until that threat is removed. Between those two events, the process of anxiety unfolds over time and involves the rapid interaction of all of the organism's information processing systems. At the behavioral level, primitive fight-or-flight action tendencies are evoked. At the physiological/affective level, physical resources are recruited in the service of fight-or-flight behavior. At the cognitive level, thoughts and images based on memories of prior confrontations with threat in general and this type of threat in particular are retrieved in the service of anticipating possible next events, possible responses, and their consequences.

All of these systems contribute to each other in a spiral of increasing anxiety that motivates behavioral avoidance. There is an asymmetry in their effects on each other, however, and the degree to which each is contributing to the anxiety spiral varies depending on the circumstances, especially those having to do with the crucialness of an immediate behavioral response. Simple stimulus-response connections can yield rapid avoidance. A swerving car on the highway can evoke a quick and effective avoidance maneuver without the contribution of much, if any, emotion or thought. If immediate avoidance is not required, these latter systems have time to become fully activated and thus can contribute further to the anxious experiences and ultimate behavioral response selection via the unfolding of meaning as further information is retrieved, is internally manipulated, and interacts among system levels. Sight of a threatening stranger approaching late at night may elicit an immediate avoidance response or action may be temporarily inhibited while a longer search among response alternatives takes place, with growing affective/physiological, memory retrieval, and conceptual processes contributing to that search. The longer behavioral action is inhibited, the more the various systems will contribute to each other and thus to the unfolding of meaning and anxious experience over time.

The phobias represent the clearest clinical example of relatively efficient, learned, motor avoidance. Perception of phobia-related cues will often lead to an immediate behavioral avoidance, reinforced by physical removal of the organism from the threat cue. Delays in this type of ordinarily successful response can occur (e.g., the physical or psychological environment at the time may prevent immediate avoidance), and until obstacles are overcome and avoidance can be released, the anxiety spiral continues. The person in such a delayed circumstance becomes aware of the growing physiological/affective activity, and thoughts and images of what might happen and what might be done to escape this situation increase in frequency in the service of ultimate escape. These systems interact, e.g., physiological/affective elicitations prime threat-related thoughts and images; images increase physiological/affective response via efferent command.

To say that anxiety begins with perception of threat and ends with successful avoidance of that threat is somewhat arbitrary. It is simply a convenient way of bracketing a series of events in time and reflects more about our experimental methods for studying anxiety than about its nature. For one thing, we know that anxious people have a pre-attentive bias to detect threat cues (Mathews, this volume). Thus, some aspects of anxious process involve continuous background activity or states of readiness to process information in particular ways. Second, once avoidance succeeds in removing the threat cue, the entire sequence of strategic processing involved in the anxiety spiral and involving all system levels and their interactions prior to successful avoidance is stored in memory. Such repeated storage strengthens the relevant associative network and thus strengthens both the predisposition to detect threat in the future and the habitual triggering of these internal sequences upon next occurrence of related threat cue.

We know from the behavior therapy outcome literature that exposure to feared objects or events with the prevention of motor avoidance is probably the most effective form of intervention. Because the strategic processing and external avoidance involved in anxiety is reinforced by successful removal of the threat upon avoidance, prevention of avoidance eliminates the reinforcement. Repeated exposures that elicit the anxiety spiral without reinforcement leads to extinction. Alternately, from a cognitive therapy perspective, the nonoccurrence of any real catastrophe disconfirms beliefs in the threatening value of the eliciting stimulus. As long as avoidance is prevented, the associative network of meaning surrounding a threat can be changed.

All of this seems straightforward in the case of phobias, wherein environmental threat cues are readily identified, overt avoidance has become the most frequent coping device, and the avoidance can be readily prevented via therapist intervention and/or client self-instruction. Not only simple phobias, but anxiety disorders considered to be intractable only 20 years ago (like panic disorder, agoraphobia, and obsessive-compulsive disorder), are now responsive to greater or lesser degrees to exposure therapies. Generalized anxiety disorder is a condition, however, wherein behavioral avoidance of threat is not so obvious. Its central threats have to do with the future, the catastrophes that may happen, and the felt sense of GAD clients that they will not be able to cope with whatever happens. The phobic individual experiences lengthy anxiety spirals in the relatively infrequent instances when behavioral avoidance is blocked; the GAD client experiences the spiral much of the time. The environment is filled with reminders of future concerns, but no behavioral avoidance will successfully terminate the threat because the thing feared does not yet exist in reality. The fearful outcomes are distant in time, are mostly low in probability of occurrence, and exist only in the illusion created by thoughts and images of what might be.

Figure 5.1 diagrams a common, generic model of anxiety process relevant to any anxiety episode: Upon perception of threat, a defensive reaction leads to interactions among behavioral, physiological/affective, and cognitive processes in an effort to terminate the threat. The duration of the spiral of interacting systems is a function of the delay in successful action for removing the threat. In most instances for phobias, effective and rapid behavioral avoidance supported by a predominance of physiological activation and catastrophic images ends the episode. When such successful avoidance is blocked in phobias or in the case of GAD most of the time, the spiral continues for a longer duration, and the opportunity for more complex types of system activity and interactions among systems arises. The types of system activity will now include a predominance of *inhibitory* processes at the behavioral and physiological levels (since no behavioral release is yet determined to be adaptive), an increase in conceptual attempts to search for a behavioral solution to this threat, and a defensive suppression of imagery and peripheral physiological activity. In the case of GAD, wherein no threat actually exists in the present and the future anticipated catastrophe has an objectively low probability of occurrence, the client is faced with an insoluble problem with no behavioral solution, although the systems continue to interact in an effort to solve that problem. At the end of any such episode of anxiety, the entire sequence of internal events is stored in memory, strengthening both the threatening meaning of the eliciting situation and the likelihood of pre-attentive bias to future, threat-related cues.

The research reviewed earlier supports this model for GAD in the following ways: Their peripheral physiological activity, especially under environmental challenge, reflects autonomic inhibition (Elliott, 1990; Hoehn-Saric & McLeod, 1988), behaviorally seen only in a subtle way in indecisiveness (Metzger et al., 1990). At the cortical level, an organ particularly inhibitory in its function, a

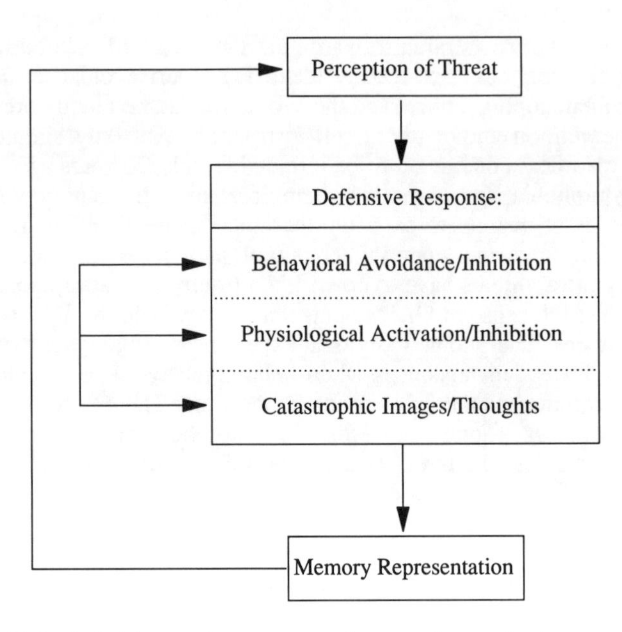

Figure 5.1. The spiral of interacting processes in an anxious episode.

variety of activation and inhibition processes are revealed, characterized by excessive left hemisphere activity and by reduced variability (inflexibility) similar to that seen in the autonomic nervous system (Inz, 1990). Simultaneously, conceptual activity (worry) increases (Borkovec & Inz, 1990) in an effort to draw on stored memories to search for a behavioral solution, with the functional and reinforcing by-product of the suppression of catastrophic imagery and thus the reduction (avoidance) of somatic anxiety experience. The costs of this spiralling process, strengthened in memory upon each reoccurrence, are twofold: (a) increases in pre-attentive bias to growing numbers of threat-related stimuli (Mathews, this volume) and (b) the suppression of emotional processing that could otherwise lead to change in the anxiety-related associative network (Borkovec & Hu, 1990).

Recent research on evaluative conditioning and unconditioned stimulus revaluation has revealed further associative processes that have relevance to our understanding of the strengthening of worry, the generalization of cues that can trigger worrisome episodes, and the reported uncontrollability of the process. Evaluative conditioning (Martin & Levey, 1987) is a process by which the affective valence of an unconditioned stimulus is acquired by a previously neutral stimulus. While such a process is commonly observed in classical conditioning preparations employing primary reinforcers such as food or shock, the useful feature of evaluative conditioning is that the emotional valence of the unconditioned stimuli used for associative learning appears to have itself been acquired in the past and mere visual perception of the unconditioned stimuli in conjunction with a neutral stimulus is sufficient to establish a shift in the latter's valence toward that of the former. The basic Martin and Levey (1987) procedure consists of pairing slides of neutral (neither liked nor disliked) human faces with slides of faces previously rated as liked or disliked. After as few as ten such pairings, the neutral slides begin to acquire the affective value of the slides with which they were paired. This demonstration suggests the possibility that images may serve the same function as pictures as long as they contain aversive or positive emotional valence. Such evaluative conditioning is also associated with other important characteristics: The conditioning is particularly capable of occurring outside of the subject's awareness, is highly resistant to extinction, but is susceptible to modification via counterconditioning (Baeyens, Eelen, & Van den Bergh, 1990; Baeyens, Eelen, Van den Bergh, & Crombez, 1989a; Baeyens, Eelen, Van den Bergh, & Crombez, 1989b).

Although research reviewed earlier suggests that conceptual activity is particularly predominant in worry and partly functions to avoid aversive imagery and its associated efferent commands, periodic images will occur as the worrier moves along the associative network links related to the worry topic. Although it has not yet been directly demonstrated, it appears likely that worry actually increases the frequency of incipient catastrophic images, even though its conceptual activity is reinforced during the episode by its immediate avoidance of those images. Thus, worry may inherently contain an evaluative conditioning process wherein conceptual activity is being paired with aversive images. Coping with threat in an abstract way becomes associated with anxious emotional state, and the very process of conceptual worry primes the occurrence of catastrophic images.

That catastrophic images can function as unconditioned stimuli has been recently demonstrated in a convincing way by Jones and Davey (1990) in their work on unconditioned stimulus revaluation effects. Neutral stimuli presented on a computer monitor were paired with aversive white noise, establishing a conditioned GSR response to those stimuli. Groups of subjects then either imagined solely the occurrence of the white noise several times, imagined solely the occurrence of a different aversive event, or engaged in a neutral control task. While the latter two groups showed reduced conditioned response upon subsequent presentations of the conditioned stimuli, the group which imagined the aversive unconditioned stimulus used in the preliminary conditioning trials displayed a maintenance of conditioned response. Thus, imagination of a catastrophic image by itself can strengthen the conditioned emotional value of any stimuli previously associated with it. For worry, this suggests another self-maintaining process: Its periodic catastrophic images may continue to strengthen the connections between worrisome conceptual activity, negative emotional states, and images of feared future events.

The processes of both evaluative conditioning and imaginal UCS revaluation also may contribute to the spread of worry activation in response to increasing numbers of environmental as well as internal cues. Worry can take place anywhere, and as it does, it can become associated with the external cues present at the time through simple pairing of those cues with worrisome activity and its attendant aversive emotional state. This process can apparently be reversed via stimulus control methods: Subjects instructed to limit their daily worrying to a specific time and place show a significant decline in worry over a four-week trial of such stimulus control instructions (Borkovec, Wilkinson, Folensbee, & Lerman, 1983). The sheer frequency of worry and its likely association with numerous environmental stimuli among anxious individuals, combined with the demonstration that evaluative conditioning readily occurs without awareness, may partly explain why GAD clients are significantly less able to identify external precipitants to the initiation of worry than nonanxious subjects (Craske, Rapee, Jackel, & Barlow, 1989). These same associative strengthening processes may also be responsible for Montalvo, Metzger, and Noll's (1989) demonstration that worry acts as a superordinate category: Worry about one topic appears to prime the worry content about other topics of concern.

The above literature thus suggests that principles of associative learning may be just as applicable to understanding both the linking of mental events among themselves and of mental events to environmental triggers or "reminders" as they are to understanding the learned associations between external stimuli commonly observed in classical and operant conditioning.

The apparent paradox of a hypothesized increased frequency of catastrophic imagery despite avoidance is partially resolvable via Schwartz and Kosslyn's (1982) suggestion that imagery involves both an imagery retrieval mechanism and a refresher mechanism. These appear to be independent operations (Cocude & Denis, 1988). Once an image has been formed from memory, a separate process is required to refresh and maintain that image. The conceptual avoidance of imagery in worry occurs in response to involuntarily retrieved aversive images triggered by worrisome associations and thus would be aimed at the refreshing mechanism. This interference would appear either as (a) a direct and complete inhibition of image refreshment resulting in the fading of the image or (b) an inhibition of some particularly affect-laden portion of the image, resulting inchanges in the image's content in a less anxiety-provoking direction (Holzman & Levis, 1989).[1] During the worry episode and upon the occurrence of such image avoidance, the spread of associations during worry then continues along verbal-linguistic pathways until another catastrophic image is encountered and the same process occurs again. Overall, moderate levels of anxiety are maintained in order to avoid the higher anxiety consequent to fully elaborated and refreshed aversive images.

As future research on thought, imagery, and affect proceeds, further elucidation of the interactions among cognitive and emotional systems will provide increasing clarity on the nature of worry process. Worry has already revealed itself to constitute a dynamic, over-time process involving several levels of system processing and responsible to some degree for the

---

[1] Indeed, Suler and Katkin (1988) have shown that fear imagery is more difficult to control and manipulate than neutral imagery, while Euse and Haney (1975) have demonstrated that high trait anxiety is associated with low control and clarity of images even of neutral quality.

perseveration of anxiety. With greater understanding of the worry process, we should be able to draw deductions useful in the development of therapeutic methods for severe anxiety disorders.

Concluding Remarks

The present volume provides a rich theoretical and empirical account of the importance and heuristic value of the concepts of vigilance and cognitive avoidance. What we attend to and how we react to those perceived stimuli form an essential dynamical sequence of events that contributes significantly to the evolution of human behavior over time. The topical area of this volume bears on an important example of this process, that having to do with threat, with implications for both general personality theories and clinical theories of adult emotional disorders.

There is also a rich diversity of perspective and method represented by the various investigators. Certainly one of the most prevalent approaches involves the categorization of subjects into predispositional groups characterized by tendencies to be high or low in vigilance and high or low in cognitive avoidance (cf. e.g., Krohne, Chapter 2 in this volume; Miller, Combs, & Kruus, this volume). Constitution and historical factors lead to the evolution of certain general strategies for responding to the world, and as can be seen in the contents of this volume, these habitual strategy choices have multiple consequences in a variety of settings. The work in this volume also draws from multiple assessments including the subjective, behavioral, and psychophysiological domains, and thus provides for opportunities to explore interrelationships among different processing systems within the human being. There is, furthermore, variability in the types of subject samples being employed, e.g., psychiatrically diagnosed clients, "normal" subjects in laboratory settings, subjects undergoing real-life medical procedures. Such diversity in the various ways described above bodes well for any research area; it promises ultimately to produce widely generalizable principles of human behavior and a more coherent view of the human organism as a whole.

Despite these positive features, there are problems in this area. One does not yet get a sense of the emergence of a single, general theory. Rarely are all of the results from a study directly derivable from its own premises. Thus, we are still very much in an empirical phase, seeking to establish empirical relationships while continuing to develop and modify our conceptualizations of the involved traits and processes in order to explain the relationships we observe. Obvious opportunities for connections among the represented perspectives do exist, however. Personality trait approaches have a great deal to say to those of us who study the moment-to-moment processing of anxious clients; personality factors provide the broader, developmental context in which to understand the etiology and maintenance of the more molecular processes which we study. At the same time, the more molecular research provides some of the potential building blocks upon which personality in its more globally assessed form is based. This potential interplay between molar and molecular perspectives is reminiscent of the concept of "self-similarity" in fractual geometry and its applications in chaos theory (Gleick, 1987). That is, at the millisecond level, some humans engage in frequent habitual, rapid cycles of vigilance (e.g., pre-attentive) and cognitive avoidance (e.g., worry). With sufficiently great frequency of this process in response to a sufficiently large number of daily events, these small cycles can be detected in the form of general personality dispositions. The self-same process is involved, irrespective of scale.

Further problems exist for us at the more specific level of individual investigator theory. Two examples will suffice. In our theory of worry, an apparent paradox exists that so far has been resolved only by unsupported speculation: Worry is primarily conceptual in nature and functions to avoid aversive imagery in order to avoid somatic activation, yet it is also likely that catastrophic imagery increases in anxious individuals. Obviously, we have a long way to go before we will thoroughly understand the process of worry and why it is that certain individuals choose this obviously unpleasant cognitive activity to cope with threat.

The second problematic example is this: How is it possible for someone to be high in cognitive avoidance without being high in vigilance to something? Cognitive avoidance implies the detection of stimuli that are avoided. It would thus seem reasonable that vigilance crucially includes temporal dimension reflecting how rapidly cognitive avoidance is evoked in response to perhaps increasingly remote cues associated with original threat and/or how far threat-stimulus detection is outside of awareness. This problem might be empirically resolvable via the use of pre-attentive bias assessment methods outlined by Mathews and applied to the vigilance/avoidance categories of Krohne and others.

References

American Psychiatric Association. (1987). *Diagnostic and statistical manual of mental disorders* (3rd rev. ed.). Washington, DC: Author.

Baeyens, F., Eelen, P., & Van den Bergh, O. (1990). Contingency awareness in evaluative conditioning: A case for unaware affective-evaluative learning. *Cognition and Emotion, 4*, 3-18.

Baeyens, F., Eelen, P., Van den Bergh, O., & Crombez, G. (1989a). Acquired affective-evaluative value: Conservative but not unchangeable. *Behaviour Research and Therapy, 27*, 279-287.

Baeyens, F., Eelen, P., Van den Bergh, O., & Crombez, G. (1989b). The influence of CS-US perceptual similarity/dissimilarity on human evaluative learning and signal learning. *Learning and Motivation, 20*, 322-333.

Barlow, D. H. (1988). *Anxiety and its disorders*. New York: Guilford.

Borkovec, T. D., & Hu, S. (1990). The effect of worry on cardiovascular response to phobic imagery. *Behaviour Research and Therapy, 28*, 69-73.

Borkovec, T. D., & Inz, J. (1990). The nature of worry in generalized anxiety disorder: A predominance of thought activity. *Behaviour Research and Therapy, 28*, 153-158.

Borkovec, T. D., Robinson, E., Pruzinsky, T., & DePree, J. A. (1983). Preliminary exploration of worry: Some characteristics and processes. *Behaviour Research and Therapy, 21*, 9-16.

Borkovec, T. D., & Sides, J. K. (1979). The contribution of relaxation and expectancy to fear reduction via graded, imaginal exposure to feared stimuli. *Behaviour Research and Therapy, 17*, 529-540.

Borkovec, T. D., Wilkinson, L., Folensbee, R., & Lerman, C. (1983). Stimulus control applications to the treatment of worry. *Behaviour Research and Therapy, 21*, 247-251.

Carter, W. R., Johnson, M. C., & Borkovec, T. D. (1986). Worry: An electrocortical analysis. *Advances in Behaviour Research and Therapy, 8*, 193-204.

Cocude, M., & Denis, M. (1988). Measuring the temporal characteristics of visual images. *Journal of Mental Images, 12*, 89-102.

Craske, M. G., Rapee, R. M., Jackel, L., & Barlow, D. H. (1989). Qualitative dimensions of worry in DSM-III-R generalized anxiety disorder subjects and nonanxious controls. *Behaviour Research and Therapy, 27*, 397-402.

Denny, M. R. (1976). Post-aversive relief and relaxation and their implications for behavior therapy. *Journal of Behavior Therapy and Experimental Psychiatry, 7*, 315-322.

Elliott, T. K. (1990). *The role of autonomic arousal in generalized anxiety disorder.* Unpublished doctoral dissertation, Pennsylvania State University, University Park, PA.

Euse, F. J., & Haney, J. N. (1975). Clarity, controllability, and emotional intensity of image: Correlations with introversion, neuroticism, and subjective anxiety. *Perceptual and Motor Skills, 40*, 443-447.

Foa, E. B., & Kozak, M. J. (1986). Emotional processing of fear: Exposure to corrective information. *Psychological Bulletin, 99*, 20-35.

Gleick, J. (1987). *Chaos: Making a new science*. New York: Penguin Books.

Gray, J. A. (1982). Precis of "The neurophysiology of anxiety: An enquiry into the functions of the septo-hippocampal system". *Behavioral and Brain Sciences, 5*, 469-534.

Hoehn-Saric, R., & McLeod, D. R. (1988). The peripheral sympathetic nervous system: Its role in normal and pathologic anxiety. *Psychiatric Clinics of North America, 11*, 375-386.

Hoehn-Saric, R., McLeod, D. R., & Zimmerli, W. D. (1988, June). *Subjective and somatic manifestations of anxiety in obsessive-compulsive and generalized anxiety disorders.* Paper presented at the annual meeting of the American Psychiatric Association, Montreal, Canada.

Holzman, A. D., & Levis, D. J. (1989). The effects of increasing the number of stimulus modalities included in a fear-eliciting imagery scene on reported imagery clarity, scene repetition, and sympathetic (fear) arousal. *Cognitive Therapy and Research, 13*, 389-405.

Inz, J. (1990). *EEG activity in generalized anxiety disorder.* Unpublished doctoral dissertation, Pennsylvania State University, University Park, PA.

Jones, T., & Davey, G. C. L. (1990). The effects of cued UCS rehearsal on the retention of differential "fear" conditioning: An experimental analogue of the "worry" process. *Behaviour Research and Therapy, 28*, 159-164.

Lang, P. J. (1985). The cognitive psychophysiology of emotion: Fear and anxiety. In A. H. Tuma & J. D. Maser (Eds.), *Anxiety and the anxiety disorders* (pp. 131-170). Hillsdale, NJ: Erlbaum.

Martin, I., & Levey, A. B. (1987). Learning what will happen next: conditioning, evaluation, and cognitive processes. In G. Davey (Ed.), *Cognitive processes and Pavlovian conditioning in humans* (pp. 57-81). London: Wiley.

Metzger, R. L., Miller, M. L., Cohen, M., Sofka, M., & Borkovec, T. D. (1990). Worry changes decision making: The effect of negative thoughts on cognitive processing. *Journal of Clinical Psychology, 46*, 78-88.

Meyer, T. J., Miller, M. L., Metzger, R. L., & Borkovec, T. D. (1990). Development and validation of the Penn State Worry Questionnaire. *Behaviour Research and Therapy, 28*, 487-495.

Montalvo, A., Metzger, R. L., & Noll, J. A. (1989, November). *The network structure of worry in memory*. Paper presented at the North Carolina Cognition Group, Davidson, NC.

Pruzinsky, T., & Borkovec, T. D. (1990). Cognitive and personality characteristics of worriers. *Behaviour Research and Therapy, 28*, 507-512.

Schwartz, S. P., & Kosslyn, S. M. (1982). A computer simulated approach to studying mental imagery. In J. Mehler, E. C. T. Walker, & M. Garrett (Eds.), *Perspectives on mental representation: Experimental and theoretical studies of cognitive processes and capacities* (pp. 69-85). London: Erlbaum.

Suler, J. R., & Katkin, E. S. (1988). Mental imagery of fear-related stimuli. *Journal of Mental Imagery, 12*, 115-124.

Velten, E. (1968). A laboratory task for the induction of mood states. *Behaviour Research and Therapy, 6*, 473-482.

Veroff, J., Douvan, E., & Kulka, R. A. (1981). *The inner American: A self-portrait from 1957 to 1976*. New York: Basic Books.

Vrana, S. R., Cuthbert, B. N., & Lang, P. J. (1986). Fear imagery and text processing. *Psychophysiology, 23*, 247-253.

York, D., Borkovec, T. D., Vasey, M., & Stern, R. (1987). Effects of worry and somatic anxiety induction on thoughts, emotion, and physiological activity. *Behaviour Research and Therapy, 25*, 523-526.

Chapter 6

Attention and Memory for Threat in Anxiety

Andrew Mathews

Introduction

The concepts of avoidant and vigilant cognitive styles in coping with anxiety is well established in psychological theory (see Krohne, Chapter 2, this volume). For present purposes, I will assume that this concept is similar to, or at least overlaps with, other dimensions referred to as repression-sensitization (Bell & Byrne, 1978) and blunting-monitoring (Miller, Combs, & Kruus, this volume). In general, it seems to have been assumed that all these proposed cognitive styles are variations in the extent that individuals typically avoid or seek out more information about anxiety-evoking stimuli, or in how they typically react to anxiety. On the basis of the predominantly self-report measures used, vigilance has sometimes been found to correlate positively with anxiety level (e.g., Cohen & Lazarus, 1973) and sometimes not (Miller, 1987). However, because both avoidance and vigilance are usually described as methods of *coping* with threat or anxiety, they are typically seen as conceptually independent from anxiety itself.

In the approach adopted here, vigilance will be considered within an information processing framework, using measures of attention, interpretation and memory for threatening information. The research to be described represents an attempt to determine the nature of processing biases that are characteristic of anxious individuals, using methods derived from studies of normal human information processing. Within this framework, information is usually thought of as being processed through several different levels or stages. The earliest stage that is relevant to the detection of threat is what Broadbent (1977) has termed the "hidden pre-attentive process". Prior to our attention being attracted to a particular stimulus, data from the environment must be automatically processed to some extent, to allow selection of significant information (e.g., our own name being mentioned). Once we attend to, and become aware of a stimulus, the personal significance of that stimulus must be evaluated; that is, we need to interpret its meaning and to decide whether it poses a personal threat or otherwise. Finally, once this primary evaluation is complete, we may chose to continue thinking about the implications of the selected interpretation, or to avoid further consideration of the personal meaning of the event. Specifically, we may choose to elabobrate on the meaning of the event in various ways ("What were they saying about me?"), seek out more information about it, or think about how we can deal with it, or we can try to avoid further thought on the subject. It is probably only this final voluntary, or controlled stage, that is capable of being tapped by self-report measures of coping strategy. Thus the acquisition of threatening information could be favored at an early (pre-attentive or attentional) stage, without necessarily implying a similar cognitive bias at later stages. Alternatively, there could be little or no attentional bias favoring the pick-up of threatening information, but either the interpretation of ambiguous stimuli, or the degree and type of later elaboration could be biased. For this reason I will use the term vigilance to refer only to a bias that favors selective attention to threatening stimuli, without assuming that subsequent voluntary processing necessarily follows the same pattern.

To anticipate the conclusions of this research, it will be proposed that: highly anxious individuals are characterized by a combination of attentional vigilance, an interpretive bias favoring the selection of threatening meaning, but also by partially successful attempts to avoid further elaborative processing of that information. Furthermore, rather than thinking of this characteristic pattern as one method for coping with anxiety, it can be seen as a cognitive mechanism involved in maintaining or perhaps causing the anxiety itself. For example, if an attentional bias has the consequence that a person processes more information about remotely possible catastrophic outcomes, this may lead to unrealistically increased subjective risk estimates about that outcome, via the availability heuristic (Tversky & Kahneman, 1973). Increased subjective risk is likely to lead to increased anxiety levels, which in turn may reinforce or maintain the attentional vigilance effect. Indeed, any cognitive bias that has the effect of enhancing the selective processing of mood congruent information (e.g., concerning danger) is potentially capable of producing such vicious circle effects. One important but unanswered question is the extent to which the voluntary adoption of a particular cognitive coping strategy can be seen as similar to a personality trait, in that it is used by some individuals more than others; or as a transient option that is adopted by all or most people under appropriate circumstances. A similar question needs to be answered about the information processing biases that are being proposed here. For example, the selective processing of threatening information can be seen as an enduring vulnerability to anxiety, similar to the trait anxiety concept, or as a transient process that can occur in those experiencing an anxious emotional state. Clearly, the type of theory that can be proposed about the mechanism linking cognitive processes and anxiety would be quite dependent on the answers to these questions.

To fully consider this issue, and to justify and defend the suggestions above, it will first be necessary to review some experiments on attention, interpretation and memory for threat in highly anxious individuals. The results of these experiments suggest that threatening distractors interfere more with the performance of anxious than non-anxious subjects, and that this is due to a tendency for the anxious subjects to attend selectively to threat cues in their environment. Furthermore, it appears that, given an ambiguous event, anxious subjects tend to select the more threatening of two possible interpretations.

However, another set of experiments suggests, unexpectedly, that anxious individuals do not always show better recall for threatening information, despite their selective attention to it. It is this apparent discrepancy that provides the main basis for arguing that anxiety involves both vigilance and avoidance, albeit at different stages of processing.

Interference and Distraction from Emotional Stimuli

One way of testing the extent to which processing resources are selectively allocated to threatening stimuli is to see how much the incidental presence of such stimuli interferes with another task. For example, the Stroop color-naming task requires that subjects name the color that a word is written in while ignoring the word's content. The version of the test that we have used (Mathews & MacLeod, 1985; Mogg, Mathews, & Weinman, 1989), contained words related to physical and social threat (e.g., "disease" or "criticized"), or were non-threatening control words. There were no significant differences in color-naming time as a function of word content for non-anxious controls, but clinically anxious subjects were significantly slower in the color-naming task when the words were threatening in content, compared with matched neutral words. Similar effects have been found with phobias (Watts, McKenna, Sharrock, & Trezise, 1986), depression (Gotlib & McCann, 1984; Williams & Broadbent, 1986), and panic (Ehlers, Margraf, Davies, & Roth, 1988), using words that matched the concerns of these individuals. Thus, the slowing effect is apparent when words match the content of the subject's worries.

In fact, it is by no means clear that slowing occurs only in response to threatening content. Recently, Martin, Williams, and Clark (1991) have shown that anxious patients (although not anxious normals) are equally slowed by highly emotional positive words, and have suggested that the "emotionality" of a stimulus, rather than threat value, is responsible for these effects. To investigate this conclusion, we (Mathews & Klug, 1991) compared the interfering effects of matched emotional positive and negative words, after dividing the word sets into those judged relevant to the likely concerns of anxious patients (e.g., safe, dying) or those less likely to be relevant (e.g., mercy, quarrel).

Consistent with the findings of Martin et al. (1991), the positive words did cause interference that was just as great as the negative words, but only for those words that had previously been judged as being relevant to those patients. One possible explanation is that the positive-related words tended to be directly opposite in meaning to relevant threat cues. Thus "safe" is the converse of "danger", so that the meaning of the latter may be activated by seeing the former. If so, then it would not be true to say that *any* emotional stimulus can cause interference; rather, only words that are closely related to a current concern of that individual should be capable of attracting processing resources, and thus slowing performance of other tasks. Further support for an explanation in terms of current concern is provided by the study of Watts et al. (1986), showing that interference from phobic words was present in phobic subjects before, but not after, successful desensitization treatment. Presumably, treatment reduced the current emotional significance of the phobic words. As might be expected from this explanation, distraction effects are not only seen in color-naming tasks. Another situation in which comparable results can be seen is dichotic listening, where a subject is required to attend to one stereo channel, while ignoring information in a second channel. If this to-be-ignored information is personally relevant, subjects may become involuntarily aware of it, supporting the assumption that even ignored stimuli are being processed out of awareness. Even when they cannot report on such ignored information, it may still take up processing resources, as shown by interference with other tasks being performed simultaneously (Bargh, 1982). In a comparison of clinically anxious and control subjects (Mathews & MacLeod, 1986), we found that controls performed a reaction task with equal efficiency, irrespective of the nature of ignored words on the unattended channel. In contrast, the anxious subjects were significantly slower when the unattended words were threatening, rather than emotionally neutral. This interference occurred despite the fact that none of the subjects was able to report accurately on the words involved. Apparently, interference can occur automatically and without the adoption of a voluntary strategy, since these subjects were hardly aware of the presence of the stimuli causing the interference.

Anxiety and Attention

Of course, interference in either color-naming or dichotic listening could be due to many causes. For example, slowing could be produced by the emotional reactions to words, or by a defensive shift in attention away from them. However, there is evidence from another experimental paradigm, showing that when the position of a target actually coincides with that of the threatening word, the target is detected *more* rapidly by anxious subjects (MacLeod, Mathews, & Tata, 1986; Mogg, Mathews, & Eysenck, 1992). Word pairs were displayed on a computer screen, and subjects were required to detect the occasional appearance of a small dot in a location just vacated by one of the two words. Since clinically anxious subjects were faster to detect the dot if it replaced a threatening (rather than neutral) word, it appears that their attention shifted towards, rather than away from, the threatening stimulus. Controls in this experiment showed the reverse effect, since they were somewhat slower to detect dots that replaced threatening words. Thus, if anything, the non-anxious controls appeared to attend less to threat and more to the neutral or positive words.

The implications of these results are that, in real life, we might suppose that anxious individuals would have their attention caught by any fleeting or inconsequential cues associated with danger, while the same cues would be neglected by those who are less anxious. Environmental information is too great in quantity and complexity for it all to be fully processed and reach awareness. Some selection must take place, and it appears that the normal mode of the cognitive system is for this selection to be biased against irrelevant threat cues. This seems adaptive, since such stimuli are present much of the time and attending to them all would make it very difficult to concentrate on anything else. In fact, highly anxious people complain of just such concentration problems and may have to exert relatively greater effort to avoid distraction (Eysenck, 1982). We propose that this arises precisely because in anxious individuals selection is biased *towards* the intake of threatening information, thus simultaneously disrupting performance and maintaining anxiety.

This raises the interesting question of causal direction. Is attentional vigilance a *cause* of anxious mood, or is it a *consequence* of it? While this remains an open question, the above line of argument suggests that, in a sense, both may be true. As was proposed earlier, anxious mood may increase attentional vigilance, and because this results in selective intake of threatening information, vigilance may in turn lead to greater anxiety. One problem with this type of vicious circle, or positive feedback model, is that of explaining why the same circumstances lead some individuals to become severely or even pathologically anxious, while others are hardly affected. Our proposed solution to this problem is to suppose that the nature of the relationship between mood and cognitive bias varies between individuals, and this variation is related to the differences in vulnerability usually described as trait anxiety. That is, we suggest that those who are more vulnerable to stress (high trait anxious individuals) have a closer relationship between level of potential danger and attentional vigilance, than do those who are less vulnerable. One way that this could arise is if vulnerable (high trait) individuals adopt a vigilant mode very readily, and thus increase their anxious mood, even at very low levels of objective threat. Less vulnerable (low trait) individuals may have a much higher threshold for entering a vigilant mode, or become *less* vigilant in the face of low threat levels. To remain biologically adaptive, even low trait anxious individuals should become vigilant when threat is imminent or severe, but could still have a lower threshold for moving from attentional indifference (or avoidance) to vigilance, thus avoiding unnecessary disturbance in the presence of cues posing no immediate threat.

Relation of Vigilance to Trait and State Anxiety

The above view makes specific predictions about the relationship between vigilance, trait and state anxiety. However, these predictions are difficult to confirm or reject based on single correlations. For example, interference scores have sometimes been found to be correlated with state anxiety, and sometimes with trait. However, in a series of studies using the dot-detection task to assess attention, Broadbent and Broadbent (1988) found evidence of a non-linear relation of vigilance with trait levels, indicating that attentional vigilance was unaffected by trait scores in the low to moderate range, but increased exponentially at the very highest levels. State anxiety only predicted vigilance when the trait score was also high, consistent with an interactive effect that only operates at the upper end of the distribution of trait anxiety scores. In other words, the results suggested that vigilance and state anxiety are highly associated only in high trait individuals; that is, in those who are persistently prone to debilitating anxiety under stress.

In a study from our own laboratory, high and low trait students were tested using the dot detection task described earlier, immediately prior to an important examination (MacLeod & Mathews, 1988). Although there had been only slight differences between high and low trait subjects in baseline levels obtained a long time before the examination, when tested under stress, the high trait students showed a significant increase in vigilance for threat words related to examinations (e.g., failure, stupid). Interestingly, however, the low trait students did not show this effect, and if anything, tended to shift attention to words that were not related to examination failure. This finding strongly supports the hypothesis of an interaction between trait and state, such that high trait anxious subjects become increasingly vigilant under stress, perhaps further enhancing their anxiety level. In contrast to this apparent positive feedback loop, low trait anxious subjects may develop a defensive response under stress, serving to restrain further anxiety increases.

A problem in the interpretation of these results is that subjects were not randomly assigned to stress conditions, but rather were tested at different points in time. For this reason we have recently carried out some experiments in which subjects grouped according to trait anxiety level were randomly assigned to a low or a high stress condition. Low stress subjects were given very easy problems from an intelligence test, while high stress subjects received extremely difficult items, to ensure they would fail. The results were not what we expected, since they were quite different from the study involving examinations. On the same dot detection task, we found that both high and low trait anxiety groups became significantly more vigilant under the high stress than under the low stress condition (Mogg, Mathews, Bird, & MacGregor-Morris, 1990); the extent of this increase in vigilance was very similar in both high and low trait groups.

The reason for this discrepancy is still uncertain, but obvious differences between the two experiments suggest possible explanations. The intensity of the stress manipulated in any laboratory session is unlikely to match that experienced before a real examination. Another possibility arises from the very different time scales involved. Perhaps the low trait subjects use effective coping strategies in the interval leading up to a long anticipated examination, that high trait subjects do not employ, or not so effectively. In the case of acute experimental stress, there might be insufficient time to see the effects of such strategies. If so, we could conclude that the initial response to a novel and unanticipated stress is one of increased attentional vigilance in all subjects. However, over time, low trait subjects become less vigilant and may even reverse attentional bias by becoming predominantly avoidant, while high trait subjects remain just as vigilant as the stressor approaches. This interpretation suggests that the hypothesis that high and low vulnerable individuals differ in their threshold for entering a vigilant mode needs to be modified somewhat. Rather, the difference may be one of the general ease with which individuals move over time into vigilant versus non-vigilant modes, with low trait anxious individuals being more able to avoid or inhibit unnecessary vigilance, and high anxiety-prone individuals being less able either to leave a vigilant mode of processing, or prevent it occurring (cf. Krohne, Chapter 2, this volume).

Can Attentional Vigilance be Controlled?

The possibilities discussed above suggest that knowledge of how low trait subjects successfully adapt to a stressor over time, while high trait subjects fail to do so, might have important implications for teaching coping skills and for understanding the mechanisms underlying effective treatment of anxiety disorders (cf. Borkovec & Lyonfields, this volume; Miller et al., this volume). Studies by Watts et al. (1986) and Foa and McNally (1986) showed that color-naming interference and dichotic listening intrusions both decreased following successful treatment, implying that some change during the process of recovery involves the elimination of attentional vigilance. However, the implication that all signs of excessive vigilance disappear with recovery is challenged by results that we have obtained when comparing clinically anxious, recovered, and control groups in a search task (Mathews, May, Mogg, & Eysenck, 1990). Subjects were required to find a neutral target (either the word 'left' or 'right'), that appeared in one of three indicated positions, while ignoring two distracting words that sometimes filled the remaining positions. The presence of non-threatening distractors slowed detection of the target more for the currently anxious patients, than for either recovered or non-anxious controls. When threatening distractors were present, however, both currently anxious and recovered subjects were slowed more, relative to the non-distractor trials, than were non-anxious controls. Perhaps therefore, even after recovery, vulnerable individuals have difficulty in avoiding the distracting effects of threatening cues at least under conditions where the task demands a search among competing stimuli. If this finding proves robust, the implication is that readiness to adopt a vigilant mode during active search, or difficulty in inhibiting it, may be a cognitive characteristic of those at risk to develop anxiety disorders.

If so, the same task (in distinction to the dot detection task which has less of a search component) might be expected to reveal differences between high trait and low trait subjects, especially under high stress conditions. Results of an experiment that we have just completed (Mathews, Thomason, & Constans, 1991) did indeed reveal significant differences between high and low trait normals, but contrary to our prediction, this was apparent only under *low* stress conditions. When given easy problems and reassured about their test scores, the subsequent search performance of high trait subjects was slowed more by threatening words than by neutral or positive distractors, in contrast to the low trait subjects. However, when anticipating failure on a difficult "IQ" task, the presence of threatening distractors had no greater effect on high than on low trait anxious subjects. Apparently, the contrived short-term stress does not reproduce the expected form of interaction between trait and high stress, even when the task is sensitive to trait effects in the absence of stress.

We do not have a convincing explanation for why these results go against predictions based on the results of previous studies. However, our hypothesis is that the search task used may be more sensitive than is the dot detection task to vigilance effects associated with high trait anxiety; but, at the same time, it is more likely to provoke subjects into making efforts to overcome the interfering consequences of these effects. This idea is based on the fact that when searching among distractors for a target, attention is easily caught by distractors that must be scanned (in order to reject them as non-targets), thus making the task quite sensitive to automatic vigilance effects. However, the slowing that results may be apparent even to the subject. The high stress condition (with its implicit demand to perform better) may provoke strenuous efforts to stop attention being captured by distractors. Thus, when high trait subjects are under performance stress, they may be able to temporarily compensate for the slowing due to vigilance, by making voluntary efforts to move their attention away from threatening distractors as rapidly as possible after capture. Such a possibility is less paradoxical than it first appears, since (as indicated previously) early detection of threat could be followed by effortful avoidance of further processing.

However, recall also that the study of examination stress suggested that the discrepancy between high and low trait subjects grows stronger over time. Just before a long-anticipated examination, high trait students had become more vigilant, but low trait students were less so. This implies that low trait anxious subjects ceased to attend to threat cues over time, whereas high trait subjects became even more vigilant, and would thus need to exert more and more effort to avoid being distracted. If so, then this could account for the greater vulnerability of high trait subjects under stress, because the effort required to avoid distraction by threat cues would eventually become excessive, leading to a breakdown in their ability to control anxiety.

To summarize, there is consistent evidence of a link between persistent vigilance for threat and anxiety level. There is less certainty about causal direction, or whether the effect of stress interacts with trait anxiety levels. However, the following hypotheses are proposed on the basis of the present pattern of results. In high trait anxious subjects, stressful events lead to increased vigilance for threat cues. To avoid loss of capacity when performing demanding cognitive tasks, they must make correspondingly greater voluntary efforts to avoid distraction by irrelevant threatening stimuli. Under chronic stress, their tendency towards vigilance persists, or may become even more marked over time. Avoidance of distraction by threat cues may thus become increasingly difficult, and eventually lead to a breakdown in ability to cope (i.e., an anxiety disorder). The initial response of low trait anxious subjects to stress appears to be a switch from a non-vigilant to a vigilant mode. Over time this pattern is readily reversed, and they cease even to attend to threat cues. An interesting question for future investigation is whether low trait subjects use voluntary strategies to effect such a beneficial change over time, and if so, what they are. Alternatively, high trait subjects may do something to make their situation worse. Either possibility would imply that even if attentional vigilance is automatic, some of the interfering consequences may be controllable. If so, this could have important implications for treatment methods, and for training in the use of effective coping strategies.

The Interpretation of Ambiguous Information

According to some theoretical views (Simpson, 1984), the various meanings of ambiguous information may be processed in parallel, until one of these meanings is selected. It is thus possible that the same mechanism which causes an attentional bias towards threat in anxious individuals may also bias the selection of meaning towards threatening interpretations. Suppose, for example, that a person perceives a bodily sensation such as their heart pounding or a feeling of dizziness. This might be interpreted as being due to several different causes, including over-exertion, intense emotion, or impending illness (Pennebaker, 1982). Anxious individuals may be more likely to attend to such sensations, to the extent that we can assume that they are processed as external threat cues are. However, whether or not sensations are interpreted as threats is likely to be influenced by prior knowledge and expectations, by immediately preceding events, similar experiences in the past, and also, by emotional state at the time. If an attentional processing bias influences the selection of alternative internal representations, as well as external stimuli, then the process of interpretation itself may also be biased in anxious individuals toward the selection of threatening meaning.

Evidence that anxious individuals do indeed select the more threatening meaning of ambiguous stimuli is provided by the results of several experiments (Eysenck, MacLeod, & Mathews, 1987; Eysenck, Mogg, May, Richards, & Mathews, 1991; Mathews, Mogg, May, & Eysenck, 1989). In two of these studies, high or low anxious subjects listened to word lists that included homophones having one threatening and one neutral meaning (e.g., "die", "dye"). Subjects were required to write down what they heard, and the spelling that they used was taken as an indication of which meaning was most available to them. Compared with controls, anxious subjects used significantly more spellings that were consistent with the threatening meaning.

In the third study, subjects listened to a series of sentences that included some which could be interpreted in different ways (e.g., "The doctor examined little Emma's growth"). In a later recognition test, subjects were required to rate new sentences for their similarity in meaning to those that they had heard previously. Some of these new sentences were a threatening version of the original ("The doctor checked little Emma's cancer"), while others were non-threatening ("The doctor measured little Emma's height"). Compared with normal controls, currently anxious (although not recovered) subjects endorsed the threatening interpretation more often. Furthermore, a signal detection analysis that included false alarms to unrelated threatening sentences in the recognition test showed that a simple response bias explanation was not sufficient to explain the results. Rather, it seems that anxious subjects are more likely to interpret ambiguous events in terms of their more threatening meaning.

The Nature and Consequences of Cognitive Avoidance

Cognitive avoidance is not a very clearly defined concept. Part of the problem may be that several different kinds of cognitive avoidance exist. From the information processing point of view, avoidance may occur at a pre-attentive level, or only after a threat has been consciously attended to. For example, the evidence reviewed above suggests that non-anxious subjects may avoid threat automatically at this pre-attentional stage of processing, so that mild or irrelevant threats never reach awareness at all. Thus some results could be interpreted as showing that low anxious subjects show "defensive" responses, and move their attention away from threatening words, although they do oot report any deliberate attempt to do so (MacLeod & Mathews, 1988; MacLeod et al., 1986).

This very early and effortless avoidance seems adaptive when the emotional stimuli thus avoided are irrelevant to current task requirements. It may often be useful to exclude such irrelevant threat cues from awareness, so as to prevent any disruption in task performance. However, to be flexibly adaptive, attention needs to be attracted by any really important or immediate threat. It therefore seems that the decision mechanisms used to allocate attention to threat should take account of threat *severity* and *urgency*. Below a certain level, we assume that threat cues are pre-attentively avoided by non-anxious subjects, while above that level, attentional resources are adaptively directed towards the threat (vigilant mode). In contrast to this, high anxious subjects tend to have their attention automatically drawn to threat stimuli, even when the "threat" is nothing more urgent than irrelevant emotional words. This suggests that very low levels of threat severity and urgency are given processing priority by high trait anxious individuals. Perhaps *any* cue associated with threat attracts attention in such anxious subjects, no matter how trivial, so that they are constantly being reminded of potential dangers under almost all circumstances (see also Miller's concept of "monitoring", cf. Miller et al., this volume).

Let us suppose that, through the process just described, highly anxious subjects have their attention continually drawn to any potential threat in their environment, and thus constantly experience thoughts about danger. How might they react to such thoughts? It is of course possible that some individuals would *not* avoid thinking about danger, and instead choose to focus on the threatening stimulus, or on the internal mental representation of it. One situation when this commonly occurs is when there is an immediate physical danger, or when a phobic stimulus is present. In this event, behavior is often inhibited ('freezing'), and attention is fixated on the threat, in order to monitor the extent of danger, until escape is possible (see Gray, 1982).

Another condition in which it appears that no attempts are made to avoid unpleasant thoughts is depression. Although the thought content in depression differs from that in anxiety, it also appears to involve selective processing of negative information, but without involving avoidance (Wenzlaff, Wegner, & Roper, 1988; cf. Weidner & Collins, this volume). The depressed person seems to lack the will or desire to avoid, perhaps because they feel hopeless about their ability to do so, that the worst has already occurred, or because they believe that they deserve to suffer. Whatever the explanation, the subjective experience of sadness seems to involve acceptance of punishment, and precludes struggle or avoidance.

Effects of Suppression and Distraction

If we make the assumption that excessive anxiety commonly leads to cognitive avoidance attempts, at a post-attentional stage of processing, there are a number of reasons to believe that these attempts may prove counter-productive. Worry is a central cognitive feature of anxiety and consists of repeated thoughts about future danger, which are experienced as aversive, but are difficult to resolve or dismiss from one's mind (Borkovec & Lyonfields, this volume). Despite this difficulty, most people report that they react to anxious thoughts and worries by trying to get rid of them, either by suppressing them, or by distracting themselves from them. Such attempts at suppression, however, are often not very effective.

A striking example of how attempts at avoidance can fail, has been documented in studies of voluntary thought suppression (Wegner, Schneider, Carter, & White, 1987; Wegner, Shortt, Blake, & Page, 1990). After a period in which they were instructed *not* to think of a particular topic (a white bear), subjects were then told that they *should* think about it; and this resulted in a greater number of thoughts about the previously forbidden topic than was seen in subjects who were encouraged to think about it at the beginning. These findings suggest that attempts at suppression produce a paradoxical rebound effect, with more thoughts than would have occurred if no suppression had been attempted in the first place. One of the difficulties reported by these subjects was that there is no way to instruct oneself *not* to think of a topic, without simultaneously reminding oneself about what that topic is. For this reason, suppression of an unwanted thought is extremely difficult.

According to the authors, the reason for the subsequent rebound was that, after trying and failing to suppress the thought, most subjects tried instead to distract themselves, by thinking of a series of unrelated topics, whenever the forbidden thought came to mind. However this tactic may have the effect of turning each of the unrelated topics into a cue for the forbidden thought, so that later, whenever any of these unrelated topics comes to mind again, the previously suppressed thought comes with it. In support of this idea, it was shown that instructing subjects to use only *one* distracting thought (a red Volkswagen) reduced, or even eliminated, the rebound effect, presumably because there were fewer topics available to cue the previously forbidden thought. If this reasoning can be taken to apply to unwanted emotional thoughts, then the common tendency to use suppression and distraction may actually make the problem worse.

These experimental studies have only been concerned with short-term effects and with artificial thought content (e.g., a white bear, mildly disturbing stories, or thoughts of sex). Most people believe, rightly or wrongly, that they can dismiss or successfully distract themselves from ordinary unwanted thoughts, without then becoming obsessed with them. It is striking, however, that the more intensely emotional a thought or memory is, the more it intrudes into awareness and the more difficult it is to dismiss. In this case, the use of unrelated distracting topics could provide many cues for the unwanted thought. When the thought is cued later on, more emotion will be produced, and the thought more difficult to get rid of again. If so, the more threatening a thought, the less effective distraction would be. Even if it works for mildly disturbing thoughts, distraction may be ineffective or counter-productive for very disturbing thoughts.

What strategy is likely to be effective for very threatening thoughts? The only remaining possibility would seem to be to modify the content of the threat representation itself. As long as its emotional threat value stays high, attempts at distraction will not work, so the representation must be modified in order to reduce the perceived threat. This might require challenging the beliefs involved, or adding some corrective and reassuring information (Foa & Kozak, 1986). Thus, rather than one coping method working best for all levels of threat, it seems possible that mildly threatening thoughts are most economically suppressed using distraction (and this will account for most of our normal experience), while only unusually severe threats will require the more effortful process of modifying threat content.

What are the implications for those who worry excessively and are vulnerable to develop anxiety disorders? The possibility suggested by these considerations is that anxiety prone individuals may be inadvertently increasing the intrusive qualities of their worries, by attempting to use inappropriate distraction methods with highly threatening emotional material. Some self-report data supports this proposal; anxious patients, even after experiencing cognitive-behavioral treatment, reported more use of cognitive distraction, and were less likely to report attempting to face the situation, than were a mixed group of general practice patients (Genest, Bowen, Dudley, & Keegan, 1990).

Memory for Threatening Information

Beyond self-report data, there is another source of evidence supporting the idea that attempted suppression of thoughts about threatening events may occur in anxious individuals. This evidence arises from results suggesting that anxious, relative to non-anxious subjects, do not always recall threatening stimuli as well as they do non-threatening stimuli. Based on the consistent finding that anxiety is associated with increased attention for threatening information, it might be expected that such information should be better represented in memory. In fact, as previously indicated, early attentional bias for threatening information is not incompatible with avoidance of processing at a later stage. However, this alternative way of looking at the issue occurred to us only after we had carried out several experiments on free recall and recognition, with negative results. In the first experiment (Mogg, Mathews, & Weinman, 1987) we compared memory for threatening and non-threatening words in clinically anxious subjects and non-anxious controls. We found no difference between groups for positive words, but paradoxically, results showed a better recall of threatening words in the controls. Several further studies of memory for words and other materials carried out by Mogg (1988) did not confirm this reverse bias but generally failed to show evidence of any consistent differences due to anxiety. One way to explain such failures is to suppose that threatening information may be poorly encoded in memory due to some form of cognitive avoidance, particularly in highly anxious individuals.

If anxious individuals do indeed avoid in some way, then our predictions become less clear-cut. Attention to threats should ensure registration in memory, but ability to recall them also depends on associative links being made with related information in memory. This process of making links in memory with related information will be referred to as elaboration (Mandler, 1980), to distinguish it from distraction, which involves thinking about unrelated topics. The distinction may have important implications, since distraction may lead to uncontrolled intrusions, as we have seen, whereas elaboration may modify the meaning of the encoded information.

Our new hypothesis is that selective attention to threat leads to activation of that information in memory, but because further elaboration of the meaning of the threat is avoided, few associative links are developed with related material, and the meaning of the threat remains unchanged. As a result, it may be difficult for anxious subjects to recall that information voluntarily, but it may recur *involuntarily* in the form of an intrusive thought. To test this idea, we relied on the distinction that has been made between implicit and explicit measures of memory (Roediger, 1990). An example of an implicit measure of memory is the word completion task, in which the subject is presented with a few letters (e.g., att...) and asked to complete them with the first word that comes to mind. Previous exposure to a word makes completion with that word more likely (so the present reader may be more likely to complete "att... " with "attend" rather than "attack", "attain", "attempt" etc.). Unlike free recall, word completion measures do not seem very sensitive to elaboration, but reflect more automatic priming effects. We found that clinically anxious subjects were more likely to complete a three-letter stem with a threatening word, relative to neutral words, while non-anxious controls showed the reverse effect (Mathews, Mogg, May, & Eysenck, 1989). Since this only applied to words that had recently been presented, it does not appear to be a permanent response bias, but instead must reflect the strength of priming, or ease of activation, for threat representations in anxious individuals. Measures of cued recall for the same material showed only a non-significant trend for anxious subjects to recall relatively more threatening words. This pattern of results suggests that the threatening words were producing more activation in anxious subjects, but that this does not always enhance recall. From our perspective, this is because the threat cues were more strongly registered due to selective attention, but less elaborated, due to cognitive avoidance at this later stage of processing.

Studies of recall in normal subjects varying in trait anxiety have produced mixed results. Several have shown no evidence of any recall bias for threatening information, although some have found a mood congruent effect, particularly in autobiographical memory (Richards & Whittaker, 1990). It therefore seems unlikely that anxiety is *never* associated with a memory bias for threatening information; instead, we would claim that whether it is observed or not depends on the way that memory is measured, and the nature of the elaboration, or avoidance of elaboration, that the subject engages in. One reason that autobiographical memory may be more sensitive to mood congruent effects is that complex real-world events may offer more scope for the operation of attentional and interpretative bias during encoding. For example, in a complex ambiguous situation, anxious individuals may attend exclusively to the most negative interpretation, and thus recall the situation as threatening, despite avoiding any further elaboration on its meaning. Non-anxious subjects may be hardly aware of the threatening interpretation in the first place, and so recall the event quite differently.

Conclusions and Implications for Coping Research

To summarize, high levels of anxiety have been shown to be associated with a mode of processing that may serve to increase the intake of threatening information from the environment. When attentional vigilance for threatening cues is compatible with the primary task that subjects are engaged in, performance may be enhanced. More commonly, such attentional vigilance effects are incompatible with the main task that subjects are trying to carry out, so that interference occurs, and performance is slowed or errors increase. Consistent with this bias in favor of external cues signalling threat, it is further suggested that a related bias operates internally so as to favor selection of the more threatening meaning of ambiguous events that can support more than one interpretation.

Despite such vigilance effects in highly anxious subjects, they may still engage in cognitive avoidance strategies. This is possible because the deployment of cognitive resources may vary at different stages of the information processing continuum, with anxious individuals encoding negative emotional aspects at an early attentional stage, but sometimes avoiding further elaborative processing of the threat at a later stage. Although it is still difficult to be certain what the full effects of this combination of vigilant and avoidant processing might be, we would speculate that it may serve to maintain, or even increase anxiety levels. This is because the early attentional bias will ensure that anxiety-prone people are constantly being reminded of possible danger, while their attempts to avoid elaboration may be counter-productive. Even if anxiety can be transiently reduced by avoidance, the strategy may fail with highly emotional material, leading instead to more frequent intrusions of worrying thoughts.

Needless to say, this interpretation of the experimental data is highly speculative. In particular, it remains possible that all the effects documented here are in fact merely secondary consequences of mood state, and have no primary causal role. To establish this would require clearer evidence that high trait (vulnerable) individuals either enter such a vigilant cognitive mode with greater ease or remain vigilant longer under stress, while also tending to use strategies involving avoidance of elaboration; and that increased anxiety results from these cognitive processes rather than vice-versa. None of the existing evidence has succeeded in demonstrating this unequivocally, although there are some suggestive findings.

At the beginning of this chapter it was suggested that research and theory in cognitive coping has raised important questions that need to be answered if further progress is to be made. These questions concern the uncertain validity of self-reports about the coping methods used by an individual, whether such reports can be taken to reflect an enduring style of coping, analogous to a personality trait, and whether it is possible to conclude that the employment of particular coping styles is related to emotional states such as anxiety. Progress has been made in validating some questionnaire measures of repressive coping style by using observable behavioral and physiological indices (Weinberger, 1990). Research in the related field of information-processing biases may offer another, and perhaps more precise way of answering these questions, or of re-casting them in a more testable form.

The research on anxiety that has been reviewed here suggests that a global designation of coping styles as vigilant or avoidant may be an over-simplification. Thus the question of which coping style is best under what conditions needs to be qualified by reference to the stage of processing being considered. Questions about the consistency with which individuals employ vigilant or avoidant processes may be better addressed using measures other than self-report. When a person says that they either want to know more about a possible threat, or to avoid worrying about it, how does this correspond to the actual attention paid to the threat, the meaning that is extracted from it, or the way in which the extracted information is further processed and stored? Experimental studies using information processing methodology offer one way of addressing such otherwise intractable questions.

References

Bargh, J. A. (1982). Attention and automaticity in the processing of self-relevant information. *Journal of Personality and Social Psychology, 43*, 425-436.

Bell, P. A., & Byrne, D. (1978). Repression-sensitization. In H. London & J. E. Exner (Eds.), *Dimensions of personality* (pp. 449-485). New York: Wiley.

Broadbent, D. (1977). The hidden pre-attentive process. *American Psychologist, 32*, 109-118.

Broadbent, D., & Broadbent, M. (1988). Anxiety and attentional bias: State and trait. *Cognition and Emotion, 2*, 165-183.

Cohen, F., & Lazarus, R. S. (1973). Active coping processes, coping dispositions and recovery from surgery. *Psychosomatic Medicine, 35*, 375-389.

Ehlers, A., Margraf, J., Davies, S., & Roth, W. T. (1988). Selective processing of threat cues in subjects with panic attacks. *Cognition and Emotion, 2*, 201-219.

Eysenck, M. W. (1982). *Attention and arousal: Cognition and performance*. Berlin: Springer-Verlag.

Eysenck, M. W., MacLeod, C., & Mathews, A. (1987). Cognitive functioning in anxiety. *Psychological Research, 49*, 189-195.

Eysenck, M. W., Mogg, K., May, J., Richards, A., & Mathews, A. (1991). Bias in interpretation of ambiguous sentences related to threat in anxiety. *Journal of Abnormal Psychology, 100*, 144-150.

Foa, E. B., & Kozak, M. J. (1986). Emotional processing of fear: exposure to corrective information. *Psychological Bulletin, 99*, 20-35.

Foa, E. B., & McNally, R. J. (1986). Sensitivity to feared stimuli in obsessive-compulsives: a dichotic listening analysis. *Cognitive Therapy and Research, 10*, 477-486.

Genest, M., Bowen, R. C., Dudley, J., & Keegan, D. (1990). Assessment of strategies for coping with anxiety: Preliminary investigations. *Journal of Anxiety Disorders, 4*, 1-14.

Gotlib, I. H., & McCann, C. D. (1984). Construct accessibility and depression: an examination of cognitive and affective factors. *Journal of Personality and Social Psychology, 47*, 427-439.

Gray, J. A. (1982). *The neuropsychology of anxiety*. Oxford: Clarendon.

MacLeod, C., & Mathews, A. (1988). Anxiety and the allocation of attention to threat. *Quarterly Journal of Experimental Psychology, 40*, 653-670.

MacLeod, C., Mathews, A., & Tata, P. (1986). Attentional bias in emotional disorders. *Journal of Abnormal Psychology, 95*, 15-20.

Mandler, G. (1980). Recognizing: The judgement of previous occurrence. *Psychological Review. 87*, 252-271.

Martin, M., Williams, R., & Clark, D. M. (1991). Does anxiety lead to selective processing of threat-related information? *Behaviour Research and Therapy, 29*, 147-160.

Mathews, A., & Klug, F. (1991). *Emotionality and interference with color-naming in anxiety.* Manuscript in preparation.

Mathews, A., & MacLeod, C. (1985). Selective processing of threat cues in anxiety states. *Behaviour Research and Therapy, 23*, 563-569.

Mathews, A., & MacLeod, C. (1986). Discrimination of threat cues without awareness in anxiety states. *Journal of Abnormal Psychology, 95*, 131-138.

Mathews, A., May, J., Mogg, K., & Eysenck, M. W. (1990). Attentional bias in anxiety: selective search or defective filtering? *Journal of Abnormal Psychology*, 99, 166-173.

Mathews, A., Mogg, K., May, J., & Eysenck, M. W. (1989). Implicit and explicit memory bias in anxiety. *Journal of Abnormal Psychology, 98*, 236-240.

Mathews, A., Richards, A., & Eysenck, M. W. (1989). The interpretation of homophones related to threat in anxiety states. *Journal of Abnormal Psychology, 98*, 31-34.

Mathews, A., Thomason, B., & Constans, J., (1991). *Effects of stress and trait anxiety on attentional search.* Manuscript in preparation.

Miller, S. M. (1987). Monitoring and blunting: Validation of a questionnaire to assess styles of information seeking under threat. *Journal of Personality and Social Psychology, 52*, 345-353.

Mogg, K. (1988). *Processing of emotional information in clinical anxiety states*. Unpublished doctoral dissertation, University of London.
Mogg, K., Mathews A., Bird, C., & MacGregor-Morris, R. (1990). Effects of stress and anxiety on the processing of threat stimuli. *Journal of Personality and Social Psychology, 59*, 1230-1237.
Mogg, K., Mathews, A., & Eysenck, M. W. (1992). Attentional bias to threat in clinical anxiety states. *Cognition and Emotion, 6*, 149-159.
Mogg, K., Mathews, A., & Weinman, J. (1987). Memory bias in clinical anxiety. *Journal of Abnormal Psychology, 96*, 94-98.
Mogg, K., Mathews, A., & Weinman, J. (1989). Selective processing of threat cues in anxiety states: A replication. *Behaviour Research and Therapy, 27*, 317-323.
Pennebaker, J. W. (1982). *The psychology of physical symptoms*. New York: Springer-Verlag.
Richards A., & Whittaker, T. M. (1990). Effects of anxiety and mood manipulation in autobiographical memory. *British Journal of Clinical Psychology, 29*, 145-154.
Roediger, H. L. (1990). Implicit memory: Retention without remembering. *American Psychologist, 45*, 1043-1056.
Simpson, G. B. (1984). Lexical ambiguity and its role in models of word recognition. *Psychological Bulletin, 96*, 316-340.
Tversky, A., & Kahneman, D. (1973). Availability: A heuristic for judging frequency and probability. *Cognitive Psychology, 5*, 207-232.
Watts, F. N., McKenna, F. P., Sharrock, R., & Trezise, L. (1986). Colour naming of phobia related words. *British Journal of Psychology, 77*, 97-108.
Wegner, D. M., Schneider, D. J., Carter, S. R., & White, T. L. (1987). Paradoxical effects of thought suppression. *Journal of Personality and Social Psychology, 53*, 5-13.
Wegner, D. M., Shortt, J. W., Blake, A. W., & Page, M. S. (1990). The suppression of exciting thoughts. *Journal of Personality and Social Psychology, 58*, 409-418.
Weinberger, D. A. (1990). The construct validity of the repressive coping style. In J. L. Singer (Ed.), *Repression and dissociation. Implications for personality theory, psychopathology, and health* (pp. 337-386). Chicago: University of Chicago Press.
Wenzlaff, R., Wegner, D. M., & Roper, D. (1988). Depression and mental control: The resurgence of unwanted negative thoughts. *Journal of Personality and Social Psychology, 55*, 882-892.
Williams, J. M. G., & Broadbent, K. (1986). Distraction by emotional stimuli: Use of a stroop task with suicide attempters. *British Journal of Clinical Psychology, 25*, 101-110.

PART III.

THE PROCESSING OF EXTERNAL AND SOMATIC INFORMATION

Chapter 7

Coping Dispositions, Attentional Direction, and Anxiety States

Michael Hock

Introduction

The theoretical models of individual differences in anxiety and coping outlined in this volume by Krohne; Mathews; and Miller, Combs, and Kruus mark a departure from the classical unidimensional conceptualization of approach and avoidance in personality and clinical research which was proposed, for example, in the construct repression-sensitization (see Bell & Byrne, 1978; Eriksen, 1966; Krohne, in press; Weinberger, 1990, for overviews). Instead of assuming an exclusive operation of approach versus avoidance, the possibility of a detached functioning of these behavior modes both across and within persons is advocated. This becomes apparent in the notion of habitual differences regarding an individual's ability to flexibly accommodate coping behavior to the opportunities and constraints inherent in different types of aversive situations, a process discussed by Krohne, Chapter 2 in this volume, and Miller et al., this volume. This is also evident in Mathews' (this volume) conception of the cognitive mechanisms underlying trait anxiety which involve approach toward as well as avoidance of threat-related information operative at different stages of processing.

The hypothesis of an independent variation of approach and avoidance, considered on both state and trait levels, has substantial implications for conceiving the role dispositional (as well as situational) factors play as determinants of anxiety states during aversive encounters. Krohne explicitly characterizes high-anxious individuals by a conflict between strong action impulses of approach *and* avoidance, leading to an unstable, fluctuating, and thereby anxiety-augmenting, rather than anxiety-reducing, coping behavior in threatening situations. Mathews specifies the process leading to and stabilizing anxiety in such persons as a combination of automatically and involuntarily activated approach toward threatening aspects of situations, followed by strategic, motivated, but only partially effective and possibly even counterproductive attempts at avoiding threat-relevant material.

The studies described in this chapter represent initial attempts to empirically address how coping dispositions are implied in the mutual dependencies of

---

I thank Jochen Hardt and Robert Schaffer for their assistance in conducting the studies.

actual emotion and cognitive coping processes. To tackle this question, there is an obvious need for establishing methods which allow for a continuous tracking of behavioral indicators of emotional and attentional changes within persons. Regarding attention, the looking behavior of individuals, directed toward or away from a source of threatening information, provides a promising starting point.

Based on assumptions of the "model of coping modes" (Krohne, 1978, 1986, 1989, and Chapter 2 in this volume), looking behavior is discussed as an indicator of attention orientation in socially threatening situations. Special emphasis is given to the notion of a two-fold function of gaze: first, as an integral part of a person's "warning system" and, second, as an important "arousal regulation device". Two studies directed at analyzing dispositional determinants of looking at or away from a source of threat are subsequently described. The last section of this chapter covers interindividual differences in the sequential relationships between looking behavior (an indicator of attention) and bodily arousal (an indicator of emotion) during the anticipation of a potentially aversive event.

Vigilance and Cognitive Avoidance

The model of coping modes considers attentional changes which are elicited when an individual is confronted with threat-related cues. When describing these changes, the constructs cognitive avoidance and vigilance are regarded to be of central importance (cf. Roth & Cohen, 1986; Suls & Fletcher, 1985). *Cognitive avoidance* denotes the diversion of attention from stimuli associated with threat. *Vigilance*, in contrast, is characterized by an intensified intake and processing of threatening information. According to the core thesis of the model, persons differ habitually regarding the degree to which both behavior tendencies are activated in anxiety-evoking situations. Since the extent of cognitive avoidant and vigilant impulses is viewed to vary independently (either one, both, or none can be present, i.e., strongly activated, in an individual), four configurations are distinguished. These become apparent in different *types* of immediate reactions following the partial identification of threat (directing attention toward or away from the source of information) and different *time courses* of attentional orientation (being either stable or variable) during the further development of an aversive encounter. Four habitually determined behavior patterns ("coping modes") are postulated: stable cognitive avoidance (strong activation of avoidant tendencies, weak activation of vigilant ones; this mode is called "repression"), stable vigilance (strong vigilant, weak avoidant tendencies; "sensitization"), unstable behavior oscillating between approach and avoidance (strong avoidance and strong vigilance; "high anxiety"), and a low tendency to manifest either a pronounced vigilant or avoidant type of reaction ("nondefensiveness").

These behavior patterns are assumed to be rooted in the differential susceptibility of individuals to two processes (or *feeling states*) which are conceived as constituents of emerging anxiety states: the *perception of bodily (emotional) arousal* and the *experience of uncertainty*. According to the model, an increased irritation caused by emotional arousal primarily stimulates cognitive avoidance of threatening information. The exclusion of such information from being noticed or fully processed is aimed at restraining or inhibiting actual or anticipated increments of emotionality. The experience of uncertainty as the primary problem, on the other hand, is assumed to be associated with vigilant action impulses. Vigilance is conceptualized as a behavioral measure which reduces or limits uncertainty. By employing vigilance, for example, a state of being surprised by suddenly appearing negative events can often be prevented. Essential for the model is the supposition that the "disturbances" caused by emotional arousal and uncertainty cannot, in general, both be attenuated at the same time. Although avoidance of threatening information may temporarily reduce an unpleasant condition of bodily activation, it is in many cases connected with an elevated state of uncertainty which becomes particularly evident in dynamic, continuously developing action fields. The intensified and prolonged intake of danger-related information may reduce uncertainty or even abolish it in the long run. The common cost of vigilance, however, is a heightened emotionality, especially in the case of long-lasting encounters, in which a rapid clarification of the situational consequences cannot be achieved. Thus, persons who preferably use either an avoidant or a vigilant mode of dealing with threat can stabilize their behavior only to the extent to which they are able to withstand the accumulating side effects of their respective attentional biases.

Following this reasoning, the manifestation of coping modes is assumed to be based on systematic differences regarding a person's ability to tolerate feelings of uncertainty and emotional arousal. The configuration "high intolerance of emotional arousal/high tolerance of uncertainty" should lead to a repressive mode of coping (stable avoidance). For sensitizers (stable vigilance), the opposite pattern is postulated (high intolerance of uncertainty, high tolerance of emotional arousal). High-anxious individuals (high vigilance and avoidance) are characterized by pronounced and about equally strong intolerance as regards both uncertainty and emotional arousal. These persons should experience a marked conflict resulting in an unstable coping behavior. Subjects who are able to tolerate increases in uncertainty and emotional arousal to a larger extent should exhibit low preferences for vigilant and cognitive avoidant strategies (nondefensives). They should therefore be able to more flexibly attune their coping behavior to the requirements of an aversive situation (see Krohne, Chapter 2, this volume, for details).

Looking Behavior in Anxiety-Evoking Interaction Situations

To empirically investigate the hypothesized links between anxiety and attentional reactions, methods have to be developed which allow for an assessment of variations in arousal and attentional direction over time. Up to now, however, most paradigms used to study attentional processes in anxiety and coping research have only provided measures which are aggregated over observations of a large number of responses in an experimental setting (e.g., reaction time data; see Mathews, this volume). Although these approaches do supply useful information about attentional mechanisms involved in the cognitive processing of threat-relevant material in different persons, they should be complemented by operations which allow for a continuous tracking of changes in attentional direction during an aversive encounter. It will be argued that gaze directed toward or away from a source of threat, observed during the anticipation period of an aversive event, could serve as a foundation for such a methodology.

My discussion of the looking behavior in anxiety-evoking situations will be limited to socially threatening situations. More specifically, dyadic interaction situations are considered, in which one of the interactants serves as a source of threat and the other is exposed to it. One part of the research concerning this issue relied on naturally occurring variations in the aversiveness of one of the interactants and involved the observation of the visual exchange between mother and child in mildly stress-inducing situations (cf. Hock & Krohne, in press). The other research, on which I will focus here, tried to experimentally manipulate the degree of threat inherent in one interactant's behavior.

The looking behavior in anxiety-evoking interaction situations is relevant from two perspectives: first, as a component of *information search* and, second, as an instrument of *arousal regulation*. Rutter and Stephenson (1979) noted that empirical and theoretical analyses in nonverbal communication research tended to neglect the informative function of gaze in favor of emphasizing its expressive function, i.e., the communication of emotions, attitudes, etc. The visual interaction was primarily viewed as an affective phenomenon; in contrast, the role of looking as a method of gaining information was ignored or considered to be trivial.

The *informative* function of gaze can be analyzed from at least three viewpoints:

1. As an integral part of the receiver's attentional orientation toward the sender during a communication, gaze contributes to *optimizing the transmission of information*. Correspondingly, the sender's looking serves to channel control as well as test the receiver's states as regards, for example, the readiness to take in information or the capacity to process information presented. This elementary aspect of information transmission is also essential with respect to the synchronization and regulation of verbal communication (Scherer, 1979).

2. In the present context, however, another aspect of looking is more important: the information conveyed about the partner's *evaluation of one's own behavior*. The detection of changes in the other's face, especially in the area of the eyes and the mouth, is of central significance in this aspect of looking. The monitoring of the partner's mimic reactions, which Efran (1968; cf. Efran & Broughton, 1966) interpreted as "looking for approval", delivers

instantaneously available feedback relating to the partner's evaluations of an interactant's ongoing behavior.

3. A third crucial facet of looking is closely connected to its feedback function: Gaze plays an important role with regard to the *anticipatory adaptation to changes in the other's behavior*. The encoding as well as decoding of visual information (such as expressive communications) are more rapid than verbal transmission processes. This enables individuals to modify their own behavior before the partner's reaction occurs or is fully established. A quick adaptation to anticipated reactions is not only relevant in view of an economical organization of verbal communication, but also with respect to preparing for possible aversive events that may occur. The partner's aversive appraisal of one's own behavior will frequently manifest itself initially in certain changes in facial expressions. Even if the occurrence of aversive acts signalled by these changes cannot be prevented, individuals who monitor the other's face are at least able to adjust themselves to the impending event and to modify its impact with preparatory reactions.

The function of gaze as a *means of arousal regulation* in social interactions is addressed, among others, in studies of mother-infant interactions. Stern (1974), for example, points to the role of gaze behavior as an instrument available at an early age for the self-regulation of physiological states. Stern notes that "the visual-motor system reaches functional maturity by the third month of life, a point in development when other motor behaviors are relatively less mature" (p. 188). The control of visual perception thus allows the infant to regulate his or her internal state within a given range. This function, which becomes particularly evident in certain play activities between mother and child, points to early precursors of coping phenomena (cf. Ainsworth, Blehar, Waters, & Wall, 1978; Grossmann & Grossmann, 1986).

The role played by gaze in regulating arousal in social interactions is also addressed by models which consider the regulation of the "psychological distance" in interpersonal interactions. Empirical research in this area was mainly inspired by Argyle and Dean's (1965) "equilibrium model" (cf. Hale & Burgoon, 1984). This model postulates that dyads, in the course of their interaction, develop an equilibrium level of immediacy, constituted by factors such as gaze, touch, facial expressions, body orientation, etc. If this optimum level is exceeded because of intervening processes which induce changes in one or more of these variables, such as when the intimacy of the communication becomes too great, anxiety is aroused and acts as a motivating force to reinstate equilibrium by making compensatory changes in other immediacy behaviors, e.g., lowering eye contact.

According to the equilibrium model, a heightened state of anxiety will influence gaze only in one direction, namely negatively. However, more complex associations have to be assumed in the model of coping modes. An enhanced as well as a lowered amount of looking can serve to reduce anxiety states. Whereas averting gaze can be assumed to be primarily aimed at reducing perceived bodily arousal, a heightened amount of looking seems to be appropriate in reducing uncertainty. Since this differentiation has not been taken into consideration until now, results of studies concerning relationships between looking behavior and anxiety are inconsistent.

Hobson, Strongman, Bull, and Craig (1973) failed to find differences in gaze behavior in an interaction between a subject and a confederate as a function of anxiety state (manipulated by different kinds of evaluative feedback, Study 1) or trait differences (Study 2). Regarding the negative results of Study 1, it is noteworthy that feedback was not given by the partner who served as the "target" person for measuring visual exchange but by a third individual. For the present purposes this point is of special importance because the assessment of actual avoidance and vigilance implies that the individual has access to threatening information. In using gaze as an indicator of approach and avoidance tendencies in dyadic interactions, this is only the case when the partner functions as the source of threat. In the interview situation realized in Study 2, the interviewer consistently showed signs of disapproval toward the subject's statements, a procedure aimed at enhancing differences between low- and high-anxious persons. Results found by Wiens, Harper, and Matarazzo (1980), however, suggest that the *clear communication of aversiveness* realized in the Hobson et al. study may well have overridden trait differences which may become apparent in more *ambiguous* threat situations. Wiens et al. varied stress in a conversation by increasing the interviewer's (confederate) answer latencies from less than one second (which corresponds to normal conditions) to 15 seconds, thus inducing speech pauses which are usually experienced as very uncomfortable. Under this condition, which may effectively induce a state of uncertainty in the interviewee, high-anxious individuals manifested an enhanced amount of looking at the confederate.

In two studies reported by Slane, Dragan, Crandall, and Payne (1980), the looking behavior manifested by repressers and sensitizers was registered under different levels and types of stress during an interview. In Study 1 repressers were found to spend more time looking at an interviewer than sensitizers, irregardless of stress condition (variations in the expected content of the interview, being either highly personal or neutral). In Study 2 the stress manipulation was intensified. In addition, a longer waiting period between stress induction and the interaction was introduced. Differences between groups were found only for the second half of the interaction. Contrary to Study 1, repressers maintained less eye contact than sensitizers. These conflicting results are interpreted in terms of the joint operation of information gathering and emotion communication functions of gaze, each becoming effective at different time points during the interaction. The shorter break between stress manipulation and interview as well as the shorter length of the interaction realized in Study 1 could have confined the measurement of gaze to the period prior to the point when looking fully reflected stress (which should be accompanied by decreases of gaze for repressers).

Two difficulties inherent in the Slane et al. studies should be mentioned: First, in Study 1, gaze behavior was measured using an estimate given by the confederate. The reliability of this unusual assessment procedure is questionable. Second, since the investigators were also interested in personal space as a dependent variable, the distance between subject and confederate could be chosen freely by the subject. Unfortunately, distance is a critical variable in determining amount of gaze (cf. Kleinke, 1986, for an overview). Whereas in Study 1 no significant differences in personal space used by repressers and sensitizers emerged, in Study 2 repressers chose to stand nearer to the confederate. Differences in looking behavior could therefore be partly due to differences in personal space.

To summarize, besides the presence or accessibility of threat-related information and the time schedule characteristic for an encounter, the ambiguity of the situation seems to play a major role regarding the manifestation of coping dispositions and anxiety in actual looking behavior. For trait differences to become apparent, an at least moderate degree of uncertainty with respect to the meaning of a communication or the consequences of a situation seems to be necessary.

Experimental Investigations

Study 1

Hypotheses

Study 1 aimed at assessing relationships between dispositional preferences (vigilance, cognitive avoidance), actual anxiety, and attentional orientation in an ambiguous situation involving different degrees of threat. To achieve this, an interaction situation was realized which was similar to an oral examination. Subjects were given either positive or negative feedback regarding their performance after a "practice period" which consisted of a series of tasks supposed to measure spatial abilities. In the subsequent "test period", tasks of the same type were administered after which the subjects expected further evaluative feedback. By administering either positive or negative feedback, the aversiveness of the confederate's behavior, which in this study served as a source of threat, should vary.

The main hypotheses concerned associations between coping dispositions and gaze behavior manifested by the subjects. Highly vigilant persons should monitor the "examiner's" face more continuously and more frequently in order to obtain clues which might help to reduce ambiguity inherent in the confederate's behavior. For highly avoidant subjects the opposite should be true: Since avoiders are primarily concerned with regulating emotional arousal, they should look at the examiner less continuously and less extensively. The conflict between approach and avoidance, which is assumed to characterize high-anxious individuals, should result in an enhanced variability of looking at the examiner. This manifests itself in frequent but comparatively short gazes. Due to low tolerances regarding uncertainty *and* emotional arousal, as soon as one of these tendencies is realized as a concrete vigilant or avoidant act, respectively, the other one is aroused and becomes prevalent very quickly.

Since the negative evaluation was assumed to lead to a comparatively strong anxiety arousal, differences between groups were expected to be more pronounced under conditions of negative as compared to positive feedback.

Method

Forty-four female students had to estimate the volume of irregularly shaped objects which they could feel but not see. The objects to be judged were handed out to the subjects by a confederate of the same sex who also removed them after the estimate was verbalized. The experiment was divided into two parallel periods, each lasting five minutes. The first period was declared the "practice period", the second the "test period". After having completed the practice period, half of the subjects were praised for their performance and encouraged to carry on in the same way. The other half were criticized; they were told that their judgments had been very wrong up to that point and that they should try to do better in the subsequent test period.

The confederate was unaware of the real intention of the experiment. She was informed that the study was aimed at investigating changes in performance after different types of evaluative feedback. The looking behavior of the confederate was standardized: She alternately looked at or away from the face of the subject for periods of five seconds each. A change in gaze direction was signalled to her via a computer monitor placed at the side of the table, so that the subjects could not see the screen. (The screen became bright when the confederate had to look at the subject and dark when she had to look away. This type of signal was easily discernible even from the corner of the eye.) The confederate was also given instructions on this monitor about the kind of feedback to deliver after the practice period was over.

Subject and confederate sat in front of each other (distance: 80 cm) at a table on which a box was placed. This box, which contained the objects to be estimated, was open on the confederate's side. On the subjects' side, the box had two openings to which sleeves had been attached and through which the subjects had to put their hands. In this way it was guaranteed that the subjects were not able to inform themselves visually about the object. The volume of the objects ranged from 2 to 120 ml. Before the start of the practice and test periods, subjects were given three reference objects.

Approach and avoidance tendencies were operationally defined as the change from practice to test period in frequency and amount (total time) of gaze directed at the confederate's face (test relative to practice period). The looking behavior was coded by an observer in a separate room via a one-way mirror. Worry cognitions (e.g., "I remembered other test situations in which I performed poorly") and perceived bodily arousal (e.g., "I was nervous") were assessed for the test period after the task was completed (cf. Morris, Davis, & Hutchings, 1981). As an objective measure of arousal, the eye-blink rate (coded from videotapes) was included. (In this case, change values were again computed.) Dispositional coping tendencies were measured by the Mainz Coping Inventory (MCI; see Krohne, 1989). As observed in previous studies (see Krohne, Chapter 2, this volume, for an overview), the scores on the vigilance and cognitive avoidance scale of this inventory varied independently ($r = -.26$ in Study 1, $r = -.04$ in Study 2, both coefficients are nonsignificant).

Correspondingly, these scales were median dichotomized and, hence, formed the levels "high" and "low". A three-way ANOVA of each dependent measure was carried out which involved type of feedback, vigilance, and cognitive avoidance as between-subject factors. If interactive effects between the dispositional variables are present, I will refer to the respective groups as nondefensives (low avoidance, low vigilance), sensitizers (low avoidance, high vigilance), repressers (high avoidance, low vigilance), and high-anxious persons (high avoidance, high vigilance).

Results and discussion

The experimental variation of the degree of stress induced by administering either positive or negative feedback after the practice period seemed to be effective, since subjective (worry, emotionality, $p < .001$) as well as objective (eye-blink frequency, $p < .10$) indicators of arousal were enhanced after negative feedback as compared to positive feedback. These general effects of type of feedback, however, were qualified by significant interactions involving coping dispositions.

With *emotionality* as the dependent variable, an interaction between feedback condition and cognitive avoidance was established, $F(1,36) = 6.38$, $p = .02$: With respect to perceived bodily arousal, high avoiders were found to be affected by the variation of feedback more than low avoiders (Figure 7.1).

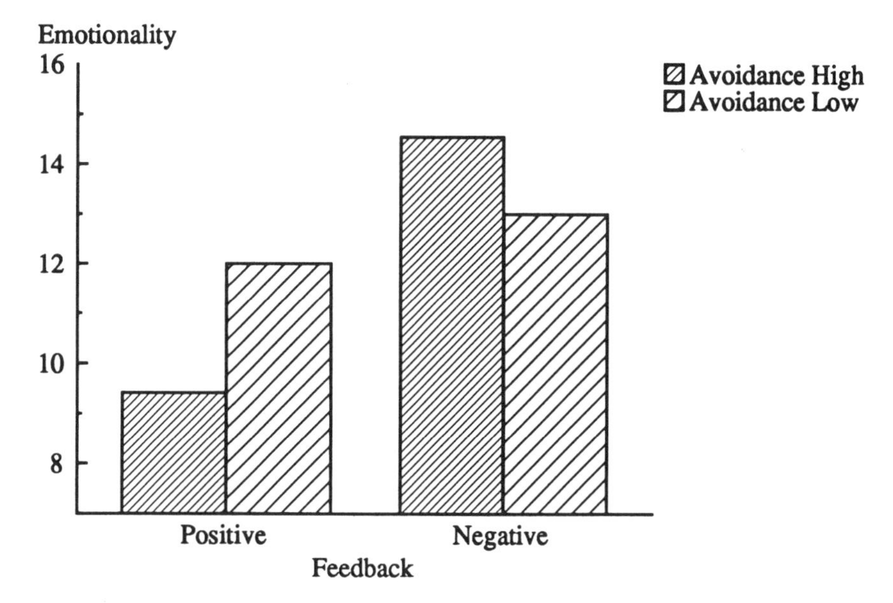

Figure 7.1. Emotionality as a function of dispositional avoidance and type of feedback.

After receiving negative feedback, high avoiders reported more emotional arousal than low avoiders. Apparently, intolerance of emotional arousal, which according to the model of coping modes underlies dispositional avoidance tendencies, manifests itself in an intensified experience of emotional symptoms when an aversive event is expected. Following positive feedback, however, high avoiders manifested a considerably lower level of emotionality which differed significantly from that of low avoiders. Obviously, positive feedback makes cues available which enable especially high avoiders to effectively prevent or reduce states of unpleasant arousal. In this case the cognitive coping operations preferred by those subjects are supported by the situation as it strengthens the expectancy that no aversive event will actually occur.

In interpreting this effect, which is specifically concerned with emotional arousal (not worry), different subprocesses connected with dispositional avoidance are assumed: 1. In stressful situations, high avoiders are primarily affected by the emotional component of anxiety. - 2. Avoiders therefore prefer to realize coping behaviors which tackle this source of discomfort. Both processes obviously have specific consequences as regards the time course of emotional arousal. When *intraindividual* changes in arousal level are considered, a heightened susceptibility of avoiders should manifest itself in a

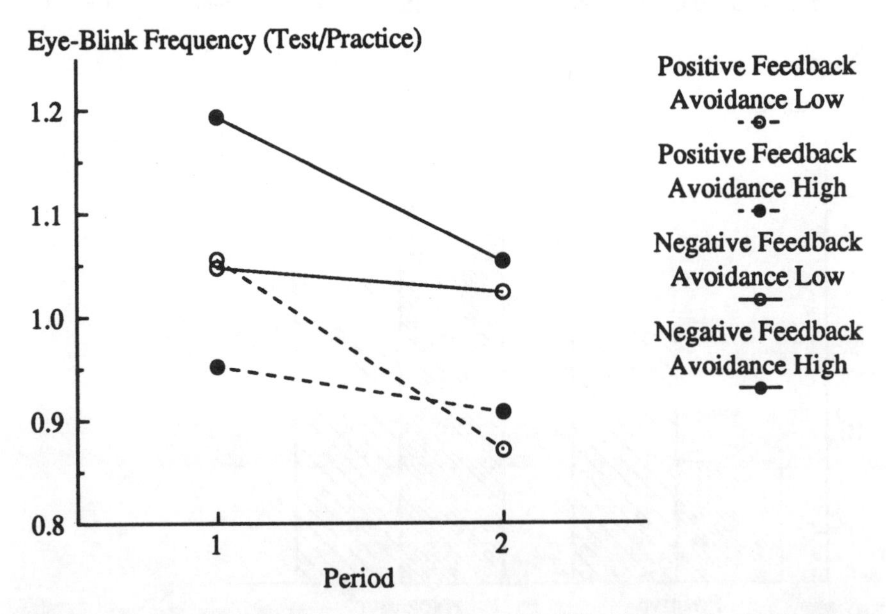

Figure 7.2. Eye-blink frequency (test divided by practice period) as a function of dispositional avoidance and type of feedback in the first and the second half of the test period.

pronounced reaction following the first contact with threatening cues. As the episode progresses, this change in arousal should be dampened by cognitively avoidant operations which are released or enhanced when the emotion is experienced. A separation of different aspects of this process is only possible via a multitemporal assessment of anxiety and actual coping behavior.

In order to collect clues regarding the operation of both hypothesized component processes, the *course of the eye-blink frequency* during the test period was analyzed. For this purpose the test period was subdivided into two halves, each lasting 150 seconds. Besides a strong main effect of the within-subject factor "subperiod", $F(1,36) = 8.44$, $p = .006$, indicating a general decline in eye-blink rate from the first to the second half of the test period, an interaction involving cognitive avoidance, feedback condition, and subperiod emerged, $F(1,36) = 3.26$, $p = .08$ (Figure 7.2). Following negative feedback, avoiders manifested a strong increase in eye-blink rate. Their eye-blink frequency was 19% above their level during the practice period. The corresponding changes for the other combinations were less marked, ranging from -4% to +5%. However, as the experiment progressed, there was a decrease with avoiders nearly approaching their baseline level as well as that of low avoiders after negative feedback. There was also a pronounced decrease in eye-blink frequency for low avoiders following positive feedback.

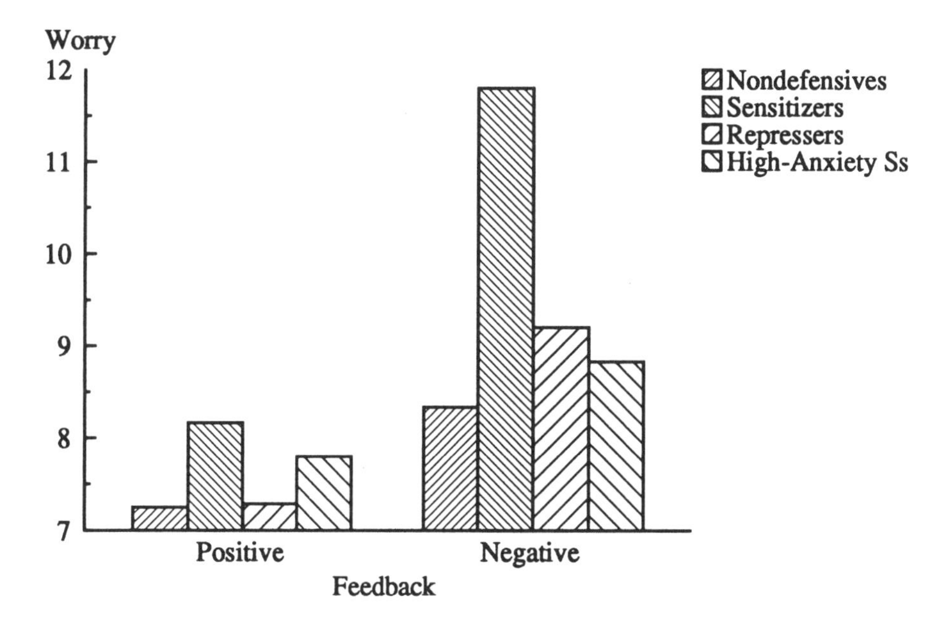

Figure 7.3. Worry as a function of coping mode and type of feedback.

With *worry* as the dependent variable, a main effect of vigilance, $F(1,36) = 5.53$, $p = .02$, as well as interactions involving vigilance and avoidance, $F(1,36) = 4.83$, $p = .03$, and vigilance, avoidance, and type of feedback, $F(1,36) = 3.17$, $p = .08$, were found (Figure 7.3). A difference between feedback conditions was generally present, but it was largely enhanced for sensitizers (vigilance high, avoidance low). This confirms the assumption that sensitizers are affected to a great extent by the degree of ambiguity inherent in threatening situations. This ambiguity primarily manifests itself in the experimental situation as the subject's uncertainty regarding the performance evaluation to be expected.

As regards the relationships between dispositions, situation, and *parameters of gaze*, no significant effects were found. Sensitizers *and* repressers manifested only a tendency to look more frequently at the examiner under conditions of negative feedback. Contrary to expectations, however, this difference was the highest for repressers.

Regarding *gaze duration*, which was the central variable in this study, no significant associations with coping dispositions could be established. With respect to dispositional vigilance, this negative result could be related to the fact that the subjects were not able to extract information from the examiner's behavior which would have allowed them to make conclusions about their level of performance. This could result in a certain number of vigilant persons refraining from an intensification of monitoring behavior after negative feedback. Since such a behavior would be incongruent with the dispositional preferences of those individuals, it should be connected with a heightened state of anxiety (cf. Kohlmann, 1990). An analysis with the median-dichotomized amount of gaze as an additional independent variable revealed an interaction of vigilance, amount of gaze, and type of feedback, $F(1,36) = 4.20$, $p = .05$. Highly vigilant individuals who tended to avert their gaze from the examiner (*incongruent vigilant persons*) did indeed manifest a pronounced degree of worry cognitions after negative feedback and differed significantly from all other groups (nonvigilants as well as vigilant subjects who enhanced their monitoring behavior, cf. Figure 7.4).

This finding can be tentatively interpreted as supporting the idea that gaze duration is an indicator of an actual coping process: Dispositionally vigilant persons who manifest a looking behavior according to their disposition are able to reduce the activation of worry cognitions which would otherwise appear. However, this result by no means provides conclusive evidence, since one can reasonably argue for other relationships which are also consistent with this result. For example, a high degree of anxiety could have inhibited the employment of actual vigilant behavior, i.e., a closer visual orientation toward the examiner. (This possibility, however, would perhaps be more plausible, if bodily arousal - in addition to or instead of worry - had been enhanced in incongruent vigilant subjects.)

The variation of feedback seems to be primarily appropriate for introducing differing levels of threat intensity. In contrast, the degree of ambiguity inherent in the situation remained at the same comparatively high level. This suggests an

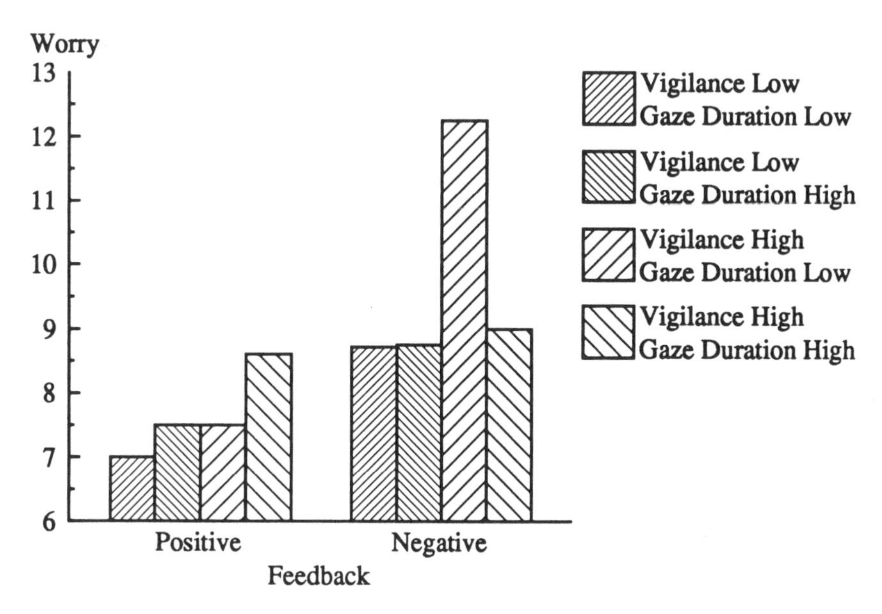

Figure 7.4. Worry as a function of dispositional vigilance, amount of gaze, and type of feedback.

extension of the design realized in this study so that it covers different levels of threat intensity as well as different levels of ambiguity. Intensity of threat may be varied - as it was done here - by using different types of feedback. Different levels of ambiguity can be realized, for example, by employing different schedules of feedback. It is this possibility which was realized in a second experiment.

Study 2

Hypotheses

Study 2 aimed at realizing an experimental situation which should allow certain aspects of aversiveness and ambiguity involved in threatening situations to be untangled. To accomplish this, the general framework of Study 1 was changed by varying two situational between-subject factors independently, namely, type of feedback (either positive or negative) and schedule of feedback (either fixed or variable). Subjects assigned to the fixed-ratio schedule were aware of the time of feedback. Subjects in the variable-ratio condition did not know when feedback would be delivered. By again giving either positive or negative feedback, varying degrees of threat originating from the examiner's behavior should have been induced. By administering feedback either according to a fixed- or a variable-ratio schedule, a specific aspect of ambiguity should vary, namely, the predictability of the time when a possibly aversive event (negative feedback) is about to occur.

Since dispositional vigilance is assumed to be based on intolerance of uncertainty and negative surprise, it was hypothesized that individuals scoring high or low on this dimension should differ in their anxiety reaction primarily according to the reinforcement schedule they were confronted with. Vigilant persons should manifest strong anxiety arousal when they were uncertain about the time of feedback and lower reactions when time of feedback was predictable. Corresponding differences were expected for gaze directed at the experimenter. Highly vigilant individuals should look at the experimenter more extensively and more continuously under conditions of uncertainty in order to (a) possibly extract information regarding their own performance (based, for example, on mimic reactions) and/or (b) be better prepared for negative events which could perhaps occur (e.g., by checking whether feedback would be given or not). With respect to differences between high and low avoiders, the variation of type of feedback should have the greatest impact. For high avoiders, negative feedback should be the main source of discomfort. They should therefore manifest comparatively strong anxiety reactions and an accordingly higher degree of gaze aversion under this condition.

Method

Eighty-eight male students served as subjects and were confronted with a male examiner. Twenty-two participants were randomly assigned to each of the four cells defined by the two between-subject factors (type of feedback: positive vs. negative; schedule of feedback: fixed vs. variable). Subjects were told that the study was aimed at assessing physiological and cognitive reactions during a test and that it was especially directed at measuring certain aspects of spatial abilities, in particular, the capacity of individuals to learn from feedback about performance level. As in the first study, subjects were instructed that they had to "blindly" estimate the volume of objects. In order to prevent extreme judgments directed at testing the appropriateness of feedback, subjects were told that the objects varied in volume from 100 to 200 ml. (Note that this was not necessary in Study 1, in which feedback was given only once.) The subjects were then instructed that three practice trials would be started in which they received feedback after each estimate. This feedback would be given in terms of their performance being "above average" or "below average" as compared to the performance of a reference group which had undergone a similar test in a previous study. It was emphasized that the feedback always concerned each respective estimate (not, for example, their average level of performance observed throughout the trials).

During the practice trials, subjects *constantly* received either positive or negative feedback according to the experimental condition to which they were assigned. The practice trials thus served to induce expectancies about the performance level of an individual. In addition, subjects should have become accustomed to the time schedule realized in the experiment.

The beginning of a trial was marked by a faint, low-pitched acoustic signal generated by the computer which controlled the course of the session. Following this signal, the object to be estimated was handed out to the subject by the experimenter. Ten seconds after the start of the trial, a second higher-pitched acoustic signal was given, after which the subjects had to immediately verbalize their estimates. The experimenter then registered the estimate using the computer keyboard in front of him. Four seconds after the second signal, the experimenter was informed via a monitor placed at the side of the table which type of feedback - either "positive" or "negative" or "no feedback" - should be given to the subject. Six seconds after feedback, the next trial was started, so that each trial lasted 20 seconds. With the exception of the time needed for entering the estimates and receiving instructions regarding which feedback to give, the experimenter constantly looked at the subjects.

Having completed the practice trials, there was a short break of 20 seconds during which the subjects in the fixed-ratio condition were truthfully informed that they were given feedback after every third estimate. Subjects of the variable-ratio condition were also truthfully instructed that feedback was administered according to a random plan determined by the computer controlling the experiment. The amount of feedback delivered to each subject was held constant, so that in each condition feedback was given in four out of 12 trials. In this study, a more precise measurement of gaze was possible, achieved by tracking the videotaped looking behavior "frame by frame". As an objective indicator of arousal, heart rate was measured continuously throughout the experimental setting.

Results and discussion

Subjective data. Under conditions of high ambiguity (variable-ratio schedule), *emotionality* was significantly enhanced, $F(1,72) = 4.26$, $p = .04$. In addition, a significant interaction between dispositional avoidance and vigilance was found, $F(1,72) = 6.38$, $p = .01$: Repressers and sensitizers generally reported higher bodily reactions than the other modes. On the whole, sensitizers were found to react most intensively.

Whereas emotionality was associated only with the schedule of feedback, *worry* was influenced only by type of feedback, $F(1,72) = 34.72$, $p < .001$. Worry cognitions were considerably enhanced after negative feedback. A marginally significant main effect of vigilance, $F(1,72) = 3.25$, $p = .08$, indicated that highly vigilant individuals tended to experience more worry during the session.

As regards the subjective data, the hypothesis concerning a differential susceptibility of avoidant and vigilant persons by type and time schedule of feedback, respectively, was not confirmed. The clear and specific effects that type and schedule of feedback exerted on different anxiety components confirm Liebert and Morris' (1967) assumption that emotionality primarily reflects the immediate uncertainty of a test-taking situation, whereas worry is related mainly to expectancies of success or failure (see also Sarason, 1984; Wine, 1982).

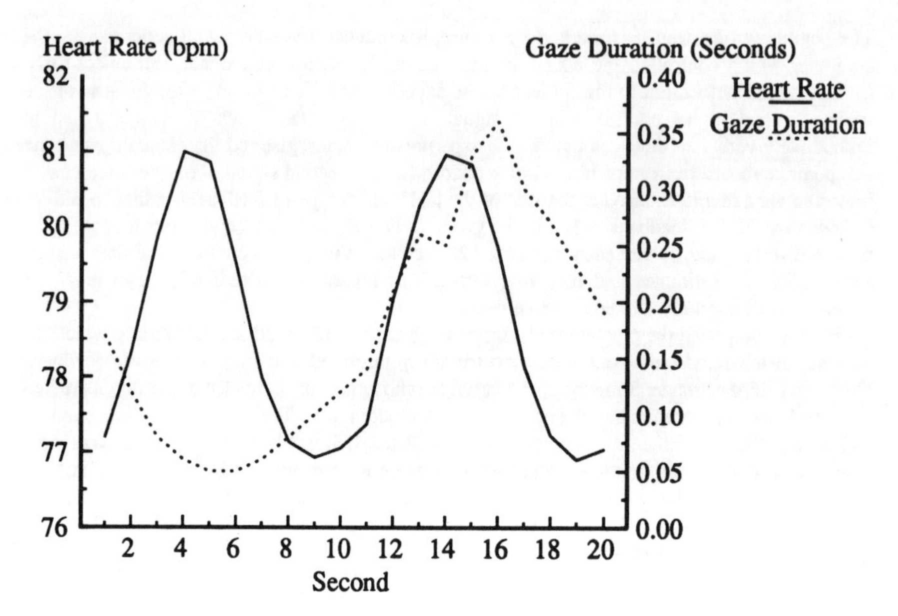

Figure 7.5. Second-by-second heart rate and gaze duration during a trial (averaged over all trials and experimental conditions).

Objective data. The general course of the objective variables is depicted in Figure 7.5. *Gaze* was found to be concentrated in the seconds around feedback, especially immediately after feedback. To analyze the gaze behavior two adjacent periods, each lasting four seconds, were considered. Period 1 covered those seconds immediately after the subjects had given their estimates and were awaiting feedback (seconds 11 to 14 of each trial). This period will be called "anticipation". Period 2 started when feedback was administered and will be labelled "confrontation" (seconds 15 to 18). These periods were entered as a repeated-measurement factor into the ANOVAs. Because the number of trials in which feedback was given differed from those without (4 vs. 8), separate analyses for both classes of trials were carried out.

For *feedback trials*, the type by period interaction, $F(1,72) = 4.54, p = .04$, as well as the schedule by period interaction, $F(1,72) = 4.21$, $p = .04$, reached significance. Regarding *no-feedback trials*, the main effect of schedule, $F(1,72) = 4.01$, $p = .05$, and the type by schedule by period interaction, $F(1,72) = 4.45$, $p = .04$, were significant (see Figure 7.6). During anticipation high ambiguity (variable-ratio) was associated with a comparatively close visual orientation toward the examiner, especially when positive expectancies had been induced. In *no-feedback trials*, gaze strongly increased from the point of anticipation to confrontation under the condition of high ambiguity (variable-ratio) and negative feedback. Also remarkable was the fact that persons in the condition high ambiguity/positive feedback, in contrast to all other groups,

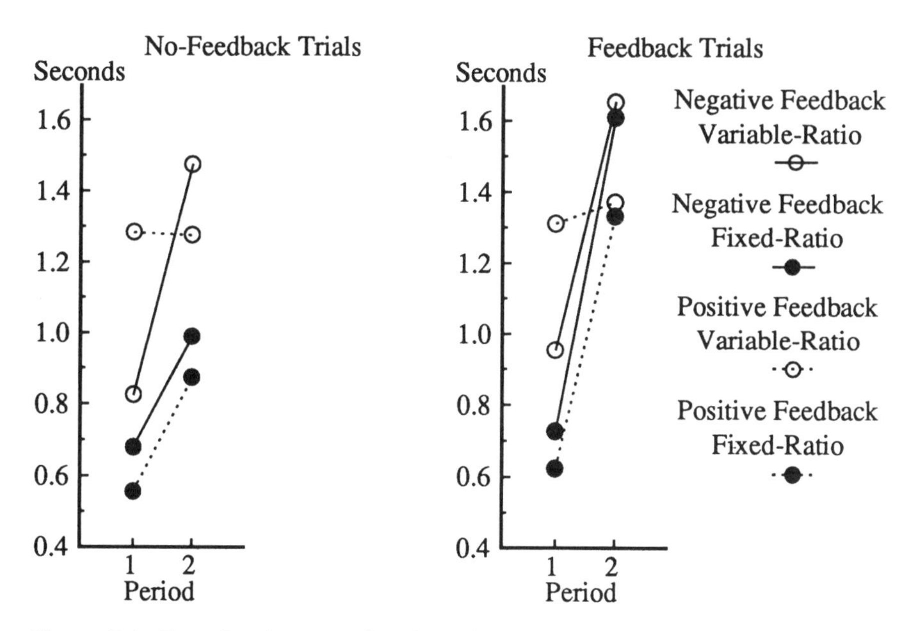

Figure 7.6. Gaze duration as a function of type and schedule of feedback during anticipation and confrontation in feedback and no-feedback trials.

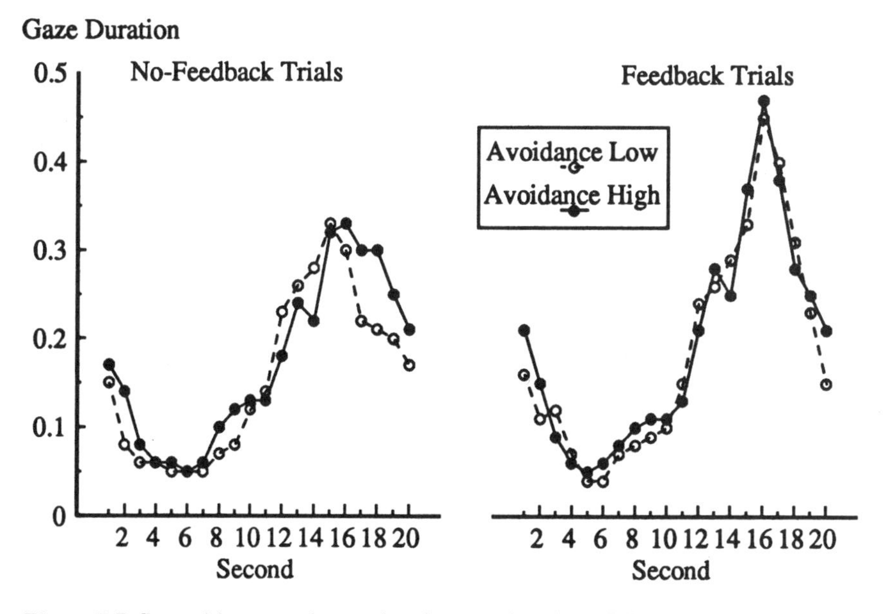

Figure 7.7. Second-by-second gaze duration as a function of dispositional avoidance in feedback and no-feedback trials.

did not intensify their looking behavior during confrontation. Whereas the results seem to support the assumption of an information-search function of gaze (looking is intensified under high ambiguity), the operation of an arousal-regulation function seems to depend on more subtle factors; looking is intensified after positive feedback, in comparison to the negative type, solely in the variable-ratio condition during anticipation.

A significant interaction between avoidance and period on *gaze duration* for trials in which *no feedback* was given, $F(1,72) = 4.47$, $p = .04$, indicated that high avoiders look less than low avoiders during anticipation (0.77 vs. 0.90 seconds) but more during (and immediately after) confrontation (i.e., when it is clear that no feedback is actually given: 1.24 vs. 1.06 seconds; Figure 7.7, left side). There was no corresponding effect for trials with feedback (Figure 7.7, right side). The plots of the second-by-second gaze duration suggest that the lower amount of looking in avoiders anticipating feedback is due to an interruption of approach apparent in the second just before feedback is administered (second 14). This is also the second in which heart rate generally reaches its maximum during the session. In contrast, a steady increase in the orientation toward the examiner was found for low avoiders.

Whereas the lower amount of looking during anticipation is in line with the hypotheses, the enhanced looking during confrontation when no feedback is given was not expected. It is tempting to relate the avoiders' behavior pattern in no-feedback trials to the time course of heart rate observed in general. During anticipation, while heart rate is accelerating, avoiders look less than nonavoiders. After the event-related deceleration of heart rate, however, they look more, i.e., they seem to be slower in reorienting attention away from the examiner. This suggests a cycle of rise and drop of tension in the seconds around feedback which may be specifically connected to avoidance and nonavoidance in those persons.

The analysis of the *frequency of gazes* directed at the experimenter showed an interaction involving avoidance, vigilance, and type of feedback, $F(1,72) = 4.13$, $p = .05$ (Figure 7.8). This interaction again emerged only in trials *without feedback*. Whereas type of feedback only slightly influenced the gaze behavior of nondefensive subjects (vigilance low, avoidance low) and sensitizers, repressers and high-anxious individuals manifested large differences between conditions. Repressers looked very frequently at the experimenter when positive expectancies had been induced and very infrequently when negative expectancies had been established. The opposite pattern was found for high-anxious individuals. These individuals check the experimenter's face more frequently after negative feedback than after positive. At the same time they do not show an enhanced total time of looking at the experimenter. This can be tentatively related to the hypothesis of a conflict between approach and avoidance tendencies in these subjects when confronted with negative feedback, resulting in an oscillating behavior characterized by frequent changes in gaze direction.

It is noteworthy that both parameters of gaze were found to depend on coping dispositions only for trials without feedback and not for those in which

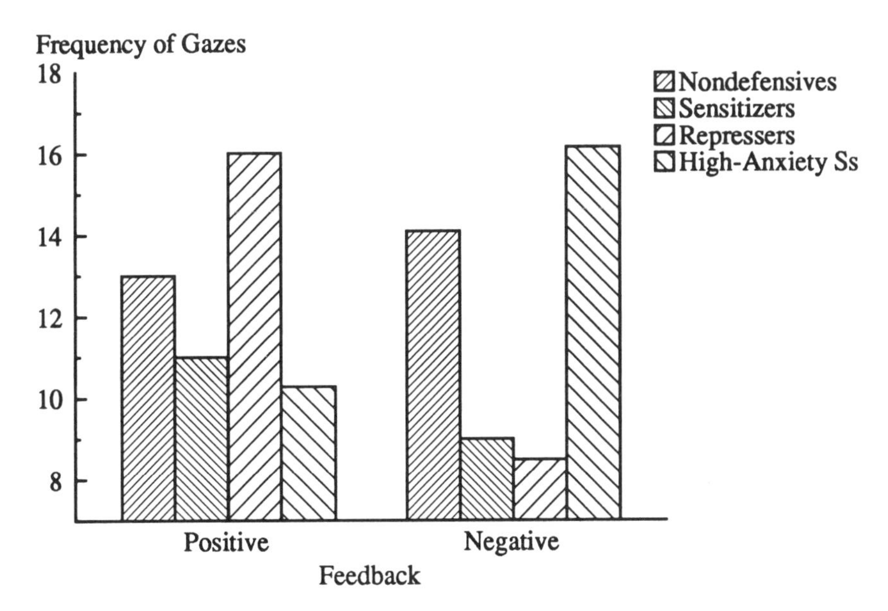

Figure 7.8. Frequency of gazes as a function of coping mode and type of feedback (no-feedback trials).

feedback was actually given. Perhaps the confrontation with feedback information tends to make the subjects' behavior uniform in a way which overrides the effects of dispositional preferences. Knowledge that feedback will be administered, which is present in the low ambiguity (fixed-ratio) condition, could also have contributed to equalizing differences between groups in feedback trials.

Contrary to expectations, vigilance was not associated with *gaze duration*. In discussing the failure to establish a vigilance effect on looking behavior in Study 1, the high level of ambiguity which characterized the test-taking situation was considered to be an important factor. In the present investigation, ambiguity was therefore varied at a more moderate level. However, vigilant and nonvigilant persons again did not differ in their looking behavior toward the examiner. Moreover, there were no interactions between vigilance and the degree of ambiguity on gaze duration. Taking these results into account, ambiguity does not seem to play a major role in determining the strength of associations between dispositional vigilance and actual looking behavior.

An alternative interpretation could refer to differences in the speed at which persons are able to extract information from the examiner's face. For one individual, a short glance at the examiner may be sufficient to reduce uncertainty or keep it within acceptable limits, while another individual needs more time to achieve this. If dispositionally vigilant persons are more skilled observers of their partners in an interaction than nonvigilant individuals, they

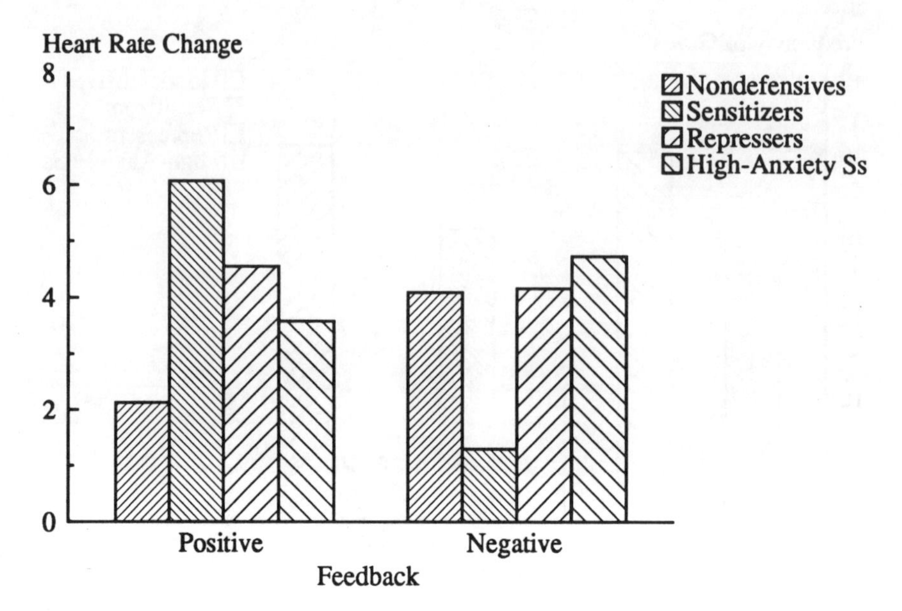

Figure 7.9. Increase in heart rate during anticipation in no-feedback trials as a function of coping mode and type of feedback.

are able to reduce uncertainty to a larger extent (and thus act according to their preferences) without necessarily *looking more*. Analyses of the within-subject consequences of intraindividual variations of looking behavior could yield support for this possibility.

Another unanticipated result was that vigilant subjects did not manifest a heightened anticipatory arousal (operationalized by the *acceleration in heart rate* observed during the anticipation period) under conditions of high ambiguity (variable-ratio). An interaction between coping dispositions and type of feedback, $F(1,72) = 7.66$, $p = .007$, emerging in trials without feedback (Figure 7.9), showed especially low heart rate changes (acceleration during anticipation) in sensitizers following the induction of negative expectancies. The failure to demonstrate a state of heightened bodily arousal in vigilant individuals (and especially sensitizers) when confronted with a possible "unpleasant surprise" could be a reason for the negative findings regarding their gaze behavior: If emotion is low, there is no internal pressure for heightened vigilance in those persons. It may be, however, that more microscopic regulation processes between emotional and attentional variations are involved. For vigilant persons, comparatively small and rapidly triggered shifts in attentional direction could be effective in controlling emotional states. This question can be addressed by intrasubject analyses of the temporal contingencies of both sequences of behavior.

Interindividual Differences in Sequential Relationships Between Attentional and Emotional Reactions

Description of a Basic Model

In this section, the within-subject relationships between indicators of attentional and emotional reactions registered in Study 2 will be examined. One aim of these analyses is to gather clues which may help clarify the lack of association between vigilance and gaze duration. The basic idea underlying the approach is that a given amount of looking has a different *meaning* or *functional significance* for persons high or low in vigilance. There are at least two possibilities: First, vigilant persons are better "information-extractors". Thus, they need not look more than nonvigilants in order to reduce uncertainty to a greater degree. Second, vigilant subjects are able to control anxiety by comparatively small shifts in looking behavior. These variations may be too small to give rise to consistent *interindividual* differences. Both possibilities do not exclude each other. Instead, the speed of information extraction may enhance the capacity to control anxiety by subtle changes in looking.

The second possibility can be addressed in a comparatively direct manner using the data obtained in Study 2. To achieve this, within-subject analyses of the sequential relationships between attentional and emotional changes are required. If direction of attention toward or away from a source of threat has a *person-specific* significance for anxiety regulation, antecedent intraindividual variations in indicators of attention (e.g., looking) have to be related to subsequent intraindividual variations in indicators of emotion (e.g., autonomic changes).

The exploration of the sequential dependencies between attention and emotion is not only relevant regarding the influence of attention on emotion but also with respect to the reverse relationship. In the model of coping modes, attentional and emotional changes are considered to be mutually dependent processes. Orienting attention toward or away from a source of threat is viewed as a means of regulating (restricting, reducing, or preventing) anxiety. On the other hand, anxiety arousal is one central determinant for the initiation and maintenance of attentional changes.

The basic assumptions of the model concerning the temporal relationships between attentional and emotional changes will be subsequently described in greater detail. A reanalysis of the data of Study 2, which aims at testing hypotheses derived from this model, will then be presented. Measures reflecting the nature and extent of the time-lagged covariations between both behavior classes are derived (within individuals) and then examined regarding their associations with situational and person variables (across individuals).

Figure 7.10 shows the functional relationships relevant in the model of coping modes and suggests a specific temporal sequence of processes involved in basic attentional and emotional reactions following the identification of threat. Processes, symbolized as rectangles, are (a) identification of an event

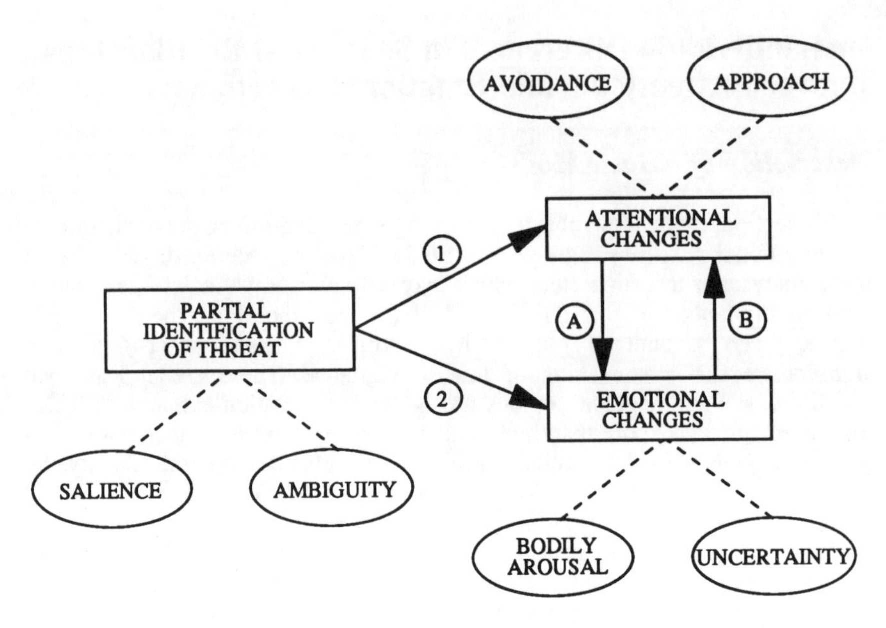

Figure 7.10. Assumed sequence of processes involved in basic attentional and emotional reactions following the identification of threat.

related to a possible danger in the future, (b) attentional reactions, and (c) emotional changes (anxiety arousal), each encompassing certain subfeatures or subcomponents indicated by ellipses. Arrows denote the involvement of a process in the initiation, maintenance, and/or intensity regulation of the processes to which they point. These influences may be facilitating or inhibitory depending on the type of information conveyed and the subcomponent processes incorporated. For example, high ambiguity should primarily give rise to a feeling state of uncertainty which, again, is assumed to motivate approach (see Krohne, Chapter 2, this volume). Figures and letters in circles refer to the postulated temporal relations (1 prior to 2; A prior to B; 1, but not necessarily 2, prior to A). Some additional assumptions are made:

1. Following and caused by the identification of threat, attentional and emotional changes start simultaneously. Therefore, for attentional biases to become apparent, preceding emotional changes are not necessary. (Although emotional changes can strengthen or even modify the focus of attentional reactions.)

2. The notion that changes in emotion and attention may be initiated simultaneously does not imply that both reach their impact at the same time. In fact, it can be assumed that attentional reactions are more rapidly established than emotional changes. The full arousal of an emotion (in the sense of a feeling state) requires the processing of internal and external stimuli to a level

at which the significance (e.g., behavioral consequences) of a stimulus can be evaluated. Attentional responses, on the other hand, do not have to await the clarification of the meaning of an environmental change and can thus be terminated or even redirected before a transformation of the emotional state is perceived.

An illustration of this process is provided by the sudden appearance of a strong, short-term event which requires instant counterreactions, such as the involvement in a dangerous traffic maneuver caused by a carelessly risky driver in another car. In this case, bodily changes are usually not noticed prior to the hopefully fortunate end of the hazardous episode.

In the initial phases of an encounter, attentional reactions are therefore likely to be the "driving force" of the transaction, i.e., they influence subsequent emotional processes more than vice versa. In the terminology used by Gottman and Ringland (1981), attention during the early phases should be "dominant" over emotion. The authors refer to the asymmetry in predictability between two behavior sequences as "dominance". In general terms, a sequence A is said to be dominant over a sequence B, if the current state of B is more predictable from the previous state(s) of A than the present state of A is predictable from the antecedent state(s) of B.

3. Once emotion is wholly aroused, either directly via external stimuli or indirectly, i.e., mediated by the operation of attentional biases, the dominance relationship between attentional and emotional responses is weakened and replaced by a bidirectional interplay. It may even be reversed, so that emotional changes become the leading processes.

4. In dispositional avoiders, the partial intake of threatening information rapidly leads to attentional diversion. The further processing of ambiguous danger stimuli is aborted early, i.e., before the emotion (in avoiders primarily a feeling state of unpleasant bodily arousal) is triggered or fully established. Only if this mechanism fails (e.g., because danger cues are too salient), does the feeling state develop. The individual now has to deal with unpleasant internal changes as a problem.

5. Attentional approach and enhanced processing of threat stimuli characteristic for vigilant persons may, as argued by Mathews (this volume), lead to increments in anxiety. On the other hand, the situation (the meaning of the stimulus) may be clarified before anxiety (in vigilants primarily caused by gradually accumulating uncertainty) is released. In this case, quickly orienting toward potential danger stimuli can certainly help to prevent or restrain anxiety increments which might be otherwise released. It can lead to a rapid reduction of uncertainty and thereby suppress the full emergence of unpleasant emotional changes. In such persons, anxiety states should be triggered when those quick attentional changes are either not effective in clarifying the meaning of a stimulus or signal the possibility of severe harm (thus transforming an ambiguous signal into a sign of clear danger).

Following these premises and regarding the short-term sequences considered in this study, it is expected that (a) looking is more effective in changing subsequent anticipatory arousal than vice versa, and (b) the direction of this effect is dependent on coping dispositions, i.e., intensified looking inhibits emotion in vigilant subjects and facilitates emotion in avoidant ones.

Empirical Analysis

Method

Both hypotheses concern time-lagged intrasubject dependencies between attention and emotion (variation of subsequent emotional reaction as a function of antecedent attentional orientation; variation of subsequent attentional orientation as a function of antecedent emotional processes). Gaze duration during the anticipation of feedback was used to indicate attention. The variations in emotion were operationalized by the corresponding heart rate changes. To analyze the sequential contingencies between bodily arousal and attentional orientation, a procedure proposed by Gottman and Ringland (1981) was employed. This technique uses within-subject regressions in which one first accounts for as much of the variance in each series by relating it to its own past and then determines how much additional variance can be explained by adding the past of the other series. The first step is important, because the existence of autodependencies within a series, which are usually present when short-term fluctuations of variables are concerned, can lead to incorrect judgments as regards the type and strength of heterodependencies between two variables of interest. The presence of dependencies within the series, for example, can generate pseudo-heterocorrelations between two series which actually have no variance in common.

The application of this procedure requires that the data are stationary, i.e., the parameters of the series (means, variances, auto- and cross-covariance) must remain relatively constant over its length. In the data from Study 2, however, strong trends for both heart rate and gaze behavior became apparent (see Figure 7.5). In order to remove nonstationarity, the original data have to be transformed. There are several methods to accomplish this, each appropriate for different sources of nonstationarity, e.g., differencing, in which the original series is replaced by changes between the adjacent values in it. Since gaze generally levels off almost to zero while the subject estimates the objects, this as well as other transformations could not be successful in removing nonstationarity in advance.

The data analysis was therefore modified in the following respects: First, only the anticipation period was considered, i.e., seconds 11 to 14 of each trial, because this is the period which is most relevant to our research question. It is also a period in which comparatively high amounts of looking were found. Subsequently, the anticipation period was divided into "early anticipation" (seconds 11 and 12) and "late anticipation" (seconds 13 and 14). In averaging over two seconds, a far better distribution of gaze duration could be achieved. In this way four variables were obtained, namely, amount of gaze and mean heart rate in seconds 11 to 12 and seconds 13 to 14, respectively, each observed over all trials.

Next, two regression analyses were carried out for each subject, in which early anticipation variables were entered as predictors and late anticipation variables as criteria. In order to estimate the degree to which the antecedent amount of gaze is associated with the consequent level of heart rate while controlling for previous level of heart rate, the early anticipation heart rate was entered into the equation as the first variable. Subsequently, the change in percentage of variance explained by adding early anticipation gaze was computed. The dependence of gaze on antecedent heart rate, while controlling for previous gaze was assessed correspondingly. In a last step, a plus or minus sign was assigned to R square change according to the direction of the relationship, either facilitating (+) or inhibitory (-).

The advantage of this method lies in the fact that one gains simple dependence measures which can be compared easily as regards interindividual and situational differences. Its disadvantage is that only a few time points are considered, so that only first-order relationships can be addressed.

Results and discussion

Generally the percentage of variance of heart rate accounted for by previous amount of gaze, and vice versa, was low: On the average, gaze accounted for 6.2% of the variance of subsequent heart rate while heart rate accounted for 6.5% of the variance of subsequent gaze. Thus, the hypothesized asymmetry in predictability between looking behavior and heart rate could not be established.

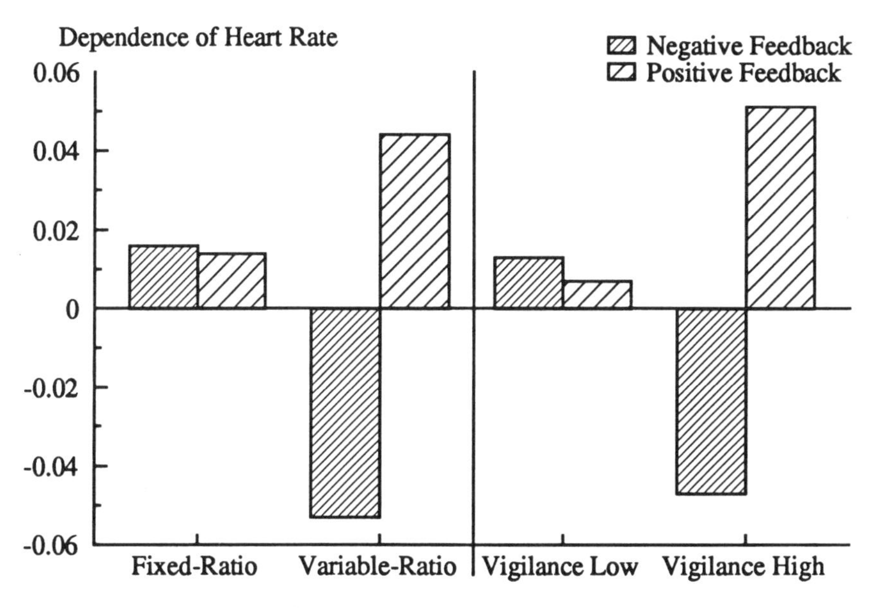

Figure 7.11. Dependence of heart rate on antecedent gaze as a function of type and schedule of feedback (left cluster) and type of feedback and dispositional vigilance (right cluster).

There were, however, large interindividual differences as regards the strength of heterodependencies observed. Both of the dependence measures were almost symmetrically distributed around $M = 0$ ($SD = .11$ in each case). Therefore, the number of facilitating and inhibitory influences established was nearly the same.

The dependence measures were analyzed by means of two ANOVAs with coping dispositions, type and schedule of feedback as independent variables.

As regards the influence of *gaze on subsequent heart rate*, an interaction of both situational variables was found, $F(1,72) = 3.98, p = .05$ (Figure 7.11). This interaction was due to the high ambiguity (variable-ratio) condition. Under negative feedback, an inhibitory influence of gaze on subsequent heart rate predominates, i.e., the higher the amount of gaze, the lower the subsequent heart rate in the anticipation period. As regards positive feedback in the high ambiguity condition, the opposite relationship was found: A high amount of gaze was associated with increases in heart rate. Weaker facilitating trends were also seen in the low ambiguity (fixed-ratio) condition.

A further interaction involved vigilance and type of feedback $F(1,72) = 4.43$, $p = .04$ (Figure 7.11): Differences between feedback conditions regarding the influence gaze exerts on heart rate were found for highly vigilant individuals. When expecting negative feedback, these persons are obviously able to reduce arousal by enhanced orientation toward the source of threat. On the other hand, they have to tolerate comparatively stronger arousal increments when they avert their gaze. Again, the pattern was reversed when positive expectancies were induced.

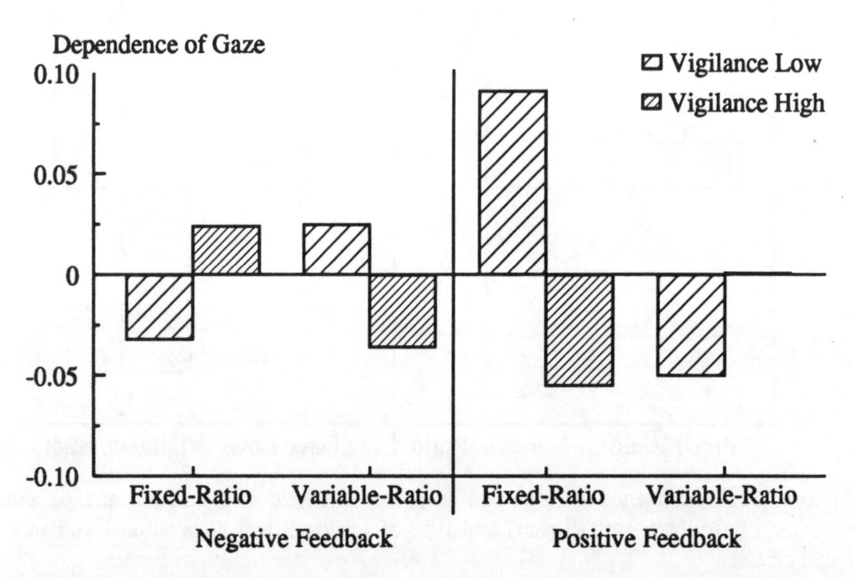

Figure 7.12. Dependence of gaze on antecedent heart rate as a function of dispositional vigilance, type of feedback, and schedule of feedback.

It is remarkable that the situational difference of low vs. high ambiguity (fixed- vs. variable-ratio) "moderates" the effects of feedback on behavior contingencies in the same way as the dispositional difference of low vs. high vigilance does. This suggests that it is the *variable degree of subjective uncertainty*, induced by situational conditions or connected with the actualization of person-specific cognitive structures, which is responsible for the interactive effects. An influence of dispositional avoidance on the gaze -> emotion contingency was not found.

With respect to the dependence of gaze on antecedent heart rate, a three-way interaction between the two situational variables and vigilance emerged, $F(1,72) = 10.51$, $p = .002$ (Figure 7.12): In low vigilant individuals, heart rate facilitates gaze under the condition of low ambiguity (fixed-ratio) and positive feedback and under the condition of high ambiguity (variable-ratio) and negative feedback. For highly vigilant persons, inhibitory influences were registered in both conditions. The facilitating influence bodily arousal exerts on low vigilant individuals under the condition of low ambiguity/positive feedback is especially pronounced. Perhaps this pattern reflects a tendency to look forward to the expected positive event, a tendency which is absent in vigilant persons and also under conditions of negative feedback or high ambiguity.

General Discussion and Conclusions

The two studies reported in this chapter were aimed at testing hypotheses derived from the model of coping modes. These hypotheses concerned the effects of dispositional avoidance and vigilance on anxiety and attention in socially threatening situations. One central intention of the studies was directed at assessing the adequacy of the looking behavior observed in a dyadic interaction situation as an indicator of dispositionally determined attentional changes.

The results of Study 1 suggested a differential susceptibility of persons classified under different coping modes with respect to perceived bodily arousal and worry cognitions following evaluative feedback to performance. Vigilant individuals generally reported more worry cognitions, an effect which was especially pronounced for sensitizers after negative feedback. In contrast, dispositional avoidance was associated with emotionality, which was found to be enhanced in high avoiders following negative evaluations and lowered following positive ones. In addition, high avoiders seemed to be able to reduce a heightened state of emotionality induced by negative feedback. This became apparent in the time course of eye-blink frequency during the test period in Study 1. Regarding the worry measure, an effect of dispositional vigilance was again found in Study 2; it was, however, only marginally significant. Emotionality was heightened in repressers and sensitizers, irregardless of situational factors. The expectations that the anxiety reaction manifested by avoiders varies primarily as a function of the type of feedback (positive vs. negative), while the anxiety state manifested by vigilant persons primarily depends on the schedule of feedback (fixed-ratio vs. variable-ratio), were not confirmed.

Whereas the results of Study 1 follow the assumptions of the model, associations registered in Study 2 cannot be easily incorporated into this framework. Several factors could be responsible for these discrepant patterns of relationships including differences in the samples employed (female sample in Study 1, male sample in Study 2), the way feedback was administered (presumably more intensively in Study 1; more frequently in Study 2), the time schedule used, as well as other procedural details. It is noteworthy that in Study 1 strong influences of type of feedback on worry *and* emotionality were found. In Study 2, however, specific relationships emerged: Type of feedback was only associated with worry. Schedule of feedback, in contrast, solely influenced emotionality. These distinct and unanticipated effects of situational variables on anxiety components could have contributed to the failure in Study 2 to clearly replicate those associations with coping dispositions uncovered in Study 1. Additionally, these effects could also be responsible for the disconfirmation of the hypothesis concerning a differential susceptibility of avoidant and vigilant individuals to type and schedule of feedback.

In future studies, a measure which more directly assesses aspects of uncertainty experienced during the session should be introduced. This would allow an empirical investigation of the proposed close association between uncertainty and worry cognitions (cf. Krohne, Chapter 2, this volume). Moreover, the functional links between both feeling states have to be conceptually elaborated in greater detail. Given that autonomic changes supposedly underlying the perception of stressful states can (at least partially) be viewed as a mobilization of bodily resources which enable an individual to better manage an ambiguous, not wholly predictable, and perhaps extremely aversive event about to occur, uncertainty may well possess some priority as regards the full emergence of the emotion.

The first investigation failed to establish significant associations between coping dispositions and looking behavior. The high degree of ambiguity in the test-taking situation realized in Study 1 was considered to be one critical factor which could have contributed to this failure. In Study 2, therefore, ambiguity was varied at a more moderate level. Congruent with the hypotheses, avoiders manifested a decreased amount of looking during the anticipation of feedback, which became apparent in trials without feedback. The results found for repressers and high-anxious individuals regarding the frequency of gazes directed at the examiner were also in line with the hypotheses. The role of situational factors in determining these person-specific attentional biases, as well as the meaning of the "rebound" effect observed in avoiders when feedback was withheld, need further clarification.

Associations between dispositional vigilance and total time of gaze directed at the examiner were again not observed. Intrasubject analyses of the sequential dependencies between antecedent looking and subsequent heart rate, however, suggested the operation of attentional mechanisms in vigilant persons which are effective in controlling emotional states. When given negative feedback, enhanced (low) monitoring during early anticipation was associated with lower (higher) heart rate during late anticipation. The significance of the reversal in direction of the influences predominant after positive feedback as well as the effects of situational and dispositional variables on the emotion -> attention contingency remain open to question.

To summarize, Study 2 did not reveal the expected relationships between coping dispositions, situational variables, and anxiety states. With respect to the looking behavior, results were only partly consistent with the hypotheses, since cognitive avoidance, but not vigilance, was associated with gaze duration while anticipating the occurrence of evaluative feedback. The inhibitory sequential effects of looking on heart rate, which were established for highly vigilant individuals in the negative feedback condition, were compatible with the assumptions. Associations with cognitive avoidance, however, were not found.

Further studies on looking behavior as an indicator of dispositional approach and avoidance tendencies should attempt to enhance the differences between the levels of the situational variables. The variations in threat as well as ambiguity were perhaps not salient enough in the experimental conditions realized to become fully effective in behavioral regulation. Correspondingly, analyses of the sequential contingencies between indicators of attention and emotion should employ procedures which allow for maximizing the within-subject variability of both classes of behavior. Regarding the assessment of interindividual differences in the intrasubject relationships, follow-up studies should be extended in two additional ways:

1. Experimental settings should be realized which allow for the incorporation of more time points in analyzing the temporal relationships between emotional and attentional processes. This is important with respect to the possibility of temporally delayed effects between the series. As suggested earlier, emotional changes may reach their maximum impact on attention comparatively slowly.
2. The operationalization of anxiety has to be extended to a broader class of indicators. This is necessary not only because various autonomic variables such as heart rate also reflect nonemotional processes (e.g., attentional changes; see Jennings, 1986, for an overview), but also with respect to the assumption made in the model of coping modes that two components of anxiety (uncertainty and emotional arousal, cf. Krohne, Chapter 2, this volume) are relevant in the reciprocal regulation of attention and emotion.

References

Ainsworth, M. D. S., Blehar, M. C., Waters, E., & Wall, S. (1978). *Patterns of attachment. A psychological study of the strange situation.* Hillsdale, NJ: Erlbaum.
Argyle, M., & Dean, J. (1965). Eye contact, distance, and affiliation. *Sociometry, 28,* 289-304.
Bell, P. A., & Byrne, D. (1978). Repression-sensitization. In H. London & J. E. Exner (Eds.), *Dimensions of personality* (pp. 449-485). New York: Wiley.

Efran, J. S. (1968). Looking for approval: Effects on visual behavior of approbation from persons differing in importance. *Journal of Personality and Social Psychology, 10*, 21-25.

Efran, J. S., & Broughton, A. (1966). Effect of expectancies for social approval on visual behavior. *Journal of Personality and Social Psychology, 4*, 103-107.

Eriksen, C. W. (1966). Cognitive responses to internally cued anxiety. In C. D. Spielberger (Ed.), *Anxiety and behavior* (pp. 327-360). New York: Academic Press.

Gottman, J. M., & Ringland, J. T. (1981). The analysis of dominance and bidirectionality in social development. *Child Development, 52*, 393-412.

Grossmann, K. E., & Grossmann, K. (1986). Phylogenetische und ontogenetische Aspekte der Entwicklung der Eltern-Kind-Bindung und der kindlichen Sachkompetenz [Phylogenetic and ontogenetic aspects of the development of the parent-child attachment and the child's competence]. *Zeitschrift für Entwicklungspsychologie und Pädagogische Psychologie, 18*, 287-315.

Hale, J. L., & Burgoon, J. K. (1984). Models of reactions to changes in nonverbal immediacy. *Journal of Nonverbal Behavior, 8*, 287-314.

Hobson, G. N., Strongman, K. T., Bull, D., & Craig, G. (1973). Anxiety and gaze aversion in dyadic encounters. *British Journal of Social and Clinical Psychology, 12*, 122-129.

Hock, M., & Krohne, H. W. (in press). Anxiety and coping dispositions as predictors of the visual interaction between mother and child. *Anxiety Research.*

Jennings, J. R. (1986). Bodily changes during attending. In M. G. H. Coles, E. Donchin, & S. W. Porges (Eds.), *Psychophysiology. Systems, processes, and applications* (pp. 268-289). Amsterdam: Elsevier.

Kleinke, C. L. (1986). Gaze and eye contact: A research review. *Psychological Bulletin, 100*, 78-100.

Kohlmann, C.-W. (1990). *Streßbewältigung und Persönlichkeit. Flexibles versus rigides Copingverhalten und seine Auswirkungen auf Angsterleben und physiologische Belastungsreaktionen* [Coping and personality. Flexible versus rigid coping behavior and its effects on anxiety and physiological stress reactions]. Bern: Huber.

Krohne, H. W. (1978). Individual differences in coping with stress and anxiety. In C. D. Spielberger & I. G. Sarason (Eds.), *Stress and anxiety* (Vol. 5, pp. 233-260). Washington, DC: Hemisphere.

Krohne, H. W. (1986). Coping with stress: Dispositions, strategies, and the problem of measurement. In M. H. Appley & R. Trumbull (Eds.), *Dynamics of stress: Physiological, psychological, and social perspectives* (pp. 209-234). New York: Plenum.

Krohne, H. W. (1989). The concept of coping modes: Relating cognitive person variables to actual coping behavior. *Advances in Behaviour Research and Therapy, 11*, 235-248.

Krohne, H. W. (in press). Repression-Sensitization [Repression-sensitization]. In M. Amelang (Ed.), *Enzyklopädie der Psychologie. Serie Differentielle Psychologie und Persönlichkeitsforschung: Band 2. Bereiche interindividueller Unterschiede.* Göttingen: Hogrefe.

Liebert, R. M., & Morris, L. W. (1967). Cognitive and emotional components of test anxiety: A distinction and some initial data. *Psychological Reports, 20*, 975-978.

Morris, L. W., Davis, M. A., & Hutchings, C. H. (1981). Cognitive and emotional components of anxiety: Literature review and a revised worry-emotionality scale. *Journal of Educational Psychology, 73*, 541-555.

Roth, S., & Cohen, L. J. (1986). Approach, avoidance, and coping with stress. *American Psychologist, 41*, 813-819.

Rutter, D. R., & Stephenson, G. M. (1979). The functions of looking: Effects of friendship on gaze. *British Journal of Social and Clinical Psychology, 18*, 203-205.

Sarason, I. G. (1984). Stress, anxiety, and cognitive interference: Reactions to tests. *Journal of Personality and Social Psychology, 46*, 929-938.

Scherer, K. R. (1979). Kommunikation [Communication]. In K. R. Scherer & H. G. Wallbott (Eds.), *Nonverbale Kommunikation: Forschungsberichte zum Interaktionsverhalten* (pp. 14-24). Weinheim: Beltz.

Slane, S., Dragan, W., Crandall, C. J., & Payne, P. (1980). Stress effects on nonverbal behavior of repressors and sensitizers. *Journal of Psychology, 106*, 101-109.

Stern, D. N. (1974). Mother and infant at play: The dyadic interaction involving facial, vocal, and gaze behaviors. In M. Lewis & L. A. Rosenblum (Eds.), *The effect of the infant on its caregiver* (pp. 187-213). New York: Wiley.

Suls, J., & Fletcher, B. (1985). The relative efficacy of avoidant and non-avoidant coping strategies: A meta-analysis. *Health Psychology, 4*, 249-288.

Weinberger, D. A. (1990). The construct validity of the repressive coping style. In J. L. Singer (Ed.), *Repression and dissociation. Implications for personality theory, psychopathology, and health* (pp. 337-386). Chicago: University of Chicago Press.

Wiens, A. N., Harper, R. G., & Matarazzo, J. D. (1980). Personality correlates of nonverbal interview behavior. *Journal of Clinical Psychology, 36*, 205-215.

Wine, J. D. (1982). Evaluation anxiety: A cognitive-attentional construct. In H. W. Krohne & L. Laux (Eds.), *Achievement, stress, and anxiety* (pp. 207-219). Washington, DC: Hemisphere.

Chapter 8

Type A Behavior Pattern and Denial of Failure-Related Information

Hasida Ben-Zur, Shlomo Breznitz,
and Ruth Hashmonay

Theoretical Considerations

The Individual and the Situation in Coping with Stress

The ways in which human beings cope with stress were extensively studied by Lazarus (1966), one of the first to describe and differentiate between two main modes of coping: active action and palliation. The first type focuses on the environment and primarily represents actions aimed at fleeing from or destroying the threatening agent. The second type focuses on the individual and represents actions or psychological mechanisms aimed at reducing or moderating both the negative emotions and the physiological arousal associated with stress. At a later stage, Lazarus and Folkman (1984) termed these two coping modes 'problem-focused' and 'emotion-focused', respectively. Moos and Billings (1982) extended Lazarus' model by adding an appraisal-focused mode, which relates to a redefinition of the situation and its significance for the individual, and by classifying coping modes according to whether they involve confrontation or avoidance of the problem. Similarly, Feuerstein, Labbe, and Kuczmierczyk (1986, p. 130) offer a matrix of coping modes characterized by the following three dichotomies: the focus (the problem or its emotional consequences), the method (active coping or avoidance), and the channel (behavioral or cognitive). In theory, this matrix produces eight possible coping responses; however, not all of them have been empirically confirmed (see Ilfeld, 1980). It then becomes apparent that one very pertinent question, recently stated by Taylor (1990), emerges from the research on coping with stress: Is the attempt to respond to a threat with avoidance, e.g., using denial, repression, or cognitive disengagement, more or less adaptive than responding with approach or attention to the threat, e.g., employing vigilance or confrontation? This question has been discussed in the context of both individual differences and situational aspects.

We would like to thank David Jenkins, author of the JAS, who gave his permission to translate the student version into Hebrew, David Glass who sent us the scoring instructions for this version of the questionnaire, and Sharon Erlich and Shmuel Weinstein who aided in organizing the study. Thanks are also due to Heinz W. Krohne for his most helpful comments.

In reference to situational aspects, it is maintained that in those cases in which the individual can do nothing to change the situation, such as intensive care patients who have suffered heart attacks or the parents of children stricken with leukemia, coping by means of denial-like processes is more adaptive, since it aids in reducing anxiety and promotes more efficient functioning (Lazarus, 1983). On the other hand, where the problem can be dealt with directly, coping by avoidance may be counterproductive. Questions have also been raised concerning the short- and long-term effects of these two coping modes, since avoidance is generally effective in the short run but less so in the long run (Mullen & Suls, 1982; Suls & Fletcher, 1985).

On the level of individual differences, Krohne (1989, and Chapter 2 in this volume) defined two main classes of coping strategies, i.e., vigilance and cognitive avoidance, and reported that both were associated with decreased physiological stress reactions (e.g., plasma concentration of free fatty acids) during a pre-surgical period. Miller (1989, see also Miller, Combs, & Kruus, this volume) refers to monitoring and blunting as two cognitive informational styles, showing that those persons defined as high monitors/low blunters constitute the vulnerable population in everyday stressful encounters.

Following current interactional approaches (e.g., Magnusson, 1982), the present study considers both the individual and the situation and focuses on whether people of a certain type respond only to specific contents with cognitive avoidance. More precisely, the aim of the study was to examine a differential denial response in relation to the personal relevance of various types of threats for individuals characterized by the Type A Behavior Pattern (TABP). Individuals with TABP have been previously shown (Friedman & Rosenman, 1974) to be highly prone to heart attack. TABP also appears to be a coping mode employed by individuals who are in constant conflict with their environment. In addition, we believe that people who exhibit the TABP (Type As) may be characterized by a tendency to deny certain types of information which are threatening on the personal level and that this behavior can aid them in the struggles encountered in their daily life. Before we consider TABP specifically, we will briefly review the current views on denial as a mechanism for coping with stress.

Denial as a Cognitive Coping Mechanism

Early psychoanalytically oriented theory (e.g., Haan, 1977) as well as the psychiatric literature regarded denial as a simple and primitive defense mechanism used by children or adults in psychotic states. More recently, denial has been seen as part of the coping process characterizing the reactions of normal stable individuals when confronted with threats that cannot be dealt with directly (Lazarus, 1983). For example, when threatened by serious illness, an individual's denial is defined as "the conscious or unconscious repudiation of all or a portion of the total available meaning of an illness in order to allay anxiety and to minimize emotional stress" (Dimsdale & Hackett, 1982, p. 1477).

The cognitive mechanism underlying denial can be understood if we assume conscious perception to be based on a multi-stage process which may be stopped at any of its stages. Indeed, it is argued that certain stimuli reach unconscious levels of sensual registration and recognition but are blocked from conscious perception (e.g., Erdelyi, 1974; Krohne, 1978). Thus, the registration of the stimulus may take place without the perception of its meaning, although some part of this meaning is absorbed (Spence, 1983) and constitutes the basis for rejecting the stimulus as a whole from full consciousness. On the basis of these arguments, Dorpat (1985) proposed the *cognitive arrest hypothesis of denial*. According to this hypothesis, an individual judges a situation preconsciously as traumatic and dangerous and therefore senses a painful affect such as depression, guilt, anxiety, or helplessness. This affect, in turn, induces the individual to divert his or her focal attention from whatever is causing the pain to something less painful or even pleasant. In a similar vein, Mathews (this volume) shows that anxious individuals are more prone to perceive threats at the early stages of encoding and registering information, although they may sometimes avoid further processing of the threatening cues at later stages.

Denial has also been viewed recently as a process which may occur at different stages of the threat and in relation to different types of information associated with it (Breznitz, 1983). Thus, individuals may deny the very fact of being exposed to the total information or the possibility that a specific threatening information was conveyed to them. This type of denial entails a severe distortion of reality. The less extreme forms of denial only relate to certain aspects of the threat, such as its personal relevance, its time urgency, or the emotion it arouses.

The present study maintains that individuals characterized by TABP will deny certain sorts of information more than others and that this tendency may serve a purpose in their dealings with everyday problems. Subsequently, we will consider those behavioral and cognitive aspects of Type As relevant to the manner in which they cope with a stressful environment.

Type A and Coping on the Behavioral Level

The TABP was first described by two physicians, Friedman and Rosenman (1974), who found that heart patients could be distinguished from other people by certain typical behaviors. They defined TABP as "an action-emotion complex that can be observed in any person who is aggressively involved in a chronic, incessant struggle to achieve more and more in less and less time, and if required to do so, against the opposing effects of other things or persons" (p. 67). Friedman and Ulmer (1984) add that the most critical aspects of Type A individuals are high aggressiveness, a sense of time pressure, and competitiveness, all of which are indications of a *struggle to overcome external obstacles*. Individuals displaying the opposite pattern, termed Type B, exhibit a calm, pleasant behavioral style, are not pressured by time, and have a sense of satisfaction in their lives. They may desire advancement and achievements but will tend to flow with the tide of life rather than struggle against it.

To summarize, TABP is a response aroused under certain environmental conditions, particularly in situations presenting serious challenges and offering social rewards for overcoming them. This is the coping style of an individual who attempts to solve his or her problems in an active and forceful manner. Indeed, Hart (1988) and Carver, Scheier, and Weintraub (1989) found that Type As are characterized by a problem-solving coping style. Moreover, the relationship between TABP and denial-like avoidance patterns is not high and generally negative. In contrast, Martin, Kuiper, and Westra (1989) found Type As to be characterized more by emotion focused coping, reporting a greater frequency of wishful thinking, self-isolation, and positive reappraisal, although the authors suggest that this is primarily a characteristic of Type A women.

While early discussions of TABP focused primarily on its behavioral traits, later studies sought to understand the psychological background underlying this behavior (Matthews, 1982; Wright, 1988). Various explanations have been offered, two of which are presented here to illustrate the premise that TABP is indeed a coping style for dealing with stress.

One of the first investigations conducted on the psychological traits of Type As was done by Glass (1977). He reported that Type As work hard to succeed, suppress subjective states which might interfere with their functioning (such as fatigue), and perform at a fast rate. Glass suggested that these behaviors represent an attempt on the part of Type As to *control the stressful aspects of their environment*. Furthermore, when faced with a stressful event, Type As will make an effort to control the event itself and will thus appear to be hard-driving, competitive, aggressive, and easily provoked. However, should their efforts to control repeatedly fail, they will give up, will not react, and will display helplessness.

According to another approach (see Matthews, 1982), an additional psychological trait characteristic of Type As is a combination of high value placed on productivity and ambiguous standards for assessing it. This combination leads to both an endless quest for achievement and a feeling of time pressure. Thus, Type As constantly try harder and better, each time according to new and higher standards (see Glass, 1977), and are therefore regarded as persons characterized by a chronic striving for achievement. According to this approach, TABP represents an attempt to reach a satisfactory self-evaluation or to improve self-esteem.

Type A and Coping on the Cognitive Level

We have seen thus far that Type As may be characterized by certain types of behavior which seem to represent specific styles of coping with the stress in their environment. In recent years attempts have also been made to characterize TABP according to certain cognitive processes. On the whole, research in this area has examined the Type A's ability to focus attention on certain aspects of their environment while ignoring or avoiding other aspects. This could occur on one of two levels. First, Type As may be able to allocate more attention to only certain task or environmental aspects. Second, where external and internal stimuli compete for their attention, Type As may be able to focus attention more on the indicators of the task they are to perform and less on bodily cues.

The Type A's ability to focus their attention on certain aspects of the stimulus was investigated by Matthews and Brunson (1979). They found that Type As perform better than Type Bs on the Stroop task, relative to their performance on a reaction-time task defined as a secondary task. Since successful performance on the Stroop task requires a person to ignore distracting or contradictory information, this suggests that Type As are better able to focus their attention on the primary stimuli and to disregard distracting ones better than Type Bs are. In contrast, Bermudez, Perez-Garcia, and Sanchez-Elvira (1990) did not find that Type As can ignore irrelevant or distracting information better than Type Bs can, a conclusion supported by Lawler and Schmied (1988) in the wake of their failure to replicate Matthews and Brunson's (1979) results.

Despite the equivocality of the above findings, Type As may be characterized by selective attention if we define this as the degree to which they attend to certain types of information. This was investigated by Lifshitz-Cooney and Zeichner (1985), who examined the Type As' preference for information on their positive assets or negative liabilities. It was found that the Type As' first preference was for negative information, to which they devoted more time, perhaps in order to correct potential flaws. Based on this and similar studies, it appears that Type As are stricter in evaluating their performance, are more attentive to negative information about themselves, and make more internal attributions regarding their performance (Smith & Anderson, 1986).

A second issue relevant to the cognitive aspects of the Type As' attention and assessment concerns the question of their attentiveness to bodily cues. Previous surveys have found that Type As respond to task performance with greater physiological arousal (Houston, 1983; Krantz & Manuck, 1984). This responsiveness, combined with selective attention, may contribute to the level of disease-proneness exhibited by such people. Indeed, it has been claimed that the relationship between stress and coronary disease may be mediated by various psychological processes (Friedman & Booth-Kewley, 1987; Holroyd & Lazarus, 1982). There are other possible explanations for the way in which this relationship is mediated. For example, a person who does not pay attention to bodily symptoms, or whose feedback regarding effort expended is delayed or distorted, may continue a destructive interaction or remain in a stressful situation, working beyond his or her capacity. Repeated episodes of this type may be expected to affect the individual's long-term proneness to disease (see Smith & Rhodewalt, 1986). Another possibility is that a person denies or does not pay attention to bodily cues or symptoms indicating an existing disease and therefore delays seeking medical treatment, a factor which could be critical in the case of heart attack, asthma attack, or early detection of cancer (Lazarus, 1983).

A review of the literature regarding the link between TABP and the report of severity of symptoms reveals that, on the whole, Type As tend to report less fatigue during task performance than Type Bs do (Offutt & Lacroix, 1988). For example, Carver, Coleman, and Glass (1976) found that Type A subjects invested more physical effort in a treadmill test but reported less fatigue than Type Bs did. Similarly, Weidner and Matthews (1978) found that Type A women did not report various symptoms during task performance despite the fact that they experienced high blood pressure and low hand temperature when exposed to aversive noise. A recent study also found that Type As displayed high physiological arousal but reported fewer symptoms related to the cardiovascular system (Roldan, 1987).

Nevertheless, research findings on the reporting of everyday symptoms remain inconsistent, with some studies showing Type As to report fewer symptoms than Type Bs do and others yielding contrary results. In a prospective study including the reporting of symptoms during examination periods, Offutt and Lacroix (1988) found no relationship between TABP and the number or severity of symptoms reported. However, one of the intriguing interpretations of their results relates back to the Type As' underlying cognitions. The authors suggest that in a study employing retrospective methodology, Type As might report fewer symptoms as a result of interpretative processes; their memory of symptoms changes over time, perhaps because of the suppression of this type of information.

Type A and Defensiveness

The studies cited above deal with the Type As' attention, undoubtedly one of the mechanisms enabling the suppression, denial, or cognitive avoidance of threatening information. Other studies offer direct evidence of the Type As' tendency for denial and suppression. For example, such individuals have been found to display greater physiological arousal when confronted with a psychological threat (negative feedback on their performance) than they do when faced with a physical threat (electric shock). While they show a tendency for suppression under both conditions, the major tendency for denial appears in a state of psychological threat (Pittner & Houston, 1980). In a more recent article, Pittner, Houston, and Spirdigliozzi (1983) show that Type A subjects use denial and projection when under the stressful condition of being threatened with electric shock. They claim that these findings may explain the Type As' ability to endure stress for long periods. In contrast, another study found no evidence for cognitive defensiveness on the part of Type As (Heilbrun & Renert, 1986). It did find however that the use of repression was associated with a stronger experience of stress among Type A persons while repression among Type Bs was associated with a lower level of stress.

Additional indications of denial by Type As can be found in Gastorf and Teevan's (1980) claim that Type A persons believe most obstacles can be overcome with sufficient effort (denial of the limits to their abilities). Alternatively, Strube (1988) describes several findings related to the Type As' attributions of success and failure, presumably resulting in the denial of personal responsibility for failure (see also Breznitz, 1983).

In sum, the available findings do not paint a coherent picture. While some indicate better performance by Type As on tasks requiring selective attention, others do not. Similarly, opinion is divided as to the Type As' tendency not to report symptoms. Furthermore, it is not entirely clear to what extent Type As employ denial nor if this is a general characteristic or a tendency to deny certain specific types of threatening information. Nevertheless, the research findings suggest that although Type A individuals tend to cope actively with stress, the avoidance of threats on the cognitive level in the form of denial, suppression, selective attention, or selective memory may be functional in maintaining an active mode of coping (see also Smith & Rhodewalt, 1986). On the physiological level, denial of bodily arousal, fatigue, or symptoms calling for medical attention may allow Type As to continue their performance related activities, thus attaining greater achievements by virtue of their persistence and efforts. On the psychological level, the denial of limited competence to perform or achieve may allow Type As to continue their efforts to cope with challenges, perhaps even those beyond their abilities. In the short run, such denial tendencies may contribute to professional and personal advancement. In the long run, they are likely to aggravate physical disorders, inhibit personal change, encourage the setting of impossible goals, and result in a poor quality of life and general dissatisfaction.

Research Aims

The findings discussed above give rise to the question of whether Type A individuals deny the personal relevance of negative information regarding achievements as well as negative information regarding health. The current study represents a preliminary attempt to investigate this issue by comparing evidence for the denial of health- and achievement-related information among Type A and Type B subjects.

The extend to which individuals deny the personal relevance of such information was examined by presenting the subjects with fabricated statistics regarding the chances of certain events occurring in the general population. These events concerned health and illness on the one hand, and success and failure on the other. Denial was indicated when the subjects stated that the chances of negative events happening to *them* were lower than those of the general population.

Previous studies employed similar instruments to assess the psychological processes involved in evaluating personal threats. Weinstein (1982) employed a questionnaire presenting a range of health problems and asked his subjects to rate their own chances of experiencing each problem in the future. He found an overall tendency to rate personal chances below average, a phenomenon which he termed "unrealistic optimism", and what we call denial (see Taylor & Brown, 1988, for a review). Zakay (1983) similarly asked subjects to rate their chances of encountering positive and negative events as well as the probability of their happening to someone else. Most of his subjects assessed their chances of encountering positive events as higher than those of others and their chances of undergoing negative experiences as lower. Finally, Butler and Mathews (1983) found that anxious patients showed higher subjective probabilities for personal negative threats when compared to threats relating to someone else or as compared to non-anxious controls. It would thus seem that the chances assessment method may be used to measure certain types of cognitive avoidance, or more specifically, denial of susceptibility to negative events, such as illness and failure, which might threaten the individual in the course of his or her life.

Method

Eighty-five paid students from various departments of Haifa University took part in this study. Of these, 25 were male and 60 female with a mean age of 23.22.

The data to be reported was collected as part of a comprehensive study of denial. Here we shall present only the data and questionnaires pertinent to our specific subject.

The TABP was assessed by the Jenkins Activity Survey (JAS; Jenkins, Zyzanski, & Rosenman, 1979), adapted by Glass (1977) for students. The student version of the JAS yields a 21-item scale for assessing TABP (A-B Scale) and shows moderate internal reliability and moderate to high test-retest reliability values (Yarnold, Mueser, Grau, & Grimm, 1986). The Hebrew translation was validated by Ben-Zur, Weinstein, and Hashmonay (1990).

The Denial of Personal Relevance Inventory was originally developed by Breznitz (1990). The version used in the present study consists of 23 items which present events associated with various threats such as health problems, e.g., recovering from meningitis; failures, e.g., getting a low grade in a semestrial exam; and physical harm, e.g., getting hurt during a tornado. Each item also includes information on the (invented) chances of the event occurring in the general population. Seventeen items are stated negatively, e.g., "The chances of getting a low grade in a semestrial exam are 30%", and six items are stated positively, e.g., "The chances of recovering from meningitis are 70%." The subjects are asked to write down the chances of the event happening *to them*. It is assumed that the lower the subjects rate their own chances of experiencing negative events as compared to those of the general population, the more they tend to deny the possibility that they themselves will experience them. Scoring is done by calculating, for each item, the difference between the percentages presented for the general population and those estimated by the subjects for themselves. For negatively-stated items, the subject's response is subtracted from the percentage for the general population. A positive difference therefore indicates that the subject rated his or her chances as lower than those of the population at large (i.e., denial of personal relevance by minimizing the possibility of suffering from the event) while a negative difference indicates the opposite. For positively-stated items, the opposite calculation is applied, so that in respect to both types of items, scoring is in the same direction. A difference of zero indicates that the subject rated his or her chances as equal to those of the general population.

Additional questionnaires were employed in the comprehensive study. Of the data collected, we will report that pertaining to Crowne and Marlowe's (1964) Social Desirability Scale (M-C Scale) and the State- and Trait-Anxiety Scales of the State-Trait Personality Inventory (STPI) developed by Spielberger et al. (1979) and translated into Hebrew by Zeidner and Ben-Zur (1988).

The questionnaires were presented to each subject individually. Subjects were asked to complete the M-C Scale first and then fill in the Denial of Personal Relevance Inventory and the STPI. The JAS was always presented last.

Results

Psychometric Data

For each subject, total scores were computed on the A-B, the M-C, and the State-Anxiety and Trait-Anxiety Scales. Table 8.1 presents the means, α values, and intercorrelations between these variables. The means and the internal reliabilities of our measures closely resemble those found for American students, as well as those reported for other Israeli samples.

Initially the total scores calculated for the Denial of Personal Relevance Inventory were based on the differences in the percentage scores described above. However, a large variance was found in the percentage scores, possibly reflecting individual differences in numerical estimations rather than an overall tendency for denial (e.g., one student might perceive a 10% difference in the same way that another perceives a 30% difference). Therefore, we used frequency scores by assigning 1 to an item difference score higher than zero and -1 to an item difference score lower than zero, with a difference of zero remaining zero. This transformation reduced variance and improved the internal reliability of the entire questionnaire (Cronbach's α = .63). When separating the items into positively- and negatively-stated ones, the internal reliability of the negative items increased further (.76; see Table 8.1). It should be noted that most findings reported here for the frequency measure were also observed for the percentage-based measure.

Table 8.1
Means, Standard Deviations, Internal Consistencies, and Intercorrelations of the Variables Employed in the Study

				Correlations				
Variable	*M*	*SD*	α	1	2	3	4	5
1. A-B Scale	7.55	3.56	.69					
2. M-C Scale	14.72	4.55	.70	-.21				
3. T-Anxiety	19.46	3.84	.75	.10	-.13			
4. S-Anxiety	16.50	4.53	.81	.12	.02	.48***		
5. Denial-P	-0.10	0.49	.63	.20	.06	-.22*	-.19	
6. Denial-N	0.31	0.34	.76	.00	.16	-.30**	-.21	-.22*

Note. α: Cronbach's α; A-B Scale: Type A Behavior Pattern based on the Jenkins Activity Survey; M-C Scale: Marlowe & Crowne Social Desirability Scale; T-Anxiety: Trait-Anxiety; S-Anxiety: State-Anxiety; Denial-P: Positively-stated items of the Denial of Personal Relevance Inventory; Denial-N: Negatively-stated items of the Denial of Personal Relevance Inventory.
$^{*}p < .05$; $^{**}p < .01$; $^{***}p < .001$.

Characteristics of the Denial of Personal Relevance Inventory

Before we turn to the data relevant to our research question, we will present several analyses performed on the responses to the Denial of Personal Relevance Inventory. These analyses were intended to assess the quality of the inventory as a denial measure. When a total score was calculated for each subject (summing over all items), it was found that over 80% of the subjects obtained scores higher than zero. When scores were calculated for each item, about 70% of the items were found to have scores higher than zero. Thus, the general trend found on this questionnaire is a reduction in one's chances of suffering a negative event. These results are in agreement with previous research findings (e.g., Weinstein, 1982; Zakay, 1983). Accordingly, we may conclude that what the inventory measures is more than a realistic, veridical estimation of the occurrences of events.

To substantiate the above conclusion, we followed the procedure of Butler and Mathews (1983) and compared high and low anxious subjects (divided at the median of the anxiety scales) by applying an analysis of variance (ANOVA) to the total frequency scores. High-anxious students displayed lower scores than low-anxious ones when anxiety was measured both as a trait [means of 0.11 and 0.27 for high- and low-anxious students, respectively, $F(1,83) = 8.60$, $p < .01$] and a state [means of 0.13 and 0.27, respectively, $F(1,83) = 6.34$, $p < .01$].

Thus, high-anxious people assess their chances of experiencing negative events as higher than low-anxious ones do. Table 8.1 shows that for both positively- and negatively-stated items the correlations with Trait-Anxiety as well as State-Anxiety are negative. These data support the notion that our measure reflects a mechanism for rejecting the possibility of aversive events occuring.

Two types of items are of particular importance here, those pertaining to illness and physical problems or recovery from them (i.e., health) and those pertaining to success or failure (i.e., achievements). The means of the health-related items, separated into positively-stated (2 items) and negatively-stated (5 items), were 0.00 ($SD = 0.61$) and 0.23 ($SD = 0.45$), respectively, and the means of the positively-stated (2 items) and negatively-stated (5 items) achievement-related items were -0.15 ($SD = 0.74$) and 0.54 ($SD = 0.42$), respectively. A two-way ANOVA, Valence × Content, where valence refers to negatively-stated vs. positively-stated items and content to achievements vs. health, showed a significant effect for valence [$F(1,84) = 42.19$, $p < .0001$] and a significant Valence × Content interaction [$F(1,84) = 19.64$, $p < .0001$]. Subjects rated their personal chances on negatively-stated items lower as compared with the positively-stated items, and this effect was higher for achievements than for health events. These tendencies lend further support to the inventory as a measure of denial.

Denial and Type A

The aim of our study was to examine possible differences between Type As and Type Bs concerning the degree of denial for different types of information - achievement- and health-related. To achieve this, subjects were divided at the median point of the A-B Scale into Type As and Type Bs (above

Table 8.2
Means and Standard Deviations of Type A and Type B Subjects on the Denial of Personal Relevance Inventory

	Type A		Type B	
Type of item	*M*	*SD*	*M*	*SD*
Health-N	.17	.48	.30	.42
Achieve-N	.60	.44	.49	.38

Note. Health-N: Negatively-stated health-related items; Achieve-N: Negatively-stated achievement-related items.

and below the median, respectively), and two-way ANOVAs (A-B Scale × Content) were conducted separately for the scores of positively- and negatively stated items. For the positively-stated items, no differences were found between Type As and Type Bs, nor were there any interactions with content. However, for the negatively-stated items, a two-way ANOVA revealed a significant interaction effect [$F(1,81) = 6.13$, $p = .01$]. Table 8.2 indicates that Type As denied failure more, i.e., saw their chances of failure as lower than Type Bs did, whereas for the chances of falling ill, the opposite held true.

Interactions with Gender and Age

As the literature contains findings on the differences between Type A men and women in coping styles (Houtman, 1990; Martin et al., 1989), we conducted the above analyses a second time, adding gender as an independent variable. No significant effect was found for gender, and no significant interaction emerged between the A-B Scale and gender.

In view of reported findings on age differences in coping processes (Folkman, Lazarus, Pimley, & Novacek, 1987), the analyses were again conducted using age as an additional independent variable. Admittedly, the age range of our subjects was relatively small, since all were university students. Nevertheless, subjects were divided into younger and older at the median (23 years), resulting in a younger group of people (range = 20 - 22) and an older one (range = 23 - 35).

Table 8.3
Means and Standard Deviations of Younger and Older Type A and Type B Subjects on the Denial of Personal Relevance Inventory

		Younger subjects		Older subjects	
Type of item		Type A	Type B	Type A	Type B
Health-N	*M*	.07	.40	.23	.25
	SD	.55	.30	.42	.47
Achieve-N	*M*	.65	.36	.58	.55
	SD	.47	.44	.43	.34

Note. Health-N: Negatively-stated health-related items; Achieve-N: Negatively-stated achievement-related items.

A three-way ANOVA produced a significant interaction between the A-B Scale, age, and content [$F(1,81) = 7.43, p < .01$] for the negatively-stated items. As can be seen from Table 8.3, the effect of differential attitudes to health and achievements by Type A and Type B subjects appears mainly among the younger students.

Type A and Coping Dispositions

Thus far we have directly considered the question of the relationship between TABP and the denial of health- and achievement related information. However, we also sought to examine whether Type As differed from Type Bs with regard to coping dispositions in general. This was done by using the measure described by Krohne (1986), i.e., dividing the subjects at the median point into high and low on both anxiety, as measured by the Trait-Anxiety Scale, and defensiveness, as measured by the M-C Scale. This division results in four possible combinations, i.e., nondefensives (low scores on both variables), repressors (low on anxiety and high on defensiveness), sensitizers (high on anxiety and low on defensiveness), and high-anxious persons (high scores on both variables). These combinations are presented in Table 8.4, which reveals that the primary difference between Type As and Type Bs is that Type B subjects tend to be repressors while those defined as Type A show a tendency towards being sensitizers ($\chi^2 = 8.39, p < .05$). Moreover, a comparison of the sensitizers' and repressors' scores on the A-B Scale showed that sensitizers had significantly higher scores than repressors [the means were 8.76 ($SD = 3.94$) and 6.32 ($SD = 2.81$), respectively, $t(41) = 2.33, p < .05$]. The finding that Type As are sensitizers is also reported by Lobel (1988) and Weidner and Collins (this volume).

Table 8.4
Coping Dispositions of Type A and Type B Subjects

Coping dispositions	Type A	Type B
Nondefensives	13	13
Repressors	8	14
Sensitizers	16	5
High-anxious persons	6	10

Discussion

The original research question concerned the degree to which Type A individuals employ denial in regard to personal health- and achievement-related information. A clear-cut prediction is problematic. Some studies show that Type As tend to report fewer bodily symptoms, such as fatigue and pain, during the performance of a task, although they experience high physiological arousal (e.g., Carver et al., 1976; Weidner & Matthews, 1978), while others have found no differences between Type As and Type Bs in reporting symptoms of everyday life (Offutt & Lacroix, 1988). Previous studies have also been unable to produce unequivocal findings in regard to the Type As' attentiveness to information pertaining to their personal achievements. According to Smith and Anderson (1986), Type As are selectively attentive to negative feedback and evaluate their achievements as lower than they actually are, thus increasing the need for greater effort in order to improve their performance. Furthermore, they tend to report the use of active coping strategies (Carver et al., 1989; Hart, 1988) and are found to generally be sensitizers (e.g., Weidner & Collins, this volume). In contrast, Pittner and Houston (1980) found that Type As deny information which threatens their self-esteem more often than Type Bs do.

The present study made use of a questionnaire examining how individuals deny the personal relevance of different sorts of threat. We found that Type As showed a stronger tendency than Type Bs to estimate their chances of failure as lower than their chances of experiencing health problems. We interpret this to mean that Type As, as compared to Type Bs, deny potential failure more than potential illness. We found no differences between Type A men and women on this differential denial. We did however find a relation to age, whereby the Type As' greater tendency to deny failure more than illness manifested itself mainly among the younger students in our sample. Finally, when we measured coping dispositions by combining anxiety and defensiveness scores, Type As generally tended towards sensitization.

The question arises as to how to reconcile our findings with those reported in the literature. At first glance, it would appear that the Type As' tendency to deny failure does not go hand in hand with the notion that Type As employ selective attention in relation to negative feedback and evaluate their achievements as lower than they actually are (see Smith & Anderson, 1986). On the other hand, Gastorf and Teevan (1980) found that Type As expressed more fear of failure than Type Bs did and suggested that the great effort and hard work that Type As invest actually reflect their attempts to defensively avoid failure. Similarly, Pittner and Houston (1980) found that Type As employ denial when confronted with a threat to their self-esteem but not when threatened with an electric shock. Furthermore, Strube (1988) says that Type As attribute their successes to their efforts and competence but deny the internal attribution of their failures. It is therefore possible that Type As cope with particularly threatening situations, those where potential failure or poor achievements are involved, by means of denial but have no need to resort to denial when negative feedback is presented as something facilitating self-improvement or better task performance.

In addition, we found that Type As did not employ denial more often than Type Bs in regard to health-related data. On the contrary, they even seemed to deny this sort of information less than Type Bs did. This follows the results of several previous studies. In their review of the literature, Suls and Sanders (1988) show that of eight studies conducted on student samples, six found a higher level of reported symptoms and slight illnesses among individuals judged to be Type As. However, other studies have demonstrated that Type A individuals report fewer symptoms and less pain and fatigue during task performance (e.g., Carver et al., 1976; Weidner & Matthews, 1978). In order to reconcile this apparent contradiction, we must consider the fact that in the present study, as in others (see Suls & Sanders, 1988), the subjects were not examined under competitive conditions or during task performance. Thus, the finding that Type A individuals tend to ignore symptoms *during the performance of a task* might reflect that denial of failure we reported on above. Such an interpretation suggests that the admission of fatigue or symptoms of illness while performing a task would in fact be an admission of poor competence. Support for this explanation comes from an additional finding by Weidner and Matthews (1978): Type As reported fewer symptoms *during* task performance than they did when it was compled. No such difference was found for Type Bs. It would therefore seem that, while performing a task, Type As allocate all of their attention to it and thus are not attentive to distracting symptoms, whereas once the task has been accomplished, they are free to turn their attention to their bodily reactions.

In sum, the main conclusion of the present study is that Type A individuals deny negative events, such as potential failures, more often than Type Bs do. This conclusion fits Pittner and Houston's (1980) results concerning the Type As' use of denial in the context of self-evaluation as well as Strube's (1988) findings which indicate that Type As tend to deny personal responsibility for failure. In order to explain the denial of potential failure among Type A persons, we rely on its functional value for these individuals: In their struggle for success and excellence, the denial of limitations and failures can enhance their faith in their competence and may eliminate any sense of helplessness or inclination to give up, thus bolstering their drive for achievement and competitiveness. Since one of the most prominent traits of Type As is the setting of high and inflexible standards which are difficult to attain (Price, 1982), such individuals may be more in need of a mechanism allowing them to deny their limitations, both objective and perceived, in order to continue to set such standards for themselves.

Support for this interpretation is given by Snow (1978), who reports that in a series of puzzle solutions, Type As displayed a higher level of ambition than Type Bs did, despite the fact that there was no difference in their level of performance. Hence, in the setting of goals for themselves, Type As seem to deny the limitations of their abilities and exhibit an unrealistic attitude. Similarly, Glass (1977) reports that when Type Bs fail to reach the high standards they have set for themselves they generally recognize their limitations and lower these standards, reflecting a realistic evaluation of their abilities. On the other hand, when Type As fail to attain their high standards, they raise them even higher. It seems reasonable to assume that in order to do so, Type As must deny their failures or adopt an overly optimistic self-evaluation.

In addition, it should be recalled that Type As are described as persons who invest considerable effort in their performance, act under time pressure, and are hostile toward others who hinder their progress. According to Glass (1977), this is their coping style or response to anything which threatens their sense of control. Both failure and ill-health constitute such a threat. However, our subjects are relatively young adults and presumably do not feel the need to deny potential illness, since this is not yet a real problem for them. More importantly, responsibility for failure is more often attributed to the individual and his or her competence than is the responsibility for illness. Thus Type As might perceive potential failure as being fundamentally more controllable than potential illness and therefore more threatening to their self-image. This, in turn, can lead to cognitive avoidance of failure on the one hand, and to greater efforts to succeed and excel on the other.

An alternative interpretation of our results could be the following: Type As rate their chances of failure as lower than average because they usually work so hard and do so well that their chances of failure are realistically lower than those of the general population. Indeed, certain studies have shown that Type A individuals do attain higher scientific achievements (e.g., Matthews, Helmreich, Beane, & Lucker, 1980). However, in our comprehensive study we also included several memory and perceptual tasks and did not find that Type As perform better than Type Bs do, a fact also reported by other researchers (Snow, 1978). Moreover, the sample as a whole displayed a greater tendency to lower the chances of personal threats. In other words, the overall findings suggest that it is more reasonable to assume that underestimating one's chances of failure reflects denial than to consider this to be a realistic view of events.

It should be noted that the differential denial of failure was more prominent among the younger Type As, while for the older subjects, Type Bs resembled their Type A counterparts. This interaction should be investigated in future research.

We also examined coping dispositions using the classification employed by Krohne (1986). Type As, as also reported by Weidner and Collins (this volume), were found to be sensitizers, in contrast to their denial tendency in respect to personal failure. These findings demonstrate the importance of investigating denial or cognitive avoidance in relation to specific situations or contents, just as in the present study.

Conclusions and Possible Implications

Type A individuals seem to have a greater tendency, in contrast to Type Bs, to deny negative information pertaining to personal achievements, or more precisely failure than to deny negative information pertaining to health, i.e., the awareness of illness. In our opinion, the most reasonable explanation for these findings is that by means of denial Type As are able to persist in their struggle for success and excellence. The less they acknowledge their limitations and the more they deny failures, the more they continue to work in order to attain the high standards they set for themselves. In this manner, they increase their chances of success and, consequently, of failure as well. However, it appears that the price of attempting to succeed at all costs may be a hyperactive sympathetic nervous system, which may in time contribute to cardiovascular disorders. The results of our study therefore appear to support that kind of relationship between TABP and coronary disease which is mediated by expending energy and strenuous efforts beyond a medically prudent level, and this may, at least in part, be promoted by the denial of failure.

The findings of this study lend support to two major claims in regard to coping processes: First, the use of coping strategies depends on both the situation and the individual. In the present study this was reflected in the interaction between TABP and the denial of certain specific threats. Second, people may employ a range of combinations of coping strategies. Thus, Type A individuals, defined as active and dynamic and therefore responsive to problems with direct-action coping modes, react avoidantly regarding the personal relevance of negative information pertaining to their achievements and progress.

References

Ben-Zur, H., Weinstein, S., & Hashmonay, R. (1990). *Jenkins Activity Survey for Evaluation of the Type A Behavior Pattern. Student Version. Manual for the Hebrew Version.* Haifa, Israel: The Ray D. Wolfe Centre for Study of Psychological Stress, University of Haifa.

Bermudez, J., Perez-Garcia, A. M., & Sanchez-Elvira, M. A. (1990). Type-A behavior pattern and attentional performance. *Personality and Individual Differences, 11*, 13-18.

Breznitz, S. (1983). The seven kinds of denial. In S. Breznitz (Ed.), *The denial of stress* (pp. 257-280). New York: International Universities Press.

Breznitz, S. (1990). *Enhancing performance under stress by information about its expected duration.* (Final Technical Report to ARI Contract No. DAJA-86-C-0048). Haifa, Israel: University of Haifa.

Butler, G., & Mathews, A. (1983). Cognitive processes in anxiety. *Advances in Behaviour Research and Therapy, 5*, 51-62.

Carver, C. S., Coleman, A. E., & Glass, D. C. (1976). The coronary-prone behavior pattern and the suppression of fatigue on a treadmill test. *Journal of Personality and Social Psychology, 33*, 460-466.

Carver, C. S., Scheier, M. F., & Weintraub, J. K. (1989). Assessing coping strategies: A theoretically based approach. *Journal of Personality and Social Psychology, 56*, 267-283.

Crowne, D. P., & Marlowe, D. (1964). *The approval motive: Studies in evaluative dependence.* New York: Wiley.

Dimsdale, J. E., & Hackett, T. P. (1982). Effect of denial on cardiac health and psychological assessment. *American Journal of Psychiatry, 139*, 1477-1480.

Dorpat, T. L. (1985). *Denial and defense in the therapeutic situation.* New York: Jason Aronson.

Erdelyi, M. (1974). A new look at the new look: Perceptual defense and vigilance. *Psychological Review, 81*, 1-25.

Feuerstein, M., Labbé, E. E., & Kuczmierczyk, A. R. (1986). *Health psychology: A psychobiological perspective.* New York: Plenum.

Folkman, S., Lazarus, R. S., Pimley, S., & Novacek, J. (1987). Age differences in stress and coping processes. *Psychology and Aging, 2*, 171-184.

Friedman, H., & Booth-Kewley, S. (1987). The "disease-prone personality". *American Psychologist, 42*, 539-555.

Friedman, M., & Rosenman, R. (1974). *Type A behavior and your heart.* New York: Knopf.

Friedman, M., & Ulmer, D. (1984). *Treating Type A behavior and your heart.* New York: Knopf.

Gastorf, J. M., & Teevan, R. C. (1980). Type A coronary-prone behavior pattern and fear of failure. *Motivation and Emotion, 4*, 71-76.

Glass, D. C. (1977). *Behavior patterns, stress, and coronary disease.* Hillsdale, NJ: Erlbaum.

Haan, N. (1977). *Coping and defending: Processes of self-environment organization.* New York: Academic Press.

Hart, K. E. (1988). Association of Type A behavior and its components to ways of coping with stress. *Journal of Psychosomatic Research, 32*, 213-219.

Heilbrun, A. B., Jr., & Renert, D. (1986). Type A behavior, cognitive defense, and stress. *Psychological Reports, 58*, 447-456.

Holroyd, K. A., & Lazarus, R. S. (1982). Stress, coping, and somatic adaptation. In L. Goldberger & S. Breznitz (Eds.), *Handbook of stress: Theoretical and clinical aspects* (pp. 21-33). New York: The Free Press.

Houston, B. K. (1983). Psychophysiological responsivity and the Type A behavior pattern. *Journal of Research in Personality, 17*, 22-39.

Houtman, I. L. D. (1990). Personal coping resources and sex differences. *Personality and Individual Differences, 11*, 53-63.

Ilfeld, F. W., Jr. (1980). Coping styles of Chicago adults: Description. *Journal of Human Stress, 6 (2)*, 2-10.

Jenkins, C. D., Zyzanski, S. J., & Rosenman, R.H. (1979). *Jenkins Activity Survey.* New York: The Psychological Corporation.

Krantz, D. S., & Manuck, S. B. (1984). Acute psychophysiologic reactivity and risk of cardiovascular disease: A review and methodologic critique. *Psychological Bulletin, 96*, 435-464.

Krohne, H. W. (1978). Individual differences in coping with stress and anxiety. In C. D. Spielberger & I. G. Sarason (Eds.), *Stress and anxiety* (Vol. 5, pp. 233-260). Washington, DC: Hemisphere.

Krohne, H. W. (1986). Coping with stress: Dispositions, strategies, and the problem of measurement. In M. H. Appley & R. Trumbull (Eds.), *Dynamics of stress: Physiological, psychological, and social perspectives* (pp. 207-232). New York: Plenum.

Krohne, H. W. (1989). The concept of coping modes: Relating cognitive person variables to actual coping behavior. *Advances in Behaviour Research and Therapy, 11*, 235-248.

Lawler, K. A., & Schmied, L. A. (1988). Allocation of attention and physiological responsivity in the Type A coronary-prone individual. *Perceptual and Motor Skills, 67*, 103-113.

Lazarus, R. S. (1966). *Psychological stress and the coping process.* New York: McGraw-Hill.

Lazarus, R. S. (1983). The costs and benefits of denial. In S. Breznitz (Ed.), *The denial of stress* (pp. 1-30). New York: International Universities Press.

Lazarus, R. S., & Folkman, S. (1984). *Stress, appraisal, and coping.* New York: Springer.

Lifshitz-Cooney, J., & Zeichner, A. (1985). Selective attention to negative feedback in Type A and Type B individuals. *Journal of Abnormal Psychology, 94*, 110-112.

Lobel, T. E. (1988). Personality correlates of Type A coronary-prone behavior. *Journal of Personality Assessment, 52*, 434-440.

Magnusson, D. (1982). Situational determinants of stress: An interactional perspective. In L. Goldberger & S. Breznitz (Eds.), *Handbook of stress: Theoretical and clinical aspects* (pp. 231-253). New York: The Free Press.

Martin, R. A., Kuiper, N. A., & Westra, H. A. (1989). Cognitive and affective components of the Type A behavior pattern: Preliminary evidence for a self-worth contingency model. *Personality and Individual Differences, 10*, 771-784.

Matthews, K. A. (1982). Psychological perspectives on the Type A behavior pattern. *Psychological Bulletin, 91*, 293-323.

Matthews, K. A., & Brunson, B. I. (1979). Allocation of attention and the Type A coronary-prone behavior pattern. *Journal of Personality and Social Psychology*, 37, 2081-2090.

Matthews, K. A., Helmreich, R. L., Beane, W. E., & Lucker, G. W. (1980). Pattern A, achievement striving, and scientific merit: Does pattern A help or hinder? *Journal of Personality and Social Psychology, 39*, 962-967.

Miller, S. M. (1989). Cognitive informational styles in the process of coping with threat and frustration. *Advances in Behaviour Research and Therapy, 11*, 223-234.

Moos, R. H., & Billings, A. G. (1982). Conceptualizing and measuring coping resources and processes. In L. Goldberger & S. Breznitz (Eds.), *Handbook of stress: Theoretical and clinical aspects* (pp. 212-230). New York: The Free Press.

Mullen, B., & Suls, J. (1982). The effectiveness of attention and rejection as coping styles: A meta-analysis of temporal differences. *Journal of Psychosomatic Research, 26*, 43-49.

Offutt, C., & Lacroix, J. M. (1988). Type A behavior pattern and symptom reports: A prospective investigation. *Journal of Behavioral Medicine, 11*, 227-237.

Pittner, M. S., & Houston, B. K. (1980). Response to stress, cognitive coping strategies, and the Type A behavior pattern. *Journal of Personality and Social Psychology, 39*, 147-157.

Pittner, M. S., Houston, B. K., & Spirdigliozzi, G. (1983). Control over stress, Type A behavior pattern, and response to stress. *Journal of Personality and Social Psychology, 44*, 627-637.

Price, V. A. (1982). *Type A behavior pattern: A model for research and practice*. New York: Academic Press.

Roldan, F. H. (1987). Type A behavior, attention, and the report of subjective arousal. *Psychotherapy and Psychosomatics, 47*, 219-226.

Smith, T. W., & Anderson, N. B. (1986). Models of personality and disease: An interactional approach to Type A behavior and cardiovascular risk. *Journal of Personality and Social Psychology, 50*, 1166-1173.

Smith, T. W., & Rhodewalt, F. (1986). On states, traits, and processes: A transactional alternative to the individual difference assumptions in Type A behavior and physiological reactivity. *Journal of Research in Personality, 20*, 229-251.

Snow, B. (1978). Level of aspiration in coronary prone and noncoronary prone adults. *Personality and Social Psychology Bulletin, 4*, 416-419.

Spence, D. (1983). The paradox of denial. In S. Breznitz (Ed.), *The denial of stress* (pp. 103-123). New York: International Universities Press.

Spielberger, C. D., Barker, L., Russell, S., Silva De Crane, R., Westberry, L., Knight, J., & Marks, E. (1979). *Preliminary manual for the State-Trait Personality Inventory (STPI)*. Tampa, FL: University of South Florida.

Strube, M. J. (1988). Performance attributions and the Type A behavior pattern: Causal sources versus causal dimensions. *Personality and Social Psychology Bulletin, 14*, 709-721.

Suls, J., & Fletcher, B. (1985). The relative efficacy of avoidant and nonavoidant coping strategies: A meta-analysis. *Health Psychology, 4*, 249-288.

Suls, J., & Sanders, G. S. (1988). Type A behavior as a general risk factor for physical disorder. *Journal of Behavioral Medicine, 11*, 201-226.

Taylor, S. E. (1990). Health psychology: The science and the field. *American Psychologist, 45*, 40-50.

Taylor, S. E., & Brown, J. D. (1988). Illusion and well-being: A social psychological perspective on mental health. *Psychological Bulletin, 103*, 193-210.

Weidner, G., & Matthews, K. A. (1978). Reported physical symptoms elicited by unpredictable events and the Type A coronary-prone behavior pattern. *Journal of Personality and Social Psychology, 36*, 1213-1220.

Weinstein, N. D. (1982). Unrealistic optimism about susceptibility to health problems. *Journal of Behavioral Medicine, 5*, 441-460.

Wright, L. (1988). The Type A behavior pattern and coronary artery disease. *American Psychologist, 43*, 2-14.

Yarnold, P. R., Mueser, K. T., Grau, B. W., & Grimm, L. G. (1986). The reliability of the student version of the Jenkins Activity Survey. *Journal of Behavioral Medicine, 9*, 401-414.

Zakay, D. (1983). The relationship between the probability assessor and the outcomes of an event as a determiner of subjective probability. *Acta Psychologica, 53*, 271-280.

Zeidner, M., & Ben-Zur, H. (1988). The Hebrew adaptation of the state-trait personality inventory. In R. Schwarzer, H. M. van der Ploeg, & C. D. Spielberger (Eds.), *Advances in test anxiety research* (Vol. 6, pp. 253-262). Amsterdam/Lisse: Swets & Zeitlinger.

Chapter 9

Heartbeat Perception, Coping, and Emotion

Volker Hodapp and Joachim F. Knoll

Introduction

The field of interoception research has only recently been developed in psychophysiology. It is concerned with the perception of internal physiological processes. How is this perceptional process to be described? What variables influence this process? What methods can be used to assess an individual's perception?

Of course, the question about the relationship between autonomic activity and its perception is a question of emotion. As early as 1884, William James claimed in his famous theory that one cannot imagine the experience of emotions without the perception of physiological changes. That which would remain without this perception would not be an emotion but merely "cold cognition".

Although the main interest in interoception research was fuelled by peripherally oriented emotion theories, this branch of research could be used profitably to answer a number of further questions. For example, the question about the role of attention to physiological processes led to the study of symptoms and physical complaints (cf. Pennebaker, 1981b). Interoception research could also be linked to studies on coping. Attention to threat-relevant characteristics of a situation is one of the key concepts in most coping theories (cf. Krohne, Chapter 2 in this volume; Mathews, this volume; Miller, Combs, & Kruus, this volume). This attention is not only focused on aspects inherent in the situation but may also be directed to bodily and physiological reactions (cf. Kohlmann, this volume). Although a connection between interoception and coping research suggests itself thematically, joint research has scarcely been conducted up to now.

In this article we will make a first attempt to bring together both research approaches. In the first section, essential methods of interoception research are considered. Using the example of heartbeat perception, various paradigms for the assessment of heartbeat perception ability are discussed and a new method is presented. In the second section, the question of the relationship between interoception, emotion, and coping is raised. Finally, in the third section an experiment dealing with the influence of heartbeat perception and coping on emotion is presented.

We are indebted to Anette Folten for her assistance with the research.

Methods of Interoception Research

Researchers in the field of interoception strive to investigate the impact of interoceptive stimuli evoked by autonomous processes on an individual's behavior and experience. Most of this work concentrates on examining the effects of afferent signals evoked by the activity of the cardiovascular system. The experiments on heartbeat perception make up the majority of this work. Additionally, there are a number of experiments studying the perception of blood pressure (Greenstadt, Shapiro, & Whitehead, 1986; Kohlmann, this volume), electrodermal activity (Diekhoff, 1976; Kerres, 1985; Lacroix, 1977), or the activities of the gastro-intestinal system (Whitehead & Drescher, 1980).

Since the experiments on interoception and emotion form part of the field of heartbeat perception research, the methods used and the problems that arise will be described in detail.

Methods of Heartbeat Perception Research

A large amount of the work on heartbeat perception published so far has not been concerned with substantial aspects of individuals' abilities to perceive their heartbeats but with the development of a suitable method for measuring this ability.

At first glance, the construction of such a method does not seem to be too problematic. First, a heartbeat is - contrary to other autonomous processes (such as fluctuations in blood pressure) - a discrete, quantifiable event; second, the measurement of heart rate does not provide any difficulties. For this purpose, an ECG recording is sufficient.

However, the last two decades have led to a "method boom" in heartbeat perception research. A variety of different methods has been presented with the intention of improving the hitherto existing methods or replacing them with new ones.

The main problem in the construction of an optimal method is the development of a procedure that is not too difficult; otherwise people with different abilities in perceiving their heartbeats could not be differentiated. On the other hand, the method must possess an adequate validity for a sensible interpretation of ability scores. "Validity" here means that a person's score solely mirrors real *perception* ability, not the ability to *estimate* the current heart rate.

An examination of the methods developed so far reveals that some of the earlier methods neglected the aspect of validity. More current methods, designed to overcome this deficit, display such a high degree of difficulty that a differentiation between people according to their perception abilities becomes impossible. It has only been during the last few years that methods have been described which seem to overcome this dilemma, at least to a certain degree.

The fact that in heartbeat perception research the development of methods is so overrepresented leads to still another problem. A vast variety of methods has not only been developed but also employed in experiments on important questions (cf. Davis, Langer, Sutterer, Gelling, & Marlin, 1986; Pennebaker & Hoover, 1984). Since parts of the methods employed differ enormously, it seems vital to relate results obtained using different procedures, especially since systematic comparisons of methods have scarcely been made. For an assessment of experimental results, knowledge of the method used is a necessity.

The existing methods for determining the quality of heartbeat perception can be roughly divided into two categories: tracking procedures and discrimination tasks.

Tracking procedures require an individual to track his or her heartbeat. By relating a subject's protocol to the actual cardiac activity, a measure of heartbeat perception ability can be derived.

The common characteristic of *discrimination tasks* is that the subject has to discriminate between two or more series of signals which have a certain temporal relation to the ongoing cardiac activity. A person's discrimination capability serves as a measure of perception ability.

Tracking procedures

In his experiment on the relationship between the ability to perceive autonomous arousal and the ability to control these processes, McFarland (1975) describes a nonverbal method for the assessment of heartbeat perception ability. A similar procedure has already been described by Brener (1974). McFarland instructed his subjects to push a button according to the rhythm of their heartbeat. The number of button pushes and the actual number of heartbeats according to the ECG were recorded, and a "heart activity perception" score (HAP) was calculated: For each trial, the absolute number of button pushes minus the number of heartbeats was divided by the number of heartbeats.

In spite of its relative simplicity, the McFarland procedure has not spread in heartbeat perception research, because doubts have arisen mainly concerning its validity. As is the case for all tracking procedures, a decision about whether a given score is based on perception or estimation of the heart rate is not possible (cf. Montgomery & Jones, 1984; Yates, Jones, Marie, & Hogben, 1985). In a carefully conducted study, Flynn and Clemens (1988) were able to confirm these doubts concerning the validity of the procedure.

The same criticism can be applied to the mental tracking procedure developed by Schandry (1981). This procedure is conceivably simple. During a time interval marked by a tone, the subject has to quietly count his or her heartbeat. After each trial, the subject informs the experimenter of the results. For each trial, the absolute value of the difference between counted heartbeats and actual heartbeats is calculated and divided by the number of actual heartbeats. The assessment of heartbeat perception ability generally consists of a number of trials separated by short breaks. The subject does not receive information about the length of the intervals. As is true for all tracking procedures, it is not possible to decide whether a given score is based on good heartbeat perception or on an adequate estimation of the heart rate (cf. Montgomery & Jones, 1984).

Discrimination procedures

The discrimination procedures presented below have been developed in an attempt to overcome the obvious deficits of the tracking procedures. As has been mentioned above, discrimination tasks require a subject to discriminate between two or more series of signals differing in their temporal relationship to the ongoing cardiac activity.

In the *S^+ series (coincident with heartbeats)*, the signal (e.g., a tone) is synchronized with the heartbeat. If the subject perceives his/her heartbeat, he/she gets the subjective experience of two simultaneously perceived stimuli, namely heartbeat and tone. The *S^- series (non-coincident)* consists of signals that are not synchronous with the heartbeat. Here, the subject gets the impression that heartbeat and external signal are perceived at different times.

The differences between varying discrimination procedures lie in the kind of external signals that are employed and above all in the way that contingent and non-contingent signal series are operationalized.

The "Whitehead Paradigm" (Whitehead, Drescher, Heiman, & Blackwell, 1977) is the one most frequently employed in experiments on heartbeat perception ability. Moreover, this method forms the basis of the paradigms created by Davis et al. (1986), Katkin, Blascovich, and Goldband (1981), and Störmer (1988).

The subject has to discriminate between two stimulus series placed in different temporal relations to the R-wave of the ECG. In the S^+ series, the delay between R-wave and signal is 128 ms, while in the S^- series, the delay is 384 ms. After each trial of 10 s duration, the subject has to decide whether the stimulus series has been presented synchronously with the heartbeat or after a delay. Tones or light flashes of short duration are usually used as external stimuli.

A person's heartbeat perception score is derived with the help of the signal detection theory (SDT), which offers the advantage of determining discrimination ability independently of non-sensoric influences, such as response tendencies.

The Whitehead paradigm attains its high validity by coupling both stimulus series with the ongoing cardiac activity. Thus, it is guaranteed that the series do not differ in their stimulus characteristics per se. These series cannot be distinguished without adequate heartbeat perception as a point of reference for their assessment. Furthermore, manipulations of cardiac activity on the subject's part will lead to identical changes in both series. Consequently, such kinds of manipulations cannot be used by the subject for the discrimination of stimulus series.

The first substantial modification of the Whitehead paradigm was presented by Katkin et al. (1981). In order to retain the advantages of the Whitehead paradigm and to enhance the distinction between the S^+ and S^- tone series, Katkin especially modified the temporal placement of the S^- stimuli. While Whitehead always placed the signals of the S^- series 384 ms after the R-wave, in the Katkin paradigm the differences between the stimuli (tones 1000 Hz, 50 ms duration) and the R-wave increase during one trial.

The most recent modification of the Whitehead paradigm has been developed by Störmer (1988). Like Katkin's method it differs from the "original" mainly in the temporal positioning of the S^+ and S^- signals (Whitehead et al., 1977). It originates from the basic assumption that the delays between successive heartbeats within a trial do not always have the same duration. Due to different cardiovascular regulation mechanisms controlled by the central nervous system, this leads to a more or less large variability in the delays between two heartbeats (IBI). If the signals of the coincident and the non-coincident tone series are always placed at constant intervals to the R-wave of the ECG, as in the previously described discrimination tasks, the relative position of the signal within the cardiac cycle is not always the same. The subject experiences that the delay between the perception of a heartbeat and the perception of the signal is not constant within a stimulus series. This could considerably increase the subjects' difficulties in discriminating between stimulus series in most paradigms.

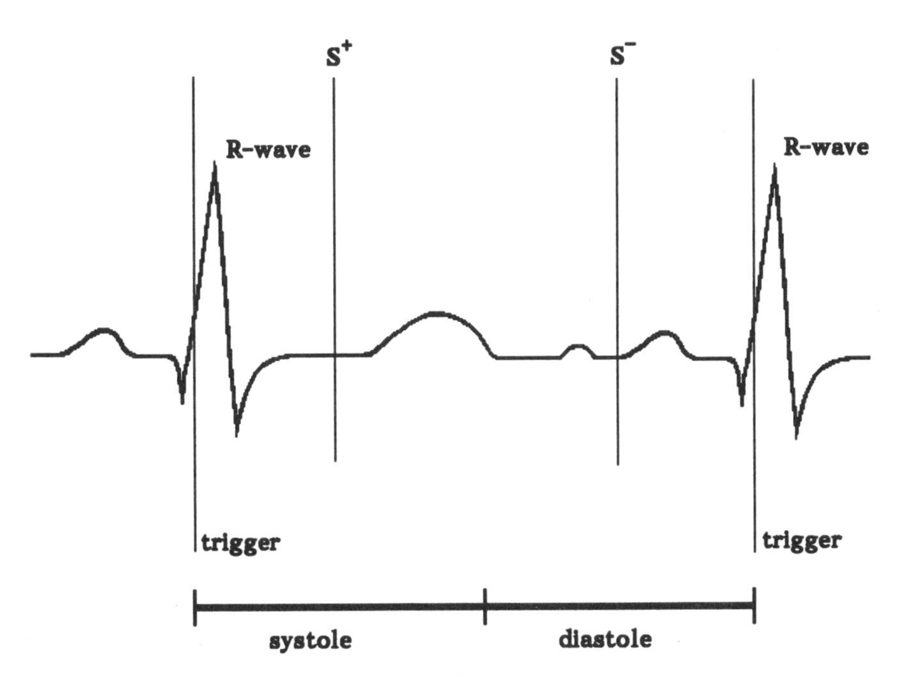

Figure 9.1. Placement of the coincident (S^+) and non-coincident (S^-) tone signals in the cardiac cycle.

In order to keep the relative position of a stimulus constant within one heart cycle, in the Störmer paradigm we start to estimate the expected duration of the ongoing IBI based on the duration of the IBI immediately before it. The signals of the S^+ series (usually eight tones within one trial) are placed after a quarter of the estimated duration of the ongoing IBI. The S^- signals are placed after three quarters of the estimated IBI duration. For example, if an IBI lasts 800 ms, an S^+ stimulus would be placed 200 ms after the R-wave of the next IBI. For an S^- stimulus, this delay would be 600 ms (cf. Figure 9.1).

A comparison between the Whitehead, Katkin, and Störmer paradigms has revealed that the highest average ability scores could be achieved with the Störmer paradigm (Störmer, Heiligtag, & Knoll, 1989). Consequently, the Störmer paradigm can be considered the easiest of the hitherto developed discrimination tasks. Although the three procedures differ only slightly in the placement of the S^+ and the S^- signals, these differences affect the difficulty levels of the procedures to a large degree.

Interoception, Coping, and Emotion

Heartbeat Perception and Emotion

Emotion theories

The methods for assessing heartbeat perception have proven to be of particular value for the research on emotion and coping. A number of emotion theories that can be labelled as peripheral emotion theories (Fehr & Stern, 1970) emphasize the role of physiological arousal. Physiological arousal is considered to be a fundamental component which is primarily involved in the onset of emotions. Curiously enough, although a key role has been ascribed to the perception of physiological arousal in these concepts of emotion, it has not been explicitly included in the model nor regarded as a variable which varies individually.

The most well-known emotion theories of interest for interoception research are those developed by James (1884) and Schachter and Singer (1962). William James claimed that an emotion is defined by the perception of a physiological process produced by a certain stimulus configuration. While James assigned a specific physiological reaction to every emotion, Schachter and Singer postulated a more common, non-specific dimension of arousal which is supposed to determine the quality of an emotion in combination with certain situationally specific cues. The perception and processing of external cues determine the experienced emotion. However, both approaches have something in common: Physiological arousal is considered a necessary condition for the onset of emotions. Moreover, the perception of arousal seems to be the crucial variable. William James considers that the perception of arousal is equivalent to the emotion itself, while Schachter and Singer claim it triggers a cognitive search for an explanation. Similarly, autonomic activity has been ascribed great importance by more recent emotion theories. According to the discrepancy/evaluation theory (MacDowell & Mandler, 1989), experienced emotions are a product of autonomic arousal and evaluative cognitions. Cognitive evaluation is supposed to determine the quality of emotion, while peripheral arousal should determine the strength of the reaction. None of the hitherto reported approaches pays attention to the fact that people might differ in their perception and that the ability to perceive physiological arousal cannot be assumed to be equal for all people.

An attempt to make more accurate predictions from these emotion theories for the field of interoception research necessitates the study of the relationship between the intensity of an emotion, the amount of physiological arousal, and the quality of its perception (Katkin, Blaskovich, & Koenigsberg, 1984). In spite of the small number of empirical results, the findings of some studies seem to justify the postulation that the intensity of physiological arousal covaries with the quality of heartbeat perception.

Arousal and heartbeat perception

Schandry and Specht (1981) conducted an experiment dealing with this problem, in which subjects were tested under three conditions: one resting condition, once immediately before a speech the subjects were expected to give, and once after 20 to 40 knee bends. In the last two conditions, the subjects not only had higher heart rates than in the resting condition, but they were also more able to precisely estimate their heart rates. Similarly, Jones and Hollandsworth (1981) and Montgomery, Jones, and Hollandsworth (1984) were able to show that increases in activity induced by physiological strain were accompanied by increases in heartbeat perception ability. However, if tonic measures of cardiovascular activity instead of phasic changes are correlated with heartbeat perception, correlations of heart rate and discrimination abilities have rarely been found (Clemens, 1984; Jones, O'Leary, & Pipkin, 1984; Knoll & Hodapp, 1991; Montgomery & Jones, 1984). On the other hand, Davis et al. (1986) found that subjects with high heart rate variability displayed higher discrimination achievements than subjects with low heart rate variability. Bestler, Schandry, Weitkunat, and Alt (1990) studied the connection between various cardiodynamic parameters and the quality of heartbeat perception. The strongest associations could be found for stroke volume (r = 0.62) and for contractility of the myocard (r = 0.45).

Emotion and heartbeat perception

At the present stage it is not clear whether the relationship between the strength of physiological arousal and the perception of the heartbeat could lead to statements about the connection between heartbeat perception and emotions. On the basis of the above-mentioned peripherally oriented emotion theories, physiological arousal should determine the strength of an emotion in a certain situation. People with better heartbeat perception are supposed to display stronger emotions than people who cannot or can only poorly perceive these processes.

From a number of empirical results, it seems reasonable to suggest a positive relationship between the strength of an emotion and cardiac perception. Schandry (1981) asked good and poor heartbeat perceivers to fill in a number of questionnaires. Good perceivers reached higher scores on the "emotional lability scale" of the FPI (Fahrenberg, Selg, & Hampel, 1978) and on the A-State scale of the STAI (Spielberger, Gorsuch, & Lushene, 1970).

In a further experiment, Schandry (1983) found an increase in correct heart rate estimation after training accompanied by an increase in state anxiety (r = 0.37). A positive connection between heartbeat perception and A-State was also reported by Ludwick-Rosenthal and Neufeld (1985).

Katkin and his research group chose a more direct approach for assessing the influence of autonomic activity and heartbeat perception on emotion. They tested the hypothesis that the presentation of aversive stimuli would lead to an increase of affective arousal, which in turn should cause an increase in cardiovascular activity and heartbeat discrimination (Katkin, Blascovich, Reed, Adamec, Jones, & Taublieb, 1982). Heartbeat perception was tested under three conditions (positive, neutral, and aversive slides). The presentation of aversive slides (mutilated victims of serious traffic accidents) led to a most distinct rise in discrimination ability. The changes in perceptional achievement, however, were accompanied by a decrease in tonic heart rate.

In another experiment (Hantas, Katkin, & Blaskovich, 1982), the influence of the accuracy of heartbeat perception on the strength of affect was investigated. First, 63 male students were divided into 17 "good" perceivers (discrimination above chance level) and 46 "poor" perceivers (chance level) on the basis of their pretest achievements. All subjects were shown the above-mentioned aversive slides. During the first presentation, the subjects only looked at the slides while changes in heart rate were recorded. During the second presentation, they rated emotional reactions on a 7-point scale ranging from "very relaxed" to "very excited". Although good and poor perceivers did not differ in heart rate, good perceivers rated themselves as excited more often than poor perceivers did. Katkin (1985) sees this as a confirmation of the basic concepts of peripheral emotion theories.

Determinants of Interoception

Present models of interoception are considered to be too simple and in need of extension. Proposals for a more accurate analysis of the perception and evaluation of internal processes have been especially made by Pennebaker (1981a; Pennebaker & Brittingham, 1982; Pennebaker & Epstein, 1983). Pennebaker (1981b) assumes three basic determinants for the perception of physiological processes: 1. the amount of internal stimulation, 2. beliefs or preconceptions about physiological activity, and 3. the amount of competing information.

The connections between internal stimulation and the quality of perception have been referred to in the previous section. However, compared with these emotion theories, Pennebaker introduces a new idea: a person's beliefs and anticipations in a situation can influence the perception of physiological reactions (Pennebaker & Epstein, 1983). Beliefs or preconceptions about physiological activity are in turn able to arouse physiological activity. Nevertheless, the decisive argument is that the perception of physiological processes can be modified by a person's implicit psychophysiology.

It is reasonable to assume that these factors reported by Pennebaker are equally important in heartbeat perception. Thus, the experiments conducted by Katkin et al. on the relationsip between emotion and cardiac perception can be viewed from this perspective. If subjects are confronted with aversive slides, their attention shifts to the perception of strong emotional stimuli, in contrast to the determination of heartbeat perception ability in a resting condition. An *estimation* of arousal could be made even without autonomic changes based solely on the emotional setting. Such an estimation becomes more likely as external cues dominate over internal cues.

A well-known theory of emotions discusses in detail the possibility of manipulating emotions solely by changing the cognitive representation of autonomic processes (Valins, 1966, 1967). Interestingly enough, this theory makes contrary predictions about the connection between emotion and heartbeat perception discussed in the previous section. Good heartbeat perceivers are not as easy to deceive with faked feedback as poor perceivers are. Therefore, people who are less proficient in heartbeat perception or people on a lower level of arousal are supposed to be especially susceptible to feedback effects and to react more emotionally to external cues than good perceivers or better-trained people do (Katkin et al., 1984). Similarly, under low arousal conditions, the connection between heartbeat perception and emotion proposed in Valins' theory is to be expected, compared to a positive connection between both variables expected under high arousal conditions. In fact, Eichler, Katkin, Blascovich, and Kelsey (1987) found negative correlations between perceptional ability and emotion ratings during the examination of aversive slides (cf. Krämer & Erdmann, 1990).

Interoception and Coping

Although several concepts of emotion have been related to heartbeat perception, it is remarkable that little attention has been paid to the connection between interoception and coping. Studies in the field of coping research could lead to the assumption that sensitizers rely more on internal sensoric information and, therefore, pay more attention to physiological processes (Pennebaker & Brittingham, 1982; see also Miller et al., this volume). However, a generalization of this relationship seems to be problematic. Although self-consciousness correlates positively with the naming of symptoms, the relationship between self-attentiveness and interoception has not yet been clarified. While Weisz, Balázs, and Adám (1988) found higher values in a heartbeat perception task under a mirror condition, Pennebaker and Epstein (1983) and Störmer (1988) were not able to demonstrate connections between heartbeat perception ability and scores on self-attentiveness.

The studies in the framework of coping research seem to be relevant for interoception research mainly under the following viewpoints: If differing coping styles refer to the way people perceive and evaluate threatening information (Krohne & Rogner, 1982), the perception and cognitive representation of internal physiological signals can be considered an indicator of coping with threatening situations. Emotional and physiological arousal is a source of information for the individual mirroring the threat of a situation and coping with a danger more or less successfully. The notion that people with a vigilant coping style ("sensitizers") are better heartbeat perceivers than people that prefer an avoidant coping style ("repressers") would correspond with empirical findings, according to which repression covaries with the amount of discrepancy between subjective and objective measures of arousal (Weinberger, Schwartz, & Davidson, 1979; Weinstein, Averill, Opton, & Lazarus, 1968; for an overview cf. Kohlmann, 1990). Taking into account the association between sensitization and anxiety, this result is in line with the finding that clinically high-anxious individuals display greater discrepancies between physiological indicators and subjective estimations than normal individuals do (Gannon, 1984).

The relationship between interoception and coping is differentiated in another way in Krohne's new conception of coping modes (Krohne, 1989, and Chapter 2 in this volume). According to this model, "people who use rigid cognitive avoidance ("repressers") can be described by their tendency to pay little attention, both mentally and instrumentally, to threat-relevant characteristics of a situation. For these people, the emotional arousal triggered by cues prior to confrontation with an aversive event should constitute a major threat. They try to cope with this threat by disregarding these particular cues" (Krohne, 1989, p. 237). In contrast to repressers, sensitizers consistently pay attention to threat-relevant (external and internal) aspects of a situation. According to this model, sensitizers should react more sensitively to physiological cues than repressers do. However, this conclusion is speculative since the exact relationship between the attention directed to internal physiological cues and the resulting perception of these cues has not yet been clarified.

An Experiment on the Influence of Heartbeat Perception and Coping Style on the Intensity of Emotions

As revealed by the discussion on the contribution of different emotion theories to the field of physiological arousal perception, different hypotheses about the connection between interoception and the intensity of emotion can be postulated. According to the peripheral physiological approach, there is a positive relationship between emotion and heartbeat perception, whereas according to Valin's cognitive approach, the opposite association is expected.

Coping theories also assume connections between coping style, perceived and actual arousal, and the intensity of emotion. Regarding the concepts of repression/sensitization, a positive relationship between sensitization and heartbeat perception can be postulated. A better autonomic perception for sensitizers may therefore be assumed. However, previously conducted studies have not taken the ability to perceive autonomic arousal into consideration. In order to examine various hypotheses about the relationship between coping style, the perception of autonomic arousal, and emotion, the following experiment was conducted.

Experimental Design and Procedure

The experiment extended over two sessions. During the first session the heartbeat perception ability was determined, whereby Schandry's (1981) "mental tracking" method and the discrimination procedure developed by Störmer et al. (1989) were used. A comparison between both methods is discussed elsewhere (Knoll & Hodapp, in press). The discrimination procedure was selected to investigate the relationship between heartbeat perception and emotion, as this method particularly registers a person's perception *ability*, independent of the possibility of that person being able to *estimate* physiological arousal according to situational factors.

The heartbeat perception ability was determined according to the discrimination procedure described by Störmer et al. (1989). After an adaptation period and the mental tracking task, the subjects underwent five 'introductory' trials of the discrimination procedure. Ninety trials followed, arranged in three blocks of 30 trials each, in which the subjects were supposed to state whether the acoustic signals were given at the same time as their own heartbeat or after a delay. The subjects did this by operating a keyboard which additionally registered the degree of certainty of the responses.

The second phase of the experiment dealt with the inducement of emotion. Several days after the first experimental session, the subjects were asked to come to the laboratory again. They were then distributed randomly into two groups. After an adaptation period, all subjects were shown two non-aversive test slides. Subsequently, the experimental group was presented with ten aversive slides and the control group with ten neutral ones. The slides with the aversive, emotionally threatening contents showed disfigured victims of traffic accidents or crimes of violence, whereas the neutral slides showed objects of daily use. All slides, shown for 20 seconds, were taken from a standardized series of slides with reference estimations concerning their valency and activating effect (Bradley, Greenwald, & Hamm, in press).

The emotional reactions to the slides were recorded using two procedures. One was the non-verbal rating procedure "Self Assessment Manikin" (SAM), which consists of several figures showing stylized representations of differing grades of valency and physiological arousal (Bradley et al., in press). After each slide, the subjects were asked to mark the manikin which best reflected their experience. In addition, a questionnaire was administered consisting of the

State-Anxiety and State-Anger subscales of the German "State-Trait Personality Inventory" (STPI; Hodapp, 1988) as well as some items describing perceived arousal of the cardiovascular system. This questionnaire was presented at the end of the slide presentation with instructions to characterize the emotional condition experienced while watching the slides.

Besides the emotional experience, physiological variables were also recorded. By continuously recording the ECG during the slide presentation, it was possible to obtain the mean heart rate over all slides. The further calculations refer to the difference between the heart rate recorded while the ten slides were shown and that recorded during the presentation of the two test slides. Blood pressure served as the second measure; it was recorded not only before but also after the slide presentation using an automatic sphygmomanometer. Here again the difference was calculated between the values taken after and before the presentation.

In addition to the variables recorded during the experimental sessions, the subjects also completed three trait questionnaires when they were registered for the experiments: the "Mainz Coping Inventory" (MCI; Krohne 1989; Krohne, Rösch, & Kürsten, 1989; cf. Krohne, Chapter 2 in this volume), the "Affect Intensity Measure" (AIM; Larsen & Diener, 1987), and the German adaptation of the "Test Anxiety Inventory" (TAI; Hodapp, 1991).

The subjects were 64 female students from various departments of Düsseldorf University. Their ages ranged from 17 to 33 years with a mean of 22.3 years and a standard deviation of 3.2 years. The subjects received payment for taking part in the experiment.

Results

First, the results of testing heartbeat perception ability will be presented. Discrimination performances are generally described using parameters from the signal detection theory. As restrictive assumptions concerning the distribution of response categories and the minimum number of trials are necessary for the application of the parametric measures ds and d', the parameter P(A), or rather its transformation $2 \times \arcsin\sqrt{P(A)}$, was used to assess heartbeat perception ability.

The transformed heartbeat perception score, determined by employing the method developed by Störmer et al. (1989), shows a mean of $M = 2.02$ ($SD = 0.38$). A value of $\pi/2 = 1.57$ corresponds to a random performance, while a performance statistically above chance over 90 trials is indicated by a score of 1.75 (59% correct responses) or higher (Jones et al., 1984). A considerable number of subjects in this experiment were thus able to achieve above-chance discriminations in the stimulus series.

The emotional reactions to the slide presentation show a very clear pattern. In all subjective parameters, the aversive slides provoke stronger reactions than the neutral slides (see Table 9.1). The aversive slides therefore induce more state anxiety, more state anger, more strongly perceived physiological arousal, and more marked negative valency than the neutral slides do.

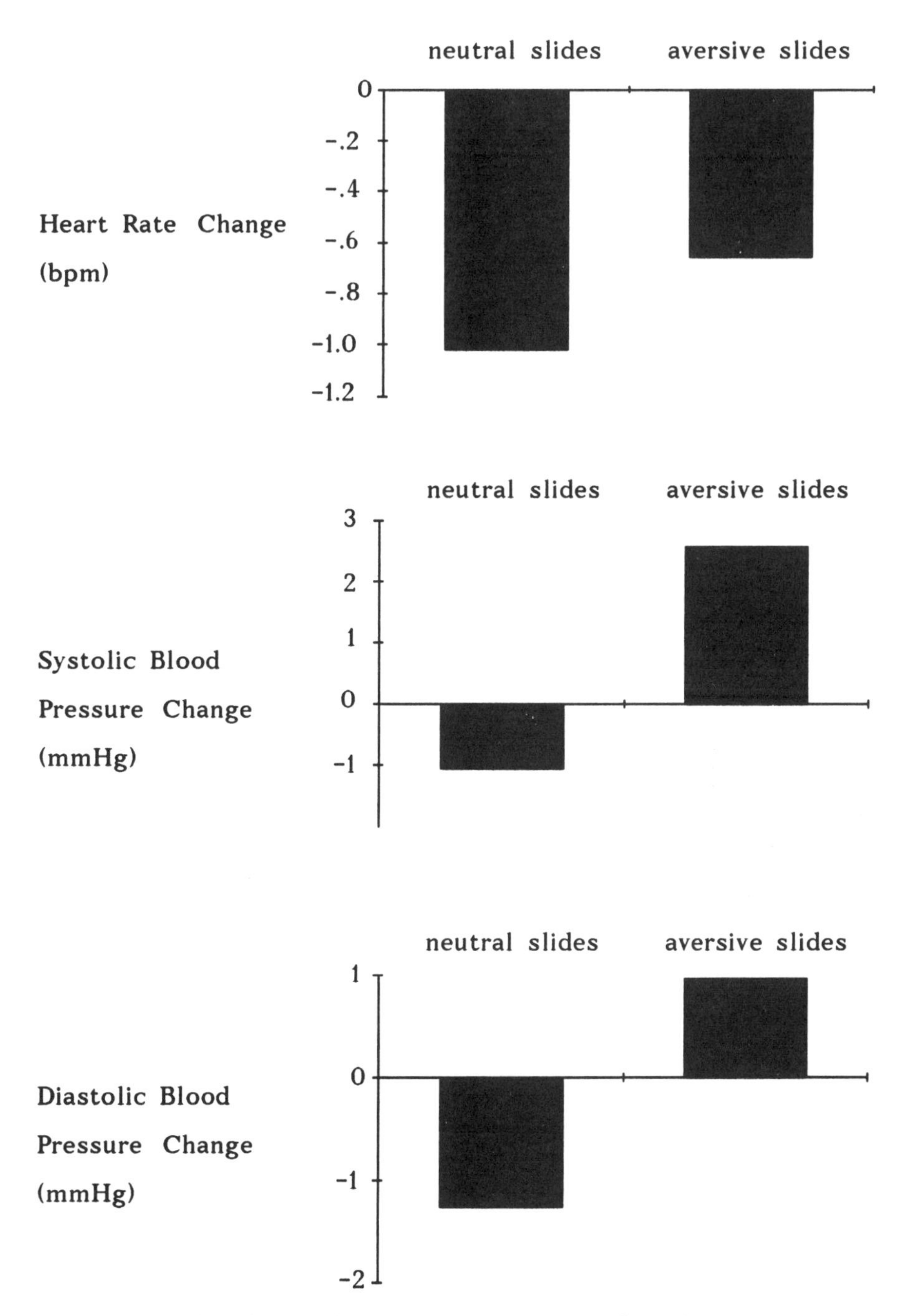

Figure 9.2. Physiological reactions during the presentation of the slides.

The physiological reactions are of greater importance for assessing the influences heartbeat perception ability and coping have on emotional experience. Figure 9.2 shows heart rate as well as systolic and diastolic blood pressure reaction values during presentation of the neutral and aversive slides. As can easily be seen, all three cardiovascular parameters show deactivation for the neutral slides. For the aversive slides, slight increases in blood pressure are found, in contrast to the decelerations in heart rate. While the heart rate differences are not statistically significant, there are significant blood pressure differences in the reactions to the neutral and aversive slides (systolic blood pressure: $t(62) = -2.49, p < .05$; diastolic blood pressure: $t(62) = -2.20, p < .05$). The physiological reactions to the slides can, however, generally be described as weak.

Table 9.1
Results of *t*-tests for the Subjective Parameters for the Neutral and Aversive Slides

		Slide				
Dependent variable		Neutral	Aversive	*t*	*df*	*p*
SAM-arousal	*M*	27.50	61.17	10.49	62	.000
	SD	12.50	13.16			
SAM-valence	*M*	49.00	78.93	14.18	62	.000
	SD	9.76	6.60			
State-anxiety	*M*	21.18	35.00	11.11	62	.000
	SD	3.94	5.93			
State-anger	*M*	14.44	21.00	3.55[a]	39.54	.001
	SD	4.49	9.03			
State-arousal	*M*	11.62	18.83	6.98[a]	35.08	.000
	SD	1.86	5.38			

[a] Separate variance estimates.

Let us now look at the subjective reactions to the slides dependent on heartbeat perception ability and coping predispositions. Multiple regression analyses were calculated to examine these influences, whereby heartbeat perception ability and the coping predispositions "cognitive avoidance" and "vigilance" were employed as predictors of emotional reactions. Due to low cell frequencies, the three-way analyses of variance we originally planned to conduct proved to be impracticable. This could be attributed to the negative correlation of $r = -.30$ between cognitive avoidance and vigilance.

Table 9.2 displays the results of the analyses of regression for the aversive slide condition. As was expected, no significant or noticeable dependencies were found for the neutral slides. In the case of the aversive slides, only the SAM-arousal variable can be significantly predicted ($R = 0.54$, $F(3,24) = 3.23$, $p < .05$). A significant contribution is supplied by cognitive avoidance, with higher values of this variable accompanying higher arousal values ($\beta = 0.56$, $t(24) = 2.91$, $p < .01$). A similar result is valid for state-anger, with cognitive avoiders again reporting stronger emotion ($\beta = 0.48$, $t(23) = 2.33$, $p < .05$).

Table 9.2
Results of the Multiple Regression Analysis: Influence of Vigilance (VIG), Cognitive Avoidance (CAV), and Heartbeat Perception (HBP) on State Measures in the Aversive Slide Condition

		Independent variables			
Dependent variable		VIG	CAV	HBP	*R*
SAM-arousal	*β*	.30	.56**	-.24	.54*
	r	.05	.39*	-.26	
SAM-valence	*β*	.29	.33	.14	.36
	r	.07	.24	.12	
State-anxiety	*β*	.29	.38	-.18	.40
	r	.08	.21	-.22	
State-anger	*β*	.00	.48*	-.29	.48
	r	-.24	.41*	-.25	
State-arousal	*β*	.23	.21	-.34	.42
	r	.16	.01	-.37*	

*$p < .05$; **$p < .01$.

Heartbeat perception ability showed no relationship to the emotional reactions; only a tendentious influence was found for the variable "state-arousal". A good heartbeat perception ability is linked with the estimation of a slighter arousal (β = -0.34, $t(24)$ = -1.75, p < .10). Apart from the valency assessment of SAM, there was also a tendency towards lower emotion values with good heart rate perception ability for the other state measures. None of the subjective reactions to the aversive slides can be predicted relying on the predisposition to vigilance.

Table 9.3
Means, Standard Deviations, and Results of *t*-Tests for the Trait Variables Vigilance (VIG), Cognitive Avoidance (CAV), Affect Intensity (AIM), and Test Anxiety (TAI) for Good and Poor Heartbeat Perceivers

Dependent variable	Heartbeat perception ability	*M*	*SD*	*t*	*df*	*p*
VIG	Poor	17.09	6.21	2.33	61	.02
	Good	14.00	4.07			
CAV	Poor	17.64	6.04	1.90	61	.06
	Good	20.50	5.89			
AIM	Poor	155.84	22.81	1.99	62	.05
	Good	145.00	20.71			
TAI	Poor	74.37	18.27	2.47	62	.02
	Good	63.94	15.38			

The last analysis concerns the relationships between heartbeat perception and the trait variables. Table 9.3 contains a comparison between good and bad heartbeat perceivers with regard to coping predispositions, the emotion intensity measurement, and test anxiety. Good and bad heartbeat perceivers are defined by scores above or below the median of the distribution of heartbeat perception (*Mdn* = 1.92). A clear pattern of relationships is revealed in such a way that good heartbeat perception ability is associated with low emotionality (AIM, TAI). This result is in accordance with the positive relationship between heartbeat perception and vigilance, as well as the inverse relationship between heartbeat perception and cognitive avoidance. Good heartbeat perception ability is thus associated with lower emotionality and a predominance of cognitive avoidant coping strategies. In the case of the trait variables, an inverse relationship between emotion and heartbeat perception is considerably clearer than at the level of the state variables.

Discussion

The results of the experiment do not give any clear and unequivocal indications for a dependency of emotional experience on heartbeat perception ability. Several aspects are, however, of importance in interpreting the results. First, it should be stated that, by selecting aversive slides, we have apparently been successful in evoking subjective emotional reactions of considerable intensity. The differences in emotional experience between the neutral and aversive slides provide evidence for the effectiveness of emotion induction in this respect.

On the other hand, only weak physiological reactions could be evoked by the presentation of slides. The aversive slides in particular did not lead to the physiological activation which had been expected and which would have enabled an investigation into the influence of autonomous arousal and its perception on the experience of emotions. In the case of blood pressure, non-continuous recordings can be made responsible for an inadequate assessment of autonomous reactions; the heartbeat results would, however, speak against such an interpretation. As already indicated in studies by Hantas et al. (1982) and Katkin et al. (1982), slides, due to their weak activating effect, appear to be rather unsuitable as emotion-inducing stimuli for testing the relationship between emotion and perceived autonomous changes. Situations which permit an active coping with stressors (Obrist et al., 1978) might possibly offer more favorable conditions for an investigation into this question. If one assumes that the presentation of slides was able to evoke emotions but that these emotions only had slight physiological effects, it appears that external rather than internal stimuli dominate as reference stimuli in inducing an emotion. Under these circumstances, a greater influence of external stimuli on bad, as compared to good, heartbeat perceivers could serve as a meaningful working hypothesis. However, the results need replication before they can really be interpreted as a clear influence of heartbeat perception ability on emotional experience.

The relationships between heartbeat perception and coping predispositions are new findings and hitherto unknown in the literature. The results are not in accordance with the hypothesis that sensitizers perceive autonomous processes more sensitively and avoidant subjects less sensitively (cf. Miller et al., this volume). This finding refers, however, to a specific aspect of the perception of autonomous processes (i.e., heartbeat perception), so that further investigations which also cover other areas of autonomous perception must follow. The finding is interesting inasmuch as it points out the necessity of differentiating more strictly between the processing of external stimuli, which can also be symbolically represented (Lazarus, 1966), and the processing of internal stimuli. Those individuals who react in a vigilant way are characterized by an increased alertness directed towards situational stimuli. On the other hand, those who react with cognitive avoidance are intolerant towards emotional arousal (Krohne, 1989, and Chapter 2 in this volume). The association of avoidance, less intensive emotional experience, and better perception of autonomous processes, e.g., heartbeats, could be related to a specific aspect of Krohne's coping model. Since avoidant persons are intolerant of emotional arousal, they might have a tendency to recognize physiological cues earlier than vigilant individuals do. Early recognition could warn them of emotional arousal and thus help to develop strategies for the avoidance of further arousal. Such a strategy could consist of removing attention from internal physiological cues in emotionally threatening situations. At the moment it does not seem possible to describe the relationship between emotion, coping, and heartbeat perception more precisely.

Conclusions

Depending on the theoretical point of view, different hypotheses concerning the relationship between heartbeat perception, emotion, and coping may be postulated. It has been argued that the traditional focus in interoception research, based on peripheral emotion theories, concentrated on a positive relationship between heartbeat perception and emotion. However, subjects who are not very emotional may also be expected to perform better when competing information from external and internal sources and preconceptions about psychophysiological processes are taken into account.

In the few investigations which have been carried out in this area, only partial aspects of the relationship between interoception and emotion have been considered. This does explain the inconsistent findings in part. In future studies, particularly the following aspects and problems should be investigated more closely:

1. How comparable are the various methods for assessing the accuracy of the perception of autonomous processes (e.g., tracking procedures, discrimination procedures)?
2. How are perception *ability* and the *estimation* of autonomous arousal related to each other? To what extent do situational cues influence perception and estimation of autonomous arousal?
3. Are correlative approaches and studies with experimental induction of emo-tions compatible with each other? Are relationships between interoception and emotion valid on the level of states as well as of traits?
4. Can general relationships between interoception and emotion be postulated, independent of the respective specific emotion? Which role does physiological activation play here?
5. In investigations concerning the associations between emotion and intero-ception, more attention should be paid to coping processes. Measures of coping, such as coping dispositions, should be included in experimental designs.

References

Bestler, M., Schandry, R., Weitkunat, R., & Alt, E. (1990). Kardiodynamische Determinanten der Herzwahrnehmung [Cardiodynamic determinants of cardiac perception]. *Zeitschrift für experimentelle und angewandte Psychologie, 37*, 361-377.

Bradley, M. M., Greenwald, M. K., & Hamm, A. O. (in press). Affective picture processing. In N. Birbaumer & A. Öhman (Eds.), *The organization of emotion.* Toronto: Hogrefe International.

Brener, J. (1974). A general model of voluntary control applied to the phenomena of learned cardiovascular change. In P. A. Obrist, A. H. Black, J. Brener, & L. V. DiCara (Eds.), *Cardiovascular psychophysiology* (pp. 365-394). Chicago: Aldine.

Clemens, W. J. (1984). Temporal arrangements of signals in heartbeat discrimination procedures. *Psychophysiology, 21*, 187-190.

Davis, M. R., Langer, A. W., Sutterer, J. R., Gelling, P. D., & Marlin, M. (1986). Relative discriminability of heartbeat-contingent stimuli under three procedures for assessing cardiac perception. *Psychophysiology, 23*, 76-81.

Diekhoff, G. M. (1976). Effects of feedback in a forced-choice GSR detection task. *Psychophysiology, 13*, 22-26.

Eichler, S., Katkin, E. S., Blascovich, J., & Kelsey, R. M. (1987). Cardiodynamic factors in heartbeat detection and the experience of emotion (Abstract). *Psychophysiology, 24*, 587.

Fahrenberg, J., Selg, H., & Hampel, R. (1978). *Das Freiburger Persönlichkeitsinventar FPI* [The Freiburg Personality Inventory FPI](3rd ed.). Göttingen: Hogrefe.

Fehr, F. S., & Stern, J. A. (1970). Peripheral physiological variables and emotion: The James-Lange theory revisited. *Psychological Bulletin, 74*, 411-424.

Flynn, D. M., & Clemens, W. J. (1988). On the validity of heartbeat tracking tasks. *Psychophysiology, 25*, 92-96.

Gannon, L. (1984). Awareness of internal cues and concordance among verbal, behavioral, and physiological systems in dysfunction. *Psychological Reports, 54*, 631-650.

Greenstadt, L., Shapiro, D., & Whitehead, R. (1986). Blood pressure discrimination. *Psychophysiology, 23*, 500-509.

Hantas, M., Katkin, E. S., & Blascovich, J. (1982). Relationship between heartbeat discrimination and subjective experience of affective state (Abstract). *Psychophysiology, 19*, 563.

Hodapp, V. (1988). *Bericht über Entwicklungsarbeiten zum deutschen State-Trait-Persönlichkeitsinventar STPI-G* [The development of the German State-Trait-Personality Inventory STPI-G]. Unpublished manuscript, Psychologisches Institut, Universität Düsseldorf.

Hodapp, V. (1991). Das Prüfungsängstlichkeitsinventar TAI-G: Eine erweiterte und modifizierte Version mit vier Komponenten [The Test Anxiety Inventory TAI-G: An expanded and modified version with four components]. *Zeitschrift für Pädagogische Psychologie, 5*, 121-130.

James, W. (1884). What is an emotion? *Mind, 9*, 188-205.

Jones, G. E., & Hollandsworth, J. G. (1981). Heart rate discrimination before and after exercise-induced augmented cardiac activity. *Psychophysiology, 18*, 252-257.

Jones, G. E., O'Leary, R. T., & Pipkin, B. L. (1984). Comparison of the Brener-Jones and Whitehead procedures for assessing cardiac awareness. *Psychophysiology, 21*, 143-148.

Katkin, E. S. (1985). Blood, sweat, and tears: Individual differences in autonomic self-perception. *Psychophysiology, 22*, 125-137.

Katkin, E. S., Blascovich, J., & Goldband, S. (1981). Empirical assessment of visceral self-perception: Individual and sex differences in the acquisition of heartbeat discrimination. *Journal of Personality and Social Psychology, 40*, 1095-1101.

Katkin, E. S., Blascovich, J., & Koenigsberg, M. R. (1984). Autonomic self-perception and emotion. In W. M. Waid (Ed.), *Sociophysiology* (pp. 117-138). New York: Springer-Verlag.

Katkin, E. S., Blascovich, J., Reed, S., Adamec, J., Jones, J., & Taublieb, A. B. (1982). The effect of physiologically induced arousal on the accuracy of heartbeat self-perception (Abstract). *Psychophysiology, 19*, 568.

Kerres, M. (1985). Objective and subjective arousal in test anxiety: Differential accuracy of internal perception. In H. M. van der Ploeg, R. Schwarzer, & C. D. Spielberger (Eds.), *Advances in test anxiety research* (Vol. 4, pp. 35-42). Lisse, The Netherlands: Swets & Zeitlinger.

Knoll, J. F., & Hodapp, V. (in press). A comparison between two methods for assessing heartbeat perception. *Psychophysiology*.

Kohlmann, C.-W. (1990). *Streßbewältigung und Persönlichkeit. Flexibles versus rigides Copingverhalten und seine Auswirkungen auf Angsterleben und physiologische Belastungsreaktionen* [Coping and personality. Flexible versus rigid coping behavior and its effects on anxiety and physiological stress reactions]. Bern: Huber.

Krämer, D., & Erdmann, G. (1990, April). *Herzschlagwahrnehmung und emotionale Reagibilität* [Heartbeat perception and emotional reactivity]. Paper presented at the 32nd meeting of the "Tagung experimentell arbeitender Psychologen", Regensburg, Germany.

Krohne, H. W. (1989). The concept of coping modes: Relating cognitive person variables to actual coping behavior. *Advances in Behaviour Research and Therapy, 11*, 235-248.

Krohne, H. W., & Rogner, J. (1982). Repression-sensitization as a central construct in coping research. In H. W. Krohne & L. Laux (Eds.), *Achievement, stress, and anxiety* (pp. 167-194). Washington, DC: Hemisphere.

Krohne, H. W., Rösch, W., & Kürsten, F. (1989). Die Erfassung von Angstbewältigung in physisch bedrohlichen Situationen [The measurement of coping in physical-threat situations]. *Zeitschrift für Klinische Psychologie, 18*, 230-242.

Lacroix, J. M. (1977). Effects of biofeedback on the discrimination of electrodermal activity. *Biofeedback and Self-Regulation, 2*, 393-406.

Larsen, R. J., & Diener, E. (1987). Affect intensity as an individual difference characteristic: A review. *Journal of Research in Personality, 21*, 1-39.

Lazarus, R. S. (1966). *Psychological stress and the coping process*. New York: McGraw-Hill.

Ludwick-Rosenthal, R., & Neufeld, R. W. J. (1985). Heartbeat interoception: A study of individual differences. *International Journal of Psychophysiology, 3*, 57-65.

MacDowell, K. A., & Mandler, G. (1989). Constructions of emotion: discrepancy, arousal, and mood. *Motivation and Emotion, 13*, 105-124.

McFarland, R. A. (1975). Heart rate perception and heart rate control. *Psychophysiology, 12*, 402-405.

Montgomery, W. A., & Jones, G. E. (1984). Laterality, emotionality, and heartbeat perception. *Psychophysiology, 21*, 459-465.

Montgomery, W. A., Jones, G. E., & Hollandsworth, J. G. (1984). The effects of physical fitness and exercise on cardiac awareness. *Biological Psychology, 18*, 11-22.

Obrist, P. A., Gaebelein, C. J., Teller, E. S., Langer, A. W., Grignolo, A., Light, K. C., & McCubbin, J. A. (1978). The relationship among heart rate, carotid dP/dt, and blood pressure in humans as a function of the type of stress. *Psychophysiology, 15*, 102-115.

Pennebaker, J. W. (1981a). *The psychology of physical symptoms*. New York: Springer-Verlag.

Pennebaker, J. W. (1981b). Stimulus characteristics influencing estimation of heart rate. *Psychophysiology, 18*, 540-548.

Pennebaker, J. W., & Brittingham, G. L. (1982). Environmental and sensory cues affecting the perception of physical symptoms. In A. Baum & J. Singer (Eds.), *Advances in environmental psychology* (Vol. 4, pp. 115-136). Hillsdale, NJ: Erlbaum.

Pennebaker, J. W., & Epstein, D. (1983). Implicit psychophysiology: Effects of common beliefs and idiosyncratic physiological responses on symptom reporting. *Journal of Personality, 51*, 468-496.

Pennebaker, J. W., & Hoover, C. W. (1984). Visceral perception versus visceral detection: Disentangling methods and assumptions. *Biofeedback and Self-Regulation, 9*, 339-352.

Schachter, S., & Singer, J. E. (1962). Cognitive, social, and physiological determinants of emotional state. *Psychological Review, 69*, 379-399.

Schandry, R. (1981). Heartbeat perception and emotional experience. *Psychophysiology, 18*, 483-488.

Schandry, R. (1983). On the relation between the improvement of cardiac perception and the increase of emotional experience (Abstract). *Psychophysiology, 20*, 468-469.

Schandry, R., & Specht, G. (1981). The influence of psychological and physical stress on the perception of heartbeats (Abstract). *Psychophysiology, 18*, 154.

Spielberger, C. D., Gorsuch, R. L., & Lushene, R. E. (1970). *Manual for the State-Trait Anxiety Inventory*. Palo Alto, CA: Consulting Psychologists Press.

Störmer, S. W. (1988). *Herzschlagwahrnehmung. Zur Meßbarkeit kardialer Interozeption* [Heartbeat perception: the measurement of cardiac interoception]. Unpublished doctoral dissertation, Universität Düsseldorf.

Störmer, S. W., Heiligtag, U., & Knoll, J. F. (1989). Heartbeat detection and knowledge of results: A new method and some theoretical thoughts. *Journal of Psychophysiology, 3*, 409-417.

Valins, S. (1966). Cognitive effects of false heart-rate feedback. *Journal of Personality and Social Psychology, 4*, 400-408.

Valins, S. (1967). Emotionality and information concerning internal reactions. *Journal of Personality and Social Psychology, 6*, 458-463.

Weinberger, D. A., Schwartz, G. E., & Davidson, R. J. (1979). Low-anxious, high-anxious, and repressive coping styles: Psychometric patterns and behavioral and physiological responses to stress. *Journal of Abnormal Psychology, 88*, 369-380.

Weinstein, J., Averill, J. R., Opton, E. M., & Lazarus, R. S. (1968). Defensive style and discrepancy between self-report and physiological indexes of stress. *Journal of Personality and Social Psychology, 10*, 406-413.

Weisz, J., Balázs, L., & Adám, G. (1988). The influence of self-focussed attention on heartbeat perception. *Psychophysiology, 25*, 193-199.

Whitehead, W. E., & Drescher, V. M. (1980). Perception of gastric contractions and self-control of gastric motility. *Psychophysiology, 17*, 552-558.

Whitehead, W. E., Drescher, V. M., Heiman, P., & Blackwell, B. (1977). Relation of heart rate control to heartbeat perception. *Biofeedback and Self-Regulation, 2*, 371-392.

Yates, A. J., Jones, K. E., Marie, G. V., & Hogben, J. H. (1985). Detection of the heartbeat and events in the cardiac cycle. *Psychophysiology, 22*, 561-576.

Chapter 10

Strategies in Blood Pressure Estimation: The Role of Vigilance, Cognitive Avoidance, and Gender

Carl-Walter Kohlmann

Basic Considerations

A central issue in health psychology concerns the question of how individuals identify their bodily states. For example, how do individuals know that their hearts are racing or that their blood pressure is high? According to previous research (cf. Barr, Pennebaker, & Watson, 1988; Baumann & Leventhal, 1985; Pennebaker, 1981; Pennebaker & Watson, 1988), self-estimations of blood pressure and heart rate can be based, as in the case of the naturalistic perception of visual and auditory stimuli, on both internal bodily and external situational cues. Internal somatic factors may be, for example, a pounding in the chest or a feeling of warmth. A possible external factor that the individual might be sensitive to is interacting in an evaluative or hostile setting. In the real world, an individual may rely on internal as well as external types of information when estimating bodily states.

Having reviewed research on visceral perception from both laboratory and field studies, Roberts and Pennebaker (1989) assume that women and men exhibit fundamental differences in their use of internal and external cues when perceiving and defining bodily states. However, a direct investigation of their assumption has not yet been conducted. Focused on the process of estimating blood pressure, this study will not only test the hypothesis of gender differences regarding the reliance on internal and external variables in estimating physiological activity but primarily address the role the personality variables vigilance and cognitive avoidance (Krohne, 1989, and Chapter 2, this volume) play in this process. Since both variables are assumed to reflect individual differences in the perception, encoding, and processing of threat-relevant information, they should be important variables in the self-estimation of bodily processes.

Two examples may illustrate the relevance of vigilance and avoidance in somatic attention. In psychological models of panic disorders (for an overview, see Ehlers, 1989) the role of vigilant processes is obvious. Panic attacks are not

---

I am indebted to Claudia Dambeck and Peter Singer for their help with the research. I would like to thank Volker Hodapp and Heinz Walter Krohne for their comments on the text.

seen as spontaneous in the sense of being unrelated to triggering stimuli. They are explained as the consequence of a positive feedback loop between internal stimuli (e.g., body sensations) and the patient's response to them. Subjective body sensations may not accurately reflect actual physiological changes. These sensations are, however, associated with immediate danger. The individual responds to the perceived threat with vigilant cognitions, which in turn leads to physiological changes and body sensations. If these symptoms are again perceived and associated with danger, further increases in anxiety occur that may escalate into a panic attack (Ehlers, 1989).

Contrarily, an avoidant or non-vigilant processing of bodily symptoms is predominant in the other example. The Type A behavior pattern (see Ben-Zur, Breznitz, & Hashmonay, this volume) seems to play a role in the etiology and course of heart disease. Regarding this personality variable, there is some evidence that Type A individuals when involved in demanding tasks, devote their full attention to the task and may have a higher threshold for noticing bodily symptoms while preoccupied than Type B individuals do (cf. Weidner & Matthews, 1978). If Type A individuals tend to ignore symptoms, they may be less likely to seek medical care or to rest when experiencing early heart disease symptoms (see Carver, Coleman, & Glass, 1976). Thus, vigilance as well as avoidance regarding bodily processes seem to be important factors in the development of various disorders.

Methodological Developments in Interoception Research

Methodological developments in laboratory research examining individuals' ability to detect their physiological activity have been primarily guided by the effort to measure "pure" accuracy in the perception of bodily processes (especially heartbeats) while controlling for all external biases in the perceptual process (see Hodapp & Knoll, this volume). Accuracy scores for the perception of cardiac activity derived from the tasks developed by Brener and Jones (1974), McFarland (1975), and Dale and Anderson (1978, see also Schandry, 1981) represent only the early stages in the development of methods to assess the quality of heartbeat detection; their scores may still be affected by the reliance on external cues (e.g., body movements, estimations of elapsed time). The state of the art in assessing heartbeat perception, however, is characterized by methods in which subjects have to differentiate between two sets of stimuli presented with different time configurations: either immediately after their heartbeat or with a short delay (Whitehead, Drescher, Heiman, & Blackwell, 1977), or after their heartbeat at fixed versus variable time intervals (Katkin, Blascovich, & Goldband, 1981; see also Davis, Langer, Sutterer, Gelling, & Marlin, 1986; Störmer, Heiligtag, & Knoll, 1989). Scores obtained from these recent signal detection tasks should depend only on the ability to perceive, encode, and process internal physiological information; a reliance on external cues cannot improve scores for interoception.[1] Unfortunately, methods free from external bias have not been developed for blood pressure estimations (for an elaborated discrimination approach, however, see Greenstadt, Shapiro, & Whitehead, 1986).

A method that has been used for a variety of physiological variables (including blood pressure) in an attempt to determine how accurately individuals perceive their physiological state is the self-report method. However, unlike the signal detection methods, there is no control for subjects' perceptual and inferential biases in this method. Since these "biases" naturally occur in the real world, the self-report method is more externally valid; it allows subjects to use all the information normally available to them in judging a bodily state (cf. Roberts & Pennebaker, 1989; see also Kohlmann, 1988). In within-subject self-report studies, subjects typically report on physiological indices several times during a laboratory session in which they are confronted with several different tasks that indirectly manipulate physiological states. Accuracy of perception is then determined by the correlation between the subjects' self-reports of bodily states and their actual physiological determinants.

Moreover, the self-report method can be applied in natural settings. This requires subjects to measure their specific physiological activity and make estimations of their respective physiological activity at specified intervals. As for the self-report studies in the laboratory, the within-subject correlations between estimated and actual physiological activity are the indices for accuracy in symptom perception.

Gender Differences in Interoception

Recently, Roberts and Pennebaker (1989) summarized the existing interoception research based on signal detection paradigms, self-report studies in the laboratory, and those in the field as follows: In general, subjects are slightly better at perceiving physiological cues in the self-report studies in the laboratory than in signal detection paradigms. However, subjects perform relatively best when estimating physiological states in their natural environments. Gender effects, with a higher accuracy score for males, arise primarily in the signal detection studies (however, see also Rouse, Jones, & Jones, 1988). In the self-report studies in the laboratory gender differences are not as robust, and no consistent gender effects have emerged in those studies in the field (see Table 10.1). Since gender differences become weaker with an

[1] Individual differences in heartbeat perception obtained during discrimination tasks (cf. Hodapp & Knoll, this volume) may not only reflect differences in "pure" accuracy but also in the ability to disregard external cues or simply the ability to concentrate solely on the discrimination task. The possibility that accuracy scores derived during discrimination tasks indicate only the lower limit of interoception ability should be directly examined. Weisz, Balázs and Adám (1988) found that subjects performed better on a heartbeat discrimination task while facing a mirror than when the mirror was absent. Self-attention enhancement, therefore, might be a powerful tool for increasing cardiac awareness.

increase in the availability of external cues for estimating physiological activity, it may be assumed that in the process of interoception women rely more on external situational cues than men and less on internal physiological cues (cf. Pennebaker, in press; Roberts & Pennebaker, 1989). One purpose of the present study is to empirically test if there is a gender difference regarding the subjects' reliance on internal and external variables while estimating their blood pressure. The idea that gender differences in perceptual style may reflect differences in dominance, socialization, hemispheric lateralization (Roberts & Pennebaker, 1989), or field dependence (cf. Kohlmann & Singer, 1991) will not be discussed. We will, however, focus on the coping strategies vigilance and cognitive avoidance (Krohne, 1989, and Chapter 2, this volume) as personality variables which may contribute to the understanding of the process of interoception.

Table 10.1
Brief Summary of Studies on Visceral Perception

Paradigm	Availability of external cues	Mean accuracy	Difference in accuracy
Signal detection	Not at all	Low	Men >> women
Self-report lab	Somewhat	Medium	Men > women
Self-report field	Fully	High	Men = women

Note. Summary is based on studies listed in Roberts and Pennebaker (1989) and their conclusions.

Coping Strategies

A link between coping dispositions and strategies in estimating one's own physiological activity might not be immediately apparent. In the traditional sense, when coping dispositions, self-reported data, and physiological activity are mentioned together, a personality psychologist might think of the so-called "discrepancy hypothesis" (cf. Lazarus, 1966; for an overview, see Kohlmann, 1990). According to Lazarus (1966), we should not necessarily expect subjective and physiological indices of anxiety to coincide. For example, in a study on actual coping during the anticipation of a cognitive task (i.e., an intelligence test) and the anticipation of the feedback of task results, subjects reporting a high amount of thoughts unrelated to the experiment (i.e., avoidant coping) exhibited high levels of electrodermal activity as compared with self-reported anxiety. On the other hand, in vigilant subjects (i.e., high amount of thoughts about the experiment) levels of electrodermal activity and anxiety were about equal (Kohlmann, Singer, & Krohne, 1989). Thus, when persons say they do not feel anxious but show marked physiological stress reactions, we assume that defensive processes are taking place.

Strategies regarding these defensive processes when coping with threat (i.e., avoidant-like responses; Roth & Cohen, 1986) have been classified under such categories as "repression" (Byrne, 1961; Eriksen, 1966), "inhibition" (Ullmann, 1958), "denial" (Lazarus, 1983), "blunting" (Miller, 1987), or "cognitive avoidance" (Krohne, 1986). On the other hand, approach-like reponses have been termed "sensitization", "facilitation", "isolation", "monitoring", or "vigilance" (cf. Krohne, Chapter 1, this volume).

According to Byrne (1964, see also Eriksen, 1966), two modes of dealing with anxiety-evoking cues can be conceptualized. One cluster of defensive strategies consists of repression and denial as ways of escaping anxiety by employing avoidance. When confronted with threat, the individual attempts to deny or to minimize its existence, fails to verbalize feelings of anxiety, and avoids thinking about the consequences of the threat. At the opposite extreme are defenses characterized by the tendency to approach the threat-relevant information. The individual is actually attuned to the presence of threatening stimuli, freely verbalizes feelings of anxiety and fear, and tries to control the danger by dwelling on its potential consequences. These two different behavior patterns have been designated as repression and sensitization.

Krohne (1986, 1989) and also Miller (1987) postulate two modes of coping with aversiveness. Since the early research on repression-sensitization (for overviews, see Bell & Byrne, 1978; Byrne, 1964, Eriksen, 1966) was conducted, theoretical and methodological progress in research on coping dispositions has emerged. This is reflected in the fact that, in both of the recent models of coping dispositions, approach and avoidant coping are conceptualized and measured separately and independently. Furthermore, the scores obtained from either the approach or the avoidance scales are, in contrast to the classical Repression-Sensitization Scale (Byrne, 1961), not highly correlated with tests of anxiety or defensiveness (cf. Krohne, Rösch, & Kürsten, 1989; Miller, 1990).

In particular, Miller (1987, 1990, see also Miller, Combs, & Kruus, this volume) postulates that there are two main modes for coping with aversiveness. The first mode, monitoring, is shown by an alertness for and sensitization to threat-relevant information. The second mode, blunting, consists of cognitively avoiding or transforming threat-relevant information.

Similarly, Krohne (1989, and Chapter 2, this volume) distinguishes two main classes of coping strategies: vigilance and cognitive avoidance. Vigilance is characterized by an approach to and an intensified processing of threat-relevant information. Its general purpose is to gain control over the main threat-related aspects of a situation, thereby protecting the individual from perceiving the threat which stems from confronting unexpected dangers. Cognitive avoidance is viewed as a withdrawal from threat-relevant information. Its general purpose is to reduce the arousal engendered by the confrontation with an aversive event.

For all three models of coping dispositions, i.e., repression-sensitization, monitoring/blunting, and vigilance/cognitive avoidance, important findings, especially regarding health-related behavior, have been documented (cf. Krohne, in press).

Byrne, Steinberg, and Schwartz (1968) found that sensitizers report more medical problems than repressers. Additionally, male sensitizers visited the health center more frequently than male repressers. Objective severity of problems, however, was not controlled.

Miller, Brody, and Summerton (1988) studied patients visiting a primary care setting for acute medical problems. Monitors (high monitoring and low blunting scores) and blunters (low monitoring and high blunting scores) differed in the *level* of seriousness of their actual medical problem. Evaluations by the physicians showed that monitors actually had less severe medical problems than blunters. Miller (1990) concludes that monitors may have a lower threshold of scanning for internal bodily cues. This would make them more inclined to detect new or changing physical symptoms.

In contrast, when considering the cognitive processes that may explain a person's preference for a cognitive avoidant coping strategy, Krohne (1989) assumes that avoidant behavior may be motivated by an "intolerance of emotional arousal" which should result in a withdrawal from internal bodily cues.

Krohne (1989) analyzed the influence of vigilant and avoidant coping strategies on self-reported and biochemical stress indicators as evidenced by patients facing surgery. Free fatty acids (FFA) and state anxiety were measured the day after admission to hospital, after the pre-op visit in the afternoon before surgery, on the morning of surgery, and prior to the induction of anesthesia. A discrepancy score between subjective and objective stress reactions was operationalized by transforming the raw data into *z*-scores and subtracting the FFA from anxiety scores. In the case of the pattern "high vigilance/low cognitive avoidance" (i.e., "sensitizers", cf. Krohne, 1989, and Chapter 2, this volume) a marked positive *z*-score emerged, indicating that the subjective presurgical stress reactions were stronger than the physiological ones (see also Slangen, Kleemann, & Krohne, this volume).

Applied to the estimation of physiological activity, it might be hypothesized that an avoidant coping style (either repression, blunting, or cognitive avoidance) will result in an *underestimation* of physiological activity while a coping style characterized by approach (either sensitization, monitoring, or vigilance) will result in an *overestimation* of physiological activity.

Regarding the process of estimating bodily states, reliance on internal variables should be relatively low for subjects high, as compared to those low, in avoidance. This hypothesis derives from the assumption of the avoidant subjects' heightened intolerance of emotional arousal (Krohne, 1989). In contrast, for highly vigilant subjects, an intensified processing of internal cues is expected which takes into account Miller's assumption of monitors having a lower threshold of scanning for internal bodily cues (cf. Miller et al., this volume).

Even though the present study is especially concerned with the role of vigilance and cognitive avoidance as the crucial variable reflecting individual differences when estimating internal states, hypotheses concerning vigilance and cognitive avoidance have also been derived from monitoring/blunting research. Besides the theoretical similarities of both conceptions, they also overlap on an empirical level. In a previous study, applying both the Miller Behavioral Style Scale (MBSS, Miller, 1987; German adaptation by Schumacher, 1990) to assess monitoring and blunting and the Mainz Coping Inventory (MCI, Krohne, 1989; Krohne et al., 1989) to assess vigilance and cognitive avoidance, associations between the corresponding scales could be demonstrated. After computing correlations between the four coping scales using the data from 72 male and female students (Kohlmann, 1990), only two significant correlations between the four coping variables emerged: While cognitive avoidance was positively associated with blunting only (r = .46), vigilance only correlated with monitoring (r = .47). Applying a principal component analysis to the four coping scores resulted in a clear two-factor solution with vigilance and monitoring as the first factor and cognitive avoidance and blunting as the second.

Blood Pressure Estimation

The question of whether individuals are able to predict changes in blood pressure has not yet been definitively answered. Although health professionals believe that blood pressure is asymptomatic, most diagnosed hypertensives are confident that they can determine when their blood pressure is elevated (cf. Meyer, Leventhal, & Gutmann, 1985). The literature available to me on within-subject correlations between estimated systolic blood pressure (EBP) and actual systolic blood pressure (SBP) basically shows that, in general, the mean within-subject correlations are significant but not very high (see Table 10.2). The variability of correlations, however, was very high in all studies. For example, in the Baumann and Leventhal (1985) study, correlations ranged from -.40 to .68. The highest mean accuracy has been found for the self-report study in the field (Smith, 1986). In this case, subjects were required to carry a portable blood pressure sphygmanometer and a questionnaire booklet with them during their daily activities for a two-week period. At least once per hour throughout their day, subjects first estimated their SBP before measuring and recording it.

The lowest accuracy, on the other hand, emerged in the self-report study in a company (Baumann & Leventhal, 1985).[2] In this study, data were collected for the subjects (insurance company employees) twice daily for ten days. This was done each day at the same time after the subjects had been sitting in the company's testing room for a few minutes. Thus, within-subject variability might have been very low. In contrast, in all the self-report studies in the laboratory, subjects participated in strenuous physical tasks (e.g., hyperventilation) as well as in relaxing tasks (e.g., viewing peaceful scenes). This procedure, however, resulted not only in the intended effect of

[2] Even though the mean within-subject correlations between EBP and SBP with r = .14 were equal for the Baumann and Leventhal study and the Barr et al. study (first testing), the percentage of subjects with significant (p < .05) correlations between estimated blood pressure and systolic blood pressure was only 15% in the Baumann and Leventhal study and a much higher 27% in the Barr et al. study.

Table 10.2
Summary of Self-Report Studies on Blood Pressure Estimation

Authors	Paradigm	Sample	*r*
Baumann & Leventhal (1985)[a]	Self-report company	Males & females:	.14
Smith (1986)[b]	Self-report lab	Males & females:	.28
		Males:	.39
		Females:	.23
	Self-report field	Males & females:	.37
		Males:	.42
		Females:	.35
Barr et al. (1988)[c]	Self-report lab		
	- first testing	Males & females:	.14
	- second testing[d]	Males & females:	.32
Pennebaker & Watson (1988)	Self-report lab	Males & females:	.25
		Males:	.33
		Females:	.22

Note. *r* = mean within-subject correlation between estimated systolic blood pressure and actual systolic blood pressure.

[a] The distribution of within-subject correlations between systolic blood pressure and prediction was used to divide subjects into three groups, representing good, fair, and poor predictors. There were no gender differences for subjects at the three different levels of accuracy.

[b] General results cited in Pennebaker (in press). Results on gender differences cited in Roberts and Pennebaker (1989).

[c] 83% of the subjects were women. No test for gender differences was performed.

[d] Three quarters of the subjects received feedback after the first testing.

manipulating blood pressure across trials but also in offering subjects situational cues they could base their estimations on (e.g., arousing = high blood pressure, neutral or relaxing = low blood pressure; see also Stewart & Olbrisch, 1986).

It is therefore necessary to confront subjects with different tasks (i.e., arousing and relaxing) to manipulate blood pressure while simultaneously *controlling for external cues*. A method to control for external cues in within-subject self-report studies has been introduced by Pennebaker and Epstein (1983).

In their study on the perception of breathing rate, finger temperature, heart rate, finger pulse volume (i.e., cool-warm hands), and skin resistance (i.e., sweaty hands), subjects participated in a series of tasks to indirectly manipulate physiological activity. During and/or following each task, subjects reported to what degree they were experiencing the physiological activity of the respective symptoms. In order to obtain a measure of beliefs regarding the impact of tasks on physiological activity, a separate "simulation group" rated the degree each task would affect their respective physiological activity. Subjects in the simulation sample only heard descriptions of the tasks rather than participating in them. Consequently, most of the task information without the bodily cues was available to them as a basis for their ratings. Multiple regressions were computed on each experimental subject's data using their estimated physiological activity as the dependent measure and their own actual physiological measure and the belief data as predictors. By examing the R^2 and R^2_{change} scores from the regression analyses, the unique and overlapping contributions from situational cues (i.e., belief data derived from simulation sample) and the subject's own physiological cues could be separated.

The present investigation attempts to study individual differences in the subjects' reliance on internal and external cues for blood pressure estimation by applying the common self-report method in the laboratory (cf. Barr et al., 1988; Pennebaker & Watson, 1988; Smith, 1986). However, in extension of the previous blood pressure studies, the focus will be on the impact of situational cues. The situational cues will therefore be treated very much like those in the Pennebaker and Epstein study.

In studies on individual differences in blood pressure estimation, *variability in blood pressure over tasks* may also be an important variable. The studies differ not only with respect to the evoked variability across tasks but also regarding the subjects within a given study themselves. Two reasons for controlling individual range of blood pressure arose in studies on blood pressure discrimination (Greenstadt et al., 1986): 1. The larger the difference to be discriminated in blood pressure is, the better the performance. 2. Information derived from the excited cuff pressure does not by itself determine performance in blood pressure discrimination tasks. It cannot however be ruled out as a factor when the difference to be discriminated is relatively large. - These results are important, because blood pressure might not be manipulated to the same degree by the tasks and rest periods for all subjects. Although subjects in the previous studies estimated their blood pressure at the beginning of cuff inflation and therefore did not have the opportunity to base their actual estimation on final cuff pressure, that final cuff pressure following verbal response (i.e., estimation) might still have been used by some of the subjects as biofeedback.[3]

For the gender differences in estimating blood pressure, which are summarized in Table 10.2, it cannot be ruled out that differences in blood pressure variability might have been a crucial moderator variable. The assumed gender difference of higher accuracy scores for men probably results only when within-subject variability of blood pressure is higher for men than women. However, within-subject variability of blood pressure was controlled in none of the self-report studies listed in Table 10.2 when testing gender differences.

Research Questions

Two types of accuracy in estimating systolic blood pressure will be measured: level accuracy and covariation accuracy. *Level accuracy* refers to the overall discrepancy between average estimated blood pressure and mean actual blood pressure levels. *Covariation accuracy* refers to the degree to which fluctuations of estimated blood pressure covary with actual blood pressure fluctuations (cf. Pennebaker & Watson, 1988). The following research questions will be pursued:

1. Do subjects high in vigilance (compared to those low in vigilance) prefer to process internal cues for estimating their systolic blood pressure?
2. Do, on the other hand, subjects high in cognitive avoidance (compared to those low in cognitive avoidance) prefer to process external cues for estimating their systolic blood pressure?
3. Do men rely more on internal cues for estimating their own systolic blood pressure than women do?
4. Do women, on the other hand, rely more on external cues for estimating their own systolic blood pressure?
5. Is there a tendency for subjects high in vigilance and/or low in cognitive avoidance to overestimate their systolic blood pressure?
6. Are there any interactions between gender and coping strategies that are related to covariation and level accuracy?
7. Is the within-subject range of systolic blood pressure related to covariation accuracy?

Method

In this study, 30 male and 30 female students (mean age = 25 years) from the University of Mainz were tested individually. They participated in eleven two-

[3] This would explain why in one study (Barr et al., 1988) covariation accuracy between estimated and systolic blood pressure also increased from one session to another for control subjects who received no verbal feedback on the accuracy of their estimations.

minute activity tasks and rest periods designed to manipulate blood pressure indirectly. Following each task, systolic blood pressure (SBP), diastolic blood pressure (DBP), and heart rate (HR) were being measured. While these variables were measured, subjects gave an estimation of their systolic blood pressure (EBP). Each task and rest period lasted about two minutes (see Table 10.3). During rest periods subjects listened to soothing Baroque music.

SBP, DBP, and HR were measured using a BOSO Oscillomat (Bosch & Sohn 751-004017, oscillometric method of blood pressure determination) with the cuff on the left arm. The subjects could not see the display during the measurements. On separate sheets of paper for each task and rest period, subjects marked their EBP on a rating scale ranging from 80 mmHg to 200 mmHg with 10 mmHg intervals. The coping variables vigilance (VIG) and cognitive avoidance (CAV) were assessed using the Mainz Coping Inventory (MCI, Krohne et al., 1989).

Table 10.3
Tasks and Baseline Periods

Situation	Description	A priori activity coding
1	Rest period	0
2	20 Knee bends	1
3	Rest period	0
4	Picture-word test	1
5	Rest period	0
6	Jumping in place	1
7	Rest period	0
8	Mental arithmetic	1
9	Rest period	0
10	Inflation of balloon	1
11	Rest period	0

Note. Coding: 0 = passive, 1 = active.

On arrival at the laboratory, subjects were seated in a comfortable chair and informed by the experimenter about the purpose of the study (i.e., ability to estimate their own systolic blood pressure). After completion of the MCI, subjects were asked if they knew their own blood pressure. Sixty percent of the males and 67% of the females said they would know their blood pressure. Two baseline blood pressure readings were taken at an interval of three minutes. Afterwards the subjects were told their mean resting SBP. The purpose of this procedure was two-fold: first, to make the subjects familiar with the measurement procedure (i.e., especially inflation of the cuff), and second, to give all the subjects a general idea of their probable SBP levels during the study.

The experimental session started with a rest period followed by the five tasks, each separated by a rest period, and concluded with a rest period. Immediately after the end of each task and rest period, SBP, DBP, and HR measurements were taken. At the beginning of the inflation of the cuff, subjects gave an estimation of their *actual* systolic blood pressure (EBP). This way it was ensured that the actual estimation of systolic blood pressure could not be based on the actual cuff pressure (cf. Greenstadt et al., 1986). In the course of the study, eleven sets of EBP, SBP, DBP, and HR were recorded for each subject.

Results

Overview of Analyses

The first question to be addressed concerns level accuracy. Was the tendency to overestimate or underestimate one's own SBP related to gender and coping dispositions?

Moreover, we sought to determine the degree to which external situational cues and internal physiological cues affected self-reports of physiological states. For the study of covariation accuracy, a combination of within-subject and between-subject designs was required. For each individual subject, we examined how estimations of a person's systolic blood pressure (EBP) were dependent on that person's actual systolic blood pressure (SBP) and/or external situational cues. Even though subjects may encode both the relative level in SBP as well as the change in SBP, we focused only on the actual physiological level. In previous studies by Pennebaker and Epstein (1983) employing a time lag regression solution, the physiological level measured at the time the estimation was made accounted for a far greater percentage of the variance in estimated physiological activity.

The external situational cues were coded in advance with *0 = passive* and *1 = active* (cf. Table 10.3). A within-subject regression approach (cf. Pennebaker & Epstein, 1983) was applied to compute the amount of internal and external information determining the EBP. Employing situational coding within a multiple regression procedure is problematic, since it is impossible to know beforehand if subjects base their blood pressure estimations more on internal physiological than on external situational cues or vice versa. Because external cues and SBP are correlated for the majority of subjects, whichever variable is forced into a regression solution first will statistically reduce the contribution of the second. This problem was dealt with by computing two regression analyses for each subject. In the first analysis, the external situational predictor was entered before the physiological data. In the second, the order was reversed. For a given subject, this procedure allowed us to compute external and internal variance components that contribute to the estimation of systolic blood pressure. The scores from these within-subject analyses (i.e., variance components that contribute to EBP) were then used as dependent variables in between-subject analyses in order to determine the influence of personality variables (i.e., gender, CAV, VIG) on the extent of the subjects' use of internal or external cues in estimating their SBP.

Descriptive Statistics

Comparisons between male and female subjects (cf. Table 10.4) indicate that men scored significantly lower on the vigilance scale of the MCI than women. Regarding the initial resting levels in the physiological variables, men exhibited a higher SBP and a lower HR than women.

Table 10.4
Description of the Sample: Means, Standard Deviations, and *t*-Tests for Gender Differences

Variable	Males ($n = 30$)	Females ($n = 30$)	t
Age	26.43 (7.10)	23.25 (5.49)	1.69
Cognitive avoidance	41.87 (13.91)	35.67 (11.91)	1.85
Vigilance	24.60 (9.56)	30.53 (9.55)	2.41*
SBP[a]	134.07 (11.87)	121.23 (16.02)	3.53***
DBP[a]	78.88 (7.84)	77.67 (11.21)	0.48
HR[a]	67.58 (12.82)	78.15 (12.90)	3.18**

[a] Based on the mean of the two initial baseline measures.
*$p < .05$; **$p < .01$; ***$p < .001$.

To control the effect of the task and rest periods on SBP, DBP, HR, and EBP, ANOVAs for repeated measurements were computed on each of the respective variables over the eleven situations. Marked changes across the situations emerged for all variables [SBP: $F(10,590) = 36.45$, $\varepsilon = .69$, $p < .001$;DBP: $F(10,590) = 2.28$, $\varepsilon = .69$, $p < .05$; HR: $F(10,590) = 28.56$, $\varepsilon = .68$, $p < .001$; EBP: $F(10,590) = 69.13$, $\varepsilon = .61$, $p < .001$]. In Figure 10.1, SBP and EBP data for the 60 subjects are displayed. The curves seem to indicate that subjects were quite good in estimating their SBP. However, the results for SBP and EBP data have been aggregated over the 60 subjects. Individual differences regarding level accuracy as well as covariation accuracy in blood pressure estimation will be the topics of the next sections.

Level Accuracy

Primarily as a test of the hypotheses regarding the discrepancies between EBP and SBP, the physiological and self-reported data for a given subject were aggregated across the eleven situations. Four different scores were computed for each subject (cf. Table 10.5). Table 10.6 gives a detailed items statistic for the mean discrepancy scale.

Separate 2×2×2 ANOVAs with the between-subject factors gender, VIG, and CAV were computed for all the mean and discrepancy scores. (Distributions of the coping variables were median-dichotomized to form the levels "low" and "high".)

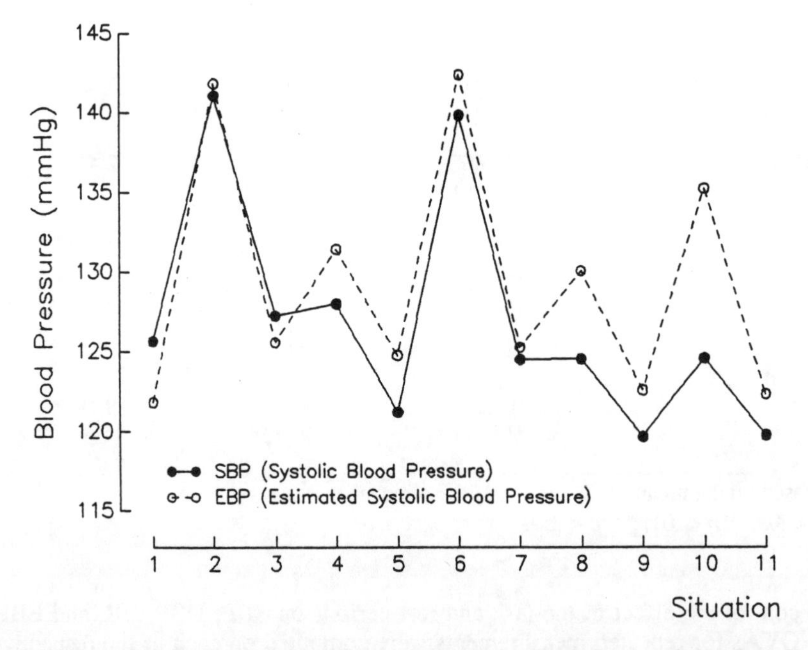

Figure 10.1. Mean SBP and mean EBP across subjects as a function of situation. (1, 3, 5, 7, 9, & 11 = rest period; 2 = knee bends; 4 = picture-word test; 6 = jumping in place; 8 = mental arithmetic; 10 = inflation of balloon.)

Table 10.5
Level Accuracy: Scales

Scale	Description	*M*	*SD*	α
Mean discrepancy	$^{1}/_{k}\ \Sigma(EBP_i - SBP_i)$	2.48	8.83	.86
Mean relative discrepancy	$^{100}/_{k}\ \Sigma[(EBP_i - SBP_i)/SBP_i]$	2.49%	8.91%	.85
Mean estimation error	$^{1}/_{k}\ \Sigma\lvert EBP_i - SBP_i\rvert$	10.57	4.85	.73
Mean relative estimation error	$^{100}/_{k}\ \Sigma(\lvert EBP_i - SBP_i\rvert/SBP_i)$	8.31%	3.98%	.70

Note. *N* = 60. α = Cronbach's α. *k* = number of situations.

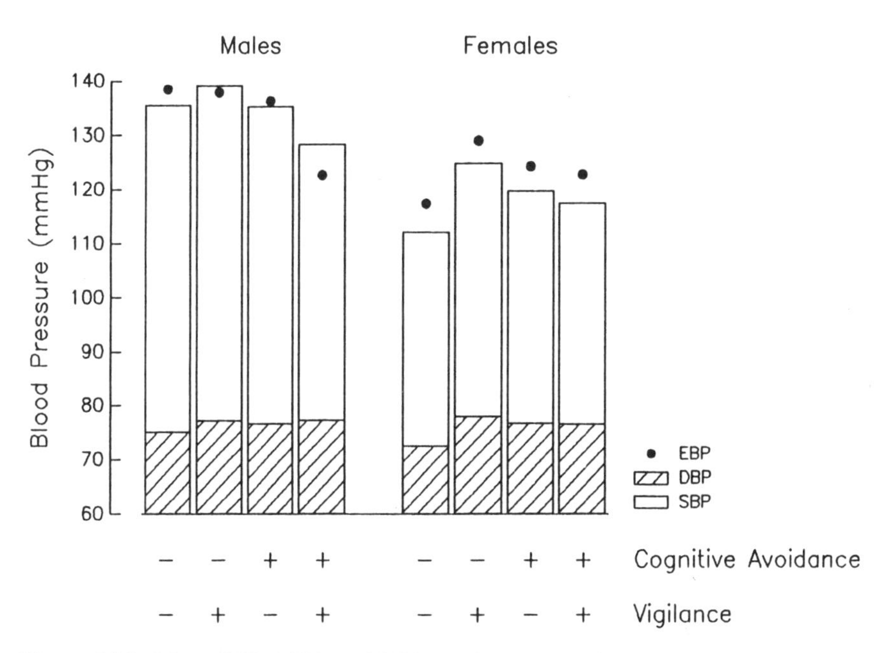

***Figure** 10.2*. **Mean SBP, DBP, and EBP, each aggregated over the eleven tasks as a function of gender, cognitive avoidance, and vigilance (-/+ = low/high scores).**

Males exhibited higher mean scores than females in SBP (134.74 mmHg versus 119.03 mmHg; $F(1,52) = 30.98$, $p < .01$) and EBP (134.88 mmHg versus 123.84 mmHg; $F(1,52) = 9.30$, $p < .01$) but lower ones in HR (71.91 bpm versus 83.92 bpm; $F(1,52) = 11.39$, $p < .01$). Regarding the discrepancy scores, women overestimated their SBP, but this was not the case for men, $F(1,52) = 5.13$, $p < .05$ (see Figures 10.2 and 10.3). This result also held when the EBP-SBP difference was related to the SBP level (mean relative discrepancy, $F(1,52) = 5.28$, $p < .05$). In detail, women overestimated their SBP across the eleven task and rest periods by about 4.87 mmHg (i.e. > 4%) while there was no discrepancy for men (0.09 mmHg, i.e. < 1%). When we consider not the direction of the difference between SBP and EBP but the estimation error scores that are based on absolute differences, the results are generally the same for men (11.07 mmHg, i.e. 8%) and women (10.07 mmHg, i.e. 8%).

An effect of the coping variables on the discrepancy scores could not be observed. Only a significant VIG × CAV interaction for mean SBP emerged, $F(1,52) = 4.52$, $p < .05$, indicating that subjects high in vigilance and low in cognitive avoidance (i.e., "sensitizers", cf. Krohne, Chapter 2, this volume) had the highest SBP scores. (The Scheffé test, however, yielded no significant group differences.)

Table 10.6
Item Statistics for the "Mean Discrepancy" Scale

	$EBP_i - SBP_i$					
	Whole sample			Males	Females	
Situation	r_{it-i}	*M*	*SD*	*M*	*M*	*t*
1 Rest period	.47	-3.83	9.69	-5.73	-1.93	1.54
2 Knee bends	.41	0.77	17.79	0.10	1.43	0.32
3 Rest period	.65	-1.67	12.12	-5.10	1.77	2.25*
4 Picture-word test	.65	3.42	13.17	-0.37	7.20	2.31*
5 Rest period	.46	3.55	12.38	2.77	4.33	0.49
6 Jumping	.62	2.55	18.27	-1.23	6.33	1.63
7 Rest period	.73	0.75	12.83	-1.50	3.00	1.37
8 Arithmetic	.49	5.53	11.36	2.73	8.33	1.95(*)
9 Rest period	.54	2.93	14.53	1.93	3.93	0.53
10 Balloon	.57	10.67	14.82	9.17	12.17	0.78
11 Rest period	.62	2.58	12.77	-1.80	6.97	2.81**

Note. $N = 60$. Males: $n = 30$. Females: $n = 30$. r_{it-i} = corrected item-total correlation. (*)$p < .10$; *$p < .05$; **$p < .01$ (two-tailed).

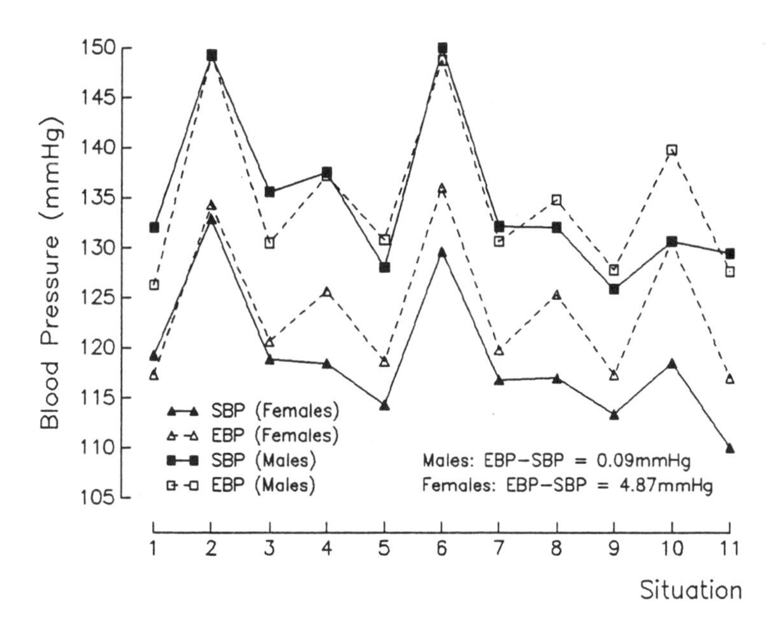

Figure 10.3. Mean SBP and mean EBP as a function of gender and situation. (1, 3, 5, 7, 9, & 11 = rest period; 2 = knee bends; 4 = picture-word test; 6 = jumping in place; 8 = mental arithmetic; 10 = inflation of balloon.)

Covariation Accuracy

Within-subject analyses

The mean summary statistics based on the within-subject multiple regressions are presented in Table 10.7. Overall, both the internal physiological information and the external situational cues contribute to actual blood pressure estimation. Although the overall variance in EBP which is accounted for by internal and external cues is generally high, the independent contribution of the external cues seems to be the more important factor. In Figure 10.4, mean percentage of EBP accounted for by situation and SBP is represented by areas of a Venn diagram (cf. Younger, 1979).[4] All the variance components show a broad variation between subjects (cf. Table 10.7). A test for normal distribution (Kolmogorov-Smirnov) of the variance components resulted in *z*-scores less than one, except for change by SBP after controlling for situation: $z = 1.32$, $p = .06$.

[4] All correlation coefficients between level accuracy scores and covariation accuracy scores were insignificant ($rs < |.17|$), suggesting some fundamental differences in the perceptual properties of the two classes of accuracy scores (cf. Pennebaker & Hoover, 1984).

Table 10.7
Summary of Within-Subject Regressions Using EBP as Dependent Measure

	R^2_{change}		Total R^2	
Predictor variable	*M*	*Min/Max*	*M*	*Min/Max*
Situation (*Step 1*)	.47	.00/.85		
SBP (*Step 2*)	.13	.00/.53	.60	.29/.91
SBP (*Step 1*)	.30	.00/.76		
Situation (*Step 2*)	.30	.01/.81	.60	.29/.91

Note. $N = 60$.

Between-subject analyses
Distributions in vigilance, cognitive avoidance, and individual range of SBP across the eleven tasks were each median-dichotomized to form the levels "low" and "high". (The mean within-subject range of SBP was 34 mmHg.) Separate 2×2×2×2 (sex × VIG × CAV × range in SBP) ANOVAs were performed for each variance component contributing to EBP.[5]

An initial result is that the total amount of variance in EBP explained by situational as well as physiological cues was unrelated to dispositional coping variables. There is a direct connection between the main effects of SBP range on both the percentage of variance in EBP which is explained by SBP as well as that percentage explained by the situation after controlling for SBP. A comparison of the subjects with a high versus low range of SBP among tasks and rest periods shows that, on the one hand, actual SBP is a significantly more important source of variance contributing to EBP for high range subjects (35%) than for low range ones (25%; $F(1,44) = 3.21, p < .10$). On the other hand, the amount of variance in EBP explained by situational cues after controlling for SBP is lower for high range subjects (25%) than for low range ones (36%; $F(1,44) = 3.23, p < .10$).

A single gender difference in variance components contributing to EBP resulted for the situational cues; $F(1,44) = 3.14, p < .10$. Situational cues were more relevant for females when predicting EBP (51% versus 44% in EBP explained by situation). A somewhat stronger effect for the reliance on situational cues resulted for CAV; $F(1,44) = 8.17, p < .01$. In estimating their

[5] The percentage of variance representing the overlap in types of information will not be used in the analyses (cf. Currie & Korabinski, 1984). For the 16 cells, counts ranged between one and eight subjects.

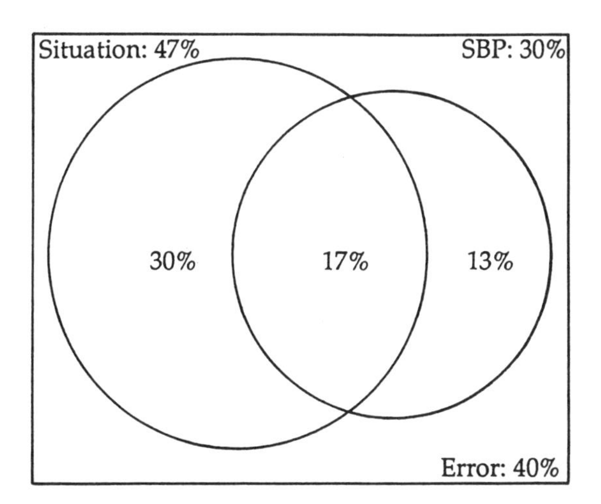

Figure 10.4. Schematic representation of sources of variance that contribute to the estimation of systolic blood pressure.

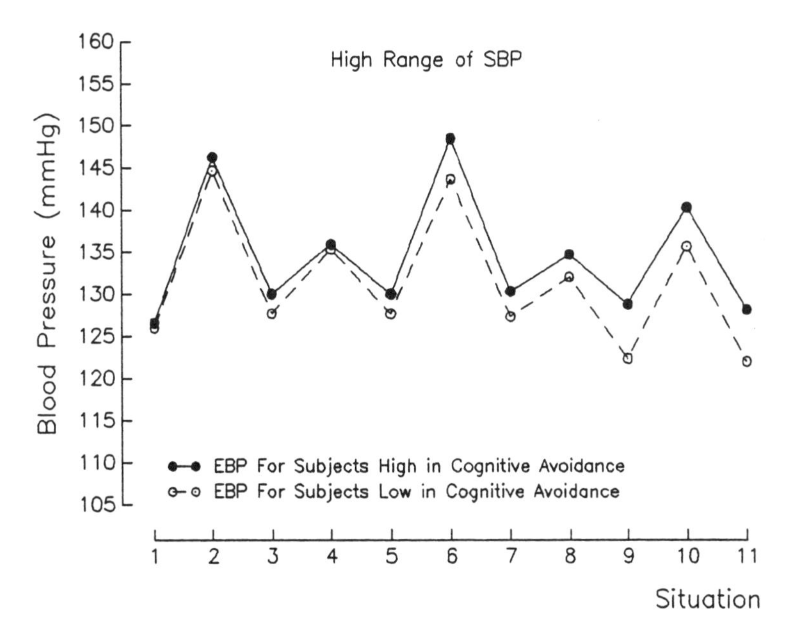

Figure 10.5. Mean EBP for subjects with a high range of SBP as a function of situation and cognitive avoidance. (1, 3, 5, 7, 9, & 11 = rest period; 2 = knee bends; 4 = picture-word test; 6 = jumping in place; 8 = mental arithmetic; 10 = inflation of balloon.)

SBP, highly avoidant subjects relied more on situational cues than low avoidant ones. (53% versus 42% in EBP explained by situation). However, this result held primarily for subjects with a low range in SBP (interaction CAV by range in SBP; $F(1,44) = 8.17, p < .01$). To demonstrate this effect in greater detail, the mean EBP curves over the eleven task and rest periods are depicted separately for low and highly avoidant subjects with a high range of SBP (cf. Figure 10.5) and those with a low range of SBP (cf. Figure 10.6). When considering subjects with a high range of SBP, the EBP curves for low and high CAV subjects are parallel while those for low range subjects differ: Highly avoidant subjects accentuated their blood pressure estimations much more according to situational cues (i.e., rest versus task) than the low avoidant ones.

While subjects high in CAV relied strongly on situational cues when estimating their blood pressure, the weight of SBP after controlling for situational cues on EBP is comparatively small; $F(1,44) = 6.33, p < .05$. The amount of variance in EBP explained by SBP after controlling for external situational cues is nearly half as great for high CAV subjects (9%) as for low CAV subjects (17%). Figure 10.7 contains the Venn diagrams for subjects high versus low in CAV.

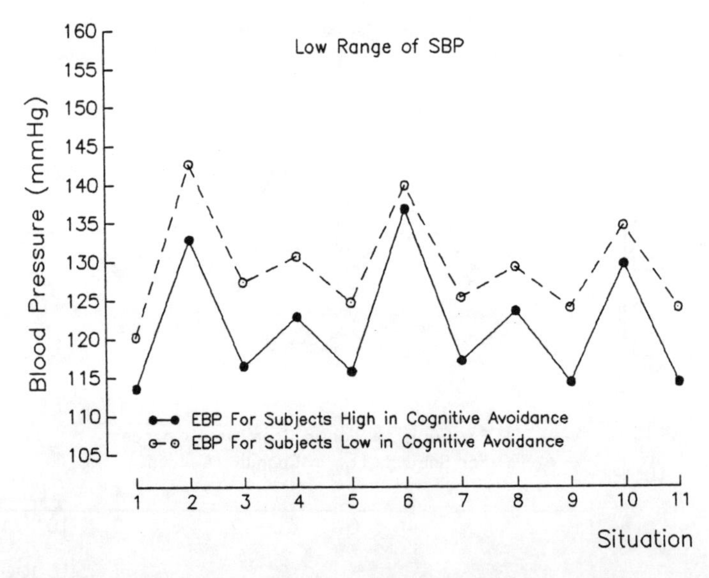

Figure 10.6. Mean EBP for subjects with a low range of SBP as a function of situation and cognitive avoidance. (1, 3, 5, 7, 9, & 11 = rest period; 2 = knee-bends; 4 = picture-word test; 6 = jumping in place; 8 = mental arithmetic; 10 = inflation of balloon.)

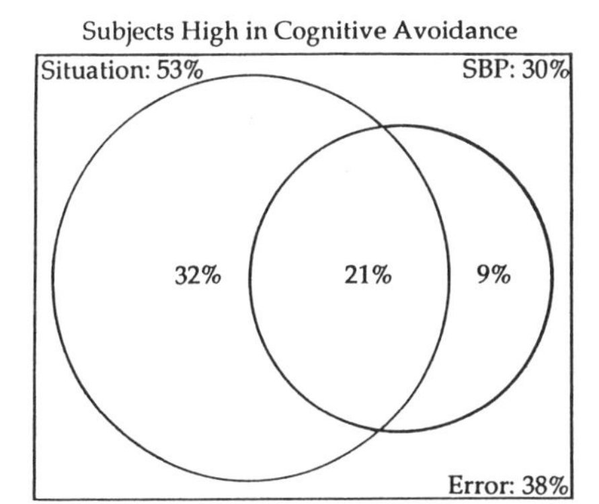

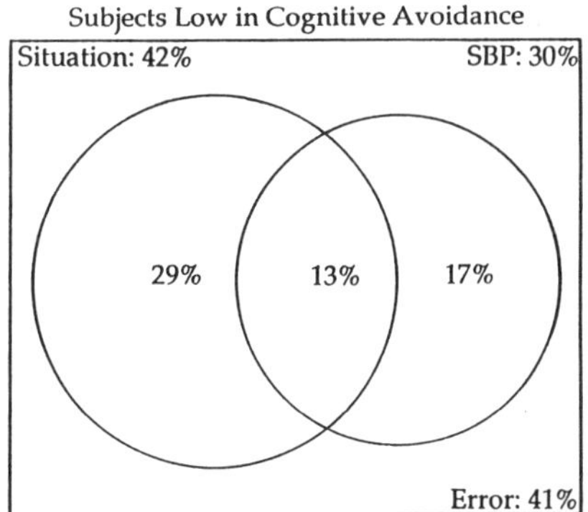

Figure 10.7. Schematic representations of sources of variance that contribute to the estimation of systolic blood pressure for subjects high versus low in cognitive avoidance.

Discussion

Within a laboratory setting, this study assessed level accuracy and covariation accuracy in blood pressure estimation and related them to gender and the coping strategies vigilance and cognitive avoidance.

The hypothesis that women rely more heavily than men on external cues when estimating their SBP could not be rejected. The percentage of variance in EBP explained by external cues was 51% in women versus 44% in men. Even though the effect was not very strong ($p < .10$), it was in the expected direction. In the previous studies on blood pressure estimation, the influence of situational cues had not been directly examined. The hypothesis concerning differences in the process of estimating physiological activity had been put forward based on gender differences in covariation accuracy which appeared only in laboratory and not in field studies (cf. Roberts & Pennebaker, 1989; Smith, 1986). In the present study, however, the mean within-subject correlation between EBP and SBP was exactly the same for men and women (mean $r = .55$, mean $R^2_{SBP} = .30$). This association is not very strong ($p < .06$, two-tailed) when one considers that this coefficient is based on only eleven tasks.

The only variable of individual difference somewhat associated with percentage of variance in EBP explained by SBP was within-subject range of SBP. (Among the men 60% had a range of SBP above the median while only 40% of the women were above it.) Following our expectations, EBP and SBP showed a stronger covariation in high range subjects (mean $r = .59$; mean $R^2_{SBP} = .35$) than in low range ones (mean $r = .50$; mean $R^2_{SBP} = .25$).

In the case of estimating SBP, there is no evidence for the Roberts and Pennebaker hypothesis that men are much better at *directly* perceiving physiological states. However, the present study has provided some evidence for the assumption that women are particularly sensitive to environmental cues.

The strongest gender effect on accuracy scores emerged for level accuracy. Based on the mean EBP-SBP discrepancy, women tended to overestimate their SBP. Further inspection of the discrepancy scores for each of the different tasks allows for a more detailed understanding of how this resulted (cf. Table 10.6 and Figure 10.3). Compared to men, women overestimated their SBP only in response to the two cognitive tasks (i.e., Situation 4: picture-word test, Situation 8: mental arithmetic) and the final rest period. By contrast, men underestimated their SBP in response to the rest period (i.e., Situation 3) following the knee bends task. These results point to the important role the selection of tasks plays in all studies of accuracy in interoception. Is it possible that women overestimate their physiological activity particularly in response to mathematical tasks, and men, conversely, tend to do so in response to verbal tasks? Self-concepts about abilities might be the crucial variables. Further research should focus on this topic.

In contrast to expectation, the coping strategies proved to be unrelated to level accuracy. Since both coping strategies concern cognitive and behavioral processes in response to *threatening* situations, the task repertoire of a study should also be guided more stringently by theory in regard to threat taxonomies; it should, for example, consist of situations in which the intensity of the threat, emanating from either the ego or a pain stimulus, is varied.

In regard to individual differences in the process of estimating one's SBP, cognitive avoidance proved to be a relevant coping dimension. For subjects high in CAV, the percentage of variance in EBP accounted for by external situational cues was comparatively high. This result does support the idea of avoidant coping preferences being motivated by an "intolerance of emotional arousal" (Krohne, 1989, and Chapter 2, this volume) and a consequent withdrawal from internal bodily cues.

This interpretation fits nicely into the assumption of the repressive coping style being associated with "low-level thinking" (i.e., a narrow perspective, a total lack of self-reflection, and no awareness of moods, cf. Pennebaker, 1989). According to Pennebaker (1989), low-level thinking during threat or stress allows for the effective blocking of emotional information; i.e., by adopting a low-level thinking strategy, the person effectively excludes affective information from linguistic processing (see also Borkovec & Lyonfields, this volume).

The type of task subjects enroll in is also of importance when covariation accuracy is considered. In estimating their physiological activity, vigilant subjects probably refer to the dimensions "threat - no threat" or "controllable - uncontrollable" rather than to "active - passive", the dimension controlled in this study. (For a comparable but much more comprehensive discussion of the potential variance between the perception of a physiological sensation and any particular interpretation of it, see Cioffi, 1991.)

In further research, much more attention should be given to task choice and task coding. It might not be necessary to code the tasks by simulation samples (cf.

Pennebaker & Epstein, 1983). For the data in Pennebaker and Epstein (1983; average of Experiment 1 and the replication), the general beliefs about HR obtained from the simulation sample correlated with a mean *r* of .62 with HR estimation. In the present study, the broad 0/1 activity coding of the situations correlated with a mean *r* of .69 with EBP. As already argued in Krohne and Kohlmann (1990), a coding of a certain task by computing the mean for the ratings of a simulation sample offers at best only a hint of *general beliefs* and does not reflect the *specific beliefs* of a given person. Effort should therefore be directed toward coding tasks along different dimensions (e.g., activity - no activity; threat - no threat; mathematical abilities required - verbal abilities required) with respect to the variables of individual difference studied.

In the present study, estimation of physiological activity was based, for the majority of subjects, mainly on external cues (external situational cues: 47%, internal physiological cues: 30%, with an overlap of 17%). A serious limitation of this analysis, however, has to be mentioned. As in most of the few studies previously conducted on the estimation of bodily state, only additive and linear, and no interactive or non-linear, influences for internal and external cues have been examined .

Several researchers (e.g., Meyer et al., 1985) point to the fact that people with chronic diseases take medication or use health facilities based on estimations of their physiological state. Because these estimations of the physiological state seem to be primarily based on the processing of external cues, interoception research attempting to increase our knowledge regarding individual differences in health-related behavior should no longer be focused exclusively on internal cues.

References

Barr, M., Pennebaker, J. W., & Watson, D. (1988). Improving blood pressure estimation through internal and environmental feedback. *Psychosomatic Medicine, 50*, 37-45.

Baumann, L. J., & Leventhal, H. (1985). "I can tell when my blood pressure is up, can't I?". *Health Psychology, 4*, 203-218.

Bell, P. A., & Byrne, D. (1978). Repression-sensitization. In H. London & J. E. Exner (Eds.), *Dimensions of personality* (pp. 449-485). New York: Wiley.

Brener, J., & Jones, J. M. (1974). Interoceptive discrimination in intact humans: Detection of cardiac activity. *Physiology and Behavior, 13*, 763-767.

Byrne, D. (1961). The Repression-Sensitization Scale: Rationale, reliability, and validity. *Journal of Personality, 29*, 334-349.

Byrne, D. (1964). Repression-sensitization as a dimension of personality. In B. A. Maher (Ed.), *Progress in experimental personality research* (Vol. 1, pp. 169-220). New York: Academic Press.

Byrne, D., Steinberg, M. A., & Schwartz, M. S. (1968). The relationship between repression-sensitization and physical illness. *Journal of Abnormal Psychology, 73*, 154-155.

Carver, C. S., Coleman, A. E., & Glass, D. C. (1976). The coronary-prone behavior pattern and the suppression of fatigue on a treadmill test. *Journal of Personality and Social Pychology, 33*, 460-466.

Cioffi, D. (1991). Beyond attentional strategies: A cognitive-perceptual model of somatic interpretation. *Psychological Bulletin, 109*, 25-41.

Currie, I., & Korabinski, A. (1984). Some comments on bivariate regression. *The Statistician, 33*, 283-293.

Davis, M. R., Langer, A. W., Sutterer, J. R., Gelling, P. D., & Marlin, M. (1986). Relative discriminability of heartbeat-contigent stimuli under three procedures for assessing cardiac perception. *Psychophysiology, 23*, 76-81.

Dale, A., & Anderson, D. (1978). Information variables in voluntary control and classical conditioning of the heart: Field dependence and heart rate perception. *Perceptual and Motor Skills, 47*, 79-85.

Ehlers, A. (1989). Interaction of psychological and physiological factors in panic attacks. In P. F. Lovibond & P. H. Wilson (Eds.), *Proceedings of the XXIV International Congress of Psychology: Vol. 9. Clinical and abnormal psychology* (pp. 1-14). Amsterdam, The Netherlands: Elsevier.

Eriksen, C. W. (1966). Cognitive responses to internally cued anxiety. In C. D. Spielberger (Ed.), *Anxiety and behavior* (pp. 327-360). New York: Academic Press.

Greenstadt, L., Shapiro, D., & Whitehead, R. (1986). Blood pressure discrimination. *Psychophysiology, 23*, 500-509.

Katkin, E. S., Blascovich, J., & Goldband, S. (1981). Empirical assessment of visceral perception: Individual and sex; differences in the acquisition of heartbeat discrimination. *Journal of Personality and Social Psychology, 40*, 1095-1101.

Kohlmann, C.-W. (1988). Persönlichkeitsspezifische Aspekte der Erfassung von Belastungsreaktionen [Personality-specific aspects in the assessment of stress reactions]. In L. Brüderl (Ed.), *Theorien und Methoden der Bewältigungsforschung* (pp. 192-199). München: Juventa.

Kohlmann, C.-W. (1990). *Streßbewältigung und Persönlichkeit. Flexibles versus rigides Copingverhalten und seine Auswirkungen auf Angsterleben und physiologische Belastungsreaktionen* [Coping and personality. Flexible versus rigid coping behavior and its effects on anxiety and physiological stress reactions]. Bern: Huber.

Kohlmann, C.-W., & Singer, P. (1991). Estimation of blood pressure: Individual differences in relying on internal physiological cues and external situational cues [Abstract]. *Journal of Psychophysiology, 5*, 113-114.

Kohlmann, C.-W., Singer, P., & Krohne, H. W. (1989). Coping dispositions, actual coping, and the discrepancy between subjective and physiological stress reactions. In P. F. Lovibond & P. H. Wilson (Eds.), *Proceedings of the XXIV International Congress of Psychology: Vol. 9. Clinical and abnormal psychology* (pp. 67-78). Amsterdam, The Netherlands: Elsevier.

Krohne, H. W. (1986). Coping with stress: Dispositions, strategies, and the problem of measurement. In M. H. Appley & R. Trumbull (Eds.), *Dynamics of stress* (pp. 209-234). New York: Plenum.

Krohne, H. W. (1989). The concept of coping modes: Relating cognitive person variables to actual coping behavior. *Advances in Behaviour Research and Therapy, 11*, 235-248.

Krohne, H. W. (in press). Repression-Sensitization [Repression-sensitization]. In M. Amelang (Ed.), *Enzyklopädie der Psychologie. Serie Differentielle Psychologie und Persönlichkeitsforschung: Band 2. Bereiche interindividueller Unterschiede*. Göttingen: Hogrefe.

Krohne, H. W., & Kohlmann, C.-W. (1990). Persönlichkeit und Emotion [Personality and emotion]. In K. R. Scherer (Ed.), *Enzyklopädie der Psychologie. Serie Motivation und Emotion: Band 3. Psychologie der Emotion* (pp. 485-559). Göttingen: Hogrefe.

Krohne, H. W., Rösch, W., & Kürsten, F. (1989). Die Erfassung von Angstbewältigung in physisch bedrohlichen Situationen [The measurement of coping in physical-threat situations]. *Zeitschrift für Klinische Psychologie, 18*, 230-242.

Lazarus, R. S. (1966). *Psychological stress and the coping process.* New York: McGraw-Hill.

Lazarus, R. S. (1983). The costs and benefits of denial. In S. Breznitz (Ed.), *The denial of stress* (pp. 1-30). New York: International Universities Press.

McFarland, R. A. (1975). Heart rate perception and heart rate control. *Psychophysiology, 12,* 402-405.

Meyer, D., Leventhal, H., & Gutmann, M. (1985). Common sense models of illness: The example of hypertension. *Health Psychology, 4,* 115-135.

Miller, S. M. (1987). Monitoring and blunting: Validation of a questionnaire to assess styles of information seeking under threat. *Journal of Personality and Social Psychology, 52,* 345-353.

Miller, S. M. (1990). To see or not to see: Cognitive informational styles in the coping process. In M. Rosenbaum (Ed.), *Learned resourcefulness: On coping skills, self-regulation, and adaptive behavior* (pp. 95-126). New York: Springer.

Miller, S. M., Brody, D. S., & Summerton, J. (1988). Styles of coping with threat: Implications for health. *Journal of Personality and Social Psychology, 54,* 142-148.

Pennebaker, J. W. (1981). Stimulus characteristics influencing estimation of heart rate. *Psychophysiology, 18,* 540-548.

Pennebaker, J. W. (1989). Stream of consciousness and stress: Levels of thinking. In J. S. Uleman & J. A. Bargh (Eds.), *Unintended thought* (pp. 327-350). New York: Guilford.

Pennebaker, J. W. (in press). Beyond laboratory-based cardiac perception: Ecological interoception. In R. Schandry & D. Vaitl (Eds.), *Advances in cardiac perception.* New York: Springer-Verlag.

Pennebaker, J. W., & Epstein, D. (1983). Implicit psychophysiology: Effects of common beliefs and idiosyncratic physiological responses on symptom reporting. *Journal of Personality, 51,* 468-496.

Pennebaker, J. W., & Hoover, C. H. (1984). Visceral perception versus visceral detection: Disentangling methods and assumptions. *Biofeedback and Self-Regulation, 9,* 339-352.

Pennebaker, J. W., & Watson, D. (1988). Blood pressure estimation and beliefs among normotensives and hypertensives. *Health Psychology, 7,* 309-328.

Roberts, T. A., & Pennebaker, J. W. (1989). *Women's and men's strategies in perceiving internal state.* Unpublished manuscript, Southern Methodist University, Department of Psychology, Dallas, Texas.

Roth, S., & Cohen, L. J. (1986). Approach, avoidance, and coping with stress. *American Psychologist, 41,* 813-819.

Rouse, C. H., Jones, G. E., & Jones, K. R. (1988). The effect of body composition and gender on cardiac awareness. *Psychophysiology, 25,* 400-407.

Schandry, R. (1981). Heartbeat perception and emotional experience. *Psychophysiology, 15,* 499-501.

Schumacher, A. (1990). Die "Miller Behavioral Style Scale": Erste Überprüfung einer deutschen Fassung [The "Miller Behavioral Style Scale": First investigation of a German adaptation]. *Zeitschrift für Differentielle und Diagnostische Psychologie, 11,* 243-250.

Smith, V. C. (1986). *Perception and estimation of blood pressure fluctuations in natural settings.* Unpublished master's thesis, Southern Methodist University, Dallas, Texas.

Stewart, H. L., & Olbrisch, M. E. (1986). Symptom correlates of blood pressure: A replication and re-analysis. *Journal of Behavioral Medicine, 9,* 271-289.

Störmer, S. W., Heiligtag, U., & Knoll, J. F. (1989). Heartbeat detection and knowledge of results: A new method and some theoretical thoughts. *Journal of Psychophysiology, 3,* 409-417.

Ullmann, L. P. (1958). Clinical correlates of facilitation and inhibition of response to emotional stimuli. *Journal of Projective Techniques and Personality Assessment, 22,* 341-347.

Weidner, G., & Matthews, K. A. (1978). Reported physical symptoms elicited by unpredictable events and the Type A coronary-prone behavior pattern. *Journal of Personality and Social Psychology, 36*, 1213-1220.

Weisz, J., Balázs, L., & Adám, G. (1988). The influence of self-focused attention on heartbeat perception. *Psychophysiology, 25*, 193-199.

Whitehead, W. E., Drescher, V. M., Heiman, P., & Blackwell, B. (1977). Relation of heart rate control to heartbeat perception. *Biofeedback and Self-Regulation, 2*, 371-392.

Younger, A. (1979). *A handbook for linear regression*. Belmont, CA: Wadsworth.

PART IV.

ATTENTION, AVOIDANCE, AND HEALTH STATUS

Chapter 11

Gender, Coping, and Health

Gerdi Weidner and R. Lorraine Collins

Effectiveness of Coping Styles

Coping has been defined as "cognitive and behavioral efforts to master, reduce, or tolerate the internal and/or external demands that are created by the stressful transaction" (Folkman, 1984, p. 843). As such, coping is multidimensional and encompasses a variety of skills and behaviors that are not necessarily related to the success of the coping efforts. While Lazarus and Folkman's (1984) conceptualization focuses on situational determinants of coping (i.e., coping efforts can shift during different stages of a stressful event), most other approaches suggest that coping may be stylistic and dispositional in nature (see Carver, Scheier, & Weintraub, 1989; Kohlmann, 1990; Krohne, 1989; Krohne, 1990).

Many formulations of coping strategies contrast attention with avoidance (see Roth & Cohen, 1986, for review). For example, Krohne (1989, and Chapter 2 in this volume) distinguishes vigilance from cognitive avoidance, Miller (1987, see also Miller, Combs, & Kruus in this volume) contrasts "monitors" with "blunters", and Suls and Fletcher (1985) review avoidant and non-avoidant coping strategies. According to Suls and Fletcher (1985), a common feature of avoidant strategies is that they "all involve a strategy that focuses attention away from either the source of stress or away from one's psychological/somatic reactions to the stressor" (p. 250). This broad definition includes a variety of coping strategies such as denial, distraction, and repression. As implied by their designation, non-avoidant strategies involve observing and attending to the source of stress and/or one's reactions to the stressor.

While many attempts to define and to measure coping strategies have been made, the issue as to which strategy is more effective is controversial. In the next section we will attempt to address the question of comparative efficacy of attention versus avoidance coping strategies, following which we will outline gender differences in coping styles. Finally, we will examine whether gender

---

Preparation of this chapter was supported by grants from the National Institutes of Health (HL-4036801), Biomedical Research Support (RR0706721), a grant from the National Institute on Drug Abuse (R01-DA05852), The American Heart Association of Suffolk County, New York, and a grant from the Swedish Medical Research Council. The authors wish to thank Gernot Gollnisch and William M. Lapp for their comments on an earlier draft of this manuscript.

men's greater risk for physical health problems as exemplified in research on differences in the use of maladaptive coping strategies could contribute to coronary heart disease, and women's greater risk for mental health problems as exemplified in research on unipolar depression.

It appears that the effectiveness of a specific coping strategy depends on characteristics of the event with which one attempts to cope. For example, in the case of ongoing marital problems, what might be effective in the short-run (e.g., denial as a means of avoiding emotional arousal) may be maladaptive in the long-run (denial prevents the elaboration of other forms of coping behaviors, such as problem solving).

Unfortunately, not many empirical studies have given consideration to situational aspects of coping (also see chapter by Miller et al. in this volume for a discussion of this problem). In a meta-analysis of the few available studies, Suls and Fletcher (1985; also see Mullen & Suls, 1982) conclude that overall, neither avoidant nor non-avoidant strategies are superior. However, when the duration of the stressor was taken into account, avoidance strategies proved to be more effective for short-term stressors (lasting no more than one week), while non-avoidant/attentional strategies were more effective when coping with long-term stressors (exceeding one week in duration). One exception was short-term physical stress, in which paying attention to sensory aspects of the situation (e.g., sensory reaction to a pain stimulus), but not to the emotional aspects of the situation, appeared to be adaptive.

In addition to the time-based distinction, controllability of the situation also determines the effectiveness of coping strategies. Generally, avoidance is seen as more adaptive when the situation is uncontrollable (e.g., paralysis), whereas attention is better when the situation is more controllable (e.g., preparing for an exam). However, in the case of transient non-physical stress, avoidance strategies are adaptive regardless of their degree of controllability. Paying attention to such stressors (especially with a focus on emotions) would be considered as maladaptive, given their brief duration and the potential wasted energy of attempting to control a series of transient events of no particular consequence. Further, the increased mental and physiological activity expended to cope with short-term stressors and the frustration engendered thereby, may result in physical and mental exhaustion, and thereby contribute to an increased risk for illness.

With regard to long-term stressors, attention is generally more adaptive in the long run, because many events are basically controllable when the individual has sufficient resources and time. The principle at work in these several instances appears to be one of putting effort into those situations that can be effectively changed and ignoring situations that are transient or cannot be reliably altered.

Gender Differences in Coping Styles

It is disconcerting to find that gender differences in coping styles have not been much studied. For example, in their attempt to summarize the literature on gender differences in cognitive coping, Miller and Kirsch (1987) wrote, "it was disappointing to find that a majority of the studies of cognitive coping and stress ... did not report on sex differences" (p. 280). Furthermore, controllability and duration of the event with which one copes are rarely assessed. Thus, even if we have information on gender, it is still difficult to draw inferences about coping style effectiveness.

We will now review studies on coping styles that have included both women and men, and in which duration and/or controllability of the stressful event have been assessed or can be inferred. Duration will be defined using Suls and Fletcher's (1985) criteria; "short-term" refers to stressors lasting one week or less, "long-term" refers to events lasting more than one week. Criteria for controllability are more difficult to specify because of the variety of conceptualizations of this construct (cf. Folkman, 1984; Lazarus & Folkman, 1984; Stone & Neale, 1984). In our use of the term, we will focus on controllability of the outcome of the stressful situation. However, because of the limited information generally available on controllability of stressors, we will not address more fine tuned distinctions concerning control and coping (cf. Folkman, 1984; Krohne, 1988; Thompson, 1981). In addition, while we have made these categorizations to highlight the situational nature of some gender differences in coping, we acknowledge that some aspects of these categorizations are arbitrary and that not all findings fit neatly within this framework.

Short-Term Events

As stated previously, avoidance would be considered an adaptive strategy when coping with non-physical threats that are short-lived and of no long-term consequence (Suls & Fletcher, 1985). A number of studies (many employ laboratory stressors) provide evidence that gender differences in coping styles appear when subjects are asked to recall (or imagine) a specific short-term stressful event. Women have been found to report more self-consoling strategies than men (Parker & Brown, 1982), are more self-critical in response to a hypothetical failure situation (Carver & Ganellen, 1983), engage in more self-blame (Frank, McLaughlin, & Crusco 1984), and focus more on their emotional response to the negative event than do men (Billings & Moos, 1981).

Of particular relevance to our question regarding maladaptive coping styles and health is the recent research reported by Nolen-Hoeksema (1987). The author argues that most people experience mild-to-moderate episodes of depressive symptoms, lasting a few hours or days. Regardless of the source of the depressive episode, women attend to the episode differently than men. According to Nolen-Hoeksema (1987), men are more likely to engage in distracting behaviors (avoidance coping) when depressed, while women are more likely to ruminate about their depressed states (attentional coping), thus amplifying and prolonging their depressive episodes. Similar results have been reported by others (Chino & Funabiki, 1984; Funabiki, Bologna, Pepping, & Fitzgerald, 1980; Kleinke, Staneski, & Mason, 1982; also see research reported by Nolen-Hoeksema, 1987).

Further support for the notion that women employ less effective coping strategies than men when coping with short-term events of a non-physical nature comes from a study by Weidner, Lapp, and Hustedt (1991). This study employed the Mainz Coping Inventory (MCI; Krohne, 1989), which assesses vigilance and cognitive avoidance to short-term hypothetical events that are threatening to one's ego and physical well-being. In contrast to behavioral avoidance, which may result from vigilant processes, cognitive avoidance aims at reducing emotional arousal (cf. Krohne, 1989, and Chapter 2 in this volume). Thus, scoring high on cognitive avoidance in the face of short-term stress would be considered adaptive, especially with regard to emotional health. The results indicated that men reported more avoidance strategies than did women regardless of the nature of the event. There were no gender differences in vigilant coping with ego-threats. However, when confronted with hypothetical events that were threatening to one's physical well-being, women reported more vigilant strategies than did men (similar results have been found by S. M. Miller; personal communication, 1990). Given the notion that attention may be more adaptive when faced with short-term physical stress (Suls & Fletcher, 1985), this finding suggests that women may engage in more adaptive coping than do men when faced with physical threats.

Stressful Events Requiring Long-Term Adjustment

While women's coping with short-term non-physical stress may not be adaptive, their adjustment to severe stress of longer duration seems to exceed that of men's. In studies on adjustment to stressful life events women were found to experience fewer negative consequences (e.g., psychological distress, physical illness) following the loss of a spouse (Sterling & Eyer, 1981; Stroebe & Stroebe, 1983) and seem to be less emotionally affected than men by financial difficulty (Kessler, 1982). Women also appear to show better adjustment (e.g., fewer negative health consequences) following marital separation and divorce when compared to men (Riessman & Gerstel, 1985; Sterling & Eyer, 1981; Wallerstein & Kelly, 1980).

It is not known what specific coping strategies women are using when encountering these types of stressors. It is conceivable that their initial reaction to stress, which is characterized by attention (or, when measured as independent dimensions, by the relative absence of avoidance), facilitates the development of more appropriate coping mechanisms, such as problem solving for situations that can be affected, and avoidance strategies for uncontrollable events. Consistent with this notion is a study by Viney and Westbrook (1982). The authors reported that among chronically ill individuals expecting to be disabled for at least six month or longer, women report "escape strategies" (e.g., "I become involved in other activities...", p. 599) more than men. The use of behavioral avoidance in the face of long-term uncontrollable stress is considered adaptive and may have resulted from vigilant processes (i.e., the realization that the situation is beyond one's control).

In contrast, men's initial avoidance reaction may not allow them to perceive and act upon early warning signs. Thus, they may be unprepared and feel overwhelmed by the problem once they realize it is of long-term consequence and indeed requires attention.

Chronic, Controllable Events

Many studies have assessed coping with daily hassles and life events. Compared to the events described in the section above, events in this category are more controllable, with varying degrees of difficulty. Thus, attention would be considered adaptive if the event was long-term, and avoidance would be adaptive if the event was short-term. Unfortunately, the exact duration of events in this category of studies is not always clear, therefore it is often difficult to determine which coping strategy is likely to be most effective.

With regard to gender differences in coping strategies with these types of events, the literature is truly "mixed". Based on their extensive program of research, Folkman and colleagues concluded that "... gender differences in coping patterns were not pronounced" (Folkman, Lazarus, Pimley, & Novacek, 1987, p. 181-182; also see Folkman & Lazarus, 1980; Folkman, Lazarus, Gruen, & DeLongis, 1986; also see Hamilton & Fagot, 1988). Similarly, Billings and Moos (1984) found that coping responses in a sample of clinically depressed women and men were generally similar, with the exception of women's greater focus on their emotions.

When gender differences in coping with chronic, controllable stress do occur, women appear to employ more avoidance strategies interfering with problem solving [e.g., positive reappraisal; seeking emotional support (cf. Carver et al., 1989)], and are engaged in strategies often labeled as "ineffective" when compared to men. For example, Folkman and Lazarus (1980) reported a tendency for men to engage in more problem-focused coping (attention) when encountering work stress than did women. Pearlin and Schooler (1978) found "a pronounced imbalance between the sexes in their possession and use of effective mechanisms" (p. 15) with men holding the advantage in the possession of effective coping responses. Similarly, Billings and Moos (1981) reported that "women are more likely to use avoidance coping, which was associated with greater impairment of functioning" (p. 154). Vingerhoets and Van Heck (1990) reported that women rated emotion-focused strategies as most characteristic of how they handled stress, and men rated problem-focused coping strategies as most characteristic (also see Stone, Lennox, & Neale, 1985; Stone & Neale, 1984).

It is of interest to note that in one of the studies (Stone & Neale, 1984) coping styles were related to perceptions of control and duration of the stressor: perceiving little control over problems and perceiving problems to be of long duration was related to the use of avoidance strategies. Unfortunately for our purposes, these data were not analyzed with respect to gender. It is possible that the women in these studies perceived (and actually had) less control over their life events and daily hassles, which may have contributed to their greater use of "ineffective" coping strategies. Generally then, when gender differences have been reported, men are described as using more effective coping strategies than do women, regardless of the particular measure of coping and/or theoretical perspective from which the measure is derived.

While the women in the studies above appear to be using less effective coping strategies when compared to men, a recent study by Rohde, Lewinsohn, Tilson, and Seeley (1990) found men to engage more in "ineffective escapism" than women. The women in this study actually engaged in more adaptive coping, such as "cognitive self-control" and "solace seeking" than did the men. The fact that subjects in this sample were 50 years of age and older raises the question whether the use of effective coping strategies changes with age to favor women. It is also conceivable that differential levels of control and duration of the stressors could have accounted for the gender differences. Thus, based on the research reviewed above, gender differences in coping with chronic but relatively controllable events are rather inconsistent. As already mentioned (page 242), it is difficult to decide which coping strategy would actually be more effective, since information on the duration and the degree of controllability of the stressful event is often lacking.

In sum, men appear better at coping with short-term events because they use avoidance. In contrast, women adjust better to less frequent but severely stressful events (e.g., death of a spouse). Women also report that they pay more attention to threats to their physical well-being than men. Gender differences in coping with chronic stress have either been minimal or men have been reported to use more attention strategies (i.e., problem solving), whereas women appear to engage in more avoidance strategies (with a focus on emotions).

Gender Differences in Health

It has been frequently observed that there are remarkable differences in health between women and men (e.g., Nolen-Hoeksema, 1987; Rodin & Ickovics, 1990; Strickland, 1988; Verbrugge, 1985; Wingard, 1984). In general, women appear to suffer more from psychological distress (e.g., depression) and minor somatic complaints when compared to men. Men on the other hand, are more susceptible to life threatening diseases, such as myocardial infarction. Several explanations for these gender differences have been offered, ranging from biological (based on genes or reproductive physiology) to psychosocial causes (e.g., stress, health behaviors; see Verbrugge, 1985; Waldron, 1983). In the remainder of this chapter, we will focus on psychosocial factors as they impact on the question of whether gender differences in the use of attention versus avoidance coping relate to gender differences in health outcomes in two areas: (1) physical health, as exemplified by the role of coping in risk for coronary heart disease (CHD); and, (2) mental health, as exemplified by the role of coping in risk for depression.

Coping Among Coronary-Prone Individuals

It is generally established that women outlive men in most countries. In industrialized countries, the major cause of premature death among men is heart disease, accounting for 41% of the gender difference in overall mortality in the U.S.A. (cf. Lerner & Kannel, 1986; Wingard, 1984). Consistent with this observation is the fact that men score higher on the three standard coronary risk factors (i.e., cigarette smoking, hypertension, elevated levels of plasma cholesterol) when compared to women. Although all three risk factors have a strong behavioral component and are influenced by stressful environments (e.g., smoking in response to stress; eating "fast foods" high in fat and salt in response to a hurried and fast pace of life; see Weidner, in press), research on coping styles as determinants of health behaviors is still rare. This is unfortunate because knowledge of the relationship between coping and health behaviors could help illuminate issues related to the efficacy of coping efforts. For example, it is conceivable that while men's greater use of avoidance strategies in the face of short-term stress is effective in relieving stress, it may be associated with escape-oriented coping behaviors (e.g., increased smoking), which place them at risk for negative health outcomes.

In addition to the traditional risk factors for coronary heart disease, men also score higher on the two psychosocial characteristics that have been implicated in CHD etiology in both genders; Type A behavior (Eaker & Castelli, 1988; Haynes, Feinleib, & Kannel, 1980) and hostility (Barefoot, Siegler, Nowlin, Peterson, Haney, & Williams, 1987). We will first turn our attention to Type A behavior, and then discuss hostility and its relevance to coping styles and risk for CHD.

Type A behavior

Type A behavior is characterized by ambitiousness, impatience, competitiveness, a rapid and emphatic speech style, irritability, and potential for a hostile response to environmental challenges. Persons without such attributes are described as displaying the alternate, Type B behavior pattern, and are more relaxed, deferent, unhurried, and less provoked by challenges in the environment than their Type A counterparts. Type A individuals report more stress in their lives and indicate difficulties with coping (cf. Suls & Wan, 1989; Weidner & Chesney, 1985). Thus, the Type A and Type B behavior patterns may be related to use of different coping strategies when confronted with environmental stress (also see chapter by Ben-Zur, Breznitz, & Hashmonay in this volume).

Indeed, a number of laboratory as well as field studies suggest that Type A individuals engage in behaviors that might elevate their risk for CHD. For example, both male and female Type As ignore symptoms of fatigue and other physical symptoms when focusing on a stressful task (Carver, Coleman, & Glass, 1976; Weidner & Matthews, 1978). Ignoring fatigue and chest pain, the prodromal symptoms of myocardial infarction, may lead to a delay in seeking medical care and thereby increase the risk of death due to CHD. Further, Type As appear to be particularly sensitive to threats to their self-esteem and are likely to employ self-handicapping strategies when they expect to fail on a task (Weidner, 1980).

In addition to focusing on specific coping behaviors, several studies have assessed dispositional coping styles among Type As and Type Bs. Overall, it appears that Type As cope actively with stress. When compared to Type Bs, Type As report more problem-focused coping (Hart, 1988), more planning and active coping (Carver et al., 1989), and more vigilance strategies in response to short-term stress (Weidner et al., 1991; cf. Ben-Zur et al., this volume). These findings are consistent with the notion of Type A behavior as a response style aimed at controlling environmental events. This hyper-reactivity in response to everyday stressors, which are usually rather minor and short-lived, may lead to physical and mental exhaustion, thus increasing their risk for illness in the long run.

There is also some evidence that Type As' chronic use of active/vigilant coping styles may be accompanied by increased activity of the sympathetic-adrenomedullary system and, possibly, also the pituitary-adrenocortical system (Henry & Meehan, 1981), which may play an important role in CHD etiology (e.g., Krantz & Manuck, 1984; Matthews et al., 1986). In a review of the research on cardiovascular stress reactivity among Type A and B individuals, Houston (1988) concluded that Type A men show greater cardiovascular reactivity to stress than Type B men. However, this difference is not consistently found for Type A and B women. It appears that in order to elicit heightened reactivity from Type A women, a verbal stressful task is necessary:... "verbal situations may appear more sex role appropriate for females, and therefore Type A women may become more engaged in such situations ..." (Houston, 1988, p. 223; also see Houston 1983).

Further support for the notion of gender influencing physiological stress reactivity and thereby risk for negative health outcomes comes from research on neuroendocrine reactivity to stress. Generally, in gender-based comparisons men are more reactive when tested within a stereotypically male area of performance (e.g., complex color-word test; Frankenhaeuser, Dunne, & Lundberg, 1976). However, this gender difference is much smaller in response to a matriculation exam, which is important to both women and men (Frankenhaeuser, Rauste-von Wright, Collins, von Wright, Sedvall, & Swahn, 1978). Also, when comparing neuroendocrine responses of women and men taking their child to a medical examination (a more traditionally female area), no gender differences were found (Lundberg, de Chateau, Winberg, & Frankenhaeuser, 1981). In addition, there is some evidence that the gender differences in physiological reactivity are greatly decreased when the responses of women in nontraditional occupations are compared with those of men (e.g., male and female engineering students; Collins & Frankenhaeuser, 1978; also see Girdler, Turner, Sherwood, & Light, 1990; Weidner & Hustedt, 1991). Based on these studies, it appears that gender differences in physiological reactivity are strongly influenced by gender roles as well as the relevance of a particular stressor to a person's gender (also see Frankenhaeuser, in press). Overall, men seem to be reactive to a broader range of stressors than women.

To conclude, both Type A women and men engage in maladaptive coping behaviors when encountering stressful events. Type As of both genders also report using vigilant coping strategies when encountering short-term environmental threats. The extent to which this behavioral hyper-reactivity is accompanied by cardiovascular arousal is influenced by gender roles and gender relevance of the threat encountered.

Hostility

The type of hostility that has been linked to CHD is usually assessed by the Cook and Medley Hostility Scale (Cook & Medley, 1954). This scale primarily measures suspiciousness, resentment, and cynical mistrust (Smith & Frohm, 1985). It is not a measure of overt aggressive behavior, which is more characteristic of Type As (Weidner, Istvan, & McKnight, 1989). Similar to the Type A behavior pattern, it is not clear how hostility asserts its influence on the disease process. It is hypothesized that highly hostile people spend a substantial amount of time in a high arousal state, overreacting to stimuli that arouse their suspiciousness. This state could be associated with increased sympathetic nervous system activity (e.g., increased release of free fatty acids, elevated cholesterol, and increased blood pressure response to stress). In fact, it has been shown that hostile women and men respond with increased systolic and diastolic blood pressure when confronted with an environmental stressor that elicits mistrust (e.g., unsolvable anagrams that had been described as "easily solvable by most people"; Weidner, Friend, Ficarrotto, & Mendell, 1989). Further, hostility among Type As is associated with elevated plasma cholesterol and low density lipoprotein cholesterol in both sexes (Weidner, Sexton, McLellarn, Connor, & Matarazzo, 1987), and the degree of coronary artery occlusion (Williams, Haney, Lee, Kong, Blumenthal, & Whalen, 1980).

Attempts to view hostility within a coping style framework are rare. Two recent presentations suggest that when imagining an anger-provoking situation, highly hostile persons reported more self-blame and escape-avoidance strategies (i.e., wishing the situation would go away; engaging in distracting behaviors, such as eating, drug use) when compared to low hostile individuals (Hart, Bliok, & Hittner, 1990; VanderVoort, Gregg, Kircher, & Rigdon, 1990). Highly hostile people were also likely to indicate lesser use of social support when compared to low hostile individuals (Hart et al., 1990). Most recently,

Weidner et al., (1991) found that Cook and Medley hostility scores were positively related to the report of vigilant coping styles among both women and men. However, this finding only applied to ego-threats and not to events threatening one's physical well-being. This latter result supports the notion of hostility as a concept of interpersonal relevance (e.g., mistrusting others, fragile self-esteem) and provides further support for the notion that hostile persons tend to use maladaptive coping strategies.

In sum, it appears that both Type A behavior and hostility are characterized by potentially pathogenic behavioral styles of coping and seem to potentiate cardiovascular responses among both genders. Since men as a group score higher on both Type A behaviors and hostility, their greater use of maladaptive coping accompanied by potentially harmful cardiovascular responses could contribute to their elevated risk for CHD.

Coping and Depression

While women live longer than men, their lives may not be as happy as those of men. Nearly twice as many women suffer from affective disorders, such as unipolar depression, when compared to men (Boyd & Weissman, 1981; McGrath, Keita, Strickland, & Russo, 1990). In her meta-analysis of this research, Nolen-Hoeksema (1987) concluded that this gender difference is quite pervasive across different countries, with the exception of the following populations: university students, the bereaved, the elderly, the Old Order Amish, and residents of some rural nonmodern cultures. While several explanations for these gender differences have been proposed, contemporary psychological explanations focus on the role of cognitive factors in depression.

Cognitive theories of depression: Implications for gender, coping, and depression

Two of the key cognitive theories of depression are Beck's cognitive triad (Beck, 1967) and the reformulated learned-helplessness approach (Abramson, Seligman, & Teasdale, 1978). Beck's theory describes depression as a chain reaction in which an initial loss is followed by cognitive changes that include an all encompassing negative view of the self, the world, and the future. This cognitive triad persists even in the face of contradictory evidence because depressed persons develop negative schemata (i.e., stable representations through which all experiences are filtered). The negative schemata include a sense of inadequacy, self-criticism, pessimism, and self-blame, which is reflected in systematic cognitive distortions and faulty information processing. For example, depressed persons appear to selectively ignore positive aspects of situations while focusing on negative features.

According to the reformulated learned-helplessness view (Abramson et al., 1978), depression may result from repeated exposure to uncontrollable events. Individuals learn that their actions have little or no impact on their environment and come to expect a lack of control in future activities. This expectation of helplessness leads to cognitive and behavioral deficits. The key cognitive feature of this theory is the tendency to attribute the cause of negative events to the self (internal, stable, and global causal attributions). A negative/pessimistic attributional style can exacerbate situational negative affect, thereby precipitating a more pervasive depressive episode.

While there is controversy as to the empirical basis for these theories of depression (e.g., Coyne & Gotlib, 1983; Robins, 1988; Sweeney, Anderson, & Bailey, 1986), our task here is to consider their relevance for coping styles and women's increased risk for depression.

Beck's theory would imply that women tend to possess maladaptive ways of thinking; see themselves and their future in more negative terms, possess negative schemata including an inclination to self-blame, and engage in cognitive distortions. Although the theory does not specify a mechanism for the development of these gender difference, one would expect that possession of these negative cognitions is likely to result in fewer adaptive coping strategies because such cognitive distortions are incompatible with the realistic thinking and problem solving required for effective coping.

Learned-helplessness theory would imply that women tend to see the world as less controllable and take more personal responsibility for negative outcomes than men. There is some evidence to suggest that women and girls possess attributional styles consistent with depression (Abramson & Andrews, 1982). In addition, feminist interpretations of learned helplessness's role in depression among women have suggested that women's powerlessness, on individual and societal levels, when compared to men, provides fertile ground for the cognitive and behavioral manifestations of depression (Radloff, 1975). To extrapolate further, if women take responsibility for negative outcomes while feeling powerless to change these outcomes they are likely to be overwhelmed with negative affect and therefore less inclined to engage in effective coping behaviors such as problem solving.

Miller and Kirsch (1987) examined the evidence for the occurrence of gender difference in the areas outlined by cognitive theories of depression and concluded that "there is little support for the existence of gender differences in the categories of negative self-evaluations/expectations/thoughts; cognitive distortion/irrational cognitions/information processing; attributions/control perceptions; and information seeking" (p. 296).

One limitation of the above conclusion is that it is based on studies of non-clinical samples only. The analogue nature of many of the studies reviewed by Miller and Kirsch limits generalizability to clinical samples. Research on clinically depressed samples may help to elucidate the links among gender, coping and depression.

Coping among depressed and non-depressed individuals

Several studies have compared coping styles of depressed individuals to those employed by non-depressed individuals. Most of the problems or stressors in clinical samples can be considered as "long-term". Based on our assumptions regarding coping style effectiveness, it is hypothesized that depressed individuals use coping strategies that prevent or interfere with problem solving. Specifically, depressed individuals may be more likely to use avoidance, which prevents the development of effective problem solving skills in the long run. They also may use vigilant strategies with a focus on emotional aspects of the problem. Thus, the depressed individual is likely to remain locked into the problem.

A number of studies suggest that depressed individuals indeed use more avoidance and focus on emotional aspects of the situation when compared to non-depressed individuals (e.g., Billings & Moos, 1984; Coyne, Aldwin, & Lazarus, 1981; Folkman & Lazarus, 1986; Perrez & Reicherts, 1986). However, theoretical and methodological limitations in much of this research makes it difficult to clarify the role of coping styles in depression. In their review of psychosocial factors in depression, Barnett and Gotlib (1990) could identify only two studies (Billings & Moos, 1985; Parker & Brown, 1982) in which the role of coping style was assessed and appropriate methods of controlling for prior depressive symptoms were undertaken. These two studies provide a starting point for our attempt to further elucidate the differences, if any, in the coping strategies used by depressed and non-depressed individuals.

Billings and Moos (1985) compared the coping strategies of three subgroups of depressed subjects (remitted, partially remitted, non-remitted) and non-depressed controls. They reported that non-remitted subjects used more emotion-focused coping strategies and less problem-focused coping. Remitted subjects (the majority of whom were women) moved from use of more emotion-focused strategy when depressed (at intake) to use of coping patterns similar to those of the control subjects (i.e., more problem solving), 12-months following treatment. Most importantly, from our perspective was the failure to find gender differences with regard to personal attributes (e.g., self-esteem, coping behaviors), life stressors, and social resources (e.g., network support).

Parker and Brown (1982) developed a measure of six classes of "anti-depressive behaviors" based on hypothetical events that were relatively chronic and required long-term adjustment (e.g., breakup of an important relationship; increasing criticism from someone important to the subject). Subjects rated their likely use of specific coping behavior and estimated the effectiveness of the behavior for handling the events. Comparisons within a clinical sample (when depressed and when symptoms had remitted) indicated that when depressed, subjects scored lower on "anti-depressive" coping strategies and their ratings of efficacy. Comparisons of remitted subjects and matched, nondepressed controls indicated only one significant difference: remitted depressives indicated a greater likelihood to engage in passive behaviors. Gender differences were not assessed in this relatively small sample of 20 depressed subjects.

Further evidence for the role of maladaptive coping strategies in depressive symptomatology comes from follow-up studies of community samples. Aldwin and Revenson (1987) assessed coping behaviors and coping efficacy in a predominantly female (62%) sample of middle class community residents who were not diagnosed as clinically depressed. Subjects rated a stressful event that had occurred in the "past month" and reported on psychological distress on each of the two occasions when data were collected. Prior distress was found to be a significant predictor of current distress and use of escape and support mobililization strategies were positively related to distress. Use of problem solving strategies was negatively related to current distress. The results were interpreted as indicating reciprocal relationships among stress, coping, and psychological distress, such that greater emotional distress and greater stress are related to the use of maladaptive coping, which in turn increased distress and the future likelihood of stress.

Most recently, Rohde et al. (1990) assessed coping (self-control, escapism, seeking solace), stress (hassles, life events), and depression in a community sample of older (> 50 years) women and men on two occasions over a 2-year period. Consistent with previous research, escapism coping (i.e., avoidance) was most strongly related to current and future depression. However, it was the men in this sample that used more escapism, while women were more likely to use self-control and solace seeking. Although gender was not predictive of increases in self-reported depressive symptoms, gender (i.e., being female), along with increased stress and prior depressive symptoms, were predictive of a future diagnosis of depression.

The results of these studies indicate that depressed individuals are less inclined to use effective coping strategies, and to perceive coping strategies as effective. This may contribute to future experience of stress, which in turn may interact with coping and depression. In addition, frequent use of ineffective coping is predictive of future depression (cf. Billings & Moos, 1985; Aldwin & Revenson, 1987). On the other hand, coping deficits seen in clinically depressed individuals seem to be state dependent, and gender differences in coping do not seem to be pervasive.

To conclude, the relative absence of gender differences in cognitive variables associated with depression in clinical as well as non-clinical samples suggests that women's increased risk for becoming depressed occurs as a function of factors other than those suggested by cognitive theories of depression.

Other psychosocial explanations for gender differences in depression

In her review of gender differences in depression, Nolen-Hoeksema (1987) provided an alternative to cognitive theories for explaining the relationship between gender and depression. She suggested that while most people experience brief episodes of mild-to-moderate depressive symptoms in the course of everyday life, *men and women handle their episodes differently and this difference could explain their differential risk for depression.* In Nolen-Hoeksema's view, men are more likely to engage in active, behavioral responses that serve to distract from and dampen episodes of depression, while women are more likely to ruminate about their depressed states. Women's tendency to ruminate amplifies and prolongs their depressive episodes and increases negative expectations for the future (also see section on short-term events, pp. 243-244).

Nolen-Hoeksema's explanation of gender differences in depression is not cast within a stress-coping framework, but it is consistent with the notion that attention to short-term stressors (implied in women's tendency to ruminate) is maladaptive, while distraction is adaptive (Suls & Fletcher, 1985). Thus, men's tendency to actively distract themselves from short depressive episodes may produce adaptive outcomes in a fashion analogous to their use of avoidance coping when faced with short-term stressful events. It shortens the duration of the depressive episode, and in doing so, may not only lessen distress, but leaves psychic energy for creating a solution to the problem. Women's tendency to ruminate produces maladaptive outcomes because by reflecting on their distress, they may help to maintain the source of stress, reinforce negative affect, and increase feelings of vulnerability.

The perspective we have employed suggests that the nature and efficacy of coping is linked to characteristics of the event. Therefore *differences in the nature and role of life events experienced by women and men could account for gender differences in coping and depression.* Examination of the nature of stressful life events may also shed some light on the notion (derived from learned-helplessness theory) that increased rates of depression in women are linked to their experience of more uncontrollable life events.

While many studies do not describe the specific nature of the life events linked to depressive symptoms in their samples, there is evidence that women and men do not differ in the number of stressful events they experience (Hamilton & Fagot, 1988; Kessler & McLeod, 1984; Vingerhoets & Van Heck, 1990), but may differ in the nature of such events (Kessler & McLeod, 1984; Wethington, McLeod, & Kessler, 1987). Kessler and colleagues argue that women are socialized to care for others and to have an increased sense of responsibility for the life events that occur to others. Thus, women experience not only the emotional effects of stressful events that occur to themselves, but also those that occur to members of their social networks. Based on data from three general population surveys, Kessler and McLeod reported that women's lives were more affected by illnesses and life crises in their social networks, than were men's. They characterized women as "doubly disadvantaged" (Kessler & McLeod, 1984, p. 628); women reported more network events and were more emotionally responsive to network events. One could imagine that for women with larger or more varied social networks, the variety and duration of various stressors could produce an almost chronic experience of stress. It is this added stress (and one would expect, the related depletion of their coping resources) that may increase women's vulnerability to depression.

Also important, given our previous analysis of the role of the controllability of stressors, is the fact that women may have little or no control over the outcome of many of the stressful events that occur to members of their networks. Since less perceived control has been associated with increased depressive symptoms in women (Warren & McEachren, 1983), it is likely that the combination of increased emotional reactivity to network events and the lack of control over outcome are potent factors in women's inclination to use maladaptive coping strategies and to experience depressive symptoms.

Kessler and McLeod's analysis suggests that *aspects of women's social roles* place them at risk for psychological distress. This notion has been echoed by other researchers who have suggested that women's socialization and limited life roles may place them at risk for depression (Repetti & Crosby, 1984; Rosenfield, 1980). For example, Repetti and Crosby have proposed a "paucity of roles" explanation of gender differences in depression. They suggest that multiple adult roles for women (e.g., career and motherhood) provide multiple sources of gratification which lessens susceptibility to depression (see also Repetti, Matthews, & Waldron, 1989). Therefore it may be the limitations of traditional female roles rather than their noxious nature that increases the potential for depression in women.

Risk factors related to women's social position could interact with both the nature of coping and coping resources available to women, to increase their risk for depression. In addition, women's social position vis-a-vis men's puts them at greater risk for experiencing lower socio-economic status, education, income and levels of employment, each of which is correlated with depression in both genders (Golding, 1988), and are likely to be related to coping. Pearlin and Schooler (1978) brought attention to the role of social factors in coping when they suggested that "coping failures, therefore, do not necessarily reflect the shortcomings of individuals; in a real sense they may represent the failure of social systems in which the individuals are enmeshed" (p. 18). Victimization of women and poverty were recently cited as "two critical, but neglected areas for understanding women's depression" (McGrath et al., 1990; p. 28). That women may lack coping resources and/or experience life as uncontrollable is a natural outgrowth of these correlates of their social position.

Summary and Conclusions

Clearly, the relationships among gender, attention versus avoidance coping, and either physical or mental health are complex and may interact reciprocally. Even so, we will attempt to summarize key aspects of these relationships as they have appeared in this review.

Gender Differences in the Use of Effective Coping Strategies

First, we pointed out that various aspects of the stressor, including duration and controllability must be considered in determining the efficacy of a particular coping strategy. It was argued (in accordance with Suls & Fletcher, 1985), that avoidance would be more adaptive if the stressor is non-physical and of short duration. With regard to long-term stress, attention would be considered more effective in case of a controllable stressor, whereas avoidance would be more adaptive when coping with a long-term problem that is beyond one's control. When these variables are considered, men report more avoidance strategies when coping with short-term transient stress than women. Women appear to attend more to short-term events (ruminate), but appear to adjust better to stressful events requiring long-term adaptation. In addition, women appear to be more attentive to threats to their physical well-being.

Generally, men's greater use of avoidance strategies, particularly for handling every day short-term stress, appears to be adaptive. It may protect them from emotional distress and contribute to their overall lower rates of depression, when compared to women. On the other hand, not paying attention to early warning signs may result in feeling overwhelmed and severely depressed when encountering relatively infrequent, but extreme threats, such as divorce or death of spouse. In this regard, it is of interest to note that the most common precursors of CHD deaths are severe feelings of depression and hopelessness, usually resulting from failure to cope with loss events (e.g., Glass, 1977; Parkes, Benjamin, & Fitzgerald, 1969; also see review by Weidner & Chesney, 1985). Also, not paying attention to early warning signs of illness decreases the likelihood of implementing appropriate coping behaviors (e.g., seeking medical care) for minimizing bodily damage.

Women's tendency to use attention strategies when encountering short-term stressors of no parÉicular consequence may be maladaptive because emotional energy (and related distress) is spent on transient events that are beyond their control. However, their greater use of attention when faced with physical threats is adaptive: Paying attention to one's physical well-being may increase the likelihood of seeking medical care early, thus preventing serious illness and increasing longevity (cf. Miller, Brody, & Summerton, 1988). Women also appear to adapt better to stressful events requiring long-term adaptation (e.g., Stroebe & Stroebe, 1983). It is possible that their initial vigilant reaction to stressful events may facilitate the development of problem solving skills required for successful coping with severely stressful life changes, such as the loss of a spouse.

With regard to coping with chronic, relatively minor stressors, such as daily hassles, gender differences are inconsistently found. Unfortunately, duration and controllability of the specific events have rarely been assessed (and often cannot be inferred) in the bulk of the literature that has analyzed for gender differences in dispositional coping styles (see section on chronic controllable events, pp. 245-246). When gender differences in coping do occur, however, it appears that men use more effective coping strategies (i.e., paying attention to the problem) than women. If we assume that the events in this category are of some long-term consequence (mostly life events), then the degree of controllability would be of extreme importance in determining which coping strategies are effective. Stone and Neale (1984) report that people in general are likely to use problem-focused strategies in controllable situations, and emotion-focused strategies in uncontrollable situations. Paying attention to controllable events (with a focus on the problem) would be adaptive, in that it could contribute to a solution of the problem. However, if there is little one can do about the event, one may come to focus on the emotions associated with this situation. To the extent that women's lives are characterized by uncontrollable events, a greater focus on emotions rather than on active problem solving would not be unexpected.

Physical Health: Coping and Coronary Risk

Although men as a group score higher on coronary-prone Type A behavior and hostility when compared to women, there appear to be no gender differences in coping styles among coronary-prone individuals. Generally, both women and men classified as coronary-prone (Type A and/or hostile) report more vigilant strategies when encountering threats. This behavioral hyper-reactivity in response to minor, uncontrollable, short-term events may lead to mental and physical exhaustion in the long run, thereby increasing the likelihood of becoming ill.

Furthermore, both Type A women and men also suppress attention to a threat if that particular threat is not the focus of their attentional field. Since Type As are busily engaged in a variety of activities, their likelihood of paying attention to physical symptoms and engaging in appropriate health behaviors (e.g., seeking medical care) is low.

In addition to showing enhanced vigilance to potential threats, coronary-prone individuals also show physiological hyperreactivity, particularly when sources of threat are self-relevant, (i.e., relaed to gender or personality). Overall, it appears that women who score high on coronary-prone behaviors exhibit excessive cardiovascular reactivity in response to a narrower range of situations than their male coronary-prone counterparts and this may mitigate against pathogenic effects on the cardiovascular system.

This issue raises the question of the physiological correlates of coping behavior and coping styles in general. There are still very few studies in which coping is assessed on multiple levels. However, given the complexity of relationships among gender, coping, and health, it would be advisable to implement a multiple-method approach in which self-reports of coping style, observable coping behavior, and physiological responses are assessed (see chapter by Slangen, Kleemann, & Krohne in this volume).

Mental Health: Coping and Depression

The role of coping in depression is complex. There is evidence that depressed individuals use more maladaptive coping styles (i.e., attention with a focus on emotion; avoidance) when compared to non-depressed individuals. However, these differences are state dependent, and gender differences appear to be minimal or non-existent.

With regard to non-clinical samples, our speculation concerning the relationship between women's greater risk for depression and their use of maladaptive coping was given some support by Nolen-Hoeksema (1987). Specifically, women's tendency to ruminate when encountering short-term, transient depressive episodes may help to maintain the source of stress, reinforce negative affect, and increase feelings of helplessness.

Generally, women's increased risk for depression is not well explained by currently popular cognitive theories of depression. Even so, notions derived from one of these theories, learned helplessness, have been interpreted to support the view that women's powerlessness on individual and societal levels places them at risk for depression (cf. Kessler & McLeod, 1984; Wethington et al., 1987). In addition, women's traditional socialization and life roles place heavy emotional demands yet limits their access to coping resources (cf. McGrath et al., 1990; Solomon & Rothblum, 1986).

In sum, the evidence we have reviewed suggests that the gender differences in depression could be due to: (a) women's greater use of maladaptive coping strategies when faced with relatively short-term, stressful, events; (b) the nature of the stressors to which women are exposed; (c) women's life and social roles.

A Recommendation to Broaden the Conceptualization of Gender in Future Research

Given the complexity of the issues related to understanding the relationships among gender, coping, and health, there are a number of areas in which recommendations for future research could be made. Previously, we have mentioned the need for a multiple-method approach to assessing coping. Others have commented on the reliance on self-report coping measures of dubious conceptual and psychometric rigor (Stone, Greenberg, Kennedy-Moore, & Newman, in press; Stone, Kennedy-Moore, Newman, Greenberg, & Neale, in press) and have called for the development of conceptually derived, psychometrically rigorous measures of coping (Carver et al., 1989; Endler & Parker, 1990).

In the coping research to date, one area of consensus is the necessity to distinguish two main classes of coping strategies: Attention (or vigilance, monitoring) and avoidance (or blunting). However, with regard to the different conceptualizations of the nature of coping, a key unanswered question is whether coping is best conceptualized as being situation-specific or more broadly seen as a style that is evident across situations (Carver et al., 1989). Despite the importance of these and other conceptual and methodological issues in research on coping and health, we close our consideration of this area of research with a focus on the conceptualization of gender.

We begin by calling for the inclusion of women in studies of coping and physical as well as mental health in sufficient numbers so that all data from such studies can be analyzed for gender differences. All too often the former occurs, but the latter does not (e.g., Carver et al., 1989; Holahan & Moos, 1987). However, in our view, the key to understanding gender differences more fully, is a more sophisticated notion of what constitutes gender. Most of the research we have reviewed focuses on the most obvious definition of gender; biologically determined masculinity and femininity. While researchers cannot be faulted for use of this readily identified marker, the reliance on biological gender may account for some of the inconsistencies in findings of research on coping and health. A fuller understanding of the role of gender is likely to result from adoption of a broader conceptualization of gender that includes socially determined aspects of identity such as life-and gender-roles.

Although this approach to defining gender has rarely been used in research on coping and health, its use has led to findings which suggest that life roles and/or gender-role identity mediate some of the relationships found. For example, Rosenfield (1980) reported on gender-based comparisons of psychiatric symptoms (including depression) and the division of labor in the marriages of 60 couples. The results indicated that overall, women had higher depression scores than men; however, within the female sample, working women were less depressed than nonworking women. More importantly, when women and men in nontraditional divisions of labor were compared, men had higher depression scores than women. Also relevant to this issue is the research by Frankenhaeuser and her colleagues, which shows that physiological reactions to stress are strongly influenced by gender roles (Frankenhaeuser, in press).

Somewhat related to the need to assess life-roles and gender-role identity are notions of the relevance of life roles, particularly in research on coping and mental health. For example, Repetti and Crosby (1984) assessed role-based explanations of depression in an adult community sample of 213 women and 181 men. Subjects participated in a structured interview which assessed areas such as positive and negative emotional experiences at home and work, occupational prestige, and depressive symptomatology. No significant differences in depression were found for women versus men, but there were significant differences related to occupational prestige. The results indicated differences within gender; low prestige single women were the most depressed and high prestige housewives were the least depressed. They concluded that "when gender is dissociated from other factors with which it is typically confounded, differences in rates of depression disappear" (p. 67). Among the merits of broadening the conceptualization of gender to include life roles and gender-role identity is the possibility that these variables could explain the failure to find gender differences in mental health when women and men have similar access to multiple roles, as has been found for example, among college students.

Also linked to broadening the definition of gender is the need to consider women's social position and how this may impact on the use of coping strategies. While the social and economic gains made by recent generations of women have broadened their roles and the coping resources to which they have access, women's social position in general remains lower than that of men. Throughout the history of industrialized countries, women have been enmeshed in a patriarchal social system in which they are socialized to serve as primary sources of nurturance in the society. As indicated in the research on the differential nature of life stressors experienced by women and men (Kessler & McLeod, 1984; Wethington et al., 1987), this facet of women's socialization represents a demanding yet undervalued responsibility. When changes in the social structure improve women's position we can expect a lessening of gender differences in mental and physical health. For women, social equality is likely to lead to decreases in risk for mental health problems, such as depression. Social equality also is likely to have advantages for men, since changes in men's social roles might produce decreases in their risk for physical health problems such as coronary heart disease.

References

Abramson, L. Y., & Andrews, D. E. (1982). Cognitive models of depression: Implications for sex differences in vulnerability to depression. *International Journal of Mental Health, 11*, 77-94.

Abramson, L. Y., Seligman, M. E. P., & Teasdale, J. D. (1978). Learned helplessness in humans: Critique and reformulation. *Journal of Abnormal Psychology, 87*, 49-74.

Aldwin, C. M., & Revenson, T. A. (1987). Does coping help? A reexamination of the relation between coping and mental health. *Journal of Personality and Social Psychology, 53*, 337-348.

Barefoot, J. C., Siegler, I. C., Nowlin, J. B., Peterson, B. L., Haney, T. L., & Williams, R. B. (1987). Suspiciousness, health, and mortality: A follow-up study of 500 older adults. *Psychosomatic Medicine, 49*, 450-457.

Barnett, P. A., & Gotlib, I. H. (1990). Cognitive vulnerability to depressive symptoms among men and women. *Cognitive Therapy and Research, 14*, 47-61.

Beck, A. T. (1967). *Depression: Clinical, experimental and theoretical aspects*. New York: Harper and Row.

Billings, A. G., & Moos, R. H. (1981). The role of coping responses and social resources in attenuating the stress of life events. *Journal of Behavioral Medicine, 4*, 139-157.

Billings, A. G., & Moos, R. H. (1984). Coping, stress, and social resources among adults with unipolar depression. *Journal of Personality and Social Psychology, 46*, 877-891.

Billings, A. G., & Moos, R. H. (1985). Psychosocial processes of remission in unipolar depression: Comparing depressed patients with matched community controls. *Journal of Consulting and Clinical Psychology, 53*, 314-325.

Boyd, J. H., & Weissman, M. M. (1981). Epidemiology of affective disorders: A re-examination and future directions. *Archives of General Psychiatry, 38*, 1039-1046.

Carver, C. S., Coleman, A. E., & Glass, D. C. (1976). The coronary-prone behavior pattern and the suppression of fatigue on a treadmill test. *Journal of Personality and Social Psychology, 33*, 460-466.

Carver, C. S., & Ganellen, R. J. (1983). Depression and components of self-punitiveness: High standards, self-criticism, and overgeneralization. *Journal of Abnormal Psychology, 92*, 330-337.

Carver, C. S., Scheier, M. F., & Weintraub, J. K. (1989). Assessing coping strategies: A theoretically based approach. *Journal of Personality and Social Psychology, 56*, 267-283.

Chino, A. F., & Funabiki, D. (1984). A cross-validation of sex differences in the expression of depression. *Sex Roles, 11*, 175-187.

Collins, A., & Frankenhaeuser, M. (1978). Stress responses in male and female engineering students. *Journal of Human Stress, 4*(2), 43-48.

Cook, W. W., & Medley, D. M. (1954). Proposed hostility and pharisaic-virtue scales for the MMPI. *Journal of Applied Psychology, 38*, 414-418.

Coyne, J. C., Aldwin, C. M., & Lazarus, R. S. (1981). Depression and coping in stressful episodes. *Journal of Abnormal Psychology, 90*, 439-447.

Coyne, J. C., & Gotlib, I. H. (1983). The role of cognition in depression: A critical appraisal. *Psychological Bulletin, 94*, 472-505.

Eaker, E. D., & Castelli, W. P. (1988). Type A behavior and coronary heart disease in women: Fourteen-year incidence from the Framingham Study. In B. K. Houston & C. R. Snyder (Eds.), *Type A behavior pattern: Research, theory, and intervention* (pp. 83-97). New York: Wiley.

Endler, N. S., & Parker, J. A. (1990). Multidimensional assessment of coping: A critical evaluation. *Journal of Personality and Social Psychology, 58*, 844-854.

Folkman, S. (1984). Personal control and stress and coping processes: A theoretical analysis. *Journal of Personality and Social Psychology, 46*, 839-852.

Folkman, S., & Lazarus, R. S. (1980). An analysis of coping in a middle-aged community sample. *Journal of Health and Social Behavior, 21*, 219-239.

Folkman, S., & Lazarus, R. S. (1986). Stress processes and depressive symptomatology. *Journal of Abnormal Psychology, 95*, 107-113.

Folkman, S., Lazarus, R. S., Gruen, R. J., & DeLongis, A. (1986). Appraisal, coping, health status, and psychological symptoms. *Journal of Personality and Social Psychology, 50*, 571-579.

Folkman, S., Lazarus, R. S., Pimley, S., & Novacek, J. (1987). Age differences in stress and coping processes. *Psychology and Aging, 2*, 171-184.

Frank, S. J., McLaughlin, A. M., & Crusco, A. (1984). Sex role attributes, symptom distress, and defensive style among college men and women. *Journal of Personality and Social Psychology, 47*, 182-192.

Frankenhaeuser, M. (in press). A biopsychosocial approach to stress in women and men. In V. J. Adesso, D. M. Reddy, & R. Fleming (Eds.), *Psychological perspectives on women's health.* Washington, DC: Hemisphere.

Frankenhaeuser, M., Dunne, E., & Lundberg, U. (1976). Sex differences in sympathetic-adrenal medullary reactions induced by different stressors. *Psychopharmacology, 47*, 1-5.

Frankenhaeuser, M., Rauste-von Wright, M., Collins, A., von Wright, J., Sedvall, G., & Swahn, C.-G. (1978). Sex differences in psychoneuroendocrine reactions to examination stress. *Psychosomatic Medicine, 40*, 334-343.

Funabiki, D., Bologna, N. C., Pepping, M., & Fitzgerald, K. (1980). Revisiting sex differences in the expression of deppression. *Journal of Abnormal Psychology, 89*, 194-202.

Girdler, S. S., Turner, J. R., Sherwood, A., & Light, K. C. (1990). Gender differences in blood pressure control during a variety of behavioral stressors. *Psychosomatic Medicine, 52*, 571-591.

Glass, D. C. (1977). *Behavior patterns, stress and coronary disease*. Hillsdale, NJ: Erlbaum.

Golding, J. M. (1988). Gender differences in depressive symptoms. *Psychology of Women Quarterly, 12*, 61-74.

Hamilton, S., & Fagot B. I. (1988). Chronic stress and coping styles: a comparison of male and female undergraduates. *Journal of Personality and Social Psychology, 55*, 819-823.

Hart, K. E. (1988). Association of Type A behavior and its components to ways of coping with stress. *Journal of Psychosomatic Medicine, 32*, 213-219.

Hart, K. E., Bliok, A. P., & Hittner, E., (1990, August). *Hostility and coping: Associations to cognitive and somatic emotional reactivity.* Paper presented at the meeting of the American Psychological Association, Boston, MA.

Haynes, S. G., Feinleib, M., & Kannel, W. B. (1980). The relationship of psychosocial factors to coronary heart disease in the Framingham study III. Eight-year incidence of coronary heart disease. *American Journal of Epidemiology, 111*, 37-58.

Henry, J. P., & Meehan, J. P. (1981). Psychosocial stimuli, physiological specificity, and cardiovascular disease. In H. Weiner, M. A. Hofer, & A. J. Stunkard (Eds.), *Brain, behavior, and bodily disease* (pp. 305-333). New York: Raven.

Holahan, C. J., & Moos, R. H. (1987). Personal and contextual determinants of coping strategies. *Journal of Personality and Social Psychology, 52*, 946-955.

Houston, B. K. (1983). Psychophysiological responsivity and the Type A behavior pattern. *Journal of Research in Personality, 17*, 22-39.

Houston, B. K. (1988). Cardiovascular and neuroendocrine reactivity, global Type A, and components of Type A behavior. In B. K. Houston & C. R. Snyder (Eds.), *Type A behavior pattern: Research, theory, and intervention* (pp. 212-253). New York: Wiley.

Kessler, R. C. (1982). A disaggregation of the relationship between socioeconomic status and psychological distress. *American Sociological Research, 47*, 752-764.

Kessler, R. C., & McLeod, J. D. (1984). Sex differences in vulnerability to undesirable life events. *American Sociological Review, 49*, 620-631.

Kleinke, C. L., Staneski, R. A., & Mason, J. K. (1982). Sex differences in coping with depression. *Sex Roles, 8*, 877-889.

Kohlmann, C.-W. (1990). *Streßbewältigung und Persönlichkeit: Flexibles versus rigides Copingverhalten und seine Auswirkungen auf Angsterleben und physiologische Belastungsreaktionen* [Coping and personality. Flexible versus rigid coping behavior and its effects on anxiety and physiological stress reactions]. Bern: Huber.

Krantz, D. S., & Manuck, S. B. (1984). Acute psychophysiologic reactivity and risk of cardiovascular disease: A review and methodologic critique. *Psychological Bulletin, 96*, 435-464.

Krohne, H. W. (1988). Coping research: Current theoretical and methodological developments. *The German Journal of Psychology, 12*, 1-30.

Krohne, H. W. (1989). The concept of coping modes: Relating cognitive person variables to actual coping behavior. *Advances in Behaviour Research and Therapy, 11*, 235-248.

Krohne, H. W. (1990). Personality as a mediator between objective events and their subjective representation. *Psychological Inquiry, 1*, 26-29.

Lazarus, R. S., & Folkman, S. (1984). *Stress, appraisal, and coping*. New York: Springer.

Lerner, D. J., & Kannel, W. B. (1986). Patterns of coronary heart disease morbidity and mortality in the sexes: A 26-year follow-up of the Framingham population. *American Heart Journal, 111*, 383-390.

Lundberg, U., de Chateau, P., Winberg, J., & Frankenhaeuser, M. (1981). Catecholamine and cortisol excretion patterns in three-year-old children and their parents. *Journal of Human Stress, 7*(3), 3-11.

Matthews, K. A., Weiss, S. M., Detre, T., Dembroski, T. M., Falkner, B., Manuck, S. B., & Williams, R. B. (Eds.). (1986). *Handbook of stress, reactivity, and cardiovascular disease*. New York: Wiley.

McGrath, E., Keita, G. P., Strickland, B. R., & Russo, N. F. (1990). *Women and depression: Risk factors and treatment issues*. Washington, DC: American Psychological Association.

Miller, S. M. (1987). Monitoring and blunting: Validation of a questionnaire to assess styles of information seeking under threat. *Journal of Personality and Social Psychology, 52*, 345-353.

Miller, S. M., Brody, D. S., & Summerton, J. (1988). Styles of coping with threat: Implications for health. *Journal of Personality and Social Psychology, 54*, 142-148.

Miller, S. M., & Kirsch, N. (1987). Sex differences in cognitive coping with stress. In R. C. Barnett, L. Biener, & G. K. Baruch (Eds.), *Gender and stress* (pp. 278-307). New York: The Free Press.

Mullen, B., & Suls, J. (1982). The effectiveness of attention and rejection as coping styles: A meta-analysis of temporal differences. *Journal of Psychosomatic Research, 26,* 43-49.

Nolen-Hoeksema, S. (1987). Sex differences in unipolar depression: Evidence and theory. *Psychological Bulletin, 101,* 259-282.

Parker, G. B., & Brown, L. B. (1982). Coping behaviors that mediate between life events and depression. *Archives of General Psychiatry, 39,* 1386-1391.

Parkes, C. M., Benjamin, B., & Fitzgerald, R. G. (1969). Broken heart: A statistical study of increased mortality among widowers. *British Medical Journal, 1,* 740-743.

Pearlin L. I., & Schooler, C. (1978). The structure of coping. *Journal of Health and Social Behavior, 19,* 2-21.

Perrez, M., & Reicherts, M. (1986). Appraisal, coping, and attribution processes by depressed persons: An S-R-S-R approach. *The German Journal of Psychology, 10,* 315-326.

Radloff, L. S. (1975). Sex differences in depression: The effects of occupation and marital status. *Sex Roles, 1,* 249-265.

Repetti, R. L., & Crosby, F. (1984). Gender and depression: Exploring the adult-role explanation. *Journal of Social and Clinical Psychology, 2,* 57-70.

Repetti, R. L., Matthews, K. A., & Waldron, I. (1989). Employment and women's health: Effects of paid employment on women's mental and physical health. *American Psychologist, 44,* 1394-1401.

Riessman, C. K., & Gerstel, N. (1985). Marital dissolution and health: Do males or females have greater risk? *Social Science and Medicine, 20,* 627-636.

Robins, C. J. (1988). Attributions and depression: Why is the literature so inconsistent? *Journal of Personality and Social Psychology, 54,* 880-889.

Rodin, J., & Ickovics, J. R. (1990). Women's health: Review and research agenda as we approach the 21st century. *American Psychologist, 45,* 1018-1034.

Rohde, P., Lewinsohn, P. M., Tilson, M., & Seeley, J. R. (1990). Dimensionality of coping and its relation to depression. *Journal of Personality and Social Psychology, 58,* 499-511.

Rosenfield, S. (1980). Sex differences in depression: Do women always have higher rates? *Journal of Health and Social Behavior, 21,* 33-42.

Roth, S., & Cohen, L. J. (1986). Approach, avoidance, and coping with stress. *American Psychologist, 41,* 813-819.

Smith, T. W., & Frohm, K. D. (1985). What's so unhealthy about hostility? Construct validity and psychosocial correlates of the Cook and Medley Hostility Scale. *Health Psychology, 4,* 503-520.

Solomon, L. J., & Rothblum, E. D. (1986). Stress, coping, and social support in women. *The Behavior Therapist, 9,* 199-204.

Sterling, P., & Eyer, J. (1981). Biological basis of stress-related mortality. *Social Science and Medicine, 15E,* 3-42.

Stone, A. A., Greenberg, M. A., Kennedy-Moore, E., & Newman, M. G. (in press). Self-report, situation-specific coping questions: What are they measuring? *Journal of Personality and Social Psychology.*

Stone, A. A., Kennedy-Moore, E., Newman, M. G., Greenberg, M. A., & Neale, J. M. (in press). Conceptual and methodological issues in current coping assessments. In B. N. Carpenter (Ed.), *Personal coping: Theory, research, and application.* New York: Praeger.

Stone, A. A., Lennox, S., & Neale, J. M. (1985). Daily coping and alcohol use in a sample of community adults. In S. Shiffman & T. A. Wills (Eds.), *Coping and substance use* (pp. 199-220). Orlando, FL: Academic Press.

Stone, A. A., & Neale, J. M. (1984). New measure of daily coping: Development and preliminary results. *Journal of Personality and Social Psychology, 46*, 892-906.

Strickland, B. R. (1988). Sex-related differences in health and illness. *Psychology of Women Quarterly, 12*, 381-399.

Stroebe, M. S., & Stroebe, W. (1983). Who suffers more? Sex differences in health risks of the widowed. *Psychological Bulletin, 93*, 279-301.

Suls, J., & Fletcher, B. (1985). The relative efficacy of avoidant and nonavoidant coping strategies: A meta-analysis. *Health Psychology, 4*, 249-288.

Suls, J., & Wan, C. K. (1989). The relation between Type A behavior and chronic distress: A meta-analysis. *Journal of Personality and Social Psychology, 57*, 503-512.

Sweeney, P. D., Anderson, K., & Bailey, S. (1986). Attributional style in depression: A meta-analytic review. *Journal of Personality and Social Psychology, 50*, 974-991.

Thompson, S. C. (1981). Will it hurt less if I can control it? A complex answer to a simple question. *Psychological Bulletin, 90*, 89-101.

VanderVoort, D. J., Gregg, C., Kircher, J., & Rigdon, M. (1990, August). *Hostility, coping styles, belief systems, and illness.* Paper presented at the meeting of the American Psychological Association, Boston, MA.

Verbrugge, L. (1985). Gender and health: An update on hypotheses and evidence. *Journal of Health and Social Behavior, 26*, 156-182.

Viney, L. L., & Westbrook, M. T. (1982). Coping with chronic illness: The mediating role of biographic and illness-related factors. *Journal of Psychosomatic Research, 26*, 595-605.

Vingerhoets, A., & Van Heck, G. L. (1990). Gender, coping and psychosomatic symptoms. *Psychological Medicine, 20*, 125-135.

Waldron, I. (1983). Sex differences in human mortality: The role of genetic factors. *Social Science and Medicine, 17*, 321-333.

Wallerstein, J., & Kelly, J. (1980). *Surviving the break-up.* New York: Basic Books.

Warren, L. W., & McEachren, L. (1983). Psychosocial correlates of depressive symptomatology in adult women. *Journal of Abnormal Psychology, 92*, 151-160.

Weidner, G. (1980). Self-handicapping following learned helplessness treatment and the Type A coronary-prone behavior pattern. *Journal of Psychosomatic Research, 24*, 319-325.

Weidner, G. (in press). Coronary risk in women. In V. J. Adesso, D. M. Reddy, & R. Fleming (Eds.), *Psychological perspectives on women's health.* Washington, DC: Hemisphere.

Weidner, G., & Chesney, M. A. (1985). Stress, Type A behavior, and coronary heart disease. In W. E. Connor & J. D. Bristow (Eds.), *Coronary heart disease: Prevention, complications, and treatment* (pp. 157-172). Philadelphia, PA: Lippincott.

Weidner, G., Friend, R., Ficarrotto, T. J., & Mendell, N. R. (1989). Hostility and cardiovascular reactivity to stress in women and men. *Psychosomatic Medicine, 51*, 36-45.

Weidner, G., & Hustedt, C. M. (1991). *The effects of sex-typed tasks and sex-role orientation on cardiovascular reactivity.* Manuscript submitted for publication.

Weidner, G., Istvan, J., & McKnight, J. D. (1989). Clusters of behavioral coronary risk factors in employed women and men. *Journal of Applied Social Psychology, 19*, 468-480.

Weidner, G., Lapp, W. M., & Hustedt, C. M. (1991). *Parental child-rearing styles, coping, and coronary-prone behaviors.* Manuscript in preparation.

Weidner, G., & Matthews, K. A. (1978). Reported physical symptoms elicited by unpredictable events and the Type A coronary-prone behavior pattern. *Journal of Personality and Social Psychology, 36*, 1213-1220.

Weidner, G., Sexton, G., McLellarn, R., Connor, S. L., & Matarazzo, J. D. (1987). The role of Type A behavior and hostility in an elevation of plasma lipids in adult women and men. *Psychosomatic Medicine, 49*, 136-146.

Wethington, E., McLeod, J. D., & Kessler, R. C. (1987). The importance of life events for explaining sex differences in psychological distress. In R. C. Barnett, L. Biener, & G. K. Baruch (Eds.), *Gender and stress* (pp. 144-156). New York: The Free Press.

Williams, R. B., Haney, T. L., Lee, K. L., Kong, Y. H., Blumenthal, J. A., & Whalen, R. E. (1980). Type A behavior, hostility, and coronary atherosclerosis. *Psychosomatic Medicine, 42*, 539-549.

Wingard, D. L. (1984). The sex differential in morbidity, mortality, and lifestyle. *Annual Review of Public Health, 5*, 433-458.

Chapter 12

Self-Focused Attention in the Face of Adversity and Threat

Sigrun-Heide Filipp, Thomas Klauer, and Dieter Ferring

Introduction

From its very beginning, research on coping processes has been concerned with the concept of "attention". This type of thinking was introduced in the conceptualizations made by Janis and his colleagues (see Janis, 1958) and Byrne (1964), and the distinction between attention and avoidance has remained a central concept in cognitive coping research (see Krohne; Chapter 1, this volume; Miller, Combs, & Kruus, this volume). Indeed, it appears that almost all coping theory, at least implicitly, distinguishes between modes of dealing with stressful experiences based on whether threatening aspects of one's life situation are attended to or kept outside one's attentional focus. Taking into consideration that confrontation with serious life events more or less *forces* the individual to process threatening information and to assimilate it with his or her models of the self and the world (Horowitz, 1980), it is not surprising that attentional processes play a crucial role within the process of coping in general.

In this chapter we will, of course, not refute such a prominent view; rather, we would like to promote the idea that speaking of "attention" in coping research - despite Ingram's (1990) recent allegation of a lack of conceptual clarity - may have at least two different meanings. When we usually refer to vigilant coping behaviors, it is implied that there is some threatening event or stimulus "in the outside world" to which the individual turns his or her attention. This can be clearly demonstrated in studies of coping with stressful medical procedures, in which vigilance is equated with a selective focus on the various anxiety-producing stimuli in the environment (see, e.g., Slangen, Kleemann, & Krohne, this volume). On the other hand, the concept of vigilant coping may also imply that the individual's attention is centered on his or her inner states and affective responses in stressful encounters rather than on the "external" threat itself (cf. Miller et al., this volume). In this latter case, the individual is obviously in a state of *self-focused attention*. The fact that attention during the coping process can be directed toward self or non-self

---

The authors would like to thank Manfred J. Schmitt for helpful comments on parts of this chapter.

aspects of a stressful person-environment-transaction has not always been differentiated, although it becomes crucially important when we try to link the coping process to the self-system (see, e.g., Carver & Scheier, 1985; Filipp, Aymanns, & Braukmann, 1986; Horowitz, 1980; cf. Carver & Scheier, this volume). From such a perspective, a theoretical approach gains importance which has not played a prominent role in coping research up to now, i.e., *the theory of self-focused attention and self-consciousness*. As will be outlined throughout our chapter, this theory provides a promising conceptual tool in the study of people dealing with crisis, and we will try to link some of its propositions to investigations on how people cope with threat and adversity in their lives.

Two main questions have guided research and theorization on self-focused attention since it was introduced by Duval and Wicklund (1972) and later elaborated in terms of a "control-theory approach to behavior" by Carver and Scheier (1981). The first question addresses the issue of how self-focus in attention is created in addition to already well-known strategies for inducing self-awareness in experimental settings. The second question refers to the behavioral consequences of self-focused attention and has stimulated hundreds of studies showing that, in general, self-focused attention does have powerful effects on an individual's behavior in a variety of domains and settings. It is our intention to add some additional insight to that body of findings by investigating, first, the role of life crisis in the creation of self-focus and, second, the role of self-focused attention in coping with serious life events.

Life Crises as Inducers of Self-Focused Attention

Despite the many studies using experimental manipulations of self-awareness, little is known about the question of when and under what circumstances individuals will turn their attention to their own selves. As we have argued earlier (see Filipp et al., 1986), it is highly plausible to assume that the exposure to serious life events is crucial to creating a self-focus in attention under natural conditions; such a view can be supported by various assumptions.

First, exposure to a serious life event represents what has been termed a "weakly scripted situation" (Abelson, 1981) in a different domain. Common to both is the experience that the exhibition of behavioral routines or "mindless" behaviors (Langer & Imber, 1979) is not accounted for; rather serious life events create dramatically altered and aversive life situations for which individuals usually have not been socialized. How to deal with the loss of a loved one has not been a topic within the curricula of schools or universities and, although we encounter many models throughout our lives who might teach us how to cope with loss, we usually prefer to look at the sunnier side of life. Unrealistic optimism (Weinstein, 1982) and belief in one's invulnerability (Perloff, 1987) hinder, in most cases, anticipatory coping efforts and prevent us from being prepared for life's difficulties and facing adversity and threat. From this viewpoint, coping with crisis is learning (new) behaviors appropriate for handling an unfamiliar, often unexpected, and highly aversive situation. This may be accomplished by rearranging commitments, by (re)establishing goals, by testing new options, or realizing whatever is at hand in the particular case.

How could this all be accomplished without turning attention to the self? Even in the face of less dramatic life events, i.e., by using relocation as a paradigm, Hormuth (1990) was able to find support for a similar assumption, namely that self-focus is created by the transition to a new environment. Contrary to what one might expect, it is not the new environment itself that attracts attention; since courses of action during transitions lack their usual smoothness, the individual is forced to direct his or her attention to the self. A similar notion can even be borrowed from one of the most prominent coping theories, although the construct of self-focused attention has never been explicitly addressed by these authors: What Lazarus and Folkman (1984), by distinguishing various phases within the coping process, termed "secondary appraisal" can simply be conceived as a phase of heightened self-focused attention, within which self-reflexive examinations of what one can or should do in a stressful encounter and evaluations of one's own coping resources are salient. Finally, Carver and Scheier (1985) have been most explicit with regard to proposing an increase in self-focus following the perception of discrepancies between one's current and desired states (in our terms: following serious life events).

A second line of reasoning can be proposed: Most critical life events exert a considerable impact on the individual, because they are directly related to the individual's *self-system*. Critical life events may attack feelings of self-worth, as is often experienced in the case of separation and divorce, or they may force the individual to alter central views of his or her self. Let us take the example of a cancer patient in his forties who, up to now, has held the self-image of being an "effective worker", an image which served as a primary organizer of his mental processes. For this patient, one of the most salient coping tasks will be to (slowly) revise that self-schema and to accommodate it to a new reality. Obviously, this process necessitates self-focused attention created by threats to self-esteem and to the sense of personal continuity and identity.

A third argument can be used to underscore our proposition: Serious life events are, by definition, accompanied by intense affective reactions; they create "affective noise" which (in addition to the absence of behavioral routines) often interferes with attempts to solve the crisis. The proposition that heightened emotional arousal creates the state of self-awareness is now widely accepted (see Wegner & Giuliano, 1980). Wood, Saltzberg, and Goldsamt (1990) have recently argued that a possible cause of self-focused attention is *affect itself*. Their prediction is based (1) on salience literature which indicates that objects that are distinctive or unexpected capture one's attention as well as (2) on theories claiming that arousal and affect promote an epistemic search for causes which, in turn, creates a high level of self-focus. Their data show that mood (induced by recalling personal events or imagining hypothetical ones that make subjects feel sad or neutral) indeed heightens self-focused attention (as measured by the number of first-person singular pronouns subjects used to fill in blanks within a series of 20 sentences). In a second experiment, using a different mood-induction procedure and a different measure of self-focus, it was shown that self-focus was created only after *dysphoric* mood had been induced; feelings of happiness had no effect. This, in addition, supports the assumption that serious life events are natural inducers of self-focused attention.

In order to gain some preliminary clues in support of our assumption, we investigated various samples of people living under difficult circumstances and having a considerable amount of problems. Unlike the studies referred to so far, self-focused attention was conceptualized as a dispositional construct, i.e., individual differences in the tendency to self-focus, rather than a situationally induced state. Furthermore, in this conceptualization *private self-consciousness* (as the disposition to direct attention towards private or "hidden" aspects of the self) and *public self-consciousness* (as the disposition to focus on aspects of the self which are accessible to everybody in one's personal context) are distinguished as presumably independent subdimensions of self-consciousness.

Such a person-oriented approach has proven to be a fruitful expansion of the theoretical scope originally proposed. It has, in the meantime, been widely accepted that individual differences in self-consciousness are almost identically related to various behavioral measures, just as has been proven for experimentally induced self-awareness (for an overview, see Filipp & Freudenberg, 1989). We administered a questionnaire measuring self-consciousness (see p. 278) to samples of (1) patients suffering from various kinds of cancer (N = 180; 78 males, 102 females), (2) alcoholics being treated in a rehabilitation center (N = 247; 184 males, 63 females), (3) unemployed workers recruited via the Unemployment Office (N = 164; 116 males, 48 females), and (4) men recently diagnosed as HIV-positive (N = 55). For means of comparisons, (5) a community sample from the city of Trier (N = 201 males) and (6) a sample of university students (N = 161; 67 males, 94 females) were also enrolled in the study.

As can be seen from Figure 12.1, the various "*problem groups*" (i.e., cancer patients, alcoholics, unemployedworkers, and HIV-positives) do have significantly higher levels of private and public self-consciousness than the community sample, with the group of HIV-positives scoring highest in private, and alcoholics scoring highest in public self-consciousness.

Although the sample of university students was originally intended to serve as a "non-crisis" control group as well, they differ significantly from the community sample and are quite similar to the sample of cancer patients and alcoholics, at least with regard to level of private self-consciousness. Taking into consideration, however, that the students had only recently joined the University of Trier and thus had experienced some life changes as well, their heightened level of self-consciousness is less surprising.

It should be mentioned, of course, that the various samples are not homogeneous with regard to age, sex, and most other characteristics;

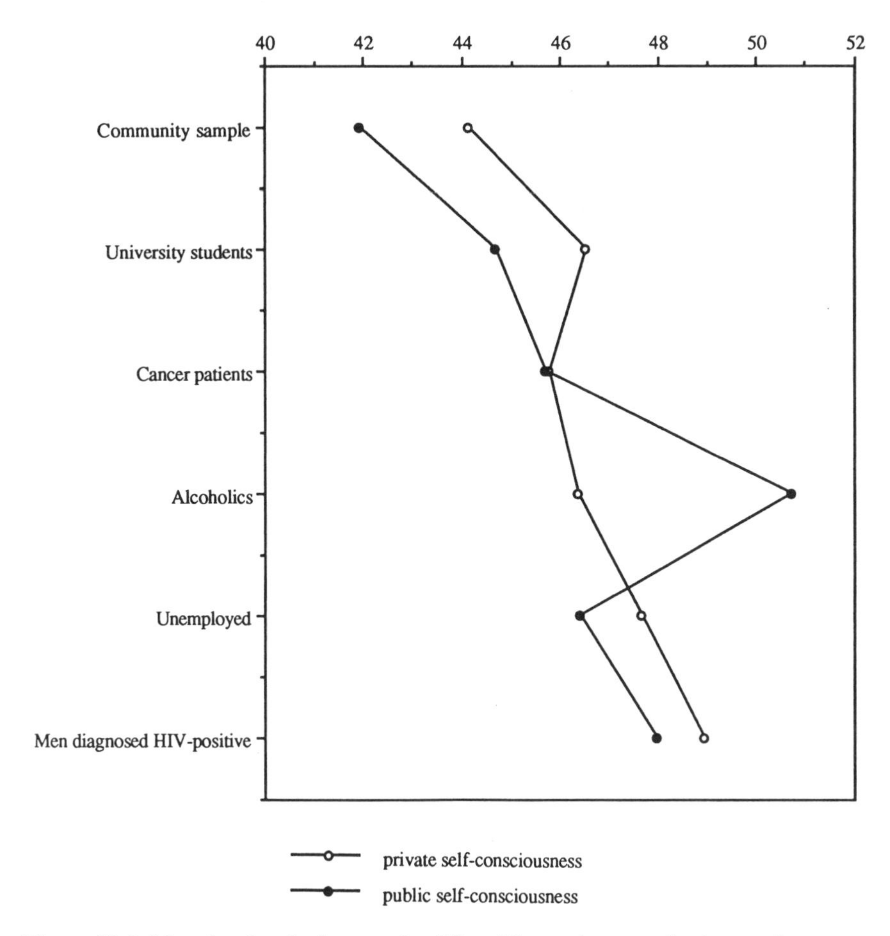

Figure 12.1. Mean levels of private and public self-consciousness in six samples.

nevertheless, we conceive of the observed differences in level of self-consciousness between the community sample and all others as primarily reflecting differences in exposure to an (extremely) difficult life situation. Age proved to be uncorrelated with levels of self-consciousness within and across various samples. Sex differences have been found in some studies indicating higher levels of (private and/or public) self-consciousness in women than in men. However, this effect could have raised the group mean in only the samples of university students, cancer patients, and alcoholics, since all other samples consisted of males only. An analysis of variance revealed both main effects (i.e., gender and group) to be independent (see Filipp, Ferring, & Klauer, 1991).

In addition, a study by Seiffge-Krenke (1984) with a sample of male and female adolescents also supports the notion that stressful experiences heighten self-focus. She subdivided the total sample into two groups differing in the level of (objective) stress and found - based on the same measure of self-consciousness - a higher level of private (though not public) self-consciousness in the group under stress, regardless of gender.

In summary, these studies illustrate that living under difficult circumstances may indeed increase self-focused attention. However, it is quite intriguing that - regardless of the nature of the threat our subjects have to deal with - *all* stressed samples are higher in private and public self-consciousness than the community sample. This can be easily related to the argument recently presented by Ingram (1990) that increased self-focused attention is related to a *diversity* of psychological disorders and that "the apparent ubiquitousness of this process in disorder makes it difficult to find anything dysfunctional that is not accompanied by increased self-focused attention" (p. 156).

After a long tradition of experimental work in which mirrors played a prominent role in creating self-awareness, there are now convincing arguments and some data available in support of the notion that natural variations in self-focused attention can be related to life stress. Since the limited data available so far are based on "natural experiments" (i.e., the onset of various critical events), we are, of course, not able to distinguish whether negative affect itself and/or the need for behavioral reorganization in the face of crisis are the crucial elements in creating self-focus.

The Role of Self-Focused Attention in Coping with Serious Life Events

While it has been argued that negative life experiences serve as a natural inducer of self-focused attention, the role of (dispositionally) focusing on the self in the *process of coping* with such experiences has been largely neglected. Besides third-variable explanations, there are various lines of reasoning that can be used to establish such a relationship including the following: (1) Self-focus intensifies ongoing negative affect associated with serious life events and is, hence, directly related to poor adaptational outcomes; (2) self-focus mediates coping responses and thereby exerts an indirect effect on adaptational outcomes; (3) self-focus is associated with higher veridicality in processing threatening information, thereby exaggerating the threat inherent in negative life situations and increasing the demands imposed on the individual. We will now turn to these assumptions, consider relevant support from the literature, and present our own data based on the Trier Longitudinal Study of Coping with Chronic Disease, which will be described in more detail below.

Self-Consciousness as an Intensifier of Negative Affect

The assumption that ongoing negative (as well as positive) affect is intensified by heightened self-focused attention is a prominent view in the literature and was already supported by experimental data several years ago (e.g., Scheier & Carver, 1977). This assumption has been promoted and elaborated by Pyszczynski and Greenberg (1986, 1987) in the formulation of their self-awareness theory of depression. According to these authors and based on the cybernetic model of self-regulation proposed by Carver and Scheier (1981), a negative discrepancy between one's current and desired state (which is *the* common element inherent in all serious life events) leads the individual to engage in behaviors aimed at reducing that discrepancy until it has been greatly reduced or eliminated. In this case, self-focus serves an *adaptive* function by providing the individual with information on current and desired states and on ways to attain (re)established goals - quite similar to Kuhl's (1981) concept of "action-orientation". If, however, the probability of reducing the perceived discrepancy is rather low, either due to low generalized outcome expectancies on the side of the individual or due to characteristics inherent in the problem itself (e.g., in the case of chronic disease), the reverse becomes true: Withdrawal from efforts directed towards reducing the discrepancy, accompanied by a *decrease* in self-focused attention, now represent an adaptive response. In either case, the onset of depression following a serious life event is highly unlikely to occur.

On the other hand, when facing traumatic and irrevocable loss, disengagement from this self-regulatory cycle and distracting attention away from the self may become extremely difficult. This is particularly true, as these authors suggest, when what has been lost served as a major source of emotional security and self-worth. As a consequence, the individual experiencing such a loss fails to withdraw from self-focus *"in the absence of any way to regain what was lost"* (Pyszczynski & Greenberg, 1987, p. 310; italics ours). In this case the development and even the exacerbation of depression are highly likely to occur (cf. Weidner & Collins, this volume).

Although the authors' theoretical propositions presented so far are primarily supported by experimental evidence (e.g., by inducing success or failure under conditions of high vs. low self-awareness), they can be easily applied to the investigation of how self-focused attention aggravates the impact of life stress which has already been proven by Hull, Young, and Jouriles (1986) in their work on the prediction of alcohol relapse. We would like to take the onset of a chronic disease like cancer as a sample case: Despite considerable individual differences in relevant belief systems (e.g., optimism) or other coping resources, it is unlikely that patients diagnosed as having cancer will easily find ways "to regain what was lost". Their life situation may be - for long periods of time - characterized by a chronic discrepancy between "current and desired state" to be coped with. Individual differences in private self-consciousness should then be even more predictive of who will develop depression as a consequence of having cancer and who will not - proposing that patients high in private self-consciousness should have more difficulties in disengaging from the above-mentioned self-regulatory cycle.

While such a view relates self-consciousness directly to depression as a non-adaptational outcome in coping with chronic disease (or any other threat), the relationship between self-focused attention and the coping process itself has been mainly neglected. However, a more thorough investigation of how coping is related to self-focus is highly warranted, since it should allow for a better understanding of the *mechanisms* that underlie the presumed association between self-focus and depression (see also Wood, Saltzberg, & Goldsamt, 1990).

Self-Consciousness as a Mediator of Coping Responses

The idea that self-consciousness affects coping by encouraging some strategies while inhibiting others is a fairly new theme in the literature and has been addressed in only a few studies (e.g., Wood, Saltzberg, Neale, Stone, & Rachmiel, 1990). There are, however, various lines of reasoning in support of such a notion, although it depends highly on how one conceives of the oping concept itself.

First, if we conceive of coping behaviors in terms of their attentional direction, relationships on the conceptual level can easily be established; high levels of (dispositional) self-focused attention should be related to an intense cogitation of one's life situation, often called "rumination". Such a mode of dealing with chronic disease presumably implies social withdrawal and a lowered tendency to mobilize and use social support; it implies behavioral inactivity and an engagement in causal reasoning and worrying about one's future; it may also imply that turning attention to the self prevents the use of social comparison information and the benefits of a "downward" perspective (see Taylor & Brown, 1988). To summarize, self-focus should encourage what others have called a "contemplative coping style" (Strack, Blaney, Ganellen, & Coyne, 1985). There is one study to our knowledge which tested a similar assumption in a middle-aged community sample (Wood, Saltzberg, Neale, Stone, & Rachmiel, 1990) and which reported in its results "that people who tend to be high in their self-focus tend to ruminate about their problems and to be less likely to take direct actions to deal with them" (p. 1031). If ruminative coping responses are, in turn, associated with or even intensify negative affect, it would be possible to prove the *indirect* effects of self-focus on depression. While, in this context, a high self-focus may represent a vulnerability factor in coping with chronic disease, patients low in private self-consciousness should, on the other hand, engage in more distracting activities, should socialize more, and, hence, suffer less from depression and negative affect.

There is a *second* line of reasoning to be taken into consideration. It has been repeatedly shown that self-focused attention leads to an overperception of the self as a target (Fenigstein, 1984); similarily, Buss and Scheier (1976) suggested that a habitual self-focus of privately self-conscious individuals leads them to attribute either positive or negative outcomes to internal causes. When one conceives of the coping process in terms of people searching for answers to the "Why me?"-question (as is without any doubt a prominent view in coping research; see Montada, Filipp, & Lerner, in press), it is highly plausible to assume that the level of self-focus may make a difference with regard to the answers which will be found. This should be particularly true for people who have to cope with a chronic disease which still has a very unclear etiology (like cancer); accordingly patients high in self-focus should be more likely to attribute the onset of cancer to internal causes or even blame themselves for it than patients low in self-focus. The question of whether self-blame is an adaptive or maladaptive strategy in coping with serious life events is controversially discussed in the literature and presumably depends on the nature of the event itself rather than on being uniformly "good" or "bad" (see Montada, in press). One of the few studies aimed at linking level of self-consciousness to causal attributions for the onset of (chronic) disease was conducted by Ferring (1987) with a sample of cancer patients and patients suffering from myocardial infarction. Attributional style as well as attributions for the onset of the disease were assessed on the causal dimensions of internality, stability, and globality and related to level of private and public self-consciousness. No mean level differences between both groups of patients could be observed. Attributional style proved to be positively related to private and public self-consciousness, however only with respect to the causal dimension of *globality*, and not to internality as well. Attributions for the onset of the disease were unrelated to self-consciousness with but one exception: Patients with high levels of *public* self-consciousness attributed the causation of their disease to external causes. Thus, the assumption about the effects of private self-consciousness on causal attributions for the onset of negative events is not confirmed by these data.

A *third and final* assumption can be described as follows: Since self-focus is most aversive under unpleasant life circumstances and since it is highly likely that patients high in self-consciousness experience higher levels of depression and dysphoric mood, they should exhibit a far greater variety of palliative coping behaviors, usually referred to as "emotion-focused coping". Obviously, this is an extremely broad category of coping responses comprised of a diversity of behaviors, all presumably equifunctional in regulating emotion and reducing distress. Thus, it is less clear which particular coping responses should be encouraged or inhibited by heightened self-focus. It might even be the case that patients high in self-focus, since they have much more "to cope with" (if it is true that ruminating and intense negative affect characterize them), should therefore exhibit a higher level of coping efforts in general, regardless of the particular mode of coping considered.

Self-Consciousness and (Non-Distorted) Perception of Threat

A last and admittedly highly speculative line of reasoning is presented as follows: We have learned from experimental work that self-focused attention also facilitates a fairly unbiased processing of information concerning the self. For example, it has been shown that individuals high in private self-focus have a much higher resistance towards experimental manipulation of physiological states using placebos (see Gibbons, Carver, Scheier, & Hormuth, 1979), and it is argued that people high in self-focus do have better access to their internal (physiological) world. Dependent on the quality of the self-relevant information to be processed, self-consciousness may play a stress-buffering role in some cases, whereas in others it may exaggerate threatening aspects inherent in self-relevant information. With regard to the first issue, a study by Mullen and Suls (1982) serves as a good example. These authors investigated private self-consciousness as a moderator of the impact of stressful life changes on physical symptoms in a sample of college students. While subjects low in private self-focus proved to be highly affected by the accumulation of stressful experiences, physical symptoms were unrelated to stressful experiences in the subsample high in self-focus. It has been argued that the latter are much more aware of their physical responses to stress and are more likely to reduce the impact of stress on their physical well-being than people low in self-focus. In a later study, also using a prospective design, Suls and Fletcher (1985) found that incidents of stressful life events predicted subsequent illness only within the subgroup of subjects low in private self-consciousness, but not for those high in private self-consciousness. Again, these findings have been interpreted in the following way: Low self-consciousness leads to a greater neglect of somatic reactions toward stressful life events and to taking appropriate preventive actions at the appropriate time.

In these cases, self-focus obviously enhanced the "veridicality" in the perception of internal states and exerted an ameliorative effect on health under stressful conditions rather than exaggerating or perpetuating the stressful experience itself. (For measuring the "veridicality" in the perception of internal physiological states, also see the chapters by Hodapp and Knoll and by Kohlmann, this volume.) However, all these studies have used college students as subjects who were exposed to, more or less, minor stressful life events (e.g., taking exams, having arguments with their friends). Thus, these results might be of limited value when predicting the impact of self-focus on adaptational outcomes in samples exposed to traumatic life events (e.g., the onset of chronic disease). What has been considered a "healthy degree of introspection" (Olbrisch & Ziegler, 1982) in students cannot, on a priori grounds, be considered "healthy" in a sample of severely and/or chronically distressed people. In contrast, it is likely that in such cases self-consciousness, by leading to non-distorted processing of information concerning the self, may even enhance the impact of serious life events on those confronted with threat. Accordingly, it is highly warranted to investigate whether self-focused attention moderates the relationship between (objective) threat inherent in stressful life situations and adaptation in a sample of severely distressed people.

Self-Focused Attention and Coping with Cancer: The Trier Longitudinal Study on Coping with Chronic Disease

The cancer diagnosis can be, without any doubt, conceived of as a prototype of traumatic life events, i.e., an experience which is highly unpredictable and uncontrollable, and which has impact on a variety of life domains and its existential plight. Accordingly, studies with cancer patients should provide better insight into the dynamics of coping with loss and threat and the various factors that might influence it.

The Trier Longitudinal Study on Coping with Chronic Disease was conducted in cooperation with several institutions for cancer care and rehabilitation in Germany (Filipp, Aymanns, & Klauer, 1983; Filipp, Klauer, Ferring, & Freudenberg, 1990)[1]. Its general aims are (1) the assessment and description of modes of coping with cancer (as well as perceived coping tasks) with special reference to the variability versus stability in coping behaviors over time, (2) the prediction of interindividual differences in coping behaviors as well as changes in coping behaviors from different sets of variables (including medical status, personality measures, etc.), and (3) the prediction of interindividual differences in a set of indicators of adjustment to cancer using longitudinal causal modeling.

Within this chapter, we will confine ourselves to the results obtained for the role of self-consciousness in the process of coping with cancer. We will present these results in two parts: The first part refers to the issue of whether self-consciousness is related to coping and to the quality of adjustment to cancer. The second part refers to the question as to whether self-consciousness moderates the relationship between severity of disease, coping behaviors, and adjustment indicators.

Analysis I: Self-Consciousness as a Determinant of Adjustment in Cancer Patients

As was outlined earlier, there are some convincing arguments for the assumption that habitual self-focused attention may represent a vulnerabilty factor in coping with threatening events for which, in particular, ways to master them are not readily at hand. Thus, suffering from cancer should be even more difficult to cope with for patients high, as compared to those low, in (private) self-focus.

[1] The research reported here was sponsored by a grant from the German Research Foundation (DFG; Fi 346/1-3)

Patient sample and procedure
On the first occasion of measurement, *N* = 332 cancer patients (178 females, 154 males), aged between 15 and 77 years (*M* = 51 years), were enrolled in the study. The largest homogeneous subsamples regarding tumor site were patients with breast cancer (*n* = 83), neoplasms in the digestive system (*n* = 63), in the area of the mouth, the throat, and the larynx (*n* = 47), and patients with cancer of the blood or lymphatic system (*n* = 43). At the time of the initial interview, half of the subjects had been diagnosed within the previous year; the time that had elapsed since diagnosis varied between one and 840 weeks (*M* = 112 weeks). The types of medical treatment most frequently applied were surgery (79.9% of the sample), radiation therapy (48.9%), and chemotherapy (27.3%). Following an initial interview, data were collected on four occasions of measurement (time intervals: three months) and at an additional follow-up two years after the initial interview.

Measures
Self-consciousness. A German modification (Filipp & Freudenberg, 1989) of the Self-Consciousness Scale developed by Fenigstein, Scheier, and Buss (1975) was used to assess *private self-consciousness* (*PRSC*; 13 items) as well as *public self-consciousness* (*PUSC*; 14 items). Both measures proved to be differentially related to various behavioral aspects in a variety of studies, although the private-public distinction has been attacked on conceptual grounds (Wicklund & Gollwitzer, 1987); within our sample of cancer patients both subscales also proved to be significantly intercorrelated ($r = .58$).

Indicators of adjustment. With regard to measuring adjustment to cancer, we tried to include a variety of indicators with particular reference to the problem that the definition of "success" in coping with serious life events is far from being established unequivocally (see Filipp & Klauer, 1991). For the present purpose, we have selected four indicators: *Hopelessness* (*HOP*) was measured by a German version (Krampen, 1979) of the Beck Hopelessness Scale (Beck, Weisman, Lester, & Trexler, 1974). *Self-esteem* (*SES*) was assessed by a German version of the Rosenberg Self-Esteem Scale (Rosenberg, 1965). *Subjective well-being* (*SWB*) was measured using a well-validated German instrument (Bf-S', Von Zerssen, 1976) comprised of 28 bipolar scales which describe positive and negative affective states; the patients' self-ratings on these scales were summed up by a single well-being score. Finally, we included a measure of dispositional *optimism* (*OPT*) employing a German version of Carver and Scheier's (1985) Life Orientation Test, well aware that the theoretical status of this construct is quite different from the other adjustment indicators included. All measures conceived to indicate adjustment to cancer revealed sufficient to high reliability coefficients between $r_{tt} = .78$ (*OPT*) and $r_{tt} = .95$ (*SWB*); intercorrelations were generally high and ranged between

r = -.81 (hopelessness and optimism) and r = .47 (optimism and subjective well-being).

Coping modes. Modes of coping with cancer were assessed by a newly developed self-report measure ("*F*ragebogen zur *E*rfassung von Formen der *K*rankheits*b*ewältigung", *FEKB*; cf. Klauer, Filipp, & Ferring, 1990). Item selection and scale development were guided by classifying coping responses a priori along three basic dimensions: (1) focus of attention (centered around vs. distracted from the disease), (2) sociability (turning towards vs. withdrawing from others), and (3) response level (overt vs. intrapsychic response). In order to elicit an "episodic" (Cohen, 1987) rather than a "dispositional" measure of coping, patients had to rate the *frequency* of each coping response within a given period of time. Such a procedure is adequate especially if one is interested in temporal variations in coping behavior rather than in coping styles.

Factor analyses revealed a structural pattern of five factors which were subsequently used for the construction of scales and the description of coping modes (see also Klauer et al., 1990): (1) *Rumination* (*RU*; 9 items) is comprised of items reflecting intrapsychic modes of coping focused on the disease and accompanied by social withdrawal, e.g., causal reasoning and engaging in temporal comparisons of one's personal past (item example: "I tried to find out whether I did something wrong"); (2) *search for affiliation* (*SA*; 9 items) is reflective of coping by turning towards others and searching for attentional diversion and distraction from the disease (item example: "I visited other people or invited them over"); (3) *threat minimization* (*TM*; 8 items) covers items that describe intrapsychic responses presumably serving palliative functions, such as self-instructions towards positive thinking and maintenance of trust in the medical regimen (item example: "I realized that physicians will do their best to help me"); (4) *search for information* (*SI*; 8 items) is comprised of overt reactions aimed at gaining knowledge about the disease and its medical treatment, particularly by interacting with other patients (item example: "I tried to establish contact with persons having similar experiences"); (5) *search for meaning in religion* (*SR*; 3 items), reflects the attempts to find meaning in the illness experience using religious resources (item example: "I imagined that there is a higher meaning in my situation").

Split-half reliability coefficients ranged between .74 (*SA*) and .90 (*SR*), Cronbach's *alpha* between .74 (*RU*) and .88 (*SI*); *RU* and *SI* as well as *TM* and *SA* were moderately intercorrelated at each of the four times of measurement. All scales were also shown to be sufficiently reliable in other samples of chronically ill adults (e.g., coronary heart disease patients, multiple sclerosis patients), although there is evidence for some intersample differences in the structure of coping (see Klauer et al., 1990).

Results

Zero-order correlations between private as well as public self-consciousness on the one hand and the various indicators of adjustment (hopelessness, optimism, self-esteem, and subjective well-being) on the other were generally close to zero or at a very modest level (e.g., $r = -.10$ for private self-consciousness and hopelessness). Thus, the hypothesis of a main effect of self-consciousness on adjustment in cancer patients, in terms of a high self-focus which intensifies negative affect, had to be rejected. However, these correlation coefficients alone may not tell us the whole story. Further analyses have therefore been conducted. First, it was not quite clear, whether the level of self-consciousness is related to the use of particular coping modes; it might be the case that *indirect* effects of self-consciousness on adjustment indicators, mediated by coping behaviors, are observable. Second, it had to be investigated whether effects of private and public self-consciousness on adjustment still remained negligible when we controlled for demographic and/or illness-related factors. Accordingly, path analysis was used to test a model in which modes of coping were analyzed as mediators of the relationship between self-consciousness and adjustment. Within these analyses, age, gender, and time elapsed since diagnosis were included as exogenous variables.

Figure 12.2 shows the model accepted for the subjective well-being measure (*SWB*) as an example (LISREL VI Goodness of fit statistics: $\chi^2_{18} = 27.36$, $p = .072$; $GFI = .98$; $AGFI = .94$); results for the criteria hopelessness, optimism, and self-esteem were very similar with a few exceptions.

First of all, these results show that both self-consciousness measures as well as all coping modes were independent of age and time elapsed since diagnosis. Gender is associated with *public self-consciousness* (*PUSC*), males being lower than females, as well as with *search for meaning in religion* (*SR*) as a coping mode which is used less often by males than by females. However, both effects are irrelevant with respect to adjustment indicators, although there is a very small, second-order indirect effect of gender on distress mediated by *PUSC* and *rumination* (*RU*).

Subjective well-being, when regressed on coping modes, on self-consciousness, and on demographic and illness-related variables, proved to be most clearly predicted by certain coping modes while being largely unrelated to time elapsed since diagnosis, gender, and level of self-consciousness. Exceptions were age, which had modestly direct effects on hopelessness (*HOP;* $\beta = .14$, $t = 2.61$, $p < .01$) and optimism (*OPT*; $\beta = -.11$, $t = -2.03$, $p < .05$), as well as private self-consciousness, which had a modestly negative relation to *HOP* ($\beta = -.17$; $t = -2.36$, $p < .05$). These few direct effects were not stable across distress measures and could be ignored when *alpha* levels of significance were adjusted.

As can be seen from Figure 12.2, private and public self-consciousness were positively related to ruminative coping behaviors, which in turn had moderate to strong effects on each of the four adjustment measures (*HOP:* $\beta = .41$, $t = 6.13$; *OPT:* $\beta = -.46$, $t = -6.69$; *SES:* $\beta = -.41$, $t = -5.75$; *SWB:* $\beta = -.31$, $t = -4.18$;

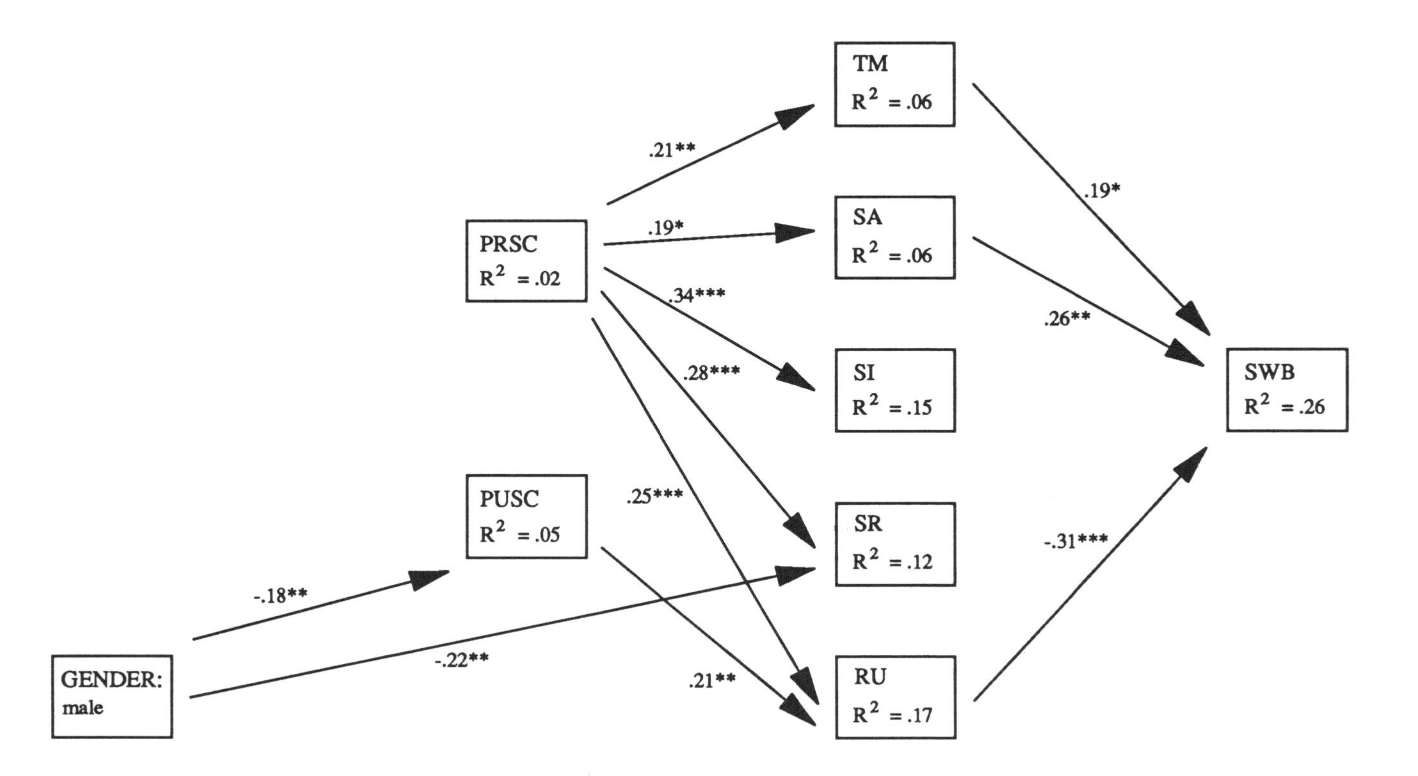

Figure 12.2. Path model of the interrelations between gender, private (PRSC) and public (PUSC) self-conciousness, coping modes (RU: rumination; SA: search for affiliation; TM: threat minimization; SI: search for information; SR: search for meaning in religion), and subjective well-being (SWB) controlling for age and illness duration: Path coefficients and explained variances (age and illness duration variables, interrelations between coping scales and insignificant paths omitted; $N = 220$ cancer patients).

all *t*-values significant at $\alpha = .001$). Our results so far correspond nicely with those presented by Wood, Saltzberg, Neale, Stone, and Rachmiel (1990) and are also in support of the notion of self-consciousness as a promoter of maladaptive, ruminative coping responses.

However, while public self-consciousness was unrelated to coping modes other than rumination, private self-consciousness had additional effects on *each* of the remaining coping measures, all of which were in a *positive* direction.

Obviously, the indirect distress-enhancing effects of private self-consciousness mediated by rumination were compensated by effects of private self-consciousness on more adaptive modes of coping: *PRSC* was most predictive of search for information (*SI*), which was unrelated to poor adjustment with the exception of self-esteem ($\beta = .15$. $t = 2.04$, $p < .05$), and also predicted search for affiliation (*SA*) and threat minimization (*TM*), which both proved to be, in general, distress-reducing modes of coping (see also Filipp, Ferring, Freudenberg, & Klauer, 1989, for a more detailed description). Search for meaning in religion (*SR*) was also related to private self-consciousness but unrelated to all adjustment indicators.

When aggregating direct and indirect effects of private and public self-consciousness on distress measures, it becomes clear that the sum of these direct and indirect effects is close to zero, although there are, in part, considerable effects of private self-consciousness on coping and coping behaviors on distress measures. It appears from these results that, in particular, *private* self-consciousness activates coping efforts in cancer patients in a fairly unspecific way rather than promoting only ruminative responses. Therefore, our data up to now do not support the notion of self-consciousness representing a risk factor in coping with cancer. In the following section some conditions are discussed under which self-consciousness may, nevertheless, affect distress.

Analysis II: Self-Consciousness as a Moderator of Stress-Distress-Relationships in Cancer Patients

An alternative perspective on self-consciousness in terms of a risk vs. protective factor in coping with chronic disease is adopted when it is investigated as a moderator of the effects of "objective" stress inherent in the disease on adjustment indicators. As has been extensively shown in research on social support, personality factors can also be considered protective or as "stress buffers" if the impact of negative life experiences depends on individual characteristics of those exposed to them (Cohen & Edwards, 1989). Self-consciousness may play such a role and was investigated here as a moderator, based on the assumption that private, but not public, self-consciousness moderates the relationships between disease-related stress (as indicated by medical data and physicians' ratings) and indicators of adjustment.

Patient sample and measures

Medical data (e.g., histological grading, recidivism, metastases as well as clinical ratings) for a subsample (n = 214) of the group of cancer patients described above were obtained from their physicians when these patients entered the study. These medical data were used as independent indicators of medical stress and were related to the various indicators of distress used in the prior analysis, i.e., hopelessness, optimism, self-esteem, and well-being. Because of listwise deletion of missing data, the size of the sample analyzed here was further reduced to N = 169 patients (75 males, 94 females; mean age: 51 years, mean illness duration: 96 weeks). Among this subsample, 69 patients (40,8%) were reported to have regional lymph node metastases, 21 (12,4%) to have metastases in other bodily areas, and 77 (45,6%) to be suffering from additional somatic complaints (multimorbidity).

Because of characteristics of their distribution in the sample, four variables were selected as "threat" indicators for the analyses to be reported here: *regional lymph node invasion* (*LNI*) at the time of diagnosis, *multimorbidity* (*MUM*), physician's rating of the patient's *overall physical impairment* (*IMP*), and physician's *prognosis for curability* (*PRG*). Impairment ratings were provided on a six-point scale ranging from 1 ("very little") to 6 ("very much"; M = 3.34; Md = 3.00; SD = 1.36); prognosis was also rated on a six-point scale with scores between 1 ("very poor") and 6 ("very good"; M = 3.69; Md = 4.00; SD = 1.46). For the present sample, ratings on both variables did not differ significantly from a normal distribution and were used as predictors in regression analyses.

Results

Zero-order correlations between level of self-consciousness, medical variables, and distress indicators (see Table 12.1) point to high consistencies within blocks of variables and, at best, weak associations between them. Interestingly enough, medical variables were almost unrelated to all distress measures, i.e., hopelessness, self-esteem, optimism, and subjective well-being, as were both self-consciousness scales.

Moderated regression analysis (Cohen, 1978; Pedhazur, 1982; Saunders, 1956) was used to test interacting effects of self-consciousness and indicators of threat on the four distress measures. To prevent problems resulting from collinearity between predictor, moderator, and multiplicative interaction term, all continuous variables were *z-standardized*. Regional lymph node invasion (*LNI*) as well as multimorbidity (*MUM*) were entered as dummy-coded predictors in separate regression analyses for each criterion (distress measures) and moderator (private and public self-consciousness), respectively.

Results for stress-by-self-consciousness interactions are summarized in Table 12.2. As can be seen, effects of *LNI* and *MUM* on all distress measures were moderated by private self-consciousness in a highly consistent way;

Table 12.1
Zero-Order Correlations Between Indicators of Medical Status, Self-Consciousness, and Distress Measures in Cancer Patients (165 ≤ *N* ≤ 169)

	Scales and coefficients[a]								
Scale[a]	PRSC	PUSC	LNI	IMP	MUM	PRG	HOP	OPT	SES
Self-consciousness scales:									
PUSC	57***								
Medical status indicators:									
LNI	12	01							
IMP	09	-10	17*						
MUM	08	-02	-06	15*					
PRG	-06	13	-33***	-47***	-01				
Distress measures:									
HOP	-15*	-08	11	10	18*	-12			
OPT	07	01	-06	-11	-18*	12	-81***		
SES	17*	04	-11	-09	-04	03	-58***	57***	
SWB	05	05	-09	-16*	-09	08	-51***	47***	52***

Note. Listed are Pearson correlation coefficients; decimal points omitted.
[a] PRSC, private self-consciousness; PUSC, public self-consciousness; LNI, lymph node invasion; IMP, impairment; MUM, multimorbidity; PRG, prognosis; HOP, hopelessness; OPT, optimism; SES, self-esteem; SWB, subjective well-being.
*p < .05; **p < .01; ***p < .001; (one-tailed).

interaction effects explained between 3.3 and 8.5 percent of variance in these measures. On the other hand, the interactive model obviously had to be rejected for physician's prognosis and impairment rating, which in our view does not necessarily contradict the general moderator hypothesis: It is likely that the validity of both of the physicians' ratings might be lower compared to the validity of *LNI* and *MUM* as indicators of medical stress - due to possible interrater differences in, for example, frame of reference or due to high levels of uncertainty in cancer prognosis in general. However, the pattern of results becomes surprisingly complicated when the directions of the effects are examined.

Table 12.2
Private and Public Self-Consciousness as Moderators of Stress-Distress Relationships in Cancer Patients: Overview of Interaction Effects ($150 \leq N \leq 156$)

Criterion[a] (Distress indicator)	Stress indicators and effect statistics[b]: Lymph node invasion				Multimorbidity				Prognosis				Impairment			
	β	*RSQC*	*t*	*F*	β	*RSQC*	*t*	*F*	β	*RSQC*	*t*	*F*	β	*RSQC*	*t*	*F*
Private self-consciousness																
HOP	-.24	.033	2.27*	3.74*	.33	.067	3.39***	6.85***	-.03	.001	.35	1.97	.04	.002	.45	1.74
OPT	.28	.045	2.62**	2.76*	-.37	.085	3.85***	7.41***	-.02	.001	.29	.95	-.02	.000	.21	.89
SES	.25	.036	2.38*	4.12**	-.29	.051	2.89**	4.37**	-.02	.000	.27	1.43	.01	.000	.13	2.04
SWB	.38	.082	3.64***	4.96**	-.31	.058	3.09**	4.13**	-.04	.002	.48	.31	.04	.002	.49	1.38
Public self-consciousness																
HOP	-.29	.048	2.76**	3.60*	.10	.006	.93	2.08	.10	.011	1.26	1.59	.03	.001	.39	.73
OPT	.41	.096	3.94**	5.49**	-.19	.021	1.84	3.30*	-.03	.001	.30	.87	.00	.000	.05	.72
SES	.16	.014	1.45	1.42	.10	.006	.97	0.43	-.13	.016	1.58	.92	.04	.002	.46	.44
SWB	.38	.083	3.67***	5.07**	-.09	.004	.85	1.12	-.02	.001	.26	.28	-.04	.003	.43	1.28

[a] HOP, hopelessness; OPT, optimism; SES, self-esteem; SWB, subjective well-being.
[b] β, standardized regression coefficient for interaction term; *RSQC*, incremental variance explained by interaction term; *t*, *t*-value for interaction term; *F*, *F*-statistic for complete equation including interaction term.
$^{*}p < .05$; $^{**}p < .01$; $^{***}p < .001$.

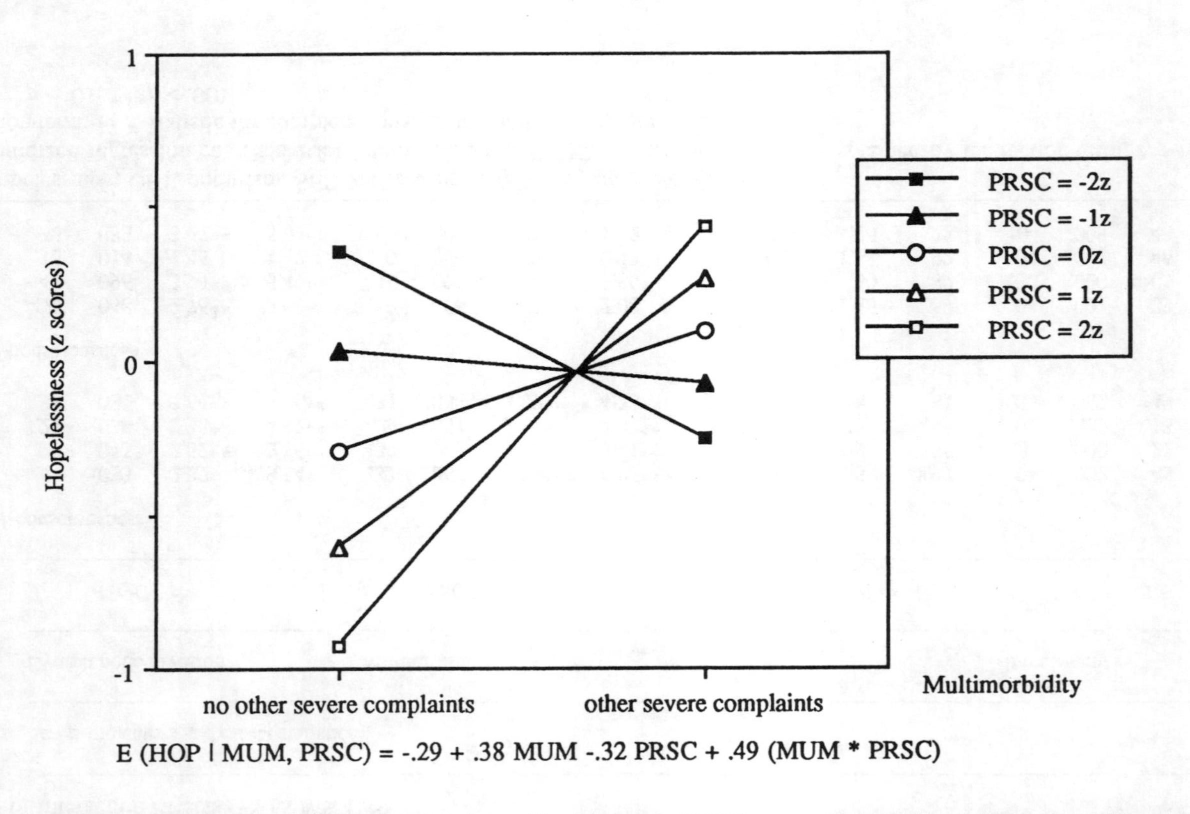

Figure 12.3. Predicted means and conditional regression of hopelessness (HOP) on multimorbidity (MUM) for different levels of private self-consciousness (PRSC; N = 156 cancer patients).

Regarding the interactions between private self-consciousness and multimorbidity, these results are consistent with the notion of private self-consciousness as a *vulnerability* factor. Let us take hopelessness as an example. Its conditional effects of multimorbidity are plotted in Figure 12.3.

As can be seen in Figure 12.3, the relationship between multimorbidity and hopelessness is positive and comparatively close for high levels of private self-focus, whereas it is modestly negative or near zero for low levels of private self-focus. The same pattern of results emerged with regard to optimism, self-esteem, and subjective well-being as distress indicators which were scored in the opposite direction: Effects of multimorbidity were close to zero at low *PRSC* levels and increasingly negative with increasing *PRSC* levels.

However, contrary to our expectations, interactions between regional lymph node invasion (*LNI*) and private self-consciousness point in the opposite direction: Having lymph node metastases at the time of cancer diagnosis is obviously rather irrelevant to the quality of adjustment to cancer (as indicated by lower hopelessness and higher optimism, self-esteem, and subjective well-being) in patients high in private self-consciousness; patients low in self-consciousness are affected in a negative manner. Figure 12.4 illustrates these results, again for the sample case of hopelessness.

In addition, the effects were in the same direction for public self-consciousness. From these results it appears that self-consciousness obviously represents a *protective* factor in coping with cancer which buffers the effects of illness severity (as indicated by lymph node invasion).

These seemingly contradictory results with respect to whether private self-focus should be regarded as a risk factor in coping with cancer deserve further consideration. It appears that multimorbidity and lymph node invasion when cancer is first diagnosed cannot be regarded as parallel indicators of global disease-related stress but as independent "stressors", as is also indicated by their near-zero correlation within our sample (*phi* = .12; n.s.). While lymph node metastases, which (in most cases) were removed during primary cancer treatment, represent some form of threat successfully overcome in the past, the presence of other illnesses and bodily complaints has an ongoing impact on patients and might permanently interfere in a negative way with the process of coping with and adjusting to cancer.

Our assumption that self-consciousness plays divergent roles in coping with the threat stemming from these medical conditions is in need of further investigation. With regard to multimorbidity, low private self-consciousness should facilitate "blunting" of the various symptoms and bodily complaints besides cancer, whereas high self-focus draws attention towards these (additional) bodily harms (cf. Miller et al., this volume). This line of reasoning is then consistent with the various results based on experimental manipulations of physiological states, indicating that highly self-conscious persons do have better access to their internal world. As a consequence, cancer patients high in self-focus do suffer more (in terms of, e.g., heightened hopelessness) under the condition of multimorbidity than those scoring low in self-consciousness. In the case of lymph node metastases which have been removed earlier and are

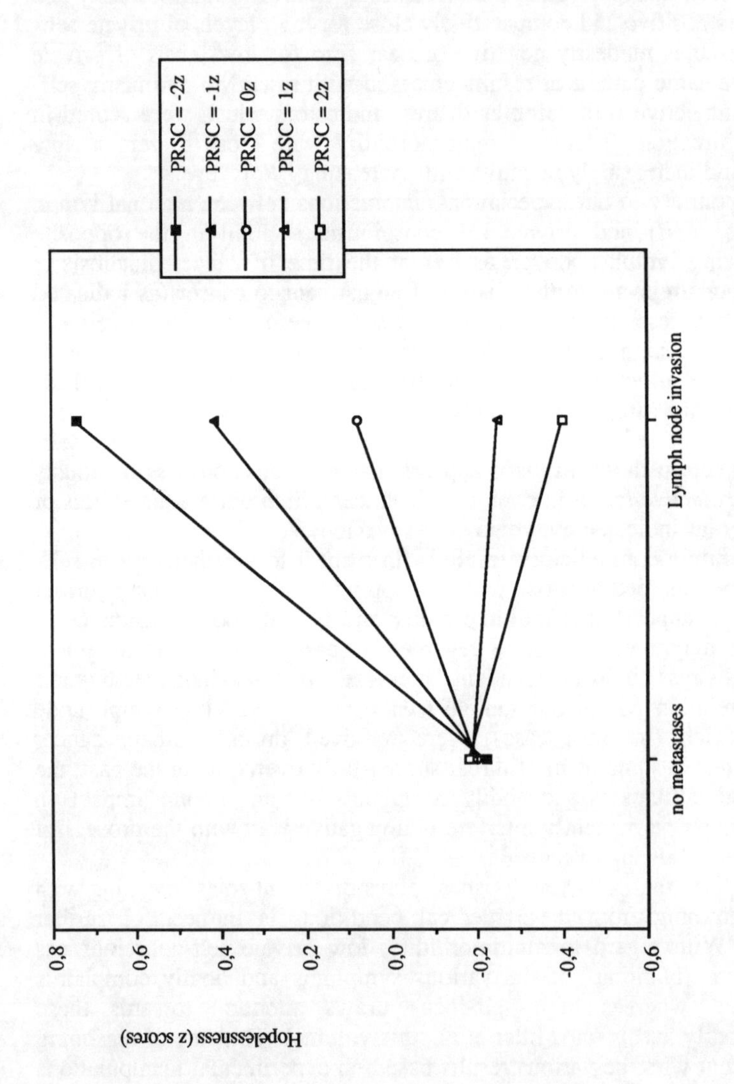

Figure 12.4. Predicted means and conditional regression of hopelessness (HOP) on lymph node invasion (LNI) for different levels of private self-consciousness (PRSC; N = 156 cancer patients).

therefore a non-present stressor, patients high in private self-consciousness might have been initially more accurate ("vigilant") in the perception of the severity of their illness (as one would also expect from other observations) and might, therefore, have initialized a variety of adaptive coping responses much faster than patients low in self-consciousness (who might have employed "avoidant" strategies). Thus, high self-consciousness might have helped to establish (perceived) control over illness consequences and to prevent hopelessness and maladjustment in the face of highly threatening cancers.

These considerations, of course, call for further analyses in which effects of self-consciousness on modes of coping under different stressful circumstances will be investigated. Preliminary analyses on the data discussed here - which cannot be reported in greater detail within this chapter - indeed suggest that, under the condition of lymph node invasion, the (positive) relationship between self-consciousness and the particularily adaptive coping modes, i.e., search for affiliation and threat minimization, is closer, whereas the relationship between self-consciousness and rumination is unaffected by lymph node metastases. In the case of multimorbidity, the positive relationship between private self-consciousness and rumination (as a maladaptive coping mode) increases, whereas the positive effects of private self-focus on threat minimization as an adaptive response disappear (all interaction terms significant at $\alpha = .05$). These results, still in need of further exploration and replication, may serve as first clues to the complicated role self-consciousness plays in coping with chronic disease.

Self-Consciousness: Resource or Risk Factor in Coping with Cancer?

Despite a fairly long tradition in the research on ways to cope with loss and adversity, we are far from having sufficient insight into the nature of resources which people can rely on in such difficult times. This is even more true when we look at chronic disease as a sample case of those negative life experiences for which we are far from being able to predict who will cope successfully or who will be psychologically overwhelmed and severely harmed. Over the past years, special interest has been directed to social resources and the notion of social support as a buffer towards disease-related stress (cf. Wortman & Conway, 1985). On the other hand, despite the search for dispositionally preferred coping strategies, personality variables have not received as much attention as predictors of individual differences in coping behaviors and coping effectiveness. This may be partly due to one widely shared assumption, namely that coping unfolds as a process over time, shaped more by the demands inherent in the stressful experience itself than the stable characteristics of the individual being threatened (e.g., Lazarus & Folkman, 1984).

We believe that this is a too narrow "situationistic" perspective; however, few concepts are available within personality research which would allow for asserting relationships between dispositional variables and modes of coping with serious life events on theoretical grounds and for deriving related hypotheses. Yet theory on self-focused attention and self-consciousness does offer a promising conceptual tool in that respect, and we have therefore included it (besides some other mainly cognitive personality variables) in our measurement battery in studying how patients cope with cancer.

In addition to the observation that self-focus is intensified during difficult life circumstances in a rather unspecific manner (as our data presented in the first part of this chapter have shown), one of the assumptions guiding our research was that coping with cancer should be impeded in patients scoring high in private self-consciousness, regardless of the various interaction effects which we had additionally proposed. One common element inherent in most of these propositions was the belief that high private self-focus should aggravate disease-related stress and threat and therefore be conceived of as a risk factor in coping with cancer. Despite the various limitations and inadequacies in defining "adjustment" or "effectiveness" in coping with cancer in general (see Filipp & Klauer, 1991), we expected that hopelessness would be enhanced by high levels of self-focus and that self-esteem and well-being should be lowered.

Our results, first of all, highlight that private self-consciousness cannot be easily or unequivocally equated with a "risk factor". Private (as well as public) self-consciousness proved to be completely unrelated to the various indicators of adjustment to cancer in the first set of analyses: Self-focus did not enhance hopelessness nor affect other outcome criteria. When taking differences in coping behaviors into consideration, self-focus did prove to exert effects on coping, but in an unpredicted manner: Although it is highly plausible to assume (even in the light of support from one previous study; see Wood, Saltzberg, Neale, Stone, & Rachmiel, 1990) that ruminative responses are more likely to be observed for patients high in self-focus, all modes of coping investigated here appeared to be positively related to self-focus, regardless of their adaptive value. Patients scoring high in self-consciousness obviously do exhibit a much higher level of coping effort in general, rather than having particular coping preferences. It is then obvious that self-consciousness exerts indirect effects on coping effectiveness; however, it does this by increasing the frequency of adaptive *as well as* maladaptive responses. As a result, differences in dispositional self-focus proved to be "irrelevant" to adjustment. However, these results hold true only when one views the whole sample of cancer patients as a "homogeneous" group in terms of disease-related stress and threat, which is, of course, a curtailed perspective.

As our second set of analyses has shown, self-consciousness does make a difference in coping effectiveness, given that patients either suffer from multimorbidity or were diagnosed as suffering from lymph node metastases during primary cancer treatment. To summarize, it was shown that self-consciousness moderates the effect of ongoing harm stemming from *multimorbidity* on, for example, hopelessness, high self-focus (compared to low self-focus) resulting in higher levels of hopelessness under the condition of multimorbidity and in lower levels of hopelessness under the condition of no other complaints. In contrast, the opposite effect emerges under the condition of *lymph node invasion*: Hopelessness is enhanced by lymph node invasion in patients scoring *low* on self-consciousness while those scoring high seem to be rather unaffected. We frankly admit that this pattern of results is hard to understand at first glance, and it seems difficult to relate them to theoretical propositions. At a second glance, however, this appears to be less difficult. We propose the following post-hoc explanation: under conditions of heightened threat (i.e., diagnosis of lymph node invasion), patients high in self-focus use many more adaptive coping responses while simultaneously showing a decrease in maladaptive ones. If this assumption holds true, it should be proven by a differential correlational pattern between self-consciousness and coping behaviors, with or without lymph node invasion.

To summarize, when the various moderator analyses are taken into consideration, the question as to whether self-consciousness serves protective or risk-increasing functions can only be answered ambiguously, namely by claiming that "It depends!" Given the complexity of (potential) influences on coping with cancer and given that, to our knowledge, this is the first study addressing this type of question, we are, however, satisfied with what we have learned from our results. In future studies we will have to place more emphasis on the various circumstances under which patients have to cope. In addition, we will have to investigate how patients' generalized control expectancies and beliefs interact with self-focus (see Scheier & Carver, 1985) and result in different adaptational outcomes. Finally, it will be of particular importance to consider how cancer (or any other disease) is mentally represented in those who suffer from it. To talk about "self-focused attention" in patients suffering from chronic disease must, by no means, imply that "disease" is the salient aspect of the self which will automatically draw attention under conditions of high self-focus. As we can learn from the work reported by Nerenz and Leventhal (1983), one of the crucial issues here may be the way in which the representation of the disease is related to the underlying self-system, i.e., encapsulated within or isolated from the self. As a consequence, self-focus in cancer patients may have quite different meanings, dependent on whether "self" and "cancer" have become interchangeable mental concepts.

References

Abelson, R. P. (1981). Psychological status of the script concept. *American Psychologist, 36*, 715-729.

Beck, A. T., Weisman, A., Lester, D., & Trexler, L. (1974). The measurement of pessimism: The Hopelessness Scale. *Journal of Consulting and Clinical Psychology, 42*, 861-865.

Buss, D. M., & Scheier, M. F. (1976). Self-consciousness, self-awareness, and self-attribution. *Journal of Research in Personality, 10*, 463-468.

Byrne, D. (1964). Repression-sensitization as a dimension of personality. In B.A. Maher (Ed.), *Progress in experimental personality research* (Vol. 1, pp. 169-220). New York: Academic Press.

Carver, C. S., & Scheier, M. F. (1981). *Attention and self-regulation: A control-theory approach to human behavior*. New York: Springer-Verlag.

Carver, C. S., & Scheier, M. F. (1985). Self-consciousness, expectancies, and the coping process. In T. M. Field, P. M. McCrae, & N. Schneiderman (Eds.), *Stress and coping* (pp. 305-330). Hillsdale, NJ: Erlbaum.

Cohen, F. (1987). Measurement of coping. In S. V. Kasl & C. L. Cooper (Eds.), *Stress and health: Issues in research methodology* (pp. 283-305). Chichester, UK: Wiley.

Cohen, J. (1978). Partialed products are interactions; partialed powers are curve components. *Psychological Bulletin, 85*, 858-866.

Cohen, S., & Edwards, J. R. (1989). Personality characteristics as moderators of the relationship between stress and disorder. In R. W. J. Neufeld (Ed.), *Advances in the investigation of psychological stress* (pp. 235-283). New York: Wiley.

Duval, S., & Wicklund, R. A. (1972). *A theory of objective self-awareness*. Orlando, FL: Academic Press.

Fenigstein, A. (1984). Self-consciousness and the over-perception of self as a target. *Journal of Personality and Social Psychology, 47*, 860-870.

Fenigstein, A., Scheier, M. F., & Buss, A. H. (1975). Public and private self-consciousness: Assessment and theory. *Journal of Consulting and Clinical Psychology, 43*, 522-527.

Ferring, D. (1987). *Krankheit als Krise des Erwachsenenalters* [Illness as a crisis of adulthood]. Regensburg: Roderer.

Filipp, S.-H., Aymanns, P., & Braukmann, W. (1986). Coping with life events: When the self comes into play. In R. Schwarzer (Ed.), *Self-related cognitions in anxiety and motivation* (pp. 87-109). Hillsdale, NJ: Erlbaum.

Filipp, S.-H., Aymanns, P., & Klauer, T. (1983). *Formen der Auseinandersetzung mit lebensbedrohlichen körperlichen Erkrankungen als Prototypen kritischer Lebensereignisse: Eine Verlaufsstudie* [Modes of coping with life-threatening disease as a prototype of critical life events: A prospective study] (Forschungsberichte aus dem Projekt "Psychologie der Krankheitsbewältigung" Nr. 1). Trier: Universität Trier, Fachbereich I - Psychologie.

Filipp, S.-H., Ferring, D., Freudenberg, E., & Klauer, T. (1989). Affective-motivational correlates of modes of coping with chronic illness: Initial results of a longitudinal study with cancer patients. *The German Journal of Psychology, 13*, 72-73.

Filipp, S.-H., Ferring, D., & Klauer, T. (1991). *Zur Bedeutung habitueller Selbstaufmerksamkeit in Prozessen der Krankheitsbewältigung* [On the role of self-consciousness in processes of coping with illness] (Forschungsberichte aus dem Projekt "Psychologie der Krankheitsbewältigung" Nr. 31). Trier: Universität Trier, Fachbereich I - Psychologie.

Filipp, S.-H., & Freudenberg, E. (1989). *Der Fragebogen zur Erfassung dispositionaler Selbstaufmerksamkeit (SAM-Fragebogen)* [Questionnaire for the assessment of dispositional self-consciousness (SAM Questionaire)] . Göttingen: Hogrefe.

Filipp, S.-H., & Klauer, T. (1991). Subjective well-being in the face of critical life-events: the case of successful copers. In F. Strack, M. Argyle, & N. Schwarz (Eds.), *Subjective well-being. An interdisciplinary perspective* (pp. 213-234). Oxford, UK: Pergamon Press.

Filipp, S.-H., Klauer, T., Ferring, D., & Freudenberg, E. (1990). Coping with life-threatening disease: Some research problems and selected findings. In L. R. Schmidt, P. Schwenkmezger, J. Weinman, & S. Maes (Eds.), *Theoretical and applied aspects of health psychology* (pp. 385-398). Chur, Switzerland: Harwood.

Gibbons, F. X., Carver, C. S., Scheier, M. F., & Hormuth, S. E. (1979). Self-focused attention and the placebo effect: Fooling some of the people some of the time. *Journal of Experimental Social Psychology, 15*, 263-274.

Hormuth, S. E. (1990). *The ecology of the self. Relocation and self-concept change*. Cambridge, UK: Cambridge University Press.

Horowitz, M. J. (1980). Psychological responses to serious life-events. In V. Hamilton & D. M. Warburton (Eds.), *Human stress and cognition* (pp. 235-263). Chichester, UK: Wiley.

Hull, J. G., Young, R. D., & Jouriles, E. (1986). Applications of the self-awareness model of alcohol-consumption: Predicting patterns of use and abuse. *Journal of Personality and Social Psychology, 51*, 790-796.

Ingram, R. E. (1990). Self-focused attention in clinical disorders: Review and a conceptual model. *Psychological Bulletin, 107*, 156-176.

Janis, I. L. (1958). *Psychological stress*. New York: Wiley.

Klauer, T., Filipp, S.-H., & Ferring, D. (1990). Development of a questionnaire for the assessment of modes of coping with severe bodily disease ("FEKB"): Construction and results on reliability, stability, and validity. *The German Journal of Psychology, 14*, 154-155.

Krampen, G. (1979). Hoffnungslosigkeit bei stationären Patienten - ihre Messung durch einen Kurzfragebogen (H-Skala) [Hopelessness in inpatients - its assessment by questionnaire (H Scale)]. *Medizinische Psychologie, 5*, 39-49.

Kuhl, J. (1981). Motivational and functional helplessness: The moderating effect of state versus action orientation. *Journal of Personality and Social Psychology, 40*, 155-170.

Langer, E. J., & Imber, L. G. (1979). Mindlessness and susceptibility to the illusion of incompetence. *Journal of Personality and Social Psychology, 37*, 2014-2024.

Lazarus, R. S., & Folkman, S. (1984). *Stress, appraisal, and coping*. New York: Springer.

Montada, L. (in press). Attribution of responsibility for losses and perceived injustice. In L. Montada, S.-H. Filipp, & M. J. Lerner (Eds.), *Life crises and experiences of loss in adulthood*. Hillsdale, NJ: Erlbaum.

Montada, L., Filipp, S.-H., & Lerner, M. J. (Eds.). (In press). *Life crises and experiences of loss in adulthood*. Hillsdale, NJ: Erlbaum.

Mullen, B., & Suls, J. (1982). "Know thyself": Stressful life changes and the ameliorative effect of private self-consciousness. *Journal of Experimental Social Psychology, 18*, 43-55.

Nerenz, D. R., & Leventhal, H. (1983). Self-regulation theory in chronic illness. In T. G. Burish & L. A. Bradley (Eds.), *Coping with chronic disease* (pp. 13-37). New York: Academic Press.

Olbrisch, M. E., & Ziegler, S. W. (1982). Psychological adjustment to inflammatory bowel disease: Informational control and private self-consciousness. *Journal of Chronic Diseases, 55*, 573-580.

Pedhazur, E. J. (1982). *Multiple regression in behavioral research*. New York: Holt, Rinehart & Winston.

Perloff, L. S. (1987). Social comparison and illusions of invulnerability to negative life events. In C. R. Snyder & C. E. Ford (Eds.), *Coping with negative life events* (pp. 217-242). New York: Plenum.

Pyszczynski, T., & Greenberg, J. (1986). Evidence for a depressive self-focusing style. *Journal of Research in Personality, 20*, 95-106.

Pyszczynski, T., & Greenberg, J. (1987). The role of self-focused attention in the development, maintenance, and exacerbation of depression. In K. Yardley & T. Honess (Eds.), *Self and identity: Psychosocial perspectives* (pp. 307-322). New York: Wiley.

Rosenberg, M. (1965). *Society and the adolescent self-image*. Princeton, NJ: Princeton University Press.

Saunders, D. R. (1956). Moderator variables in prediction. *Educational and Psychological Measurement, 16*, 209-222.

Scheier, M. F., & Carver, C. S. (1977). Self-focused attention and the experience of emotion: Attraction, repulsion, elation, and depression. *Journal of Personality and Social Psychology, 35*, 625-636.

Scheier, M. F., & Carver, C. S. (1985). Optimism, coping, and health: Assessment and implications of generalized outcome expectancies. *Health Psychology, 4*, 219-247.

Seiffge-Krenke, I. (1984). Formen der Problembewältigung bei besonders belasteten Jugendlichen [Coping modes of highly stressed adolescents]. In E. Olbrich & E. Todt (Eds.), *Probleme des Jugendalters: Neuere Sichtweisen* (pp. 353-386). Berlin: Springer-Verlag.

Strack, S., Blaney, P. H., Ganellen, R. J., & Coyne, J. C. (1985). Pessimistic self-preoccupation, performance deficits, and depression. *Journal of Personality and Social Psychology, 49*, 1076-1085.

Suls, J., & Fletcher, B. (1985). Self-attention, life stress, and illness: A prospective study. *Psychosomatic Medicine, 47*, 469-481.

Taylor, S. E., & Brown, J. D. (1988). Illusion and well-being: A social psychological perspective on mental health. *Psychological Bulletin, 103*, 193-210.

Von Zerssen, D. (1976). *Die Befindlichkeitsskala* [Well-being Scale]. Weinheim: Beltz.

Wegner, D. M., & Giuliano, T. (1980). Arousal-induced attention to the self. *Journal of Personality and Social Psychology, 38*, 719-726.

Weinstein, N. D. (1982). Unrealistic optimism about susceptibility to health problems. *Journal of Behavioral Medicine, 5*, 441-460.

Wicklund, R. A., & Gollwitzer, P. M. (1987). The fallacy of the private-public self-focus distinction. *Journal of Personality, 55*, 491-523.

Wood, J. V., Saltzberg, J. A., & Goldsamt, L. A. (1990). Does affect induce self-focused attention? *Journal of Personality and Social Psychology, 58*, 899-908.

Wood, J. V., Saltzberg, J. A., Neale, J. M., Stone, A. A., & Rachmiel, T. B. (1990). Self-focused attention, coping responses, and distressed mood in everyday life. *Journal of Personality and Social Psychology, 58*, 1027-1036.

Wortman, C. B., & Conway, T. L. (1985). The role of social support in adaptation and recovery from physical illness. In S. Cohen & S. L. Syme (Eds.), *Social support and health* (pp. 281-302). Orlando, FL: Academic Press.

Chapter 13

Vigilant and Avoidant Coping in Two Patient Samples

Charles S. Carver and Michael F. Scheier

Introduction

What tactics do people use to cope with adversity and difficult circumstances in life? Which ways of coping are most effective in the short run and in the longer run? Do different tactics work better for different people? These questions (and others like them) pose a conceptual and empirical puzzle that can be approached from a variety of different angles, as is reflected in the diversity among the chapters in this volume.

Our contribution to the central issue underlying this volume - the effects of vigilance and avoidance in coping with aversiveness - has somewhat unusual origins. The line of thought that led eventually to our research began not from an interest in vigilance and avoidance as processing styles, or even an interest in coping per se. Rather, we began with an interest in the structure of behavior, an interest that stemmed in part from an effort to understand the divergent consequences of self-focused attention (e.g., Carver & Scheier, 1981, 1983, 1986). Our interest in broad principles of behavioral self-regulation led us to a particular view on the nature of stress and coping. Some of the research prompted by that view on coping, in turn, provides information on the question that underlies this volume.

We begin this chapter by sketching the conceptual background to our work, and the perspective this background gives us on the nature of coping. Then we turn to a brief description of two studies we have recently conducted in which the correlates of different coping responses were examined. We close the chapter with a few comments concerning research tactics used in examining the nature of vigilant and avoidant coping.

Background: Self-Regulation and Coping

Our view on behavior begins with the assumption that behavior is goal directed, an assumption that characterizes many contemporary theories (e.g., Elliott &

Preparation of this chapter was facilitated by NSF grants BNS90-11653 and BNS90-10425 and American Cancer Society grant PBR-56.

Dweck, 1988; Emmons, 1986; Klinger, 1977, 1987; Little, 1983; Pervin, 1983, 1989). People have long-term and short-term goals, narrow and broad goals, plans for their attainment (strings of subgoals), and strategies to use in implementing the plans. In this view on behavior, people's goals give form to their lives.

We believe that when people are acting in pursuit of their goals, their self-regulatory efforts take the form of a hierarchy of feedback loops. People monitor their actions, periodically assess whether the actions are producing the intended results, and make adjustment in their actions (as necessary) to remedy any discrepancy sensed between the two values (Carver & Scheier, 1981, 1990a). In this way behavior proceeds smoothly in the direction of the intended result, and the person's goals are realized in his or her actions. Higher order goals are attained through a continuing process of attaining the lower goals that contribute to them (cf. Vallacher & Wegner, 1987).

Sometimes, however, things do not go as smoothly as this. Sometimes people encounter difficulties in their efforts to move toward their goals. The difficulty can derive from any of several sources. External impediments can disrupt behavior, and so can internal doubts or conflicts. Another source of difficulty is the perception that the effort to move toward one goal is creating an undesired discrepancy with respect to another important goal (cf. Emmons & King, 1988; Van Hook & Higgins, 1988).

We have argued that when movement toward desired goals is sufficiently difficult, the person interrupts his or her current action (cf. Mandler, 1984; Mandler & Watson, 1966; Simon, 1967) and assesses the likelihood of being able to complete the intended behavior successfully. This usually is an implicit assessment and is not necessarily made in probabilistic terms. More commonly it is felt subjectively as a sense of confidence versus doubt.

We assume that what follows from this assessment process depends critically on this dimension of confidence versus doubt (see Figure 13.1). People whose confidence is above some quasi-threshold will continue to engage their efforts toward taking steps in the direction of the goal they are trying to attain. People whose confidence is lower - who are doubtful about eventual success - experience a conflicting impulse to withdraw.[1] In Klinger's (1975) phrase, commitment to the incentive gives way to disengagement from it. This disengagement impulse can be expressed overtly, by leaving the field of action. It can be displayed as a reduction in effort. It can also be displayed less overtly, in off-task thinking or daydreaming. Since several of these manifestations interfere with task performance, doubtful people often display performance impairments.

---

[1] We should note a distinction between withdrawal of effort at goal attainment and the social withdrawal described by Repetti (1989) in an examination of air traffic controllers. An air traffic controller sufficiently doubtful about performing adequately under conditions of high volume and poor visibility may withdraw goal directed effort while on task. This response is what we are focusing on here. A controller who has been burdened by these conditions (not necessarily to the point of impaired effort) and needs time to recover from the experience may withdraw *from an off-task activity* such as social interaction. This response, which is one focus of Repetti's work, is quite different both in its origins and in its consequences, and is outside the scope of our present discussion.

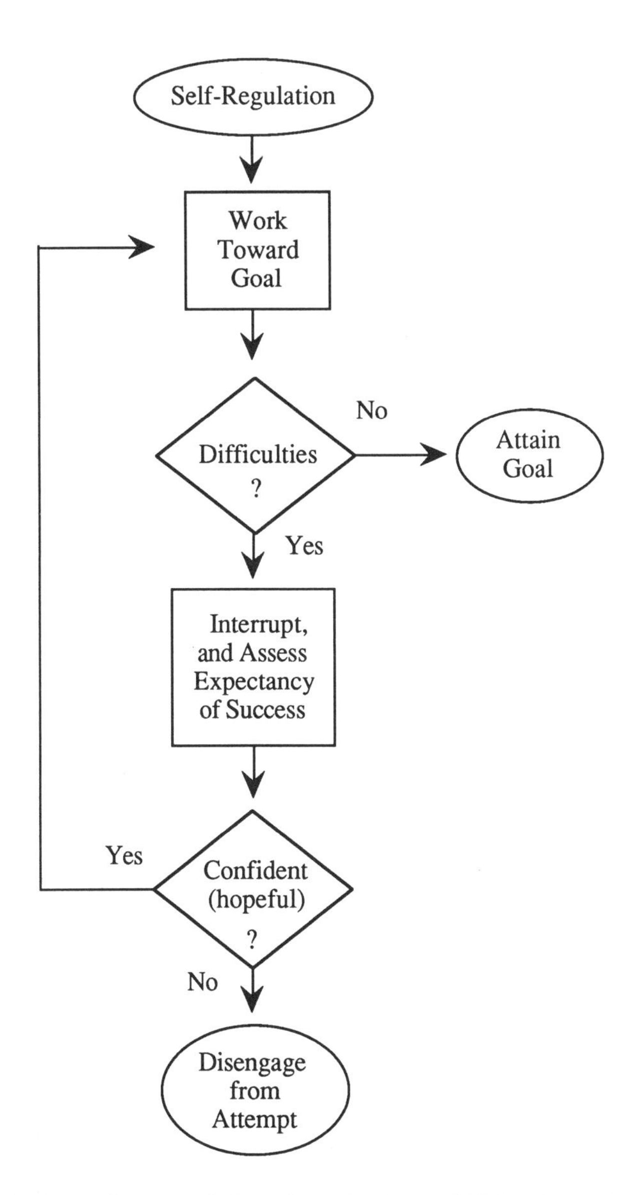

Figure 13.1. Flow diagram of three behavioral possibilities. Sometimes behavior proceeds unimpeded, leading to attainment of the desired goal. Sometimes difficulties of one or another type cause behavior to be interrupted and the person to evaluate (explicitly or implicitly) the chances of successful goal attainment. Confidence leads to further effort; sufficient doubt leads to a tendency to disengage.

The idea that confidence versus doubt plays an important role in determining people's behavior is an idea that has been used widely in contemporary models of behavior (e.g., Bandura, 1986; Kanfer & Hagerman, 1985; Kirsch, 1990; Klinger, 1975; Mischel, 1973; Seligman, 1975), though there are several variations in emphasis from theory to theory (see Carver & Scheier, 1990a). As an example of these variations, we have tended to view behavioral responses to adversity as forming a rough dichotomy - that is, striving vs. giving up (see also Klinger, 1975; Kukla, 1972; Wortman & Brehm, 1975). This dichotomous quality among behaviors is not as obvious in every theory that incorporates expectancy assumptions. Nevertheless, a conceptual disjunction between continued striving and abandoning the struggle seems to be inherent in all such theories.

The broad theme of confidence versus doubt (and the corresponding behavioral responses) is reflected in a wide range of specific constructs such as helplessness, optimism, and pessimism (to name only a few). Optimism, for example, is a case in which a person is confident not just about one aspect of life, but about one's personal future more generally, whereas pessimism is a broad sense of doubt about one's personal future (Scheier & Carver, 1985, 1987). Similar qualities of confidence and doubt play a role in a variety of other constructs, such as learned helplessness (Seligman, 1975), learned resourcefulness (Rosenbaum, 1990), coherence (Antonovsky, 1987), and self-esteem (Brockner, 1988; Rosenberg, 1979).

A Closer Look at Effort and Disengagement

Discussions of confidence and doubt often focus on task performance, and they tend to emphasize the debilitating effect of doubt. It is worth noting, though, that continued effort and giving up are both adaptive aspects of behavior - when they occur in the right circumstances. Continued effort is adaptive in any situation where continued effort will produce the desired outcome (assuming, of course, that this effort does not create a debilitating drain on one's resources). In such cases, giving up prematurely works against the person. By the criterion of successful goal attainment, at least, disengaging in such a situation is dysfunctional.

There are also cases, however, in which disengagement is the more adaptive response. In situations where continued effort is futile, the sooner the person disengages from pursuit of the goal the better. Giving up in such a case permits the person to take up an alternative goal and to move forward with life. This is true whether the alternative goal is a lower aspiration in the same domain or a new goal in a new domain altogether. Thus, optimal functioning across a lifetime (or even a day) requires that the person sometimes stay locked onto goals and sometimes abandon them.

Abandoning a goal is not always easy to do, however, even given the impulse to do so. There are times when a person wants to give up but can not. Sometimes this is because the goal in question is deeply connected to the person's implicit definition of self. Disengagement from such a goal thus represents disengagement from oneself. As an example, consider the person who dreams of a career as a physician, but who is unable to gain admission to medical school. This person may experience a strong impulse to stop applying. Expressing that impulse, however, means living with a large and permanent discrepancy with respect to an important goal of the self. This makes it difficult to disengage from the behavioral goal (getting into school), despite the impulse to do so.

A situation that is structurally similar to this one is posed by serious illness (see also Filipp, Klauer, & Ferring, this volume). The goal (or set of goals) that is threatened in this case is continuation of one's life as a healthy human being, and all the activities thereby implied. The diagnosis of a life-threatening illness implies that continuing one's life on its present course may be impossible, prompting a giving-up response with respect to that goal. Giving up in this case, however, means giving up on one's life. To manifest such a response would have very adverse consequences and thus is extremely difficult to do.

To feel that it is impossible to continue to move toward a goal to which you remain commited is a particularly difficult situation psychologically (cf. Pyszczynski & Greenberg, 1987). In such cases the disengagement response tears at the very fabric of the self. We have argued, for reasons that are more complex than need be addressed here, that this combination of circumstances yields a high degree of emotional distress (Carver & Scheier, 1990a, 1990b).

Coping as Self-Regulation

The viewpoint on behavior sketched out in the preceding sections is the view we bring to the topic of stress and coping. This view on self-regulation appears compatible with the approach to stress and coping taken by Richard Lazarus and his colleagues (e.g., Lazarus, 1966; Lazarus & Folkman, 1984), though there are some differences in emphasis. Discussions of stress tend to emphasize the occurrence of harmful or unpleasant events (actual or impending), whereas models of self-regulation tend to focus more on issues concerning the impending non-occurrence of positive events (Carver, Scheier, & Pozo, in press). Thus, a person can be threatened by sudden movement in a dark alley, the sound of a tornado, or the diagnosis of a major illness, but the person can also be threatened by doubt about receiving a sought-after promotion. This difference in emphasis should not obscure the fact that the approaches share a concern with how people respond to adversity or difficulty.

Another link between models concerns the role of expectancies. The Lazarus model holds that people do not always respond automatically to the perception of threat, but often weigh options and consider the consequences of responding in various ways before responding. The choice of coping response is based partly on judgments about its likely effectiveness. The broader models of behavior suggest further that expectancies influence the extent to which the person continues to engage at all in efforts to overcome the threat.

We believe that thinking in terms of general self-regulatory principles when analyzing stress brings several points to mind that would not otherwise be as apparent. First, the goal-based approach to behavior suggests that many of the stressors that people experience are stressful precisely because they threaten the attainment - or continued attainment - of important goals in the person's life. The more goals that are threatened, and the more central those goals are to the overall sense of self and continuation of the person's activities, the more stressful is the experience (cf. Millar, Tesser, & Millar, 1988).

A second set of issues concerns the effect of confidence versus doubt regarding the attainment of those goals. To the extent the stressful transaction yields doubt, the person can be expected to display manifestations of the disengagement response. This implies that it is desirable for research on coping to collect data concerning responses that reflect disengagement from goals with which the stressor is interfering. Although one might argue that such responses do not represent "coping" per se, such responses constitute an important part of the overall picture of behavioral self-regulation. Another, more specific implication of this line of thought is that when people experience the disengagement impulse but cannot express it fully, the result should be an especially high level of distress.

Vigilance and Avoidance

The ideas described thus far form a broad background to our view of stress and the coping process. Let us now consider more explicitly vigilance and avoidance as coping tactics. As described in greater detail elsewhere (e.g., Krohne, 1989, and Chapter 2 in this volume; Mathews, this volume; Miller, 1990; see also Miller, Combs, & Kruus in this volume; Slangen, Kleemann, & Krohne, this volume), most analyses of vigilance and avoidance focus on two points. The first concerns the extent to which people actively direct attention toward threat-relevant aspects of a situation. Presumably engaging in this *vigilance* response renders the situation more predictable, even if the threat is something for which no active coping is possible. The second point of focus concerns the extent to which people divert attention from threat-relevant aspects of the situation. This *avoidance* response is presumably aimed at reducing the emotional impact of the threat.

These two tendencies can be described as momentary differences in deployment of attention, as we have just done, and they can also be conceptualized as dispositional preferences. When assessed as dispositions, the two tendencies have been found to be relatively independent of one another (Krohne, 1989), which permits examination of the effects of the two tendencies both separately and in interaction with each other.

The effects of vigilance and avoidance have not been an explicit focus of our own research. There are, however, two aspects of our research that do seem to bear on these cognitive responses to threat. First, in two recent studies involving surgical patients, we asked subjects a series of questions about their cognitive responses to the situations they were confronting. Several of these questions asked subjects to indicate the extent to which they had been thinking about certain topics, some of which constituted threatening aspects of their situation. Other questions asked subjects to indicate the extent to which they had been making an effort *not* to think about the same topics. These two sets of questions would seem to tap situational vigilance and avoidance, respectively.

The second aspect of this research that is relevant to a discussion of vigilance and avoidance stems from our attempt to measure coping strategies more broadly (Carver, Scheier, & Weintraub, 1989). The second study that is described below incorporated a series of scales devised to measure several aspects of coping. We had not conceptualized these facets of coping in terms of vigilance and avoidance, but one of the scales seems quite comparable in some ways to avoidance as an attentional response. This scale assesses the extent to which subjects engaged in activities intended to create a *mental disengagement* from the threat. Items measuring mental disengagement include "Daydreaming about things other than this," and "Going to movies, watching TV, or reading, to think about it less," (where "it" refers to the stressful event). Another scale that may also be relevant to this discussion assesses conscious efforts at *denial* (which presumably also reflects an avoidance response). Items measuring denial include "Refusing to believe that it has happened," and "Acting as though it hasn't even happened."

One further difference should also be noted between our measures in these studies and the measures used by Krohne and his colleagues and other researchers (e.g., Miller, 1987). In our studies we assessed the extent to which subjects were using a given response during a specific period of time in the course of a stressful transaction. Other than the scales just mentioned, the cognitive tendencies we assessed were also extremely concrete and specific (for a similar approach see also Slangen et al., this volume). This differs somewhat from the strategies used by other researchers. We will consider the possible implications of this difference later on in the chapter.

With this discussion as background, then, let us consider the research projects. In the following sections we describe aspects of two studies, the subjects of which were people facing serious threats to their health. One study examined the adjustment of men undergoing coronary artery bypass surgery (CABS). The other study examined the adjustment of women undergoing surgery for breast cancer (see also Filipp et al., this volume). Both studies assessed aspects of psychological well being as an outcome; the CABS study also incorporated physiological and behavioral measures.[2]

---

[2] The two studies described here actually focused most closely on aspects of coping other than those now under discussion. In particular, both studies concern differences between optimists and pessimists in the manner and success with which they deal with the health crisis they are undergoing. For greater detail on the rationale behind that aspect of the research, see Scheier et al. (1989).

Coronary Artery Bypass Surgery

Subjects in the CABS study were 51 men who were undergoing first-time nonemergency bypass surgery (see Scheier et al., 1989, for greater detail on the sample and the procedure). Each subject was interviewed on the day prior to surgery, again six to eight days after surgery, and again six months later. Medical data were gathered at baseline and at several points during the recovery process; a record of surgical complications at six weeks postsurgery was also obtained.

The initial interview included a measure of negative mood, or distress, and a set of items intended to provide insight into the cognitive strategies subjects were using to cope with the upcoming surgery and its aftermath. The postsurgical interview repeated the mood measures and the items on coping. Also assessed at this stage was the subject's rate of recovery, both in terms of behavioral milestones and in terms of evaluations made by the cardiac rehabilitation staff. These evaluations included ratings of the patient's pace of recovery compared to other CABS patients, the patient's morale, and the patient's prognosis for normalizing his life after leaving the hospital. Finally, at six months postsurgery, subjects reported on their quality of life, and on the extent and pace with which their life's activities had returned to normal.

The self-report items of greatest interest at present are items that suggest either a vigilance or an avoidance response. Presurgically, subjects were asked to indicate the extent to which they were thinking about (a) their physical symptoms, (b) their negative emotions, and (c) the events of the operation and hospitalization period. Subjects also reported the frequency with which they had requested information from the medical staff about their operation and recovery. Responses to these items were taken as indicators of vigilance across these domains. As measures of presurgical avoidance in these same domains, subjects were also asked to indicate the extent to which they had been trying *not* to think about these things.

The same vigilance and avoidance questions were asked again six to eight days postsurgically, with two exceptions. First, rather than ask how much subjects were thinking (and trying not to think) about the events of the operation, we asked how much they were thinking (and trying not to think) about their period of recovery in the months ahead. Second, the item dealing with information search was altered to embrace the next several months following discharge (rather than the next few days of recovery and hospitalization).

We describe findings pertaining to vigilance first, and then turn to avoidance. Within each of these broad sections, implications for psychological well-being are considered first, then other implications.[3]

[3] We might note at the outset that the use of vigilance and avoidance strategies were largely unrelated to indices of presurgical physical health in this study. Thus it is difficult to account for results pertaining to these two classes of variables in terms of differential physical health.

Vigilance

The first question to ask concerns the extent to which responses to the vigilance items covaried. Stated differently, if a patient was vigilant in one domain, was he also likely to be vigilant in other domains? The answer here seems largely to be "no." Among presurgery items, three significant associations arose - between thinking about emotions and thinking about the operation, between thinking about emotions and requesting information about the operation, and between thinking about the operation and requesting information about the operation - but the correlations were all modest (average r = .33). The other correlations among items were considerably weaker (average r = .15).

The pattern of associations among items was even weaker postsurgically, with one exception: thinking about physical symptoms and thinking about emotions were strongly associated (.62). The average among the remaining correlations was .06. Nor were the vigilance items very highly correlated from pre- to postsurgery (the average r was .20). Taken together, these data suggest a considerable degree of selectivity in terms of where patients focused their vigilance, both at a given time and across time. Given that the measures pertaining to vigilance do not appear to have a clear common core, it seems necessary to consider them separately in subsequent analyses.[4]

Psychological well-being

Several associations emerged between vigilance and negative mood or distress. Presurgically, there was a strong positive correlation (.67) between thinking about emotions and distress. The correlation between thinking about the operation and distress was also significant, but weaker (.36). Thinking about physical symptoms and requesting information were unrelated to presurgical distress.

Postsurgically, the concurrent association between thinking about emotions and distress was again strong (.62). An association also emerged between thinking about physical symptoms and distress (.40). In contrast, requesting information about the recovery period to come was inversely associated with postsurgical distress (-.30). That is, the patients who were requesting information postsurgically were the ones lowest in distress. Postsurgical thinking about future recovery was also negatively related to postsurgical distress, albeit only marginally so (-.26).

The pattern reflected in patients' self-reports of postsurgical distress was echoed in ratings the cardiac rehabilitation staff made of patient morale (just prior to discharge). That is, postsurgical thinking about physical symptoms and thinking about emotions were inversely related to staff ratings of morale (-.30 and -.47, respectively), whereas postsurgical thinking about the recovery period tended to be positively associated with staff ratings of morale (.27).

[4] It might be argued that the low correlations among these items are simply a reflection of measurement unreliability. This is a possibility we cannot discount. Readers will have to evaluate this issue for themselves and temper their inferences from the data accordingly.

The fact that distress was measured both before and after surgery made it possible to conduct prospective analyses to see whether presurgical vigilance predicted *post*surgical distress, after controlling for presurgical distress. Distress ratings from presurgery to postsurgery were only modestly correlated in this study (.31), which should permit any prospective association to emerge relatively easily, but none did. Prospective analyses were also conducted to determine whether presurgical distress predicted postsurgical vigilance. One such effect emerged: distress before surgery was a significant predictor of postsurgical thinking about symptoms (.50).

We turn now to data collected six months postsurgery. Two measures of presurgical vigilance - thinking about physical symptoms and thinking about emotions - correlated inversely with quality of life at six months (-.27 and -.47, respectively). With regard to postsurgical measures, only one association emerged as significant. People who sought out more information during the immediate postsurgical period reported a higher quality of life six months later (.52).

Physical well-being

Several associations emerged between vigilance and reports of physical well-being. First, thinking about emotions before surgery was related to less satisfaction with rate of recovery during the immediate postoperative period (-.39), to less satisfaction with improvement at six months (-.55), to less satisfaction with overall physical health at six months (-.43), and to less of a belief at six months that the operation had improved their health (-.55).

A second set of findings related to the tendency to seek out information before the operation. People who sought information before surgery were more likely to be rated by members of the cardiac rehabilitation unit as having a poor prognosis for rate of normalizing their lives (.29). Indeed, these patients did take longer to normalize their lives across several domains (.34), including returning to sexual activities (.39).

Postsurgical vigilance items were also related to several recovery variables (indeed, were generally better predictors than presurgical vigilance). In general, thinking about symptoms and thinking about emotions were tied to adverse effects on recovery. In contrast, thinking about the recovery period after leaving the hospital and requesting information about this period tended to have more positive effects.

Consider first the adverse effects. People who reported thinking about physical symptoms postsurgically reported at the 6-month follow-up taking longer to return to work full-time (.39) and less satisfaction with their physical health (-.30). Similarly, people who reported thinking about their emotions postsurgically were less satisfied with their rate of recovery in the immediate postoperative period (-.47) and more likely to say that their recovery rate during this time was not matching their expectations (-.49). This felt dissatisfaction appeared to have some basis in fact. People who spent a lot of time thinking about their emotions were slower to begin walking for prolonged periods around their hospital rooms (.36) and were hospitalized longer (.34). They were rated by the rehabilitation staff as slower in their recovery than other patients (-.29) and as having a poorer prognosis for rapid normalization of their life activities (-.31). It also took them longer to return to work full-time after discharge (.34).

In contrast to these effects, postsurgical thinking about the recovery period to come was associated with positive outcomes. People showing this tendency reported more satisfaction with their rate of recovery during the immediate postoperative period (.36) and believed that they were recovering faster than other patients. These positive reports also had some basis in fact. These people began walking around their rooms sooner after surgery, both for brief periods (-.29) and for prolonged periods (-.41). By the 6-month follow-up, they were more likely to have resumed vigorous physical exercise (.29). Patients who requested information about the recovery period while in the hospital were also more likely to report that their operation had improved their health by the 6-month follow-up (.29) and to report having been free of chest pain for the 4-month period preceding the follow-up.

To summarize, the measures that we are treating here as indices of vigilance were associated with concurrent distress, both before surgery and afterward, though there were also variations among the items. Vigilance also was related to a wide variety of other outcome measures, both postsurgery and at the 6-month follow-up, with two diverging sets of effects. Focusing on emotions and symptoms was linked to adverse consequences. In contrast, focusing postsurgically on the events of the upcoming recovery period was associated with positive outcomes. Quite obviously there is an important difference between these two contents, or domains, of attention.

Avoidance

Measures of presurgical avoidance were more highly correlated than were the measures of vigilance (averaging .43). This relative homogeneity diminished, however, postsurgery. The strongest correlation was between not thinking about physical symptoms and not thinking about emotions (.33), but trying not to think about the events of the recovery period diverged from these two items (correlating with them an average of .13). Correlations between presurgical and postsurgical avoidance items were also low (averaging .20). Taken together, these findings suggest that patients were not avoiding *in general*, but were avoiding very specific thought contents, which differed from one measurement to the other. Once again, then, the measures had to be treated separately in subsequent analyses.

Psychological well-being

Each aspect of presurgical avoidance correlated highly with presurgical distress (the average r was .43). Correlations between aspects of postsurgical avoidance and postsurgical distress were quite small, however (the average *r* was only .14). Further, there was little association between presurgical avoidance and postsurgical distress (the average *r* was .23). Given these findings, it should come as no surprise that avoidance failed to predict changes in distress prospectively. Nor did distress predict avoidance prospectively. In sum, except for the associations between presurgical avoidance and presurgical distress, there was little evidence that use of avoidance tactics covaried much with subjective distress.

Nor was the impact of avoidance much more consistent on other aspects of psychological well-being, though several potentially important associations did emerge. Trying not to think about emotions presurgically and postsurgically were both related to staff ratings of low morale prior to discharge (-.29 and -.39). Several items also predicted self-reports of poorer quality of life six months later: trying not to think about emotions presurgically (-.45), trying not to think about physical symptoms presurgically (-.43), and trying not to think about symptoms postsurgically (-.38).

Physical well-being

When physical well-being is considered, a very different pattern of effects appears. That is, avoidance was related in important and pervasive ways to the physical health of the patients and their recovery over time. Patients who actively tried to not think about symptoms or emotions presurgically reported doing worse than expected in their recovery during the immediate postoperative period (-.31 and -.46, respectively); they had a greater number of surgical complications six weeks postoperatively (.27 and .35, respectively); and they took longer to return to fulltime work following discharge (.28 and .38, respectively).

Trying not to think about emotions presurgically was also linked to several other effects: being more likely to have applied for disability (.36) and less likely to have begun vigorous exercise (-.29) by the 6-month follow-up; being less likely to have resumed normal life activities by the 6-month follow-up (-.33); feeling less improvement as a result of the surgery by the 6-month follow-up (-.49); and being less likely to report that the surgery had improved overall health (-.47). These negative outcomes seem to have been anticipated by the cardiac rehabilitation staff just prior to discharge, who gave these patients a poorer prognosis with respect to the rate at which they expected their lives to normalize (-.29).

Patients who tried not to think about their negative emotions *post*surgically were less likely to have returned to full-time employment by the 6-month follow-up (.35) and were less likely to have enrolled in a cardiac rehabilitation program (.38). These patients were also rated by the rehabilitation staff as recovering more slowly than other patients (-.31) and as having a poorer prognosis for normalizing their life activities (-.32). On the other hand, they were also less likely to report significant chest pain during the four months preceding the follow-up (.29).

Trying to avoid thinking about the recovery period postsurgically yielded mixed effects. On the negative side, people who did this tended to be less likely to enter a cardiac rehabilitation program (.27). On the positive side, they were quicker to attain several milestones of recovery during the first few postoperative days. That is, people who tried not to think about the recovery period ahead were faster to begin sitting up in their beds (-.39), to begin sitting without assistance in a chair (-.41), and to start walking around the rooms for brief intervals (-.29) than those who were not trying to block out thoughts of the recovery period. There was also an indication that trying not to think about emotions aided recovery during this time, as well, in that this variable also predicted shorter times to begin sitting up in bed (-.29).

To summarize the effects of avoidance, the data were generally consistent in indicating that trying to suppress thoughts about symptoms and especially emotions was linked to adverse outcomes. The outcomes in question were less likely to involve subjective distress, however, than other indices, including poor quality of life, slowness to resume activities, and doubt that the surgery had been beneficial. As was true of vigilance, there was a great difference between the correlates of trying not to think about emotions and the correlates of trying not to think about the upcoming recovery period. Trying to suppress thoughts of recovery during the months ahead was, in general, associated with positive effects, all of which had to do with faster improvement in the week postsurgery. This pattern hints that efforts to suppress thoughts of the more extended recovery period may reflect an effort to focus more fully on the present, in order to concentrate on immediate steps toward recovery. If so, it would further suggest that this item may not have constituted a measure of avoidance in the sense that we have been using that word thus far (i.e., avoidance of threatening cues).

Combinations of Vigilance and Avoidance

Correlations between thinking items (vigilance) and the corresponding trying-not-to-think items (avoidance) were quite strong before surgery (averaging .55). The comparable correlations were considerably lower after surgery, however (averaging .20). Wherever the correlations were not prohibitively high, we proceeded to treat the two tendencies as distinct from each other and to consider their simultaneous effects, in two different ways. First, we set about creating situational versions of the four combinations of vigilance and avoidance portrayed in Krohne's (1989) model. We did this by dividing subjects by median split into highs and lows with respect to one facet of vigilance (e.g., thinking about symptoms) and the corresponding avoidance (trying not to think about symptoms). These two variables then were used as separate factors in analyses of variance, predicting various dependent measures. These analyses yielded no evidence of meaningful interaction between vigilance and avoidance.[5]

We also conducted regression analyses in which vigilance and avoidance items were permitted to enter separately, to determine whether vigilance and avoidance tendencies made separate contributions to outcomes. These analyses (which were limited to cases where univariate tests had found effects for both vigilance and avoidance) revealed one such instance. Thinking about emotions after surgery and trying not to think about emotions made distinct contributions to predicting postsurgical staff ratings of morale (βs = .40 and .28, respectively), together accounting for 16% of the variance.

Breast Cancer Surgery

The second study in which we have been involved looks at the adjustment process among a group of early-stage breast cancer patients. This study (Pozo et al., 1990) is still in progress as of this writing. The associations outlined here are those that emerged from preliminary analyses of a nearly final sample of 65 women. Subjects are women who have been diagnosed with Stage I or Stage II breast cancer. A diagnosis of Stage I or Stage II implies a relatively good prognosis, though the cancer clearly poses a threat to future health and survival. In addition, the remedy for the disease is a disfiguring surgical procedure, which is often followed by adjuvant therapy that has a variety of unpleasant side effects. Thus, this experience incorporates many sources of potential distress.

Patients in this study are first interviewed at the time of diagnosis. They are interviewed again on the day before surgery, and again seven to ten days after surgery. Follow-up interviews are conducted three months later. All interviews beyond the initial one include a measure of negative mood, or distress, which is the primary outcome variable in these analyses. Subjects also complete an instrument called the COPE (Carver et al., 1989) at these measurement points. The COPE asks respondents to indicate the extent to which they have been engaging in each of a series of behavioral or cognitive tactics as a way of dealing with the stresses surrounding (in this case) the experience of diagnosis and surgery. At presurgery the patient indicates how much she used each tactic since learning she would need surgery, at postsurgery she refers to the time since surgery, and at follow-up she reports on the prior month. The scales of greatest interest at present are those assessing mental disengagement and denial.

In the presurgery and postsurgery interviews, subjects are also asked to respond to attentional items similar to those used in the CABS study described earlier. Subjects indicate the extent to which they have been thinking about their physical symptoms, their emotions, and (presurgery only) the events of the

[5] The procedure involved a relatively large number of tests, a few of which did yield statistically significant interactions. However, the rate of occurrence of significant effects was not quite at the level of chance, and those that did occur were inconsistent in their form, suggesting that the effects were random.

operation and recovery room. Subjects also indicate the extent to which they have been trying *not* to think about each of these things. Subjects are also asked to indicate the extent to which they have asked the doctors and nurses (presurgery) for information about the operation and what will be involved in recovery, and (postsurgery) for information about the regimen they will be following in the months ahead.

Vigilance

As in the CABS study, correlations revealed considerable divergence among the indices of vigilance. Thinking about symptoms correlated moderately strongly with thinking about emotions (.45 before surgery, .42 after surgery), but presurgery thoughts about the upcoming operation were less related to these two measures (averaging .33). Seeking of information from nurses and doctors was poorly correlated with any thought measure before surgery (averaging .11), but the associations increased a bit after surgery (averaging .30). The measures did not stay especially stable from pre- to postsurgery: thoughts about symptoms and emotions correlated at about .40 from pre to post, but information seeking correlated only .28. Since vigilance again did not have a clear common core, the items were considered separately in subsequent analyses.

Most measures of presurgery vigilance correlated moderately strongly with concurrent distress. Thoughts about symptoms, emotions, and the events of the operation correlated an average of just over .50 with presurgical distress. Presurgery requests for information, however, were unrelated to presurgery distress. The postsurgery measures of vigilance correlated with concurrent distress and physical pain at about the same level as the presurgery associations (average .50). In contrast to the presurgical data, however, postsurgery seeking of information about the recovery period was positively associated with both postsurgical distress (.38) and pain (.43).

We also tested for prospective effects, using vigilance at one time point as a predictor of distress at the subsequent measurement, partialling out the earlier distress level. Prospective tests in this data set were hampered, however, by high correlations between distress levels from one measurement to the next (about .80, in each case). Given this, partialling out the association of the earlier distress level left relatively little variability to be accounted for by the other predictor variable. Thus, although presurgery thoughts related to later distress, the association disappeared when the initial relation between thoughts and distress was controlled for. Similarly, prospective effects for the measures of vigilance at postsurgery were absent in all but one case. Postsurgery seeking of information about the recovery period remained a significant predictor of higher levels of follow-up distress, even after controlling for postsurgical distress (.34).

Finally, we examined the extent to which vigilant attentional strategies themselves were influenced prospectively by the experience of distress. These analyses revealed that distress before surgery prospectively predicted both vigilance about one's emotional reactions during the postsurgery period (.32) and information seeking postsurgery (.36).

In summary, the self-reports that we are treating here as indices of vigilance were associated with high levels of concurrent distress (and postsurgical pain). Initial distress was also a prospective predictor of greater degrees of two measures of subsequent vigilance. One of these measures of subsequent vigilance (information seeking) was itself a prospective predictor of greater amounts of distress at follow-up (though this was the only instance of vigilance predicting distress prospectively). These data suggest a cycle in which initial distress led to more vigilance postsurgery, which in turn resulted in higher distress later on.

Avoidance

There was much greater consistency among the indices of avoidance than among the indices of vigilance, particularly before surgery. The average correlation among reports of trying not to think about symptoms, emotions, and the upcoming operation was .73. The associations between these items and the COPE scales measuring mental disengagement and denial were lower, however (averaging .30). The latter two scales also correlated poorly with each other before surgery (.17). At postsurgery, trying not to think about emotions remained fairly highly correlated with trying not to think about symptoms (.55) and was now more strongly related to denial (.48). The other associations were minimal, however. None of these indices was especially stable across these two measurement points (averaging .30).

Correlations between avoidance and distress before surgery were positive but generally lower than the correlations between vigilance and distress. The correlations between trying-not-to-think items and distress averaged .29, and a comparable correlation emerged for the mental disengagement scale. The denial scale correlated much more strongly with distress, however (.58). Postsurgical avoidance of symptoms and feelings correlated with concurrent distress at roughly the same level as at presurgery (average .33). Denial was strongly related to distress postsurgery (.48), but mental disengagement was unrelated to postsurgical distress.

As was true of vigilance measures, prospective prediction from avoidance to later distress did not yield a great deal of information. The presurgery trying-not-to-think items all related to postsurgical distress, but only one item - trying not to think about symptoms - remained tied to postsurgical distress after controlling for presurgery distress (.25). Presurgery denial also related to later distress, but these associations disappeared when controlling for presurgery distress. Prospective prediction of distress at the 3-month follow-up from avoidance at postsurgery yielded no significant effect.

Prospective prediction of avoidant responses from emotional distress yielded three significant effects. Distress presurgery was related to reports of denial postsurgery after controlling for denial presurgery (.29), and also to trying not to think about emotions postsurgery after controlling for presurgery suppression of the same thoughts (.31). This latter finding parallels a finding noted earlier for the comparable vigilance item. Thus, distress presurgery seems to have induced both a tendency to think about emotions and a tendency to suppress thoughts about emotions after surgery. These two tendencies seem to have occurred in different sets of women, though, since the two postsurgery measures were not highly correlated with each other (.26). Finally, distress postsurgery predicted mental disengagement at 3-month follow-up, after controlling for mental disengagement postsurgery.

In summary, the self-report indices of avoidance were positively associated with concurrent distress (and postsurgical pain), though generally less strongly than the indices of vigilance. One index of vigilance was a prospective predictor of greater amounts of subsequent distress, and distress was also a prospective predictor of three aspects of avoidance, two at postsurgery and one at follow-up.

Combinations of Vigilance and Avoidance

Correlations between thinking items (vigilance) and the corresponding trying-not-to-think items (avoidance) were not strong, either before surgery (averaging .20) or after surgery (averaging .25). This permitted us again to treat the two tendencies as distinct from each other, and to consider their simultaneous effects, in the same ways as in the CABS study. First, we set about creating situational versions of the four combinations of vigilance and avoidance portrayed in Krohne's (1989) model of dispositional tendencies. We did this by dividing subjects by median split into highs and lows with respect to one facet of vigilance (e.g., thinking about the upcoming operation) and the corresponding avoidance (trying not to think about the upcoming operation). These two variables then were used as separate factors in analysis of variance, with concurrent distress as the dependent measure. These analyses yielded no evidence of any interaction between vigilance and avoidance.

We also conducted regression analyses in which vigilance and avoidance items were permitted to enter separately, to determine whether vigilance and avoidance tendencies made separate contributions to distress. These analyses revealed two such instances. Thinking about the events of the operation beforehand and trying not to think about these same events made distinct contributions to predicting concurrent distress (βs = .49 and .26, respectively), together accounting for 31% of the variance. Thinking about one's emotions after surgery and trying not to think about emotions also made independent contributions to prediction of concurrent distress (βs = .57 and .35, respectively), accounting for 54% of the variance.

Disengagement from Goals

As a point of comparison for the effects of vigilance and avoidance in this study, we include brief description of one additional aspect of women's responses to the surgery: the extent to which they reported experiencing a tendency to give up on the goals with which the diagnosis and surgery was interfering. This tendency is assessed by the COPE scale termed *behavioral disengagement* (with items such as "Giving up the attempt to cope" and "Just giving up trying to deal with it"). These responses were not made frequently in this sample, but recall from earlier in the chapter that our theoretical analysis holds this to be a response with considerable emotional impact.

Reports of behavioral disengagement were unrelated to any index of avoidance before surgery except for denial, to which it was related rather strongly (.51). Behavioral disengagement presurgery was also related to one index of vigilance before surgery, thinking about emotions (.36). Behavioral disengagement was a strong correlate of presurgical distress (.50), as expected. This association remained significant when partialling out the concurrent effects of denial (.29) and thinking about emotions (.40), but it slipped to a marginal level when controlling for both simultaneously (.22).

Behavioral disengagement after surgery was again uncorrelated with any index of postsurgical avoidance other than denial (.34). There were associations, however, between disengagement and three indices of vigilance: thinking about symptoms, thinking about emotions, and information seeking (average r = .36). Behavioral disengagement was strongly related to distress after surgery (.57), an association that remained significant after controlling for denial (.50), after controlling for all indices of vigilance (.39), and after controlling for all these variables together (.29). A multiple regression analysis indicated that thinking about emotions, denial, and behavioral disengagement all made significant independent contributions to predicting concurrent distress, accounting as a group for 63% of the variance.

Postsurgical behavioral disengagement also served as a significant prospective predictor of distress at three months. That is, it remained related to 3-month distress after controlling for postsurgical distress (.28). Not surprisingly, this relationship was bidirectional. That is, distress postsurgery also predicted higher levels of behavioral disengagement three months later (.32).

In sum, behavioral disengagement is a reaction to adversity that seems to have an important emotional impact. As was suggested by the theoretical model of behavior outlined earlier in the chapter, experiencing a tendency to give up, in a situation in which giving up is not really feasible, is linked to higher levels of distress.

Similarities and Differences Between Studies

The results of these two studies are similar in several ways, though differing in others. In both studies, measures of vigilance were related to high levels of concurrent distress. This was true both before the surgery and afterward, and was true even though the vigilance measures were not highly correlated from pre- to postsurgery. Indeed, the CABS data even suggested that thinking about symptoms and emotions early (before and just after surgery) was tied to adverse health effects six months later. In contrast to these findings for health effects, there was little evidence that vigilance was prospectively related to subjective distress after controlling for previous distress. Vigilance was not uniform in its effect, though. Tendencies to focus on emotional reactions and physical symptoms were far more likely to relate to distress than was the seeking of information about the upcoming surgery.

One difference between studies concerns the role played by postsurgical information seeking. We initially viewed this as a type of vigilance, reasoning that the events of the postsurgical period have threatening aspects, and that thinking about those events means confronting the threat. This appears to have been far more true for the cancer patients than the CABS patients. Among the cancer patients this focus of thinking was tied to concurrent distress and was even a significant prospective predictor of distress three months later. Among CABS patients, in contrast, thinking about the recovery period was inversely associated with concurrent distress, and was associated with a variety of positive outcomes six months later.

This difference almost certainly derives from an important difference in the postsurgical experiences of the two sets of patients. Most of the cancer patients must look forward to radiation and/or chemotherapy, which are quite threatening. For most of the CABS patients, in contrast, recovery is relatively uneventful. Thinking about the events of that period are likely not to be nearly as threatening. This reasoning, in turn, suggests that this item may not even be assessing vigilance among the CABS patients in the same sense as vigilance has been used throughout this discussion (i.e., attention to threatening cues).

The two studies also yielded a picture of the effects of avoidance, which diverged in some respects from study to study. The differences, however, emerged primarily in measures that were present in one study but not the other. Generally speaking, avoidance was associated with distress, but at lower levels than was vigilance. One notable exception was denial as an avoidant tactic, which was strongly tied to distress. The fact that this measure was not included in the CABS study precluded obtaining a similar effect there.

Other differences concerning the effects of avoidance stem from measures that were included in the CABS study but not the cancer study. For example, among CABS patients trying not to think about symptoms and emotions during the period surrounding surgery was associated with a variety of adverse health and well-being effects both at postsurgery and at the 6-month follow-up. In contrast, trying to avoid thinking ahead to the recovery period was related to faster progress through milestones of recovery immediately postsurgery. None of these outcome measures was included as part of the data set from the cancer study, precluding similar effects emerging there.

Vigilance and Avoidance Reconsidered

One aspect of the findings of these studies deserves additional comment. Specifically, we found that both vigilance and avoidance were positively associated with distress. Avoidance has often been conceptualized as a process whereby the person is able to reduce emotional arousal (e.g., Krohne, 1989, and Chapter 2 in this volume), but this conceptualization does not reflect well what emerged among our subjects. There was only one instance in which avoidant coping responses were associated with lower levels of subjective distress, and there is some question as to whether that response really reflected avoidance as it is being discussed here. In most instances avoidance was linked to higher levels of distress. Nor are these the only instances in which avoidance coping (as a broad category) has been ineffective for distress reduction (Aldwin & Revenson, 1987; Billings & Moos, 1984; Holahan & Moos, 1985; Wills, 1986). It seems clear, then, that the hypothesized function of avoidant attentional strategies as a way of reducing distress needs further scrutiny, with an eye toward establishing limiting conditions, or perhaps examining variations among aspects of avoidance or the context in which the avoidance takes place (see also Cioffi, 1991).

Krohne (Chapter 2 in this volume) points to a number of considerations that are surely important in analyzing this issue, including the fact that one can not always infer correctly the intention that lies behind a particular action. Thus, for example, there are many reasons why a person awaiting an operation may try to suppress thoughts about the surgical procedure or the emotions being experienced. These reasons include (obviously) the fact that the surgery is threatening, but also the fact that thinking about the surgery distracts one from events taking place prior to the surgery that may urgently need close attention. Thus, even a simple response concerning the extent to which a person is trying not to think about something can be ambiguous.

As another example, being watchful and vigilant about threat cues - and thus thinking a good deal about the threat - differs considerably from experiencing undesired intrusions of threat-related thoughts (cf. Horowitz, Wilner, & Alvarez, 1979; see also Borkovec & Lyonfields, this volume). It is important to note, in this regard, that the questions that we asked our subjects - how much they had been thinking about a specific aspect of their experience - were ambiguous as to whether the thoughts reported had been intentional or had been unwanted intrusions.

What Constitutes Vigilance and Avoidance?

The question of ambiguity in a given response is an important one, but there are other issues as well. The argument that Krohne (1989, and Chapter 2 in this volume) has made concerning the functions served by vigilance and cognitive avoidance is an interesting and plausible one. All conceptual arguments, however, are ultimately tested through operationalizations. In discussing his operationalization, Krohne describes an Eysenckian hierarchy of levels of abstraction, in which coping *behaviors* are aggregated into coping *strategies*, which in turn are aggregated into higher order *superstrategies*. As does Eysenck in the domain of personality, Krohne places his greatest emphasis on the highest level (superstrategies). Thus, what he terms cognitive avoidance is actually a very broad category, which is roughly akin to what Lazarus and Folkman (1984) call emotion focused coping.

As we have noted elsewhere (e.g., Carver et al., 1989), emotion focused coping involves a range of tactics that diverges quite considerably. The same issue can be raised for the superstrategy called cognitive avoidance. Among the contributors to cognitive avoidance are *attentional diversion* (which to us seems to be at the heart of the concept of avoidance) and *denial* (which we, as well, treated here as a facet of avoidance). Also among the constituents of cognitive avoidance, however, are *reinterpretation*, *accentuating positive aspects*, *self-enhancement*, and *emphasizing one's own efficacy*. Although it can certainly be argued that each of these tactics does in some manner diminish (or modify) the person's awareness of threat cues, it also seems clear that these tactics are quite different from attentional diversion (see also Wack & Turk, 1984). It is somewhat disconcerting that the elements that load most highly on the cognitive avoidance superstrategy are not attentional diversion and denial, but reinterpretation, accentuating positive aspects, emphasizing one's efficacy, and self-enhancement (Krohne, 1989, Table 2). Attentional diversion, which is central to the avoidance concept, is reported to be the poorest loading contributor to that factor (though its loading is by no means trivially small).

A similar question can be raised about vigilance as a superstrategy (the closest comparable concept in the Lazarus model seems to be primary appraisal, though the fit between concepts is not perfect). Vigilance is a process of clarification of the meaning of the situation (Krohne, Chapter 2 in this volume), by attempting to obtain information relating to a threatening event (Krohne, 1989). Yet, despite this conceptually clear depiction, the three highest loading contributors to vigilance as a superstrategy do not involve either clarification of meaning or attempting to obtain information. Rather, they are *self-pity*, *escape tendencies*, and *anticipation of negative events* (Krohne, 1989).

One aspect of the question we are raising here concerns the level of abstraction at which it is most useful to think and work. In this instance, we are arguing for the greater usefulness of a level of abstraction below that of superstrategy (though we do not inevitably prefer to use a low level of abstraction, cf. Carver & Scheier, 1989). We are concerned in this case that blending too many qualities in a single measure may reduce the measure's intelligibility (cf. Carver, 1989).

Another aspect of the question (and another reason for our concern) is empirical. Although we have never used the Mainz Coping Inventory (MCI, Krohne, 1989) in our research, our COPE inventory has distinct scales that are labeled in ways that resemble several of the constituents of the MCI. Apart from mental disengagement (which shares some conceptual substance with the MCI's attentional diversion) and denial, the COPE also includes a number of other scales, one of which assesses positive reinterpretation (which in the MCI contributes to cognitive avoidance).

We have never found this reinterpretation scale to correlate significantly in a positive direction with denial or mental disengagement, and the correlations are often inverse. Indeed, in the sample of cancer patients discussed earlier, positive reinterpretation was inversely related to denial presurgery (-.28), though the correlation fell short of significance postsurgery. Positive reinterpretation was also inversely related to concurrent distress (-.46 before surgery, -.41 afterward). Quite clearly, if our operationalization of cognitive avoidance had included (or emphasized) positive reinterpretation, the pattern of results would have said something quite different about the relation between avoidance and distress. For this reason, we think it is important to separate these qualities from each other.

In sum, we believe that contemporary knowledge about the many aspects of coping remains at a stage where careful attention must be paid to possibly meaningful variations within any broad domain of coping. Doing this requires assessing the variations separately from each other and examining their effects separately.

Attention, Vigilance, and Giving Up

We close by noting that the data from the cancer study reported above seem to suggest that the effects of vigilance and avoidance can both be distinguished empirically from the effects of at least one other response to the diagnosis and surgery. This response, which we were drawn to examine by our interest in the self-regulation of behavior, is the experiencing of an impulse to give up on one's goals. We said earlier in the chapter that giving up is functional and adaptive in certain contexts, but that it leads to serious distress when the threatened goals are goals that can't be given up easily. Consistent with that reasoning, behavioral disengagement as a response to the situation confronted by these patients made an important contribution to the picture of distress and its causes.

This finding is important in two respects. First, it confirms the usefulness of broader self-regulatory ideas in examining the processes of stress and coping. But the finding is also important for a second reason. Specifically, the data appear to suggest that this effect is not just a vigilance or a cognitive avoidance effect under another name, nor are vigilance and cognitive avoidance simply proxies for giving up. That is, the disengagement effect appeared separately from effects of vigilance and avoidance. In one case, all three tendencies made separate contributions to prediction of distress. These findings suggest, then, that relationships between distress and aspects of coping emerge at several different points along the psychological stream, for several different reasons. This seems not to be a case in which there are competing theoretical models, only one of which is right and the others wrong. Rather, there seems to be usefulness in all of them.

References

Aldwin, C. M., & Revenson, T. A. (1987). Does coping help? A reexamination of the relation between coping and mental health. *Journal of Personality and Social Psychology, 53*, 337-348.

Antonovsky, A. (1987). *Unraveling the mystery of health: How people manage stress and stay well.* San Francisco: Jossey-Bass.

Bandura, A. (1986). *Social foundations of thought and action: A social cognitive theory.* Englewood Cliffs, NJ: Prentice-Hall.

Billings, A. G., & Moos, R. H. (1984). Coping, stress, and social resources among adults with unipolar depression. *Journal of Personality and Social Psychology, 46*, 877-891.

Brockner, J. (1988). *Self-esteem at work: Research, theory, and practice.* Lexington, MA: Lexington Books.

Carver, C. S. (1989). How should multifaceted personality constructs be tested? Issues illustrated by self-monitoring, attributional style, and hardiness. *Journal of Personality and Social Psychology, 56*, 577-585.

Carver, C. S., & Scheier, M. F. (1981). *Attention and self-regulation: A control-theory approach to human behavior.* New York: Springer-Verlag.

Carver, C. S., & Scheier, M. F. (1983). A control-theory approach to human behavior, and implications for problems in self-management. In P. C. Kendall (Ed.), *Advances in cognitive-behavioral research and therapy* (Vol. 2, pp. 127-194). New York: Academic Press.

Carver, C. S., & Scheier, M. F. (1986). Functional and dysfunctional responses to anxiety: The interaction between expectancies and self-focused attention. In R. Schwarzer (Ed.), *Self-related cognitions in anxiety and motivation* (pp. 111-141). Hillsdale, NJ: Erlbaum.

Carver, C. S., & Scheier, M. F. (1989). Social intelligence and personality: Some unanswered questions and unresolved issues. In R. S. Wyer, Jr. & T. K. Srull (Eds.), *Advances in social cognition: Vol. 2. Social intelligence and cognitive assessments of personality* (pp. 93-109). Hillsdale, NJ: Erlbaum.

Carver, C. S., & Scheier, M. F. (1990a). Origins and functions of positive and negative affect: A control-process view. *Psychological Review, 97*, 19-35.

Carver, C. S., & Scheier, M. F. (1990b). Principles of self-regulation: Action and emotion. In E. T. Higgins & R. M. Sorrentino (Eds.), *Handbook of motivation and cognition: Foundations of social behavior* (Vol. 2, pp. 3-52). New York: Guilford.

Carver, C. S., Scheier, M. F., & Pozo, C. (in press). Conceptualizing the process of coping with health problems. In H. S. Friedman (Ed.), *Hostility, coping, and health.* Washington, DC: American Psychological Association.

Carver, C. S., Scheier, M. F., & Weintraub, J. K. (1989). Assessing coping strategies: A theoretically based approach. *Journal of Personality and Social Psychology, 56*, 267-283.

Cioffi, D. (1991). Beyond attentional strategies: A cognitive-perceptual model of somatic interpretation. *Psychological Bulletin, 109,* 25-41.

Elliott, E. S., & Dweck, C. S. (1988). Goals: An approach to motivation and achievement. *Journal of Personality and Social Psychology, 54,* 5-12.

Emmons, R. A. (1986). Personal strivings: An approach to personality and subjective well-being. *Journal of Personality and Social Psychology, 51,* 1058-1068.

Emmons, R. A., & King, L. A. (1988). Conflict among personal strivings: Immediate and long-term implications for psychological and physical well-being. *Journal of Personality and Social Psychology, 54,* 1040-1048.

Holahan, C. J., & Moos, R. H. (1985). Life stress and health: Personality, coping, and family support in stress resistance. *Journal of Personality and Social Psychology, 49,* 739-747.

Horowitz, M., Wilner, N., & Alvarez, W. (1979). Impact of Event Scale: A measure of subjective stress. *Psychosomatic Medicine, 41,* 209-218.

Kanfer, F. H., & Hagerman, S. M. (1985). Behavior therapy and the information-processing paradigm. In S. Reiss & R. R. Bootzin (Eds.), *Theoretical issues in behavior therapy* (pp. 3-33). New York: Academic Press.

Kirsch, I. (1990). *Changing expectations: A key to effective psychotherapy.* Pacific Grove, CA: Brooks/Cole.

Klinger, E. (1975). Consequences of commitment to and disengagement from incentives. *Psychological Review, 82,* 1-25.

Klinger, E. (1977). *Meaning and void: Inner experience and the incentives in people's lives.* Minneapolis: University of Minnesota Press.

Klinger, E. (1987). Current concerns and disengagement from incentives. In F. Halisch & J. Kuhl (Eds.), *Motivation, intention, and volition* (pp. 337-347). Berlin: Springer-Verlag.

Krohne, H. W. (1989). The concept of coping modes: Relating cognitive person variables to actual coping behavior. *Advances in Behaviour Research and Therapy, 11,* 235-248.

Kukla, A. (1972). Foundations of an attributional theory of performance. *Psychological Review, 79,* 454-470.

Lazarus, R. S. (1966). *Psychological stress and the coping process.* New York: McGraw-Hill.

Lazarus, R. S., & Folkman, S. (1984). *Stress, appraisal, and coping.* New York: Springer.

Little, B. R. (1983). Personal projects: A rationale and methods for investigation. *Environment and Behavior, 15,* 273-309.

Mandler, G. (1984). *Mind and body: Psychology of emotion and stress.* New York: Norton.

Mandler, G., & Watson, D. L. (1966). Anxiety and the interruption of behavior. In C. D. Spielberger (Ed.), *Anxiety and behavior* (pp. 263-288). New York: Academic Press.

Millar, K. U., Tesser, A., & Millar, M. G. (1988). The effects of a threatening life event on behavior sequences and intrusive thought: A self-disruption explanation. *Cognitive Therapy and Research, 12,* 441-457.

Miller, S. M. (1987). Monitoring and blunting: Validation of a questionnaire to assess styles of information seeking under threat. *Journal of Personality and Social Psychology, 52,* 345-353.

Miller, S. M. (1990). To see or not to see: Cognitive informational styles in the coping process. In M. Rosenbaum (Ed.), *Learned resourcefulness: On coping skills, self-regulation, and adaptive behavior* (pp. 95-126). New York: Springer.

Mischel, W. (1973). Toward a cognitive social learning reconceptualization of personality. *Psychological Review, 80,* 252-283.

Pervin, L. A. (1983). The stasis and flow of behavior: Toward a theory of goals. In M. M. Page (Ed.), *Nebraska symposium on motivation* (Vol. 30, pp. 1-53). Lincoln: University of Nebraska Press.

Pervin, L. A. (Ed.). (1989). *Goal concepts in personality and social psychology.* Hillsdale, NJ: Erlbaum.

Pozo, C., Carver, C. S., Robinson, D. S., Ketcham, A. S., Legaspi, A., Moffat, F., & Scheier, M. F. (1990). [Adjustment process among a group of early-stage breast cancer pationts]. Unpublished data, research in progress.

Pyszczynski, T., & Greenberg, J. (1987). Self-regulatory perseveration and the depressive self-focusing style: A self-awareness theory of reactive depression. *Psychological Bulletin, 102*, 122-138.

Repetti, R. L. (1989). Effects of daily workload on subsequent behavior during marital interaction: The roles of social withdrawal and spouse support. *Journal of Personality and Social Psychology, 57*, 651-659.

Rosenbaum, M. (Ed.). (1990). *Learned resourcefulness: On coping skills, self-regulation, and adaptive behavior*. New York: Springer.

Rosenberg, M. (1979). *Conceiving the self.* New York: Basic Books.

Scheier, M. F., & Carver, C. S. (1985). Optimism, coping, and health: Assessment and implications of generalized outcome expectancies. *Health Psychology, 4*, 219-247.

Scheier, M. F., & Carver, C. S. (1987). Dispositional optimism and physical well-being: The influence of generalized outcome expectancies on health. *Journal of Personality, 55*, 169-210.

Scheier, M. F., Matthews, K. A., Owens, J. F., Magovern, G. J., Sr., Lefebvre, R. C., Abbott, R. A., & Carver, C. S. (1989). Dispositional optimism and recovery from coronary artery bypass surgery: The beneficial effects on physical and psychological well-being. *Journal of Personality and Social Psychology, 57*, 1024-1040.

Seligman, M. E. P. (1975). *Helplessness: On depression, development, and death.* San Francisco: Freeman.

Simon, H. A. (1967). Motivational and emotional controls of cognition. *Psychological Review, 74*, 29-39.

Vallacher, R. R., & Wegner, D. M. (1987). What do people think they're doing? Action identification and human behavior. *Psychological Review, 94*, 3-15.

Van Hook, E., & Higgins, E. T. (1988). Self-related problems beyond the self-concept: Motivational consequences of discrepant self-guides. *Journal of Personality and Social Psychology, 55*, 625-633.

Wack, J. T., & Turk, D. C. (1984). Latent structure of strategies used to cope with nociceptive stimulation. *Health Psychology, 3*, 27-43.

Wills, T. A. (1986). Stress and coping in early adolescence: Relationships to substance use in urban school samples. *Health Psychology, 5*, 503-529.

Wortman, C. B., & Brehm, J. W. (1975). Responses to uncontrollable outcomes: An integration of reactance theory and the learned helplessness model. In L. Berkowitz (Ed.), *Advances in experimental social psychology* (Vol. 8, pp. 277-336). New York: Academic Press.

Chapter 14

Coping with Surgical Stress

Kerstin Slangen, Peter P. Kleemann,
and Heinz Walter Krohne

Theoretical Background

Patients who must undergo an aversive medical intervention (surgery or an unpleasant, possibly painful treatment or diagnostic procedure) are exposed to a multitude of stressors (cf. e.g., Guggenheim, 1986; Höfling, 1988; Janis, 1958; Johnston, 1980; Tolksdorf, 1985; Van der Ploeg, 1988; Vögele, 1988; Volicer, 1970; Volicer & Bohannon, 1975; see also the chapters by Carver & Scheier and by Miller, Combs, & Kruus in this volume). Besides the primary stressor of a potential or actual physical injury caused by the intervention, an additional important stressor is the significantly *reduced control the patient has over the central threat-relevant elements of such a situation.* This reduced control includes a *restricted behavioral controllability* of these elements as well as the *lacking predictability* of important situational factors, e.g., in the case of a surgical intervention, the exact time of surgery, the course of anesthesia, or the consequences of surgery (for a general overview of these stressors cf. e.g., Averill, 1973; Krohne, 1986; Miller, 1981; Prystav, 1979, 1985).

In this chapter, we will concentrate on the stressors inherent in a *surgical procedure* and the ways they are coped with. As for *predictability* (or uncertainty), the loss of control varies to different degrees throughout the individual dimensions of this category. The socalled *general* predictability, i.e., knowing whether the stressful event will even occur at all, is naturally high. The information about the onset of the event (*temporal* predictability) is limited until the actual scheduling of surgery. Since surgery is often scheduled only a day or two in advance, many patients perceive this state as particularly stressful. As for *event-related* predictability, information about the *nature of the confrontation* (the concrete circumstances of undergoing surgery) is available to different degrees, dependent on the type of procedure, the patient's general medical knowledge, and his/her actual prior experiences with surgery (see Steptoe & O'Sullivan, 1986, for more information on this topic). In contrast, information about a number of possible *consequences of this event* (e.g., condition after surgery, pain, success of the healing process) is largely

We are indebted to Susanne Stellrecht, Barbara Frisch, and those persons on the medical staff of the Mainz University Clinic who assisted us in conducting this research.

unavailable. A *behavioral controllability* of the situation is practically impossible prior to surgery, but becomes increasingly more feasible (at least in general) afterwards.

To what extent these objectively existing stressors also lead to intensified stress reactions (e.g., anxiety) in the patient depends on a multitude of variables and their interactions. Obviously, we first think of the type of *premedication* as one important factor (Höfling, 1988; Tolksdorf, 1985). The different methods of *psychological intervention* correspondingly constitute the second major source of influence (for recent reviews cf. Auerbach, 1989; Miller, Combs, & Stoddard, 1989; Yap, 1988). In addition to these externally implemented factors, the third determinant of objective and subjective stress reactions is represented by the *coping strategies* developed and employed by the patient. According to the findings of different studies, the pre- and intraoperative stress level and especially the quality of postoperative recovery depend on the actions and cognitive operations the patient employs before the surgical procedure (Miller & Mangan, 1983; Phipps & Zinn, 1986; Scott & Clum, 1984; see also Carver & Scheier, this volume; Miller et al., this volume; for a review cf. Cohen & Lazarus, 1982).

Since a behavioral (instrumental) influence on the situation before the medical procedure is practically impossible, the central goal of coping strategies must be to change the *perception of the situation*, i.e., to use cognitive operations like attentional diversion, reinterpretation, or the construction of a schema of the expected confrontation, in order to reduce the aversiveness of the situation (cf. e.g., Breznitz, 1983; Krohne, 1986, 1989; Lazarus, 1983; Rothbaum, Weisz, & Snyder, 1982). Such cognitive operations *formally* have the same function in reducing stress that premedication or psychological interventions do.

It can be assumed that every person will employ some kind of coping strategy in a highly stressful situation. We must therefore take into consideration that the possible effect of every external intervention interacts with the type of coping strategy employed. Hence, a certain (medical or psychological) intervention with the goal of reducing surgical stress may be counterproductive in view of the patient's preferred and actually employed coping strategies. Regarding this problem, our research group has set the following general goals:

1. Analyzing different parameters (measured on the experiential, expressive-motoric, and biological level) in regard to their function in indicating the actual amount of stress,

2. acquiring criteria for assessing the patient's intraoperative as well as (short- and long-term) postoperative adaptive status,

3. determining which coping strategies prove to be especially efficient with regard to the reduction of stress as well as the improvement of the patient's (short- and long-term) adaptive status,

4. planning interventions whose content is coordinated with the patient's preferred and actually employed coping strategies. The goal of this program,

which should be implemented in the sense of an aptitude-treatment interaction (Cronbach & Snow, 1977), is to minimize stress for every patient during the entire surgical situation and the long-term adaptation.

In a series of previous studies, we analyzed the influence of fundamental types of coping behavior on subjective and objective stress indicators before and after surgery. Among the coping strategies considered were such operations in which cognitive processes were used in an attempt to reduce the situational aversiveness.

The theoretical foundation of these studies is provided by the *model of coping modes* developed by our research group. This model, described elsewhere in more detail (Krohne, 1989; cf. Krohne, Chapter 2 in this volume), is based on two dimensions of cognitive orientation in face of an aversive situation: *vigilance* and *cognitive avoidance*. Vigilance is characterized by an intensified search for and processing of threat-related information. This should reduce the subjective uncertainty which is triggered by the ambiguity present in practically all threatening situations. Cognitive avoidance is, in contrast, characterized by withdrawing from threat-relevant cues. In this manner, the emotional arousal triggered by these cues, i.e., by the anticipated confrontation with an aversive event, should be reduced. Of course, both of these dimensions also play a central role in other researchers' investigations on coping with surgical stress, for example, as "monitoring" and "blunting" (Miller, 1987; Miller & Mangan, 1983; Phipps & Zinn, 1986; Steptoe & O'Sullivan, 1986; cf. Miller et al., this volume) or "attention" and "rejection" (Mullen & Suls, 1982). A fundamental difference between our approach and those mentioned is that, in the model of coping modes, both dimensions, conceived as *personality variables*, are considered to vary independently. Since this hypothesis could be repeatedly confirmed by means of a newly constructed inventory (Krohne, 1989; Krohne, Rösch, & Kürsten, 1989; cf. Krohne, Chapter 2, this volume), it is thus possible to systematically analyze the simultaneous influences of vigilance and avoidance on stress.

Empirical Investigations

In an initial study, Krohne, Kleemann, Hardt, and Theisen (1990), analyzed the influence of dispositional and actual vigilant and avoidant coping on preoperative stress reactions. Forty men and women who underwent elective maxillofacial surgery took part in this investigation. None of the patients received any anxiolytic premedication. The amount of preoperative stress was recorded as subjective (*self-reported state anxiety*) and objective (*plasma concentration of free fatty acids*) data. The stress variables were measured at four times: 1. in the morning after admittance to the hospital ward, 2. in the afternoon before surgery, 3. on the morning of surgery, and 4. immediately prior to induction of anesthesia. At all four points of time the state anxiety (A-State) scale of the "State-Trait Anxiety Inventory" (STAI; Laux,

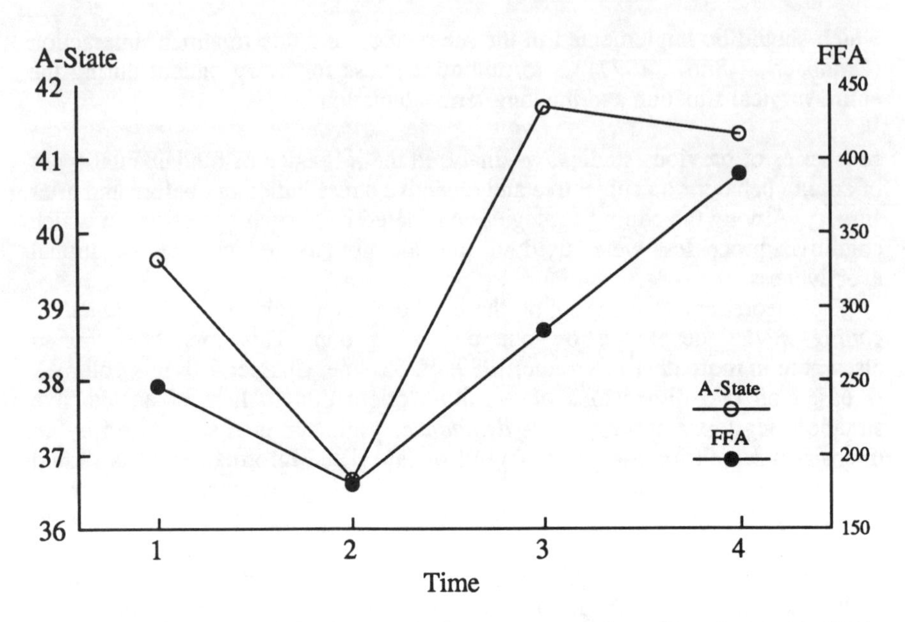

Figure 14.1. State anxiety (A-State) and plasma concentration of free fatty acids (FFA, µmol/l) as a function of time of measurement ($N = 40$).

Glanzmann, Schaffner, & Spielberger, 1981) was administered, and in addition, blood samples were taken to determine the plasma concentration of free fatty acids. Dispositional and actual coping on the dimensions *vigilance* and *cognitive avoidance* were measured at time 1 using the "Mainz Coping Inventory" (MCI; Krohne et al., 1989).

The results showed a clear influence of the time of measurement as well as the coping variables on the stress reactions. For both stress indicators, significant changes over time could be verified (see Figure 14.1). For example, *state anxiety* decreased from the first measurement (after admittance to the ward) to time 2 (after the anesthetist's pre-op visit), increased significantly on the morning of surgery, and remained at this high level until anesthesia was induced. *The free fatty acids* manifested an almost identical course until time 3 (on the morning of surgery) but, in contrast to state anxiety, a further significant increase was found until time 4.

Both stress indicators were also significantly influenced by the coping variables. *State anxiety* was especially low when the patients employed (actual) cognitive avoidant strategies before surgery. For the dispositional measures, a significant interaction could be confirmed: Patients who were characterized by high vigilance and low avoidance manifested more state anxiety than all other groups. The stress parameter *free fatty acids* revealed a significant interaction between actual cognitive avoidance and vigilance. Patients who employed neither vigilant nor avoidant coping strategies before surgery reached a

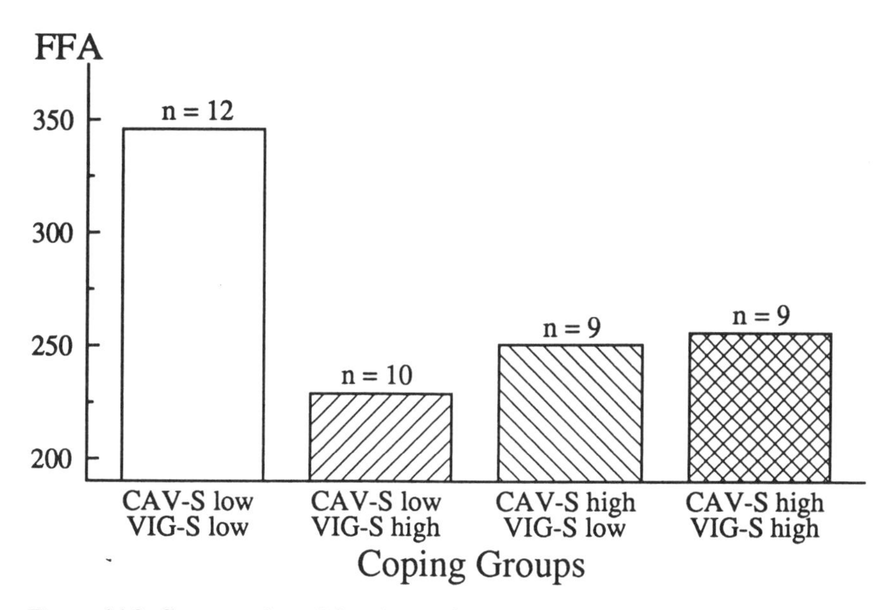

Figure 14.2. Concentration of free fatty acids (FFA) as a function of actual vigilance (VIG-S) and cognitive avoidance (CAV-S).

substantially higher concentration of this stress parameter than those patients who relied on either one or both of the coping forms (cf. Figure 14.2). The course of free fatty acids was also influenced by an interaction between dispositional cognitive avoidance and time of measurement: After admittance to the hospital (time 1), dispositional avoiders showed stronger stress reactions than nonavoiders. At time 2, both groups reached identically low values while on the morning of surgery (time 3 and 4) persons with lower avoidance showed a substantially higher stress increase than high avoiders.

In view of this data we can reach the following tentative conclusions: The patient's stress decreases distinctly after the anesthetist's pre-op visit. This situation obviously exerts an uncertainty-reducing and calming effect. As the aversive confrontation draws near on the morning of surgery, the stress level increases again. This increase continues until immediately before the begin of surgery for the physiological parameter *free fatty acids*, but not for the subjective (*cognitive*) variable *state anxiety*. This could indicate the onset of psychological anxiety control mechanisms immediately prior to the aversive confrontation, a process described by Epstein (1972) within the framework of his anxiety-control theory. These mechanisms first inhibit the cognitive and then later (if at all) the somatic stress reactions.

The key result of this analysis is the observation that the highest concentrations of free fatty acids in the plasma were found for patients who preoperatively react in a neither markedly cognitive avoidant nor vigilant manner. This special configuration of coping with stress can be interpreted in two ways. On the one hand, we may be dealing with persons who (at least in regard to the stressors realized here) are characterized by a general coping deficit (cf. Krohne, Chapter 2, this volume). Such persons should not be as successful as those patients who attempt to reduce situational aversiveness by employing certain, yet individually unique (i.e., vigilant or avoidant), coping strategies. On the other hand, it can be argued that persons with the configuration "low vigilance and low avoidance" attempt to change the situation with coping mechanisms of a different kind. In the model of coping modes (Krohne 1986, 1989; cf. Chapter 2, this volume), persons with this configuration are characterized as "nondefensive". It was postulated that they primarily attempt to influence the situation using direct (instrumental) behavior instead of only employing cognitive operations in an attempt to change the perception of the situation. If such people are confronted by a situation in which practically no instrumental control is possible (as before surgery), they should experience a certain helplessness and hence increased stress. Future studies must therefore employ measurement instruments expanded to distinguish between those persons who manifest stress reactions as a consequence of a generally deficient coping repertoire and those who experience stress because they use coping strategies not appropriate for this specific situation.

In a second investigation (cf. Krohne, 1990), the times of measurement were extended into the postoperative phase so that pre- as well as postoperative stress reactions could be recorded. Furthermore, *cortisol*, which has been established as a valid stress indicator in numerous studies (see, e.g., Berger, 1983), replaced free fatty acids as a parameter for measuring physiological stress reactions.

Forty male and female patients (orthopedic surgery which lasted at least one hour and was performed under local anesthesia) participated in this investigation whose formal structure corresponded to that of the first study. As in the first study, none of the patients received any anxiolytic premedication. The stress indicators were measured at five times; however, state anxiety and cortisol were not assessed at every time point. At time 1 (in the afternoon before surgery), both stress indicators as well as dispositional and actual coping on the dimensions *vigilance* and *cognitive avoidance* were measured. Both stress reactions were also measured before the local anesthesia was induced (time 3) and on the day after surgery (time 5). Subjective stress (A-State) was recorded two additional times on the day of surgery (early in the morning, time 2, and in the afternoon after surgery, time 4).

The results again show clear influences of the time of measurement and the coping variables on the stress reactions. For both parameters there were highly significant changes over time (cf. Figure 14.3). *State anxiety* increased significantly from time 1 to 2, remained at this high level for time 3, and fell back to the original level after surgery, reaching at time 5 the level of the standardization sample reported by Laux et. al. (1981). *Cortisol* showed a highly significant increase from time 1 to 3 and remained constant at this high level into the postoperative phase (time 5).

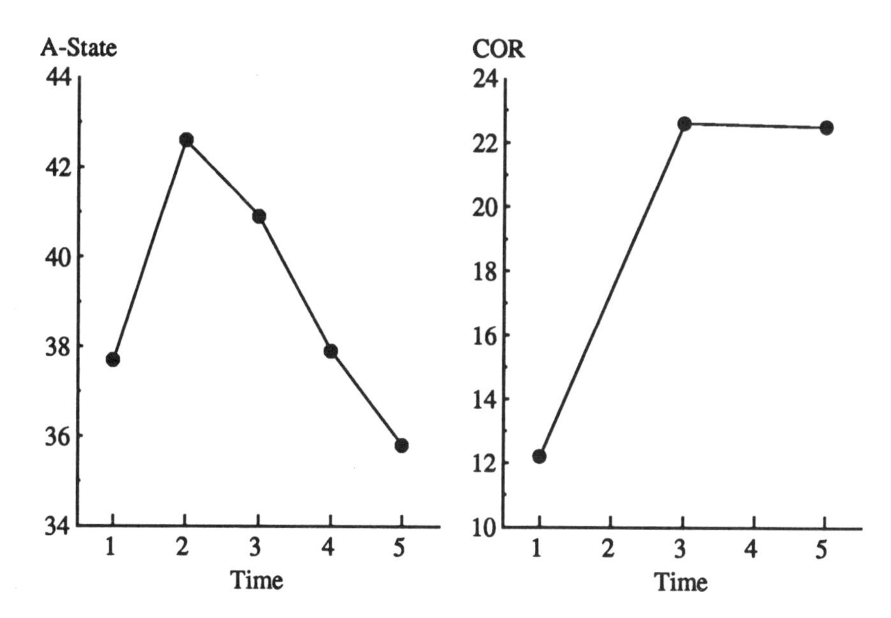

Figure 14.3. State anxiety (A-State) and cortisol level (COR, µg/100ml) as a function of time of measurement ($N = 40$).

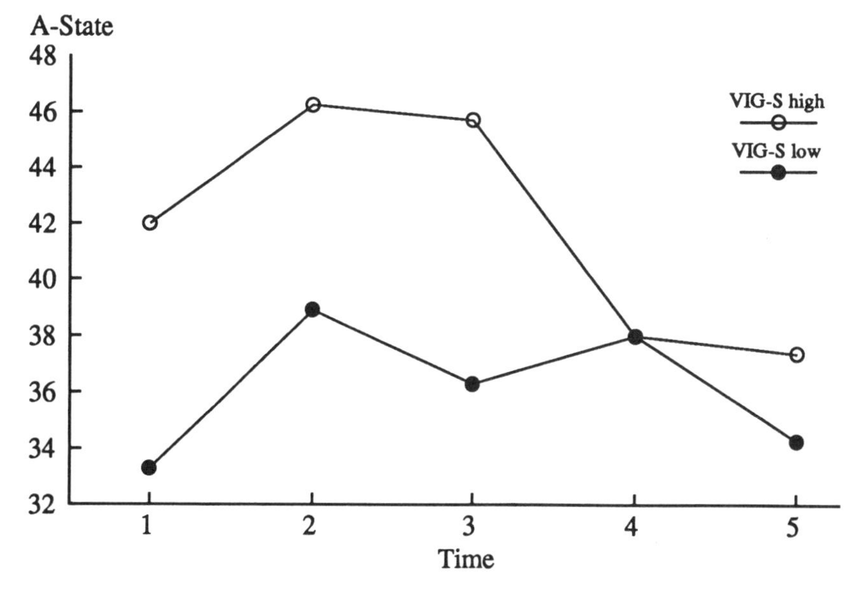

Figure 14.4. State anxiety (A-State) as a function of actual vigilance (VIG-S) and time of measurement (high VIG-S: $n = 20$, low VIG-S: $n = 20$).

As in the first study, the stress indicators were also significantly influenced by the coping variables. For example, significant effects of dispositional and actual vigilance on *state anxiety* were found, whereby this influence for actual vigilance was dependent on the time of measurement (cf. Figure 14.4): Patients who employed vigilant strategies manifested an increased anxiety level only *before* surgery.

For *cortisol*, similar to the case of state anxiety, persons who employed increased cognitive avoidance before surgery manifested significantly lower values than patients who did not. For the dispositional measures, however, an interactive effect of both coping variables on cortisol could be registered (cf. Figure 14.5). Patients who prefer to cope using cognitive avoidance (in the terminology of the model of coping modes "repressers") as well as persons who primarily react vigilantly ("sensitizers") showed lower cortisol values than patients who are habitually low in vigilance *and* avoidance. (As already mentioned, persons with this coping configuration are classified as "nondefensive" in the model of coping modes.) However, the highest stress was manifested by those patients who are characterized by high levels of both vigilance *and* avoidance. (In the model such people are classified as "high-anxious"; cf. Krohne, Chapter 2, this volume.)

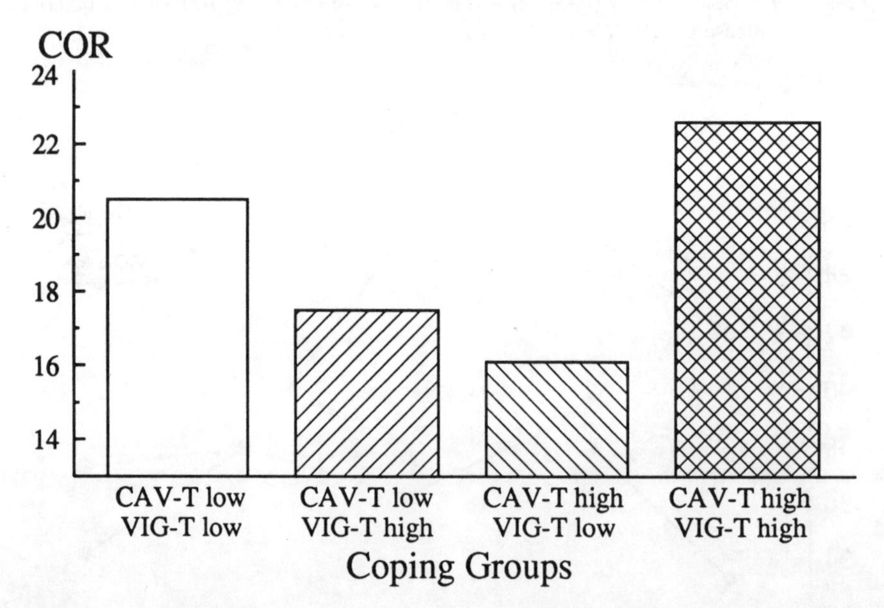

Figure 14.5. Cortisol level (COR) as a function of dispositional vigilance (VIG-T) and cognitive avoidance (CAV-T).

Compared with the results of the first study, the second investigation revealed several convergent, but also some divergent, findings. One *convergent finding* is that the self-reported anxiety reaches its maximum in the early morning before surgery and then decreases as the aversive confrontation draws near. A further drop can be observed for the postoperative period. In contrast to the subjective (or cognitive, respectively) anxiety reactions, the values for the somatic stress parameter remain at a high level in the postoperative phase.

This clear difference in the levels of cognitive and somatic anxiety reactions *after surgery* can be interpreted in view of theoretical considerations concerning the differential importance of the cognitive and somatic (emotional) anxiety components (cf. e.g., Borkovec, 1985; Morris & Liebert, 1970). According to these considerations, reactions in the cognitive component primarily reflect the apprehension and uncertainty in a threatening situation while changes in the somatic (emotional) anxiety component are more a function of the experienced general stress (in our study probably also a function of the physiological strain of surgery). Correspondingly, it is expected that apprehension is especially high in the preoperative phase, i.e., at the point of maximum uncertainty, and decreases soon after the successfully completed surgery. On the other hand, emotionality should reflect the general stress throughout the hospital stay and the surgical procedure and, hence, decrease only at a later time. If one assumes that in the present study the cognitive component was operationalized mainly in the items of the A-State Scale of the STAI, while the physiological indicator tapped the somatic (emotional) component, then the observed courses correspond to the theoretical expectations.

The high levels of the physiological stress indicator registered in the first study (free fatty acids) for patients with the configuration "low vigilance *and* low avoidance" were also recorded in the second study (cortisol), though with certain modifications. Again, it is persons with either primarily cognitive avoidant or vigilant coping who manifest the lowest stress reactions. In contrast, persons who employ low vigilance and low avoidance (so-called "nondefensives") show clearly stronger reactions. This time, unlike the results in the first study, they are surpassed by the so-called "high-anxious" patients, i.e., persons with the configuration "high vigilance *and* high avoidance". This result actually corresponds better to theoretical expectations which can be derived from the model of coping modes (cf. Krohne 1986, 1989; Chapter 2, this volume). Accordingly, persons who employ vigilance *as well as* cognitive avoidance comparatively more often in a stressful situation should manifest an instable coping behavior which entails a rather inefficient control of the stressors and hence higher stress reactions. In contrast, individuals with the configuration "low vigilance and low avoidance" should, as already mentioned, prefer to control the situation instrumentally. If this control largely fails, as in the surgical situation, it should lead to intensified stress reactions, just as in the case of instable copers, yet for a different reason. This assumption has important consequences for the psychological as well as medical treatment in the surgical situation: Patients can obviously manifest increased stress for very different reasons. Therefore the respective treatment must be tailored to these specific conditions, i.e., to the patient's respective coping tendencies.

A further important result which conforms to the model could be determined because the time of measurement in the second study was extended into the postoperative phase: Only *before* surgery do highly vigilant patients show more state anxiety than those who do not employ vigilance. According to the model of coping modes, highly vigilant persons are primarily affected by the uncertainty (especially the lacking predictability) in a threatening situation. After surgery most of the uncertainties have been eliminated, so that stress (and hence anxiety) decreases again.

A Study on Surgical Stress, Coping, and Intraoperative Adaptation

Objectives of the Study

In view of the promising (although complex) findings of the two studies reported, a third investigation was planned whose central results will now be presented. As it became increasingly clear in both of the first studies that the contingencies between anxiety control processes and the course of cognitive and somatic anxiety reactions had to be more precisely analyzed, the following broader objective was pursued:

In an attempt to replicate and extend results of the two earlier studies, relationships between the dispositional coping variables vigilance and cognitive avoidance, actual surgery-related coping, and stress indicators from different levels of measurement and assessed at different times during the aversive confrontation were analyzed. Self-reported state anxiety was differentiated according to the cognitive (worry) and the affective components. Moreover, expressive-motor manifestations of anxiety during the anesthetist's pre-op visit were rated by independent observers. We also wanted to determine whether coping variables can differentially predict indicators of patients' adaptation. The doses of the narcotic agents used for induction of anesthesia and the alveolar concentration of the volatile anesthetic were used as parameters of *intra*operative adaptation.

Method

Sample

Forty male patients (ages between 17 and 57, M = 30.15) who underwent elective maxillofacial surgery participated in this study. Emergency surgery or surgery due to terminal or chronic illnesses was excluded. Only patients with an overall good medical status (ASA groups 1 and 2), in particular those who did not manifest any endocrine disorders or who were not being treated with hormones or psychoactive drugs, participated in the study. None of the patients received any anxiolytic premedication.

Table 14.1
Design of the Study

	Times of measurement	Variables	
t1	After admittance to ward (one day before surgery)	A-State Cop-act	Self-reported state anxiety Actual coping behavior
t2	During and after the anesthetist's preoperative visit (afternoon before surgery)	Beh-Rat A-State Cop-act	Observer-rating of anxiety and coping
t3	On the morning of surgery (about 1 h before induction of anesthesia)	A-State Cop-act	
t4	In the anesthesia induction room (about 5 min before induction of anesthesia)	A-State	
t5	Intraoperatively	THIO FENT M AC-E	Dose of thiopentone for induction of anesthesia/kg body weight Dose of fentanyl for induction of anesthesia/kg body weight Mean alveolar concentration of the volatile anesthetic (enflurane) during surgery
t6	One day after surgery	A-State Cop-act	
t7	One day before discharge	CAV VIG	Dispositional cognitive avoidance Dispositional vigilance

Procedure

Table 14.1 gives an overview of the variables measured at different times. Self-reported state anxiety as well as actual coping behavior were recorded five (or four, respectively) times before and after surgery: 1. after admittance to the hospital ward, 2. in the afternoon before surgery during and after the anesthetist's pre-op visit, 3. on the morning of surgery, about one hour before it began, 4. immediately before induction of anesthesia (state anxiety only), and 5. on the day after surgery.

The *dispositional coping behavior* was recorded on the dimensions *cognitive avoidance* (CAV) and *vigilance* (VIG) at time 7 by use of the "Mainz Coping Inventory" (MCI; cf. Krohne, 1989; Chapter 2 in this volume). The *actual coping behavior* was measured with a newly constructed inventory which permits the recording of the patients' individual coping reactions in the surgical situation (cf. Slangen, Krohne, Richter, & Stellrecht, 1991). Unlike the "actual" part of the MCI, which only measures vigilant and avoidant coping, the items of this new inventory were selected so that they would represent the greatest possible range of cognitive and instrumental coping reactions in order to most extensively address all possible behaviors in the hospital situation. Since responding to this questionnaire is very time consuming, we dispensed with a measurement at time 4 (immediately before induction of anesthesia). Factor and item analysis of the data of a sample of N = 126 patients awaiting surgery yielded four scales of coping reactions which can be labeled *positive restructuring*, *passive coping*, *actual vigilance*, and *actual cognitive avoidance*, the latter scale (*range* 0 - 10) including typical avoidance items as well as items describing attempts to control emotional arousal (e.g., "I talk to somebody about my feelings", "I try to mentally focus on something other than surgery"). Item examples for vigilance (*range* 0 - 8) are "I talk to somebody in order to find out more about my situation", and "I turn the problem over and over in my mind". In this analysis only the scales "actual cognitive avoidance" (CAV-AC) and "actual vigilance" (VIG-AC) will be considered. Reliabilities (alpha coefficients) for the present sample range between .67 and .75 (CAV-AC) as well as .73 and .83 (VIG-AC) for the four times of measurement.

Self-reported state anxiety was assessed by a newly constructed instrument with two scales factor-analytically derived from the data of the above-mentioned sample of N = 126 patients awaiting surgery. An *affectivity* (AFF) scale consists of five items dealing with affective aspects and six items concerning somatic symptoms of anxiety (*range* 11 - 44). A *worry* (WOR) scale consists of eight items describing cognitive anxiety reactions (*range* 8 - 32). The reliabilities of the individual scales in the present sample were separately determined for the different times of measurement. Alpha coefficients range between .80 and .92 for AFF and from .85 to .91 for WOR (for more details see Slangen, Krohne, & Kleemann, 1991).

To record some *expressive-motor aspects of state anxiety*, a psychologist-observer assessed several indicators during the anesthetist's preoperative visit on six-point rating scales. Signs of anxiety in the patient's *verbal behavior* (SPE) were rated, such as a hoarse voice, lack of concentration, hesitant replies, and confused speech. In addition, we rated the *intensity of anxiety concerning surgery* (ANX) explicitly stated by patients towards the anesthetist. Also, the frequency of patients' *requests for information* (INF) concerning preparation for surgery, surgery itself, and their postoperative well-being, which we regard as indicative of vigilant coping, was assessed. This measurement yielded three scales: speech (SPE; 4 items; a = .64), anxiety (ANX; 3 items; a = .70), and requests for information (INF; 3 items; a = .51).

The parameters of *intraoperative adaptation* were evaluated retrospectively using the anesthesia record. The *doses of the narcotic agents used for anesthesia induction, thiopentone* (THIO) and *fentanyl* (FENT), were recorded relative to the patient's weight in kilograms with high doses indicating higher arousal at anesthesia induction. The *mean alveolar concentration of the volatile anesthetic* (enflurane; M AC-E) was calculated by averaging the concentration levels registered in 15-minute intervals. This score served as a measure of the amount of narcotic agent required by the individual patient in order to maintain an adequate depth of anesthesia during surgery.

Statistical analysis

The bivariate linear relationships between variables were determined using Pearson correlations. The influences of dispositional and actual coping and time of measurement on the different aspects of state anxiety and intraoperative adaptation were tested by multiple analyses of variance (ANOVAs) according to the regression-analytical model. The dispositional coping dimensions VIG and CAV as well as the scales for actual avoidant and vigilant coping reactions, VIG-AC and CAV-AC, served as independent variables. Each had two levels (high and low). For the dispositional variables, these groups were defined by sex-specific split at the median of a sample of 330 male patients whose MCI data were already available. For VIG-AC and CAV-AC, the data at times 1 and 2 from our patient sample were averaged and split at the sample-specific median. Patients with data on the median were excluded from the analyses, resulting in reduced sample sizes for several analyses. With the exception of the variables which were only recorded once, the four- or five-level factor "repeated measurement" constituted the third independent variable. If variance homogeneity in the cells was missing, degrees of freedom were corrected according to Greenhouse and Geisser (1959). When effects were significant, multiple mean comparisons between the individual groups and the time of measurement were conducted using tests for simple main effects or Tukey's HSD-test, respectively (Kirk, 1968).

Results

The correlation between dispositional vigilance (VIG) and cognitive avoidance (CAV) is as low as expected (r = -.12; see also Krohne, Chapter 2, this volume). Therefore both variables can be considered independent factors in the analyses of variance.

In order to facilitate an overview of the correlational analyses, the number of times of measurement was reduced for the variables with repeated measures, i.e., affective and cognitive aspects of anxiety as well as actual coping. For that purpose the values at times 1 and 2 were averaged (T1), yielding a score for each AFF and WOR which represents the *stress level on the day before* surgery. Likewise, the averaging of the scores at times 3 and 4 (T2) resulted in scores for the *morning of surgery*. The value for time 6 (*first postoperative day*) was not changed. The scores for VIG-AC and CAV-AC were averaged for times 1 and 2 only.

Table 14.2
Correlations Between Dispositional (CAV, VIG) and Actual Coping Behavior (CAV-AC, VIG-AC)

	CAV	*N*	VIG	*N*
CAV-AC-T1	.36*	37	.24	37
CAV-AC-t3	.34*	39	.26	39
CAV-AC-t6	.24	40	.21	40
VIG-AC-T1	.09	37	.58**	37
VIG-AC-t3	.29	38	.52**	38
VIG-AC-t6	.21	40	.48**	40

Note. CAV-AC: actual avoidant coping, VIG-AC: actual vigilant coping; T1: mean for time 1 and 2; t3 = time 3; t6 = time 6.
*p < .05; **p < .01 (two-tailed).

Table 14.2 gives an overview of the correlations between dispositional coping (CAV, VIG) and the two scales of actual coping behavior (CAV-AC, VIG-AC) for the different measurement times. There are substantial and significant correlations between dispositional and actual vigilant coping at all times of measurement (*range* from r = .48 to r = .58). In contrast, the associations between dispositional and actual cognitive avoidance are somewhat lower (*range* from r = .24 to r = .36) and reach significance only for the preoperative times of measurement. The coefficients for CAV and VIG-AC as well as VIG and CAV-AC are, however, expectedly low and insignificant.

The correlations between the two subscales of state anxiety (AFF, WOR) at corresponding times of measurement are rather strong but not consistently high enough to justify combining both scales into one total score. The coefficients are $r = .72$ (day before surgery), $r = .63$ (morning of surgery), and $r = .78$ (first postsurgical day), $p < .01$. The correlation between the two anxiety-components aggregated over the four preoperative times of measurement is $r = .66$. Therefore, both subscales were entered as separate variables in all further analyses.

Table 14.3
Correlations of Self-Reported Affectivity and Worry with Observer-Rated Anxiety Variables and Criteria of Intraoperative Adaptation ($N = 40$)

	Observer-rated variables			Criteria of intraoperative adaptation		
	SPE	ANX	INF	THIO	FENT	M AC-E
AFF-T1	.13	.17	.07	-.12	-.14	.22
AFF-T2	-.05	.33*	.24	-.47**	-.08	.22
AFF-t6	.08	.28	.24	-.44**	-.02	.26
WOR-T1	.33*	.23	.16	-.21	-.14	.02
WOR-T2	.13	.40*	.24	-.45**	-.10	.09
WOR-t6	.10	.26	.32*	-.30	-.03	.01

Note. Abbreviations cf. text; T1: mean for time 1 and 2; T2: mean for time 3 and 4; t6 = time 6.
*p < .05; **p < .01 (two-tailed).

As to *correlations between the stress variables from different data levels*, Table 14.3 shows the *associations between self-reported and observer-rated anxiety variables*. There is a significant association between *verbal indicators of anxiety* (SPE) and self-reported worry at T1 ($r = .33$, $p < .05$): Patients who report more worry the day before surgery also show stronger speech-related signs of anxiety. As one would expect, there are also consistent positive correlations between *anxiety concerning surgery* (ANX) stated explicitly during the anesthetist's visit and both self-report anxiety components at all preoperative times of measurement, reaching significance only on the day of surgery itself (AFF: $r = .33$; WOR: $r = .40$; for both coefficients $p < .05$): Patients who expressed anxiety when talking to the anesthetist also report higher anxiety on the morning of surgery. Concerning patients' requests for information about preparation for surgery, surgery itself, and their postoperative state (INF, vigilant coping), there is one significant relationship with self-reported anxiety: Postoperative worry is significantly higher in patients who asked more questions when talking to the anesthetist (cf. results reported by Carver and Scheier, this volume).

The *correlations between self-reported anxiety variables and criteria of intraoperative adaptation* are also summarized in Table 14.3. Thiopentone (THIO), one of the narcotics needed for induction of anesthesia, is consistently negatively correlated with state anxiety reports, the correlation being more pronounced with the affective component, i.e., men who report higher levels of emotional distress and worry on the morning of surgery need a *smaller* dose of thiopentone for anesthesia induction (AFF: $r = -.47$; WOR: $r = -.45$, for both coefficients $p < .01$). Correspondingly, those patients who received less thiopentone report more anxiety postoperatively ($r = -.44$, $p < .01$). In contrast, neither the fentanyl dose (FENT) nor the criterion of adaptation during surgery (*M AC-E)* show any significant associations with anxiety.

As to the *associations between observer-rated anxiety variables and medical variables*, only one significant negative association between ANX and thiopentone dose can be reported ($r = -.39$, $p < .05$). Men who explicitly express anxiety during the anesthetist's visit receive significantly *less* thiopentone during anesthesia induction than those not expressing anxiety. All other associations between these groups of variables are low and insignificant.

In examining the ANOVAs of the self-reported anxiety variables, the *effects of the factor "time of measurement"* will be considered first (for an overview of the results cf. Table 14.4).

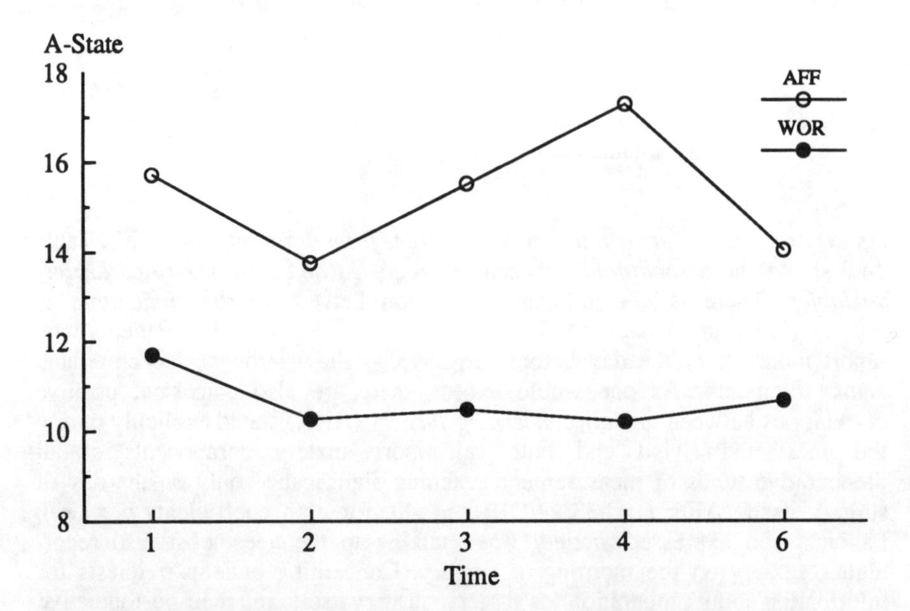

Figure 14.6. State anxiety components affectivity (AFF) and worry (WOR) as a function of time of measurement.

Table 14.4
Self-Reported Affectivity and Worry as a Function of Dispositional and Actual Coping Variables and Time of Measurement

Dependent variable	Source of variation	*F*	*df*	*p*
AFF	Cognitive avoidance (A)	1.15	1,30	n.s.
	Vigilance (B)	9.56	1,30	**
	A x B	4.19	1,30	*
	Time (C)	5.02	3,91	**
	A x C	.23	3,91	n.s.
	B x C	1.09	3,91	n.s.
	A x B x C	.55	3,91	n.s.
WOR	Cognitive avoidance (A)	1.11	1,30	n.s.
	Vigilance (B)	40.88	1,30	**
	A x B	.61	1,30	n.s.
	Time (C)	3.29	2,68	*
	A x C	.41	2,68	n.s.
	B x C	1.65	2,68	n.s.
	A x B x C	.40	2,68	n.s.
AFF	CAV-AC (A)	1.53	1,25	n.s.
	VIG-AC (B)	.24	1,25	n.s.
	A x B	.28	1,25	n.s.
	Time (C)	4.32	3,66	**
	A x C	.75	3,66	n.s.
	B x C	.18	3,66	n.s.
	A x B x C	.88	3,66	n.s.
WOR	CAV-AC (A)	.99	1,25	n.s.
	VIG-AC (B)	3.08	1,25	n.s.
	A x B	1.73	1,25	n.s.
	Time (C)	2.02	3,76	n.s.
	A x C	2.58	3,76	n.s.
	B x C	.34	3,76	n.s.
	A x B x C	.22	3,76	n.s.

Note. Abbreviations cf. text.
*p < .05; **p < .01 (Greenhouse-Geisser corrected).

For both anxiety variables there are significant main effects of time (Figure 14.6). Marked changes, however, occur only for AFF while WOR remains at essentially the same level with one significant difference between time 1 and time 4 ($p < .05$), indicating that the patients worry more after admittance to ward than immediately before surgery.

The decrease in AFF from time 1 (after admission to ward) to time 2 (after the pre-op visit), which can be seen in Figure 14.6, is marked but does not quite reach an acceptable level of statistical significance. The further course of *affectivity* is characterized by an increase from time 2 to time 3 and again to time 4, immediately before anesthesia induction, with values at time 4 being significantly higher than on the afternoon before surgery ($p < .01$). Postoperatively, a significant decrease ($p < .01$) to values that compare to those from the afternoon before surgery can be registered.

The significant *main and interaction effects of the coping variables* will be reported next (cf. Table 14.4). For AFF, an interaction between *dispositional* CAV and VIG could be confirmed, $F(1,30) = 4.19$, $p < .05$ (cf. Figure 14.7): Patients who are habitually high in vigilant coping and low in cognitive avoidance ("sensitizers") report more affectivity than the group with the reversed pattern of dispositional coping ("repressers", $p < .05$) and those patients low on both dimensions ("non-defensives", $p < .01$).

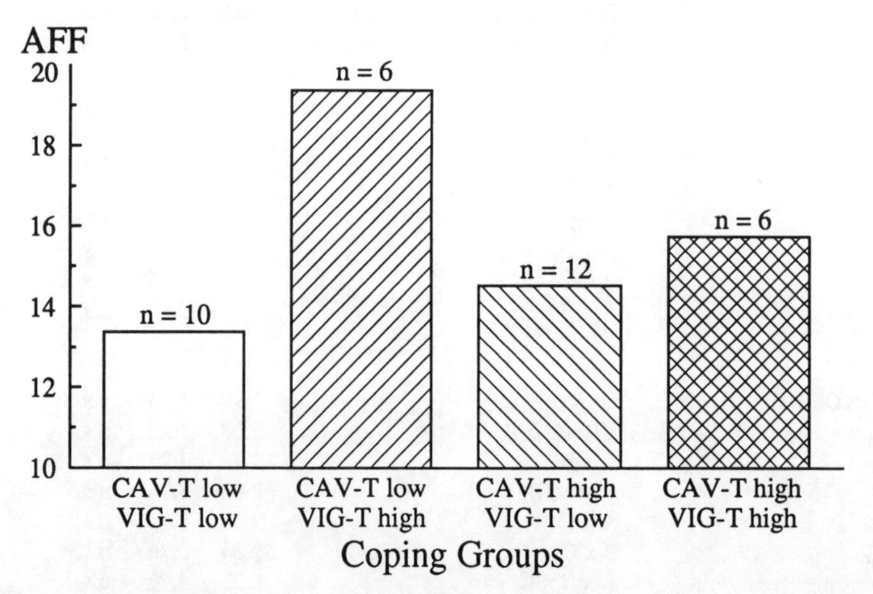

Figure 14.7. Affectivity (AFF) as a function of dispositional vigilance (VIG-T) and cognitive avoidance (CAV-T).

In addition, a highly significant main effect of vigilance on the cognitive aspect of anxiety (WOR) could be confirmed, $F(1,30) = 40.88$, $p < .01$: Patients low in vigilance generally do not worry at all ($M = 8.76$, $SD = 1.25$), while patients high in vigilance worry to a considerably greater extent ($M = 14.19$, $SD = 3.22$).

In order to determine the *influences of actual coping behavior on the self-reported anxiety variables*, additional ANOVAs with CAV-AC and VIG-AC as independent variables were calculated (cf. Table 14.4). There are no effects of the actual coping behavior assessed on the day before surgery on *affectivity*. Concerning *worry* there is a tendency for an interaction between CAV-AC and time, $F(3,76) = 2.58$, $p < .10$ (after adjusting for degrees of freedom). It indicates that while there are no significant differences between persons high and low in actual avoidance, changes over time occur only in the group that reports employing many cognitive avoidant reactions on the day before surgery. Those patients worry considerably more after admittance to hospital than on the day after surgery (cf. Figure 14.8).

Next, the results for the dependent variables which were assessed only once will be reported. For two *observer-rated indicators of anxiety* (ANX and INF), no significant effects of dispositional or actual coping could be registered. However, for speech-related signs of anxiety (SPE), there are significant interactions between both CAV and VIG, $F(1,30) = 5.26$, $p < .05$, and CAV-AC and VIG-AC, $F(1,25) = 4.72$, $p < .05$ (cf. Figure 14.9). Patients high in both dispositional CAV and VIG ("high anxiety") show significantly more verbal signs of anxiety than the other three groups, which do not differ at all.

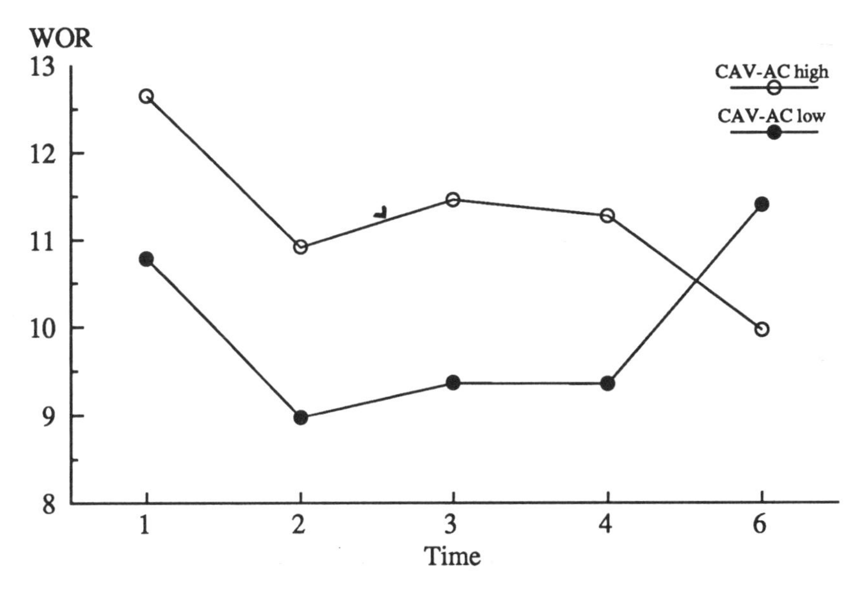

Figure 14.8. Worry (WOR) as a function of actual cognitive avoidance (CAV-AC) and time of measurement (high CAV-AC: $n = 13$, low CAV-AC: $n = 16$).

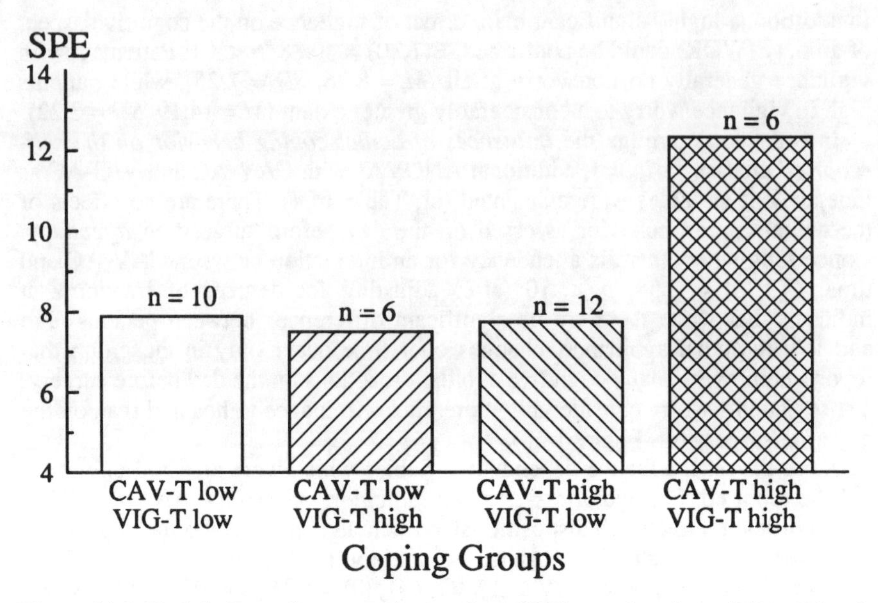

Figure 14.9. Verbal signs of preoperative anxiety (SPE) as a function of dispositional vigilance (VIG-T) and cognitive avoidance (CAV-T).

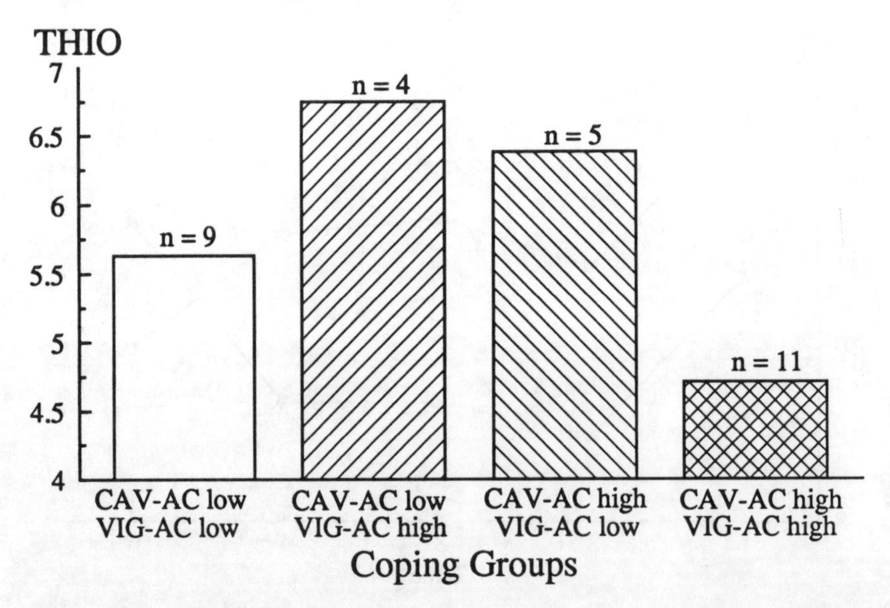

Figure 14.10. Thiopentone dose (THIO) as a function of actual vigilance (VIG-AC) and cognitive avoidance (CAV-AC).

Similarly, patients who employ both types of coping strategies on the day before surgery show significantly more speech-related signs of anxiety than the group using *either* cognitive avoidance or vigilance preoperatively.

Concerning *criteria of intraoperative adaptation*, there are no differences for dispositional coping groups. However, the data yielded significant interactions between CAV-AC and VIG-AC on thiopentone dose (THIO), $F(1,25) = 4.68$, $p < .05$, and M AC-E, $F(1,25) = 7.26, p < .05$. Patients who use mainly vigilant coping preoperatively receive significantly higher thiopentone doses during anesthesia induction than those patients who frequently employ both cognitive avoidance and vigilance (cf. Figure 14.10). The mean alveolar concentration of enflurane during surgery is significantly higher in patients who use mainly cognitive avoidant coping before surgery as compared to the two groups with either high or low values on both scales (cf. Figure 14.11).

Finally, the dimensions of actual coping behavior, CAV-AC and VIG-AC, will be considered as a function of dispositional avoidance, vigilance, and time of measurement (cf. Table 14.5 and Figure 14.12). For *actual cognitive avoidance*, a main effect of time could be observed, indicating that patients cope more avoidantly immediately after admittance to ward than on the morning of surgery, $F(3,81) = 3.56$, $p < .05$. This can be further differentiated by looking at the (marginally significant) three-way-interaction between CAV, VIG, and time, $F(2,65) = 2.48$, $p < .10$ (after adjusting for degrees of freedom).

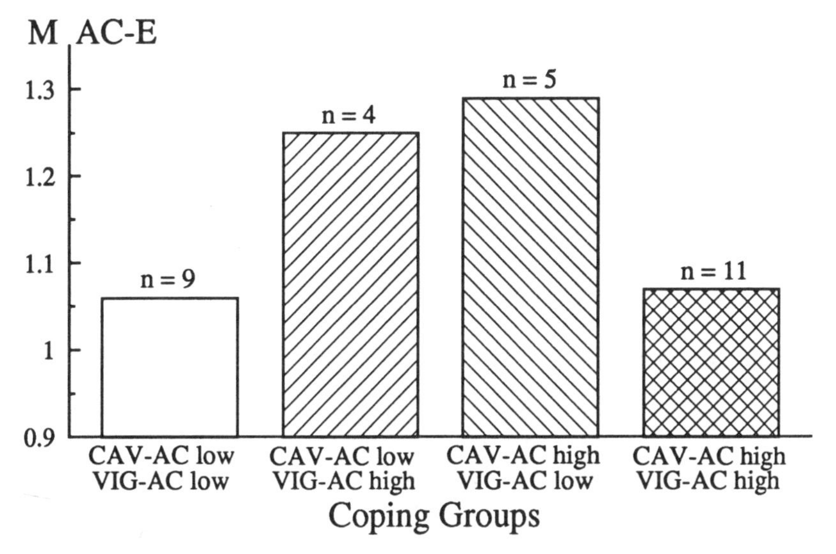

Figure 14.11. Mean alveolar concentration of the volatile anesthetic (M AC-E) as a function of actual vigilance (VIG-AC) and cognitive avoidance (CAV-AC).

The difference in level of actual cognitive avoidance is most pronounced in patients who are dispositionally high in both cognitive avoidance *and* vigilance ("high-anxious" persons).

Table 14.5
Actual Coping Behavior as a Function of Dispositional Coping and Time of Measurement

Dependent variable	Source of variation	*F*	*df*	*p*
CAV-AC	Cognitive avoidance (A)	3.83	1,27	n.s.
	Vigilance (B)	.16	1,27	n.s.
	A x B	.09	1,27	n.s.
	Time (C)	3.56	2,65	*
	A x C	1.18	2,65	n.s.
	B x C	1.03	2,65	n.s.
	A x B x C	2.48	2,65	n.s.
VIG-AC	Cognitive avoidance (A)	6.22	1,26	*
	Vigilance (B)	11.53	1,26	**
	A x B	.96	1,26	n.s.
	Time (C)	3.59	2,65	*
	A x C	.49	2,65	n.s.
	B x C	.18	2,65	n.s.
	A x B x C	1.18	2,65	n.s.

Note. Abbreviations cf. text.
*p < .05; **p < .01 (Greenhouse-Geisser corrected).

For *actual vigilant coping* there are main effects of all three predictors. The main effect of time implies that at time 1 (after admittance to ward) actual vigilance is significantly higher as compared to all later times, $F(2,65) = 3.59$, $p < .05$. The main effects of CAV and VIG indicate that both, patients who dispositionally prefer cognitive avoidance ($M = 2.86$, $SD = 2.02$) and patients who prefer vigilance ($M = 3.72$, $SD = 1.88$) show more vigilant coping reactions than patients low on either of the two dimensions (CAV: $M = 1.71$, $SD = 1.67$; VIG: $M = 1.64$, $SD = 1.6$). The overall level of actual vigilance is, however, rather low with values in the lower third of the scale's potential range. In contrast, cognitive avoidance is used more often, with values ranging in the middle third of the scale.

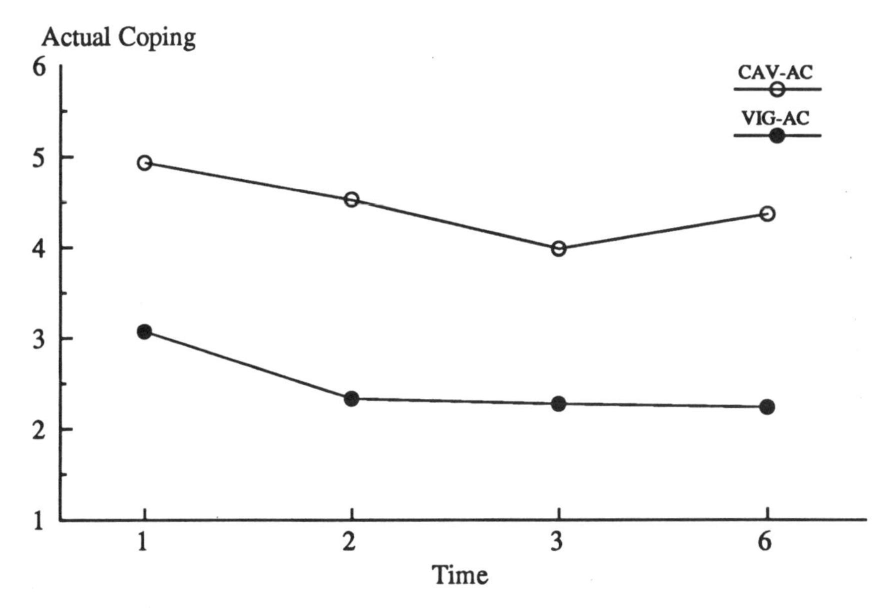

Figure 14.12. Actual vigilance (VIG-AC) and cognitive avoidance (CAV-AC) as a function of time of measurement.

Discussion

First of all, the study demonstrated that it is meaningful to separately assess an affective (somatic) and a cognitive component of state anxiety. The affective component yielded significant changes throughout the different phases of the stress event: First, it decreased from time 1 to time 2, i.e., it indicated a calming effect of the anesthetist's pre-op visit. It rose again immediately prior to surgery, and, finally, dropped again after completion of surgery. The cognitive component, however, which reflects apprehension and worry regarding surgery and its consequences, showed almost no fluctuation over time. Employing behavior-observation methods, it could be demonstrated that those patients whose verbal behavior indicated a higher level of stress are not necessarily identical with those individuals who score high on self-report scales of anxiety. Analysis of verbal-expressive behavior could therefore help identify "leakage cues" (Ekman & Friesen, 1974) concerning stress reactions of those persons who tend to present themselves as relatively anxiety-free (cf. Laux, 1986).

Regarding the effects of coping variables on stress reactions and intraoperative adaptation, it could be demonstrated that dispositionally vigilant patients manifested higher levels of worry and affectivity than nonvigilant persons. Similarly, persons who predominantly relied on vigilant strategies in the actual preoperative situation received higher doses of the narcotic agents used for anesthesia induction than patients who either employed both vigilant *and* cognitive avoidant strategies or who manifested low levels for both types of strategies. Similar relationships could be confirmed for the mean alveolar concentration of enflurane, the narcotic agent necessary to maintain an adequate depth of anesthesia during surgery.

These results in total confirm the frequently reported maladaptive effects of a predominantly vigilant style of coping with short-term (lasting no more than one week) health stressors (for an overview see Suls & Fletcher, 1985; cf. chapters by Carver & Scheier, this volume, and by Weidner & Collins, this volume). On the other hand, cognitive avoidant strategies did not prove to be more effective than nonavoidance, since patients who primarily employed avoidance prior to surgery also received higher doses of narcotic agents.

Concerning the intraoperative variables, fentanyl showed only a low interindividual variability and therefore did not prove to be a good indicator of adaptation. For thiopentone, however, marked correlations with self-reported anxiety could be confirmed. Since the individual thiopentone dose is set according to certain physiological criteria (extinction of the eyeblink reflex, cardiovascular status), an explanation of this finding, albeit still speculative, could be that patients who freely report their anxiety on the morning of surgery manifest less physiological arousal than patients who express little anxiety. Of course, this hypothesis needs confirmation by assessing physiological stress reactions in the preoperative phase.

Regarding the repeatedly assessed variables of actual coping, vigilance yielded comparatively low scores with the one exception of the measurement after admittance to hospital. Obviously, this is a phase where patients still have to orient themselves and therefore manifest intensified search for information. It should be pointed out again that the surgery our subjects had to undergo was generally minor with few threatening implications, so that vigilant coping was really not required. A decrease in cognitive avoidance could be observed as the time of surgery drew near. This result was to be expected as avoidance becomes less feasible when the confrontation is imminent.

Conclusions

All three studies demonstrated significant *changes in the stress indicators* throughout the different phases of the stress event. Self-reported state anxiety, free fatty acids, and cortisol can therefore be regarded as sensitive indicators of the course of surgical stress. With state anxiety, the separate assessment of an affective (somatic) and a cognitive component (worry, apprehension) proved to be meaningful. In the investigation presented, the cognitive component showed almost no fluctuation over time, while self-reported somatic arousal reacted sensitively to the differential stress load of the measurement phases. It should be kept in mind, however, that we were only dealing with minor surgery. With the anticipation of more severe consequences (as would be the case, e.g., with heart surgery, cf. chapter by Carver & Scheier, this volume), a higher level and a different course of the worry component could be expected.

In addition to the stress variables already described, observer-rated anxiety also proved to be a valid stress indicator. The signs of anxiety observed by the psychologist are associated with coping variables as well as with the status of intraoperative adaptation, the latter relationship being of special interest: the more freely the anxiety is expressed preoperatively, the lower the doses of the narcotic agent used for induction of anesthesia, i.e., the lower the level of stress reactions immediately before surgery.

In all three studies the pattern of relationships among the stress variables was complex and not very consistent. Moreover, stress indicators from different data levels (self-report, physiological) did not vary synchronously over time. These findings point to the necessity of a *multilevel-multitemporal assessment* of stress reactions (cf. Krohne, 1986). Multilevel refers to the fact that stress reactions should be assessed on the subjective (self-descriptive), expressive-motoric, and physiological level. Multitemporal means that these parameters have to be measured at different, theoretically relevant points in a time sequence. In addition, on the subjective level, anxiety should be differentiated according to an affective (somatic) and a cognitive component (worry, rumination). In the first two studies described, state anxiety has been measured by the STAI (Laux et al., 1981), which stresses the cognitive component. In contrast, our newly developed instrument puts equal emphasis on the measurement of the affective component, and the wording of the items makes them more suitable for use in physically threatening situations such as surgery.

With respect to the assessment of stress on different data levels, it would be promising to classify patients according to registered discrepancies between their reactions on different levels. As our data indicate, individuals who openly express little stress but, on the physiological or expressive level, manifest comparatively high stress reactions should only be poorly adapted to the surgical situation. In the terminology of our model of coping modes (cf. Krohne, 1989, and Chapter 2, this volume), those persons are called "repressers" (see also Singer, 1990).

On the whole, results of the third study did not confirm the stress-reducing effect of cognitive avoidance which had been established in the first two studies (see also Lazarus, 1983; Miller & Mangan, 1983; Suls & Fletcher, 1985). Obviously, the hypothesis of a stress-reducing effect of avoidant coping needs further scrutiny. For example, it is questionable whether this effect is valid for the long-term postoperative recovery (cf., e.g., Davies-Osterkamp, 1982; Goldstein, 1973; Lazarus, 1983; Mathews & Ridgeway, 1981). In addition, the result that highly vigilant patients report higher state anxiety than persons low on vigilance only *before* surgery could not be replicated in the third study (cf. results reported by Carver and Scheier, this volume). Considering both vigilance and cognitive avoidance, the following fields should be investigated in future studies: limiting conditions of an established relationship (e.g., the specific structure or temporal extension of the stress event), the context in which coping takes place, and different aspects of vigilance and avoidance as well as their functional relationships with different stress parameters (cf. Cioffi,

1991; see also chapters by Carver & Scheier, Leventhal, Suls, & Leventhal, Miller et al., and Weidner & Collins, this volume).

References

Auerbach, S. M. (1989). Stress management and coping research in the health care setting: An overview and methodological commentary. *Journal of Consulting and Clinical Psychology, 57*, 388-395.

Averill, J. R. (1973). Personal control over aversive stimuli and its relationship to stress. *Psychological Bulletin, 80*, 286-303.

Berger, M. (1983). Neuroendokrinologie der Angst [Neuroendocrinology of anxiety]. In F. Strian (Ed.), *Angst - Grundlagen und Klinik* (pp. 71-85). Berlin: Springer-Verlag.

Borkovec, T. D. (1985). Worry: A potentially useful concept. *Behaviour Research and Therapy, 23*, 481-482.

Breznitz, S. (1983). Anticipatory stress and denial. In S. Breznitz (Ed.), *The denial of stress* (pp. 225-255). New York: International Universities Press.

Cioffi, D. (1991). Beyond attentional strategies: A cognitive-perceptual model of somatic interpretation. *Psychological Bulletin, 109*, 25-41.

Cohen, F., & Lazarus, R. S. (1982). Coping with the stresses of illness. In G. C. Stone, F. Cohen, & N. E. Adler (Eds.), *Health psychology - a handbook* (pp. 217-254). San Francisco: Jossey-Bass.

Cronbach, L. J., & Snow, R. E. (1977). *Aptitudes and instructional methods: A handbook for research on interactions*. New York: Irvington.

Davies-Osterkamp, S. (1982). Angst und Angstbewältigung bei chirurgischen Patienten [Anxiety and coping in surgical patients]. In D. Beckmann, S. Davies-Osterkamp, & J. W. Scheer (Eds.), *Medizinische Psychologie* (pp. 148-167). Berlin: Springer-Verlag.

Ekman, P., & Friesen, W. V. (1974). Detecting deception from the body or face. *Journal of Personality and Social Psychology, 29*, 288-298.

Epstein, S. (1972). The nature of anxiety with emphasis upon its relationship to expectancy. In C. D. Spielberger (Ed.), *Anxiety: Current trends in theory and research* (Vol. 2, pp. 291-337). New York: Academic Press.

Goldstein, M. J. (1973). Individual differences in response to stress. *American Journal of Community Psychology, 1*, 113-137.

Greenhouse, S. W., & Geisser, S. (1959). On methods in the analysis of profile data. *Psychometrika, 24*, 95-112.

Guggenheim, F. G. (Ed.). (1986). *Advances in psychosomatic medicine: Vol. 15. Psychological aspects of surgery*. Basel: Karger.

Höfling, S. (1988). *Psychologische Vorbereitung auf chirurgische Operationen. Untersuchungen bei erwachsenen Patienten mit elektiven Eingriffen* [Psychological preparation for surgery. Studies with adult patients undergoing elective surgery]. Berlin: Springer-Verlag.

Janis, I. L. (1958). *Psychological stress*. New York: Wiley.

Johnston, M. (1980). Anxiety in surgical patients. *Psychological Medicine, 10*, 145-152.

Kirk, E. R. (1968). *Experimental design: Procedures for the behavioral sciences*. Belmont, CA: Wadsworth.

Krohne, H. W. (1986). Coping with stress: Dispositions, strategies, and the problem of measurement. In M. H. Appley & R. Trumbull (Eds.), *Dynamics of stress. Physiological, psychological, and social perspectives* (pp. 209-234). New York: Plenum.

Krohne, H. W. (1989). The concept of coping modes: Relating cognitive person variables to actual coping behavior. *Advances in Behaviour Research and Therapy, 11*, 235-248.

Krohne, H. W. (1990, July). *Coping dispositions and stress reactions before and after surgery.* Paper presented at the 5th annual meeting of the International Society for Research on Emotions, New Brunswick, NJ.

Krohne, H. W., Kleemann, P. P., Hardt, J., & Theisen, A. (1990). Relations between coping strategies and presurgical stress reactions. In L. R. Schmidt, P. Schwenkmezger, J. Weinman, & S. Maes (Eds.), *Theoretical and applied aspects of health psychology* (pp. 423-429). London: Harwood.

Krohne, H. W., Rösch, W., & Kürsten, F. (1989). Die Erfassung von Angstbewältigung in physisch bedrohlichen Situationen [The assessment of coping in physical-threat situations]. *Zeitschrift für Klinische Psychologie, 18*, 230-242.

Laux, L. (1986). A self-presentational view of coping with stress. In M. H. Appley & R. Trumbull (Eds.), *Dynamics of stress. Physiological, psychological, and social perspectives* (pp. 233-253). New York: Plenum.

Laux, L., Glanzmann, P., Schaffner, P., & Spielberger, C. D. (1981). *Das State-Trait-Angstinventar (STAI)* [The State-Trait Anxiety Inventory (STAI)]. Weinheim: Beltz.

Lazarus, R. S. (1983). The costs and benefits of denial. In S. Breznitz (Ed.), *The denial of stress* (pp. 1-30). New York: International Universities Press.

Mathews, A., & Ridgeway, V. (1981). Personality and surgical recovery: A review. *British Journal of Clinical Psychology, 20*, 243-260.

Miller, S. M. (1981). Predictability and human stress: Toward a clarification of evidence and theory. In L. Berkowitz (Ed.), *Advances in experimental social psychology* (Vol. 14, pp. 203-256). New York: Academic Press.

Miller, S. M. (1987). Monitoring and blunting: Validation of a questionnaire to assess styles of information seeking under threat. *Journal of Personality and Social Psychology, 52*, 345-353.

Miller, S. M., Combs, C., & Stoddard, E. (1989). Information, coping and control in patients undergoing surgery and stressful medical procedures. In A. Steptoe & A. Appels (Eds.), *Stress, personal control and health* (pp. 107-130). Chichester, England: Wiley.

Miller, S. M., & Mangan, C. E. (1983). Interacting effects of information and coping style in adapting to gynecologic stress: Should the doctor tell all? *Journal of Personality and Social Psychology, 45*, 223 - 236.

Morris, L. W., & Liebert, R. M. (1970). Relationship of cognitive and emotional components of test anxiety to physiological arousal and academic performance. *Journal of Consulting and Clinical Psychology, 35*, 332-337.

Mullen, B., & Suls, J. (1982). The effectiveness of attention and rejection as coping styles: A meta-analysis of temporal differences. *Journal of Psychosomatic Research, 26*, 43-49.

Phipps, S., & Zinn, A. B. (1986). Psychological response to amniocentesis: II. Effects of coping style. *American Journal of Medical Genetics, 25*, 143-148.

Prystav, G. (1979). Die Bedeutung der Vorhersagbarkeit und Kontrollierbarkeit von Stressoren für Klassifikationen von Belastungssituationen [The importance of predictability and controllability of stressors in classifying stressful situations]. *Zeitschrift für Klinische Psychologie, 8*, 283-301.

Prystav, G. (1985). Der Einfluß der Vorhersagbarkeit von Streßereignissen auf die Angstbewältigung [The influence of the controllability of stress events on coping]. In H. W. Krohne (Ed.), *Angstbewältigung in Leistungssituationen* (pp. 14-44). Weinheim: edition psychologie.

Rothbaum, F., Weisz, J. R., & Snyder, S. S. (1982). Changing the world and changing the self: A two-process model of perceived control. *Journal of Personality and Social Psychology, 42*, 5-37.

Scott, L. E., & Clum, G. A. (1984). Examining the interaction effects of coping style and brief interventions in the treatment of postsurgical pain. *Pain, 20*, 279-291.

Singer, J. E. (Ed.). (1990). *Repression and dissociation. Implications for personality theory, psychopathology, and health.* Chicago: University of Chicago Press.

Slangen, K., Krohne, H. W., & Kleemann, P. P. (1991). *Beziehungen spezifischer Dimensionen der Zustandsangst und der aktuellen Streßbewältigung zur perioperativen Belastung* [Relationships of specific dimensions of state anxiety and actual coping with perioperative stress]. Manuscript in preparation.

Slangen, K., Krohne, H. W., Richter, S., & Stellrecht, S. (1991, March). *Aktuelles Bewältigungsverhalten chirurgischer Patienten in der prä- und postoperativen Situation - Beziehungen zu perioperativer Belastung* [Actual coping of surgical patients in the pre- and postoperative situation - Relationships with perioperative stress]. Paper presented at the 3rd Congress of the Deutsche Gesellschaft für Verhaltensmedizin und Verhaltensmodifikation (DGVM), Trier, Germany.

Steptoe, A., & O'Sullivan, J. (1986). Monitoring and blunting coping styles in women prior to surgery. *British Journal of Clinical Psychology, 25*, 143-144.

Suls, J., & Fletcher, B. (1985). The relative efficacy of avoidant and non-avoidant coping strategies: A meta-analysis. *Health Psychology, 4*, 249-288.

Tolksdorf, W. (1985). *Der präoperative Streß* [Presurgical stress]. Berlin: Springer-Verlag.

Van der Ploeg, H. M. (1988). Stressful medical events: A survey of patients' perceptions. In S. Maes, C. D. Spielberger, P. B. Defares, & I. G. Sarason (Eds.), *Topics in health psychology* (pp. 193-203). Chichester, England: Wiley.

Vögele, C. (1988). *Perioperativer Streß. Eine psychophysiologische Untersuchung zu prä- und postoperativen Reaktionen chirurgischer Patienten* [Perioperative stress. A psychophysiological study of pre- and postoperative reactions of surgical patients]. Frankfurt a.M.: Peter Lang.

Volicer, B. J. (1970). Hospital stress and patient reports of pain and physical status. *Journal of Human Stress, 4(2)*, 28-37.

Volicer, B. J., & Bohannon, M. W. (1975). A hospital stress rating scale. *Nursing Research, 24*, 352-359.

Yap, J. N.-K. (1988). A critical review of pediatric preoperative preparation procedures: Processes, outcomes, and future directions. *Journal of Applied Developmental Psychology, 3*, 359-389.

Author Index

Numbers in *italics* indicate pages with complete bibliographic information.

Subject Index